Patriarchs, Angels &

The exhibition (20 December 1996 - 9 March 1997) was made possible
with the financial support of the Mondriaan Foundation

Cover: Rembrandt, *The Sacrifice of Isaac*, 1655,
*Museum het Rembrandthuis, Amsterdam (see cat. no. 12)*
Backcover: *Christoffel II van Sichem after Tobias Stimmer,*
*Joseph and Potiphar's Wife, in: Flavii Josephi..., Amsterdam 1626.*
*University Library Nijmegen (see cat. no. 70)*

'Patriarchs, Angels and Prophets' forms part of the series
Studies in Dutch Graphic Art

# PATRIARCHS, ANGELS & PROPHETS

The Old Testament in Netherlandish Printmaking
from Lucas van Leyden to Rembrandt

Peter van der Coelen

with contributions by
Christian Tümpel
(University of Nijmegen)
and
Gerlinde de Beer
Marlies Enklaar
Judith van Gent
Aernout Hagen
Marloes Huiskamp
Petra Jeroense
Netty van de Kamp
Jeroen Kuppens
Gabriël Pastoor
Astrid Tümpel

MUSEUM HET REMBRANDTHUIS - REMBRANDT INFORMATION CENTRE AMSTERDAM 1996

# Contents

# Foreword

These days the Bible is enjoying something of a revival - not just among churchgoers, but among non-believers too. Popular versions of Bible stories enjoy a wide and enthusiastic audience. Indeed, lectures by churchmen about biblical issues are increasingly well-attended. Hardly a coincidence then, that Dutch Churches have called on 1998-1999 to be dedicated as the Year of the Bible.

It is the dramatic stories of the Old Testament that have a particular appeal. For printmakers, these stories, with their patriarchs, angels and prophets, provided an inexhaustible source of inspiration throughout the centuries and especially in the Netherlands of the sixteenth and seventeenth centuries. In the work of artists such as Lucas van Leyden, Maarten van Heemskerck and later Goltzius and Rembrandt, the Old Testament stories are no longer only shown as prefigurations or references to events in the New Testament, but in their own right as series or individual prints. It was in the period in which these masters flourished that print books first appeared. These books depicted the Old Testament systematically, starting at the Creation and ending with the Israel's return from exile and the struggle for freedom.

The books of Judith and Tobit, like the thirteenth chapter of Daniel, are not part of the Hebrew Bible but rather of the Apocrypha. Nevertheless, they certainly formed part of the iconographical 'canon' of Netherlandish printmaking of the sixteenth and seventeenth centuries. For that reason these stories have been included in this catalogue.

*Patriarchs, Angels & Prophets. The Old Testament in Netherlandish Printmaking from Lucas van Leyden to Rembrandt* has a long history. In 1990 Professor Christian Tümpel of Nijmegen University set up a research team on the subject of the Old Testament in Dutch painting of the Golden Age. Their findings resulted in an exhibition in the Jewish Historical Museum in Amsterdam (1991-92). This show was later exhibited, albeit in a modified form, in 1993 in the The Israel Museum in Jerusalem. A year later the two exhibitions led in the Westfälisches Landesmuseum in Münster to *Im Lichte Rembrandts. Das Alte Testament im Goldenen Zeitalter der niederländischen Kunst.* Unlike the previous exhibitions, this show featured a section on prints and picture books. It is especially gratifying that the Rembrandthuis Museum was been given the opportunity by the Nijmegen research team and the Westfälisches Landesmuseum to take this section as a basis for the museum's own exhibition. I would like to express my special thanks to Christian Tümpel and his colleagues, as well as Klaus Bußmann and Angelika Lorenz, director and curator of the Westfälisches Landesmuseum, for their generous cooperation. In addition, I would like to thank Judith Belinfante (Jewish Historical Museum, Amsterdam) and Martin Weyl (The Israel Museum, Jerusalem) whose contribution helped make the work of the Nijmegen team possible.

*Patriarchs, Angels & Prophets* is the first exhibition to be entirely dedicated to Old Testament prints and book illustrations of the Golden Age. Naturally, the focal points of the show are the prints by Rembrandt and those of his principal predecessors, such as Lucas van Leyden, Maarten van Heemskerck and Hendrick Goltzius.

The development of the exhibition concept was the work of Peter van der Coelen, specialist in sixteenth- and seventeenth-century graphic art. In this he was helped by Christian Tümpel, who provided both advice and assistance. Van der Coelen was also largely responsible for the concept of the catalogue, which appears as the second volume in the *Studies in Dutch Graphic Art* series. Moreover, apart from his numerous entries, he has contributed two major introductory essays. In the first, he provides a stimulating survey of the development of Old Testament prints in the Northern and Southern Netherlands in the sixteenth and seventeenth centuries, at the same time outlining its European context. No survey of the subject has been available until now. His second contribution deals with the profusion of Old Testament prints that could be found in seventeenth-century print- and bookshops. Rembrandt's limited but unparalleled oeuvre is the subject of the third introductory essay, written by Christian Tümpel, who has published numerous important studies on Rembrandt. He provides incisive analyses of Rembrandt's Old Testament prints, which are rightly recognized as being among the most outstanding works ever produced in the field.

Most of the catalogue entries were written by Professor Tümpel's Nijmegen research team consisting of Gerlinde de Beer, Jacqueline Boonen, Peter van der Coelen, Judith van Gent, Marloes Huiskamp, Petra Jeroense, Netty van de Kamp, Jeroen

Kuppens, Gabriël Pastoor, Astrid Tümpel and Ulrike Wegener. Additional texts were written by Marlies Enklaar and Aernout Hagen. Some of the catalogue entries had already been featured in the Münster catalogue. Where necessary these were extended and adjusted to bring them up to date with the latest art-historical research. Around a quarter of the entries on the prints are completely new. The first section of the catalogue focuses on single prints on Old Testament themes, the second section features picture Bibles and other illustrated books. The catalogue section is ordered according to the chronology of the Old Testament stories.

Final editing of the catalogue was the responsibility of Marlies Enklaar. She was assisted by Peter van der Coelen. Their inventive solutions and extensive skills have led to countless improvements, both in form and content. Marlies Enklaar was also in charge of the photo editing, highly intensive because of the large number of illustrations.

The translations, by Donald Gardner, Sammy Herman, Henry Lake, William Mickens and Bob Ordish, were coordinated and, where necessary, perfected with the patient and dedicated assistance of Sammy Herman. The design was in the reliable hands of Vincent van Baar (Barlock) and once again Orientaliste in Herent, Belgium, has ensured the excellent technical production of the book. During the compilation of the catalogue, the authors received valuable advice and assistance from Arie van den Berg, Nico Boerma, Jan-Piet Filedt Kok, Peter Fuhring, Julia Gerasimova, Huigen Leeflang, Jan Pluis, Jean-Pierre van Rijen,

Gerard Rooijakkers, Peter Schatborn, Els Scholtens, Christiaan Schuckman, Ilja Veldman, Jan van der Waals and Margreet Wolters. I would like to extend my gratitude to Marjolein de Boer, Ger Feyen, Maartje de Haan, Iman Heystek, Wim Hofman, Ger Luijten, Bart Makken, Henk Medema, Paul Nieuwenhuizen, Henk-Jan Oudenampsen, Peter Poldervaart, Ida Schuurman and Manfred Sellink, and all those who have helped in any way towards the realization of this catalogue and to the success of the project.

The educational programme accompanying the exhibition was made possible by a grant from the Mondriaan Foundation. Their support is for us an encouragement in our attempt to allow as wide as possible a section of the Dutch public to enjoy these splendid sixteenth- and seventeenth-century prints of Old Testament subjects.

Finally, I would like to thank all the institutions and individuals who have lent objects for this exhibition. I am particularly grateful to the Rijksprentenkabinet in Amsterdam and Museum Boijmans Van Beuningen in Rotterdam, both of which have made numerous works available. Without their generous cooperation it would certainly not have been possible to realize either the exhibition or the accompanying publication in the present form.

Ed de Heer
Director
Museum het Rembrandthuis

Right: detail of cat. no. 40

6

# Netherlandish Printmakers and The Old Testament

*Peter van der Coelen*

From the book of Genesis with its stories of the Creation and the patriarchs to the canonical and apocryphal books about Israel in exile and its liberation struggle - the Old Testament was ideal material for artists in search of engrossing, moving and instructive tales. In it they found narratives with a whole range of human themes - seduction and adultery, murder and slaughter, war and hatred, famine and drought, doubt and disobedience; but also love and affection, loyalty and obedience, faith and constancy, penitence and courage, hospitality and kindness to strangers. In sixteenth and seventeenth century Netherlandish printmaking, it was a source of countless scenes that appeal to the imagination, such as 'The Fall', 'Hagar in the Wilderness', 'The Sacrifice of Isaac', 'The Journey of Tobias and the Angel' and 'Susanna and the Elders'. The vicissitudes of Jacob and Joseph and the courage of the heroes and heroines of the Old Testament are recorded in etchings, engravings and woodcuts. The artistic riches of these Old Testament prints are conveyed by highly dramatic compositions and others that are more tranquil, in scenes with a wide variety of gestures, facial expressions and emotional states.

The Old Testament was of quite exceptional importance for the literary and visual culture of the early modern age. The young Dutch Republic saw its own history to an important extent as resembling that of Israel as described in the Bible. In his play *Het Pascha* (1612), for instance, the poet Joost van den Vondel compared the Dutch Revolt against the Spanish with the Crossing of the Red Sea by which the Israelites escaped from their Egyptian oppressors (cf. cat. no. 75). This notion of a 'Netherlands Israel' left its mark in the fine arts too. By decorating public buildings with scenes from the Old Testament, a mirror of exemplary behaviour was held up to regents and governors. In the field of book illustration we find a striking example in the publisher Pieter Mortier who dedicated his picture Bible of 1700 (cat. no. 63) to Anthonie Heinsius, the Pensionary of Holland, advising him that even the greatest statesman could still learn something from the valour of Joshua and the wisdom of Solomon. Ordinary citizens too were often urged to follow the example of Old Testament protagonists. The behaviour of the patriarch Abraham in particular - his faith, his perseverance and his hospitality - were held up as an example in numerous prints.[1]

Identification like this assumed a widespread knowledge of the Bible. Long before the publication of the States Bible of 1637, that became the standard version for Dutch Protestants, the Bible was already available in various editions. Dutch translations began to appear in both the Southern and Northern Netherlands from the end of the fifteenth century, and in increasing numbers from the second quarter of the sixteenth century. Even though their publication was hampered by censorship and repression, the Bible eventually became available to a fairly broad public of both Protestants and Catholics. Both translations and editions of the original Hebrew text were published of the Old Testament - the part of the Bible that was common to both the Jewish and Christian faiths (cf. cat. nos 67-69).[2]

The Golden Age in the Northern Netherlands is also known as the time of Rembrandt and his works certainly form a highpoint in this period, not excepting his Old Testament prints. In this essay, however, it is not Rembrandt's etchings that occupy a central position, but the works of his predecessors, beginning with Lucas van Leyden. In the sixteenth and seventeenth centuries there were at least three hundred other Northern and Southern Netherlands artists actively involved - in a more or less original manner - making prints based on the Old Testament - either as designers, *peintre-graveurs* or reproductive engravers.[3] Obviously it is impossible to discuss all these artists individually. This introduction aims instead to present the main trends in the production of Old Testament prints for the whole period in both the Northern and Southern Netherlands, without losing sight of the European context. It does this through a description of the main artists, groups of artists and 'schools'. In what way did they depict the Old Testament? What themes did they favour and how did they present them? How important was the Old Testament in their work, compared with the New? I will discuss not only separate prints but also the series of prints - their rise, their highpoint and their decline - and picture Bibles. Emphasis is placed on the line that leads from Lucas to Rembrandt. This line will take us to various cities - Antwerp, Haarlem and Amsterdam - but it begins in Leiden.

## Lucas van Leyden: tradition and innovation

The father of printmaking in the Netherlands, Lucas van Leyden (Leiden 1494? - Leiden 1533), started his career as a child prodigy

**1.** Cf. for the political and social interpretation and function of Old Testament scenes: Huiskamp 1991 & 1994. For the role of the Old Testament in seventeenth-century Dutch painting: Amsterdam 1991-92 & Münster 1994. Cf. for the place of the Bible in Dutch culture during this period: Frijhoff 1995, pp. 314-350.
**2.** For Dutch translations of the Bible see: De Bruin 1993. For the reading of the Bible in the seventeenth century in Holland: Van Deursen 1974, pp. 180-187. Cf. Groenendijk 1989.
**3.** The figure is based on the artists included in the Hollstein volumes. It is a minimum number not only because the Hollstein series is unfinished, but also because the early volumes are incomplete. Furthermore it does not include the numerous printmakers who only made quick and mediocre copies. For Rembrandt's Old Testament prints see Christian Tümpel's article in this book.

1. Jacob Cornelisz. van Oostsanen and Lucas van Leyden, *Abraham and Isaac, Christ Carrying the Cross, Elijah and the Widow of Zarephath* (above); *The Judgement of Solomon, The Last Judgement, David Condemning the Amalekite* (below), woodcuts; photographic reconstruction of sheet M (c. 38 x 27 cm) in: Biblia Pauperum, Amsterdam (Doen Pietersz.) c. 1530. Rijksprentenkabinet, Amsterdam

who was probably already producing masterpieces at the age of fourteen. He also played a pioneering role in depicting the Old Testament. Obviously he did not start from nowhere. Old Testament tales had been illustrated before his time and he still had one foot in the medieval tradition. With his other foot, however, he stepped out towards the future: his engravings, woodcuts and series of prints were a major influence in opening up the whole domain of the Old Testament printmaking.[4]

Unlike his older contemporary, Albrecht Dürer, whose prints were mainly concerned with the life of Jesus (cf. fig. 2.1), Lucas who was active in Leiden, a relatively small city that hitherto had not had any tradition in printmaking, showed a considerable interest in the Old Testament. We know of more than seventy prints by him that have Old Testament subjects: engravings (33), woodcuts (12) and illustrations for books and framed picture series

(28). They were made in a period of some twenty-five years. The earliest of his Old Testament prints were produced in 1506, the last in about 1530.[5]

In terms of iconography a number of these prints clearly still belong to the medieval tradition. This is certainly true of the 24 Old Testament scenes that Lucas made in 1525-30 that were commissioned by the Amsterdam publisher Doen Pietersz. For his *Biblia Pauperum* (fig. 1). Besides Lucas' woodcuts, this 'Bible of the poor' that was printed in roughly 1530 also contained 48 scenes by Jacob Cornelisz. van Oostsanen. It is a series of prints in a large format with twelve sheets, each of which has two rows of three scenes set in ornamental frames. The layout is a traditional one that became standard in the fifteenth century: a New Testament subject appears in the middle with scenes from the Old Testament on either side.[6]

The Old Testament subjects in the *Biblia Pauperum* were not chosen so much for their value as stories as for their correspondence with episodes in the New Testament. Old Testament scenes alluded typologically to events in the New Testament; that is, they were interpreted as prefigurations or 'types' of New Testament events. The depiction of *Christ Carrying the Cross*, for instance, at the top of sheet M, has *Abraham and Isaac on the Way to Mount Moriah* (Gen. 22:6) on one side, showing Isaac carrying the wood in a similar way to Christ bearing the cross, while on the other side is *Elijah and the Widow of Zarephath* (1 Kings 17:12), showing the widow gathering wood for kindling, holding the twigs in the shape of a cross. In the centre at the bottom of the sheet we see *The Last Judgement*, with an Old Testament story of a judgement on either side - *The Judgement of Solomon* (1 Kings 3:28) and *David Condemning the Amalekite* (2 Sam. 1:16). The two latter woodcuts were designed by Lucas, while the remaining scenes are the work of Jacob Cornelisz.

The edition of Doen Pietersz. comes at the end of a long tradition. It is one of the last examples of a *Biblia Pauperum*. The form in which the series is published diverges from the norm in that it consists of large woodcuts on loose sheets. Traditionally the *Biblia Pauperum* was published in book form, originally in manuscripts, but after the middle of the fifteenth century also as a blockbook (with woodcuts and text being cut out of a single block).[7] A type of book with a similar history is the *Speculum Humanae Salvationis* (fig. 2, p. 10). Like the *Biblia Pauperum* this 'mirror of salvation' belongs to the genre of typological picture books of the late Middle Ages. Here, however, instead of two Old Testament prefigurations, there are three for every New Testament scene. In the Dutch edition of c. 1479 we see *The Betrayal of Christ* (Matthew 26:47-50) with three Old Testament examples of treacherous behaviour: *Joab Killing Amasa* (2 Sam. 20:9-10), *David Playing the Harp before Saul* (1 Sam. 18:10-11) and *Cain Killing Abel* (Gen. 4:8).[8]

4. For Lucas van Leyden as printmaker see: New Hollstein, Lucas van Leyden; Filedt Kok 1978; Parshall 1978; Washington/ Boston 1983. For his Old Testament prints: Gibson 1983; Gibson 1989, pp. 10-11. For a general survey of Netherlandish

printmaking in the sixteenth century see: Munich 1979.
5. New Hollstein, Lucas van Leyden, nos 1-33, 175-177, 181-185, 187-190, 213, 222, 239, 278, 287-310.
6. New Hollstein, Lucas van Leyden, pp. 213-237, nos 287-310.

For the Biblia Pauperum of Doen Pietersz., see: Filedt Kok 1988.
7. For the Biblia Pauperum see: Henry 1987; Mainz 1991, pp. 263-310.
8. For the Speculum Humanae Salvationis see: Wilson/ Wilson 1984; Mainz 1991, pp. 311-317.

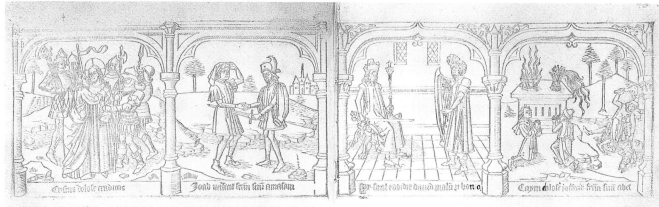

2. Anonymous, *The Betrayal of Christ, Joab Killing Amasa, David Playing the Harp before Saul, Cain Killing Abel*, woodcuts, in: *Speculum Humanae Salvationis*, second Dutch edition, Northern Netherlands, c. 1479, blockbook and letterpress. Stadsbibliotheek, Haarlem

The typological approach in which the Old Testament is not treated as an independent source of subject matter, but is seen from the perspective of the New Testament was common in the late Middle Ages. There were also some other approaches in fifteenth century art. Again the choice is often not determined by the subject matter of the Old Testament as such but by a general theme such as 'the power of women' or 'heroes of history'. Lucas van Leyden also explored both these subjects; the former, in two 'Power of Women' series where scenes such as the *Fall*, *Samson and Delilah* and *Solomon's Idolatry* were depicted showing how men in all ages have been deceived or ruined by women; the latter are presented in his woodcuts series of the *Nine Heroes*, in which, besides three Old Testament heroes (Joshua, David and Judas Maccabeus), three classical and three Christian heroes are portrayed.[9]

Not all late medieval depictions of the Old Testament originate in a typological or thematic treatment like this. In book illustra-

tion scenes from the Old Testament were also common; they were arranged in historical order, so that the important thing was the story itself. Manuscripts of history Bibles, for instance, were lavishly illustrated, especially the Old Testament part. The same can be said of the incunabular Bibles of the second half of the fifteenth century, such as the *Cologne Bible of c. 1478*.[10]

Before Lucas van Leyden's time we come across few cases of Old Testament narratives being depicted for their own sake apart from textual illustrations like these; the same is also true of loose-leafed prints. Dürer, for instance, hardly took any notice of the Old Testament, with the exception of the Fall. One obvious reason why this theme was such a favourite with artists - it occurs a good eight times in Lucas' work (cf. fig. 2.2) - was that it gave them the opportunity to portray both male and female nudes, a typical predilection of the Renaissance. Lucas went further than Dürer, making a six-part series about the Creation (cat. no. 1). He tells the story of Adam and Eve and their sons Cain and Abel in six

9. For the *Power of Women* series (c. 1514 and c. 1517) see: New Hollstein, Lucas van Leyden, pp. 157-164, nos 175-180, pp. 164-170, nos 181-186; *Nine Heroes* (c. 1520): ibid, pp. 173-175, no. 190. Related to the latter series is Lucas' woodcut frieze *The Twelve Kings of*

Israel (c. 1520): ibid., pp. 173-175, no. 189.
10. For the illustration of the Netherlandish history and incunabular Bibles, see: Hindman 1977, pp. 41-99; Rosier 1992, Vol. I, pp. 1-3.

scenes, displaying a variety of nude poses. Lucas took on the challenge set by the Italian engravings of the school of Raphael here, taking, for instance, some motifs from the prints of Marcantonio Raimondi.[11]

Lucas had previously devoted a series of five engravings to the story of Joseph (cat. no. 16). Here we see: *Joseph Telling his Dreams* (Gen. 37:1-11), *Joseph and Potiphar's Wife* (Gen. 39:7-20), *Potiphar's Wife Accusing Joseph* (Gen. 39:7-20), *Joseph Interpreting the Dreams in Prison* (Gen. 40:5-19), *Joseph Interpreting Pharaoh's Dreams* (Gen. 41:15-26). In a fluent and richly varied visual idiom Lucas tells the story of the young and virtuous Joseph. He portrayed Joseph's skill in interpreting dreams in no less than three scenes. Joseph's virtue is in sharp contrast with the deceitful conduct of Potiphar's wife that we see illustrated in the other two prints.

Series such as these were not new in themselves; Dürer, for instance, had already produced some celebrated examples. All the preceding series, however, were devoted to themes from the New Testament, and in particular to the Passion (fig. 2.3). Lucas' decision, after producing series based on the New Testament, to focus on an Old Testament history was revolutionary. His Joseph series is a milestone and inaugurates a new period in Old Testament printmaking.

Besides these two series Lucas also produced isolated prints with Old Testament themes; there are, for instance, engravings such as the *Banishment of Hagar and Ishmael*, the *Triumph of Mordecai* and *David in Prayer* (cat. nos 7 and 40 and fig. 32.1) and also woodcuts such as *Abraham and Isaac before the Sacrifice* and *Joseph's Coat Shown to Jacob* (figs 11.1 and 18.1). One of his most impressive prints is an engraving of *c.* 1508, with an episode from the history of Saul and David (fig. 3).[12] King Saul is tormented constantly by 'evil spirits' who take possession of him. On his courtiers' advice the young David is brought to the court to calm the king by playing the harp whenever he is suffering from these fits (1 Sam. 16:14-23). At first the remedy is effective, but after David has defeated Goliath and the Philistines, Saul becomes jealous of him. This leads to two incidents when David plays the harp and Saul seizes the javelin to kill him (1 Sam. 18:10-11; 19:9-10).

Lucas chose the moment immediately before the incident. Although there are some soldiers and courtiers present, spectators like us, it is the protagonists who are emphasized. On the left we see David, a model of calm, concentrating on the harp, while keeping an eye on the king. On the right sitting on a richly decorated throne we see Saul, 'looking frenzied, appearing really mad', as Karel van Mander described him so accurately in 1604. Clenching his fists and gnashing his teeth, he is barely able to control his rage, while his frenzied expression indicates that the story is about to take a dramatic turn.[13]

The decision not to illustrate the climax of the tale but the moment immediately before can be regarded as typical of Lucas' approach. As for the theme, the artist could draw on the *Speculum Humanae Salvationis* (fig. 2, p. 10); there too Saul has not yet moved to action. The portrayal of his psychological state is, however, lacking in drama. The comparison with the illustration of *c.* 1479 also shows how effective and innovatory Lucas' formal idiom was. His portrayal of his figures is both vigorous and monumental. His meticulous modelling creates chiaroscuro effects that make for a remarkable plasticity and a naturalistic rendering of textures. Lucas' imaginative power can also be seen in his skill in creating variety in people's features and facial expressions, in their hairstyles, their clothes and headgear. This was also a quality that Van Mander admired in him: 'In [...] all his [...] prints, one sees many subtle variations of faces and costumes after the old style: hats, caps and veils which for the most part differ one from another [...]'.[14]

While the theme is common in medieval typological series, there is no reason to assume with either Lucas' *David Playing the*

3. Lucas van Leyden, *David Playing the Harp before Saul*, *c.* 1508, engraving, 25.7 x 18.5 cm, Rijksprentenkabinet, Amsterdam

11. For Lucas' illustrations of the Fall see: New Hollstein, Lucas van Leyden, nos 3, 7-10, 175, 181, 287. *Cf.* Silver/ Smith (1978, esp. pp. 239-240, 244-260) who stress the connection between the choice of subject matter and the aim of conveying a moral message.

12. For the print, see: New Hollstein, Lucas van Leyden, pp. 56-57, no. 27 and the literature mentioned there. See also: Parshall 1978, pp. 206-207; Filedt Kok 1978, p. 27; Gibson 1983, p. 128.
13. Van Mander/ Miedema 1994-95, Vol. 1, p. 114.

14. Van Mander/ Miedema 1994-95, Vol. 1, p. 106. *Cf.* for Lucas' original choice of subject matter: Parshall 1978, esp. pp. 212-213.

4. Jan Swart, *Abraham and Melchizedek*, woodcut, *c.* 11 x 8.3 cm, in: *Den Bibel...*, Antwerp (Willem Vorsterman) 1528. University Library, Amsterdam

5. Heinrich Aldegrever, *Joseph Telling his Dreams*, 1532, engraving, 11.7 x 7.6 cm, Rijksprentenkabinet, Amsterdam

*Harp before Saul*, or with his two Old Testament series that he had any other aim than to tell the tale as such with all its drama and emotions. The same is true of most of his other Old Testament subjects.[15] Lucas concentrated above all on the events of the early chapters of Genesis and the history of the patriarchs, though he also had a special interest in David and Solomon. The apocryphal Book of Tobit, later such a frequent subject in Dutch prints, is completely absent. Compared with Dürer and his Netherlandish contemporaries Lucas' interest in the Old Testament was exceptional, resulting in 73 prints. As was the case with his predecessors the New Testament, however, remains dominant with 188 prints out of a total of 326 engravings, etchings and woodcuts.[16]

## The Little Masters

While a number of Lucas van Leyden's contemporaries in the Netherlands made Old Testament prints - for instance Jan Gossaert and Jacob Cornelisz. van Oostsanen, mentioned earlier - their contribution remained a modest one. A notable exception is the *Vorsterman Bible*, printed in Antwerp by Willem Vorsterman in 1528. Lucas only contributed a small number of prints, all of them of New Testament scenes, while Jan Swart was responsible for the lion's share. His Old Testament woodcuts are distinguished by their inventiveness and originality (fig. 4), certainly by comparison with the illustrations in other Netherlandish Bibles of the period, that were often no more than copies of German woodcuts.[17]

For the further development of loose-leafed prints we should in the first instance turn our attention to Germany. Lucas' initiative

with Old Testament prints and print series was continued by Sebald and Barthel Beham, Georg Pencz, Heinrich Aldegrever and Jacob Binck - artists who due to the small format of their prints are known as the Little Masters (*Kleinmeister*). They were born in around 1500 and were partly trained by Dürer. From the point of view of style, technique and composition, the influence of the master of Nuremberg prevails with all of them. Like Lucas these artists differed from Dürer in terms of their choice of subject matter, depicting a variety of Old Testament stories, for instance 'Judith and Holofernes' and 'Joseph and Potiphar's Wife'.[18]

After *c.* 1528, and particularly during the 1540s and 1550s, Heinrich Aldegrever and Georg Pencz devoted a number of print series to Old Testament figures such as Adam and Eve, Abraham, Lot, Joseph, Amnon, Tobit and Susanna.[19] The earliest series is by Aldegrever and consists of four prints; it is surely no coincidence that like Lucas' first series, it concerns the life of Joseph. We are shown in turn: *Joseph Telling his Dreams* (fig. 5), *Joseph and Potiphar's Wife*, *Potiphar's Wife Accusing Joseph* and *Joseph Selling Corn to his Brothers*. The engravings of these Little Masters are indeed smaller than those of Lucas van Leyden. Aldegrever's prints without exception have a vertical format and they measure roughly 12 x 8 cm; Pencz usually adopted an oblong, somewhat smaller format. Like Lucas, their narrative style is simple and sharply defined and stresses the human rather than the heroic; similar too is the variety of groups of figures, clothing and headgear. Among other qualities, this feature of Aldegrever's work was praised by Van Mander: 'These prints of his are, with regard to the nudes, composition,

**15.** Interpretations such as that of Busch (1982), who treats Lucas' *Banishment of Hagar* (B. 17), as though it were a complex theological treatise are therefore not subscribed to by this author. Cf. Van der Coelen 1996-97.
**16.** Lucas' New Testament scenes (including Mary, the Apostles and the Evangelists): New Hollstein, Lucas van Leyden, nos 34-107, 179, 186, 191, 195-201, 204-205, 207-211, 209-217, 219, 223-227, 240-247, 275, 279-286.
**17.** For sixteenth-century illustrated Bibles in the Netherlands see: Rosier 1992. For the *Vorsterman Bible*: Beets 1915.
**18.** For the Little Masters see: Lawrence 1988. For their Old Testament prints: Gibson 1989.
**19.** Series by Aldegrever: Joseph (1528-32; TIB XVI, pp. 143-144, nos 18-21), Lot (1555; TIB XVI, pp. 141-142, nos 14-17), Adam and Eve (1540; TIB XVI, pp. 136-138, nos 1-6), Amnon and Thamar (1540; TIB XVI, pp. 145-148, nos 22-28), Susanna (1555; TIB XVI, pp. 150-151, nos 30-33). Series by Pencz: Abraham (*c.* 1543; TIB XVI, pp. 84-85, nos 1-5), Joseph (1544-46; TIB XVI, pp. 88-89, nos 9-12), Tobit (1543; TIB XVI, pp. 90-92, nos 13-19).

exotic costume and handsome, precise manner of engraving, 'most outstanding and worthy of preservation'.[20]

This preference for a small format is not an exclusively German trait but is typical throughout European printmaking in the period around 1550. In the Netherlands it occurs especially in the engravings of Cornelis Matsys and Cornelis Bos, two artists who presumably both spent a short period in Nuremberg, then the centre of graphic art in Germany. After *c.* 1537 the painter Cornelis Matsys produced engravings, adopting a wide range of subjects. Besides the obvious Italian influences we also see a definite influence of the German Little Masters in Matsys' work. It is clearly present in the three Old Testament series he engraved in the 1540s: *The History of Abraham* (1545), *The History of Samson* (1549) and *The History of Tobit* (1544-56; see fig. 6), in three, twelve and eight parts respectively.[21] The latter series, for instance, can be compared with the Tobit series by Pencz. Not only are they small with a similar horizontal format; they also resemble each other in the stress placed on the figures that are relatively small and lively in appearance. The scenes, moreover, are usually set in sober interiors with glimpses outside.

Cornelis Bos, who like Matsys was exiled from Antwerp as a heretic in 1544, also produced work that in format, iconography and composition resembles that of the German Little Masters. His sole Old Testament series, the twelve-part *History of Abraham* (1555), consists, however, of literal, if mirror-image copies of woodcuts by Bernard Salomon.[22] In the early 1550s this French artist explored the Bible in systematic fashion. His scenes had a fundamental influence on European printmaking during the third quarter of the sixteenth century; the work of Maarten van Heemsckerck is a good example.

6. Cornelis Matsys, *Tobias Taking Leave of his Parents, c.* 1544-56, engraving, 7.1 x 9.5 cm, Stedelijk Prentenkabinet, Antwerp

## Maarten van Heemskerck

In 1548, even before Salomon, the Haarlem painter Maarten van Heemskerck (Heemskerk 1498 - Haarlem 1574) began systematically to cover the biblical material in prints and print series. Van Heemsckerck's known production consists of a total of 599 engravings, etchings and woodcuts of which some 423 prints depict biblical subjects and 278 are devoted to the Old Testament.[23] This enormous production was only possible since Van Heemskerck - unlike Lucas van Leyden and the Little Masters - did not engrave his own designs but let them be executed by professional engravers. With Van Heemskerck the age of reproductive printmaking made its appearance in the Netherlands. These reproductive prints are not reproductions of existing independent works of art; rather they are engravings and etchings from drawings that were specially made to be reproduced as prints. It was not the drawings, but the prints that reproduce them that are the final product, the finished work of art.[24]

Compared with Lucas van Leyden, Maarten van Heemskerck - who was incidentally only four years younger - was a late developer as a printmaker, only starting to make designs for prints when he was forty. In the first ten years of his career as a printmaker he designed only one engraving on an Old Testament subject. However, after he began collaborating with the etcher and engraver Dirck Volkertsz. Coornhert, he became more productive, to put it mildly. After 1548 the two of them launched a veritable illustrations campaign; starting with Genesis, they illustrated large parts of the Bible. This mainly took the form of multipartite series of etchings, usually with one individual figure from the Bible as the theme. While they did not stick rigidly to the biblical chronology, it seems that after 1549 their approach was systematic. In 1549-50 they produced six series with themes from Genesis, namely the histories of Abraham, Isaac and Rebecca, Jacob, Judah and Tamar and Joseph, as well as *The Twelve Sons of Jacob* (figs 22.1-22.12).[25] After treating Genesis in this fashion Van Heemskerck and Coornhert went on to the prophets and apocryphal books respectively in 1550-52: the stories of the Disobedient Man of God, Jonah, Judith and Holofernes and Susanna.[26]

One distinguishing feature of these series by Coornhert and Van Heemskerck is the vertical format measuring *c.* 25 x 20 cm, noticeably larger than the work of the Little Masters. One typical work is *The Meeting of Abraham and Melchizedek* (Gen. 14:17-20) in the Abraham series (1549; fig. 7, p. 14). The composition is powerful and, like the Little Masters, Van Heemskerck stresses the figures. They occupy almost the entire picture plane, while the background only receives summary treatment. It was clearly Van Heemskerck's aim to introduce variety both in the clothing and the poses. The dynamic movements of his figures, their energetic gestures and muscular bodies betray the influence of

**20.** Van Mander/ Miedema 1994-95, Vol. 1, p. 169. Aldegrever's Joseph series: Holl., German, I, p. 13, nos B. 18-21.
**21.** Abraham: Van der Stock 1985, pp. 37-38, nos 34-36; Samson: ibid., pp. 38-42, nos 39-50 (cf. Münster 1994, p. 310, no. 86);

Tobias: Van der Stock 1985, pp. 45-48, nos 73-80.
**22.** Cf. Van der Coelen 1995, pp. 143-146.
**23.** Biblical scenes: New Hollstein, Heemskerck, nos 1-417, 468-73; Old Testament: nos 1-270, 273-274, 468-473 (see also series

nos 313-320, 436-443, 521-523). For Van Heemskerck see: Veldman 1977. For his Old Testament prints: Saunders 1978; Veldman 1991-92, pp. 30-37.
**24.** For the rise of reproductive engraving in the Netherlands see: Munich 1979, pp. 25-34; Evanston

1993, pp. 1-17, 102-104.
**25.** New Hollstein, Heemskerck, nos 8-13, 17-22, 23-30, 35-38, 47-50, 52-63. For the collaboration between Van Heemskerck and Coornhert see: Veldman 1977, pp. 53-93; Saunders 1978, pp. 4-5; Veldman 1989, pp. 115-130.

**26.** New Hollstein, Heemskerck, nos 123-126, 174-177, 199-206, 215-218.

7. Dirck Volkertsz. Coornhert after Maarten van Heemskerck, *The Meeting of Abraham and Melchizedek*, 1549, etching, 24.8 x 19.7 cm, Museum Boijmans Van Beuningen, Rotterdam

Michelangelo, whose work he had come to know during his visit to Rome. Stylistically, the whole composition is somewhat sketchy. The outlines are emphasized more than the hatching, which is still used in a relatively limited fashion. All this definitely has to do with Coornhert's reproductive technique - that of etching.[27]

It is not certain where and by whom these series by Van Heemskerck and Coornhert were published. Perhaps the designer and his engraver in Haarlem acted as publishers themselves, either separately or in partnership, but it is also possible that some of the series were distributed by Cornelis Bos in Groningen.[28] What we do know is that Antwerp, as the main commercial and artistic centre in the Netherlands during this period, must have played an important role in the distribution of Van Heemskerck's prints for the international market. It is hardly suprising then that after 1553 the artist had his work published by Hieronymus Cock, the renowned printseller who was based in Antwerp.

It was with Cock, who in 1548 began to build up an extensive stock, that print publishing in Northern Europe was first profes-

sionalized. Henceforth three people were involved in the production of a print - the designer, the engraver and the publisher. It was the latter who usually took the initiative, made the necessary investments and organized the distribution. Cock presumably had a certain influence on Van Heemskerck's choice of subject matter, possibly including that of his Old Testament series. Between 1554 and 1556 Van Heemskerck designed four of these series for him which were executed by two anonymous engravers. The subjects were stories for which no engravings by Van Heemskerck were yet available, namely those of the kings Saul, David and Solomon and that of the apocryphal Book of Tobit.[29]

During these years Van Heemskerck came increasingly to prefer a horizontal format (c. 20 x 25), as in *The History of Tobias* (1556), including the print *Tobias Catching the Fish in the River Tigris* (Tobit 6:2-5; fig. 8, p. 15). The figures have become markedly smaller, making space for a more detailed landscape. In it we now also see a detailed side-scene, showing the next episode in the history: the fish that has been caught is cut open and its heart, liver and gall are removed. The change in technique - engraving instead of etching - goes with a more elaborate style of drawing. More detailed hatching made for a greater variety in shading as well as a subtler rendering of textures than one finds in the earlier prints.

In the years 1559-64 Cock commissioned six more series, comprising the Book of Judges (Gideon and Samson) that Van Heemskerck had not treated previously, a number of new histories from Genesis, Samuel and Kings and finally - once again - Susanna.[30] Three of these series were engraved by Philips Galle, an engraver of Haarlem who worked for Cock in that city. After 1563, when Galle set himself up as an engraver and publisher independently of Cock, Van Heemskerck probably had many of his Old Testament series executed by his fellow townsman. Between 1563 and 1567 these comprised the histories of Elijah and the priests of Baal, Esther (cat. no. 39), Job and Judith (cat. no. 45), all of which were engraved personally by Galle.[31]

Finally between 1565 and 1569 eight series were produced after designs by Van Heemskerck - four of them engraved by Galle and four by Herman Jansz. Muller - which were to be included in 1579 in the *Thesaurus*. This picture Bible by the Antwerp publisher Gerard de Jode will be discussed in more detail below. Some of the series were also ordered by De Jode, but the majority had already been published earlier by Galle and Cock. They include the histories of Dinah and Shechem, and Judah and Tamar, the *Ten Commandments*, the histories of Joash and Athaliah, of Josiah, of Shadrach, Meshach and Abed-Nego, of Jonah and Daniel, Bel and the Dragon.[32]

In the 1560s series the format becomes horizontal once and for all, this being more suitable for the inclusion of additional scenes. These are now usually included in the composition in a somewhat more harmonious manner. Van Heemskerck seems also to pay

**27.** Cf. for stylistic development in Van Heemskerck's prints: Veldman 1986A, p. 15; New Hollstein, Heemskerck, p. 11.
**28.** Cf. Veldman 1977, pp. 55, 106-107 and New Hollstein, Heemskerck, Vol. 1, pp. 11-12 (Coornhert/ Van Heemskerck);

Van der Coelen 1995, pp. 123, 138-139 (Bos?).
**29.** New Hollstein, Heemskerck, nos 94-103, 104-109, 117-122, 189-198. Coornhert and Van Heemskerck had already produced a series of woodcuts on the theme of Tobit in around 1548: ibid.,

nos 183-188 (cf. fig. 50.2). For Cock see: Münster 1976, pp. 1-93; Riggs 1977. For the prints he published after Van Heemskerck see: ibid., pp. 337-346.
**30.** New Hollstein, Heemskerck, nos 2-7, 78-83, 85-90, 110-115, 132-137, 219-224.

**31.** New Hollstein, Heemskerck, nos 128-131, 151-158, 161-168, 207-214. Cf. for the collaboration between Van Heemskerck and Galle: ibid., pp. 11-12; Sellink 1992, pp. 13-14.
**32.** New Hollstein, Heemskerck, nos 31-34, 39-42, 65-74, 139-142,

143-150, 170-173, 179-182, 226-235.

increasing attention to the details. In *The History of Esther* (cat. no. 39), for instance, the presentation and the staging of the tale are elaborately detailed. The king and his courtiers are wearing fantastic, heavy and luxurious garments, so that the shape of their bodies is less clearly defined than before. The palaces are impressive with richly decorated interiors.

It was these elements - the lavish and imposing character that could also be called pompous and pretentious - as well as the abundant compositions with their lively and muscular figures that later earned Van Heemskerck a bad name. In the sixteenth and seventeenth centuries, however, he was still admired. His works, in which many episodes from the Old Testament were eloquently illustrated for the first time, exercized a fundamental influence on the iconography of Baroque painting and printmaking. A quotation from Karel van Mander (1604) shows just how much Van Heemskerck's versatility was admired: 'He was an excellent designer, yes: a man who, in a manner of speaking, filled the world with his inventions, added to which he was also a good architect as all his works make abundantly clear. There would be no end to it if one wanted to relate how many prints have already been published by him [...]'.[33]

Van Heemskerck's exceptional number of designs were made in a comparatively short period of time. His 38 series on Old Testament themes were produced in a period of twenty years (1549-69), roughly between the ages of fifty and seventy. With ceaseless imaginative power he applied himself to illustrating nearly all aspects of the Old Testament. Van Heemskerck also produced fifteen New Testament series between 1548 and 1575. He was, however, one of the few printmakers who depicted Old Testament stories more frequently than those from the New.

While in the art of the late Middle Ages the Old Testament was often depicted in relation to the New Testament, sixteenth century artists such as Van Heemskerck - following Lucas van Leyden and the Little Masters - saw it as an independent field in its own right. They were no longer concerned with the prefigurative meaning of the Old Testament, the foreshadowing of the events of the New Testament, but rather in the content of the stories as such. This can clearly be seen in the numerous multipartite series in which the lives of the patriarchs and the Old Testament heroes and heroines are told in detailed, even exhaustive fashion.

An approach of this sort presupposes a thorough knowledge of the Bible, on the part of artist and public alike. This was already the case with Lucas van Leyden whose unusual choice of subjects could sometimes only be fully appreciated when one was aware of the preceding moment in the narrative and that which followed. By Lucas' time, translations of the Bible - that had appeared in print from the late fifteenth century on (Delft, 1477; Cologne, 1478) - had made it accessible to a somewhat broader public.[34] Van Heemskerck's series, that often deal in detail with lesser known passages from the Bible, presuppose an even greater scriptural knowledge, something that was fostered in his time by the translations published in Antwerp and elsewhere from the 1520s on. Humanism and the Reformation encouraged the popularity of the Bible considerably. The fact that its readership was not limited to that part of the population with Protestant leanings is illustrated by Van Heemskerck himself who, working in a humanist milieu in Haarlem, remained a Catholic all his life.[35]

### Picture Bibles: the 'Thesaurus' and Maarten de Vos

In the mid-sixteenth century the only artist to be interested in systematically depicting the Old Testament in loose-leafed series of engravings was Maarten van Heemskerck. A parallel figure in France in the field of book illustrations was Bernard Salomon. This artist produced an extraordinary amount of work in an exceptionally small format. He designed a series of almost 350 woodcuts with biblical scenes that were published from 1553 on. None of the 248 woodcuts that deal with Old Testament subjects measures more than c. 6 x 8 cm. Naturally they include well-known themes such as the 'Sacrifice of Isaac', but little known stories also appear - for instance 'The Israelites Resting at the Oasis of Elim' (Ex. 15:27; fig. 9, p. 16). Salomon's woodcuts were published by Jean de Tournes in Lyon. This was done in the form of picture Bibles. In these books the Bible is told with the aid of images. The biblical text itself is not included, but its content is often summed up in short verses. A total of 26 editions of

8. Unknown engraver after Maarten van Heemskerck, *Tobias Catching the Fish in the River Tigris*, 1556, engraving, 20 x 24.4 cm, Museum Boijmans Van Beuningen, Rotterdam

**33.** Van Mander/ Miedema 1994-95, Vol. 1, p. 245. For examples of Van Heemskerck's influence in the seventeenth century: Münster 1994, *passim. Cf.* also cat. nos 22 and 50.
**34.** *Cf.* Gibson 1983, p. 128 (who in fact only emphasizes the importance of history Bibles). For the relation between the interpretation of the Scriptures and biblical illustration see: Tümpel 1980, pp. 129-135.
**35.** In this period, however, the Bible was definitely not yet a popular book and its readership should not be overestimated. See: Gawthrop/ Strauss 1984. For Van Heemskerck's religious views, see: Veldman 1987B.

EXOD. XV.

*In Helin fie ir läger fchlügen,*
 *Sibentzig beum, fchön palmen trügen:*
 *Zwölff fchöner bruñen auch dartzü,*
 *Da fand Ifraël gûte rů.*

9. Bernard Salomon, *The Israelites Resting at the Oasis of Elim*, woodcut, c. 6 x 8 cm, in: *Wol gerissnen vnd geschnidten figuren Ausz der Bibel...*, Lyon (Jean de Tournes) 1554. Herzog August Bibliothek, Wolfenbüttel

Salomon's picture Bible were published in no less than seven languages, including German, Dutch and English.

The first picture Bibles had been published in the first half of the sixteenth century.[36] All of them, however, were much more modest in scale. Salomon opened up the whole domain of the Bible in unprecedented fashion. His contemporaries must have greeted his picture Bible with astonishment. It had an enormous influence, not least on Netherlandish art. We have seen that Cornelis Bos copied part of Salomon's woodcuts in his *History of Abraham*. Maarten van Heemskerck, who had already embarked in 1548 on systematically illustrating the Bible in print series soon got to hear about the book and it served as a fresh stimulus for his own work.[37]

During the period from 1550-85 the systematic almost encyclopaedic exploration of the Bible was at its height. Salomon's example inspired artists in France (Pierre Eskrich; fig. 43.2) and in the German-speaking territories (Virgil Solis, Tobias Stimmer

and Jost Amman; figs 53.1 and 73.2). Commissioned by publishers such as Guillaume Rouillé (Lyon) and Sigmund Feyerabend (Frankfurt), they illustrated a whole series of picture Bibles. Like Salomon, these artists worked in a small format, using woodcuts as their medium. At the same time something unprecedented was occurring in Antwerp. Hieronymus Cock, who published the work of numerous Netherlandish and Italian artists (cf. fig. 59.1), led the way in making this city the centre for copper engraving. The Old Testament series by Van Heemskerck that Cock published were emulated by several artists, including Hans Bol, Frans Floris and Crispijn van den Broeck. Their work was published by various Antwerp printsellers, including Gerard de Jode.[38]

In 1579 the latter devised a plan to compile a large number of Bible series and publish these as a book. The result was a new picture Bible, the *Thesaurus Veteris et Novi Testamenti*. Unlike previous picture Bibles, the *Thesaurus* is a large-format work with engravings instead of woodcuts. The first edition was published in the same year. The definitive edition appeared in 1585 and consists - as we can see from the two supplementary lists of contents - of 61 print series covering 341 sheets. The table of contents for the Old Testament lists 218 sheets comprising a total of 42 series from the Creation to the Prophets (fig. 10, p. 17). Stories from Genesis and the books of Kings are the most common subjects. Like Van Heemskerck, the *Thesaurus* artists usually give a single biblical protagonist pride of place in the series, showing the most important deeds in his or her life in separate scenes.[39]

The basis for the *Thesaurus* was formed by some older series that had previously been published separately. For his picture Bible, however, De Jode specially commissioned many new series. The *Thesaurus* therefore offers a sample of Netherlandish graphic art from the years around 1580. The series were designed by Maarten de Vos, Jan Snellinck, Ambrosius Francken, Gerard van Groeningen, Marten van Cleve, Pieter van der Borcht, Hans Bol, Crispijn van der Broeck, Hans Vredeman de Vries (fig. 42.3), Frans Menton, Michiel Coxie, Adriaen de Weerdt and Maarten van Heemskerck. Here too we are dealing with reproductive prints: the designs by these artists were executed by the best engravers of Antwerp, including Johannes Sadeler I, Anton, Johannes and Hieronymus Wierix and Adriaen and Hans Collaert.

Maarten de Vos (Antwerp 1532 - Antwerp 1603) contributed the largest number. He was responsible for about a third of the Old Testament (14 series), namely the histories of Abraham, Jacob and Esau, Balaam, Gideon, Samson (see cat. no. 58), David and Abigail, David and Absalom, Hezakiah and Sennacherib, Jeremiah, Jonah (fig. 9, p. 46), Esdras, Tobit and Judith and Holofernes and the series featuring the kings of Judah. De Vos' designs were engraved by the Wierix brothers and a number of anonymous artists.[40]

**36.** Engammare 1994, pp. 556-573. *Cf.* Van der Coelen 1993. For Salomon's picture Bible see: Schubart 1932.
**37.** For Salomon's influence on Van Heemskerck see: Saunders 1978, pp. 98-103; Veldman 1986B, pp. 265-266.

**38.** For printmaking in Antwerp in the second half of the sixteenth century see: Munich 1979, pp. 34-52; Savelsberg 1992; Evanston 1993, pp. 8-30, 104-111. There is no room here to discuss the prints made after Floris' designs. For this important work

see instead: Van de Velde 1975, pp. 389-434.
**39.** For the *Thesaurus* see: Mielke 1975; Van der Coelen 1991 and 1994, pp. 170-171. An extensive article about the recently discovered first edition of 1579 (*cf.* Münster 1994, p. 329, no. 117;

Van der Coelen 1994-95, p. 111) will be published in 1997 in the *Bulletin van het Rijksmuseum*. *Cf.* also: cat. no. 58.
**40.** Holl. XLIV, nos 62-67, 68-71, 83-86, 87-90, 91-97, 114-117, 118-121, 128-131, 138-141, 158-161, 162-165, 166-171, 172-174, 185-186.

*Cf.* for De Vos' share in the *Thesaurus*: Zweite 1980, pp. 186-189.

The series designed by De Vos, *The History of Jacob and Esau*, that had already been included in the 1579 *Thesaurus* edition, consists of four parts and was engraved by an unknown artist (fig. 11, p. 18). We see repectively *Esau Selling his Birthright to Jacob for a Pottage of Lentils* (Gen. 25:29-34), *Blind Isaac Blessing Jacob Disguised as Esau* (Gen. 27:26-29), *Jacob's Dream* (Gen. 28:10-15) and *The Meeting of Jacob and Rachel* (Gen. 29:11).[41] While De Vos' illustrations with their wealth of detail, varied poses, lavish clothing and hair styles recall Van Heemskerck's work, the differences are fundamental. The compositions show a greater harmony, the lines are flowing and the modelling is softer and more refined. De Vos' figures are tall and slender and their gestures are generally speaking more graceful and elegant than those of the Haarlem artist. The clothing seems to cling less to the body and is often loose and wind-blown. The whole is also more painterly, something that can be seen, for instance, in the landscapes of the third and fourth prints and in the procession of well-proportioned angels with their elegant feathered wings in *Jacob's Dream*. The work of Michelangelo that Van Heemskerck admired so greatly was also an influence on De Vos but his main source of inspiration was Venetian masters like Tintoretto.

In 1604, Maarten de Vos' inventiveness was praised by Karel van Mander, who compared his productivity with that of Maarten van Heemskerck: 'The design of his pictures, the manner and posture of his figures and, in short, his talent is amply to be seen in the prints which were published after him by various engravers and in such quantities that they exceed, or at least equal in number, those of the other Marten, that is Hemskerck; for he was very productive, quick and sure in designing [...]'. Only recently has it become clear just how much more productive De Vos' was than Van Heemskerck. Almost 1,600 prints have been identified as being based on his designs, a thousand more than Van Heemskerck's![42]

As far as the Old Testament was concerned De Vos did not confine himself to the fourteen *Thesaurus* series. He was involved in the production of a total of 35 Old Testament series, being responsible himself for 243 sheets.[43] These series, where the dated ones come from the years 1579-91, were presumably produced in an even shorter period than Van Heemskerck's. De Vos could only do this because he worked for a number of publishers simultaneously - besides De Jode, he was employed, for instance, by Johannes Sadeler I, Philips Galle and Crispijn de Passe I - and his designs were executed by various engravers, in particular Crispijn de Passe I and members of the engraver families of Sadeler, Wierix and Collaert.

In many of his Old Testament series De Vos treated the same subjects as Van Heemskerck. What is striking, however, is his interest in the early chapters of Genesis. While Van Heemskerck really only began with Noah and Abraham, De Vos also produced five series illustrating the histories of Adam and Eve and their direct descendants.[44] In quantity the Old Testament and New Testament series almost balance each other in his oeuvre. If we

10. Engraved table of contents for the Old Testament, in: *Thesaurus Sacrarum Historiarum Veteris Testamenti...*, Antwerp (Gerard de Jode) 1585. Rijksprentenkabinet, Amsterdam

**CATALOGVS HISTORIARVM, quæ hoc libro compræhenduntur.**

| No. | Entry | fol. | No. | Entry | fol. | No. | Entry | fol. |
|---|---|---|---|---|---|---|---|---|
| 1 | Creatio mundi. | 8 | 21 | Dauid & Abigael. | 4 | 41 | Ionæ prophete. | 4 |
| 2 | Fratricidium Caini. | 3 | 22 | Dauid & Bersabea. | 4 | 42 | Prophetæ. | 4 |
| 3 | Diluuium. | 3 | 23 | Dauid & Abselon. | 4 | | | |
| 4 | Turris Babilonica. | 3 | 24 | Salomon. | 4 | | | |
| 5 | Abraham. | 6 | 25 | Roboã & Ieroboam. | 6 | | | |
| 6 | Lothus. | 4 | 26 | Helias & Sacer.Baal. | 4 | | | |
| 7 | Iacob et Esau. | 4 | 27 | Helias & Heliseus. | 4 | | | |
| 8 | Dina filia Iacob. | 4 | 28 | Regina Athalia. | 4 | | | |
| 9 | Duodeci Patriarchæ. | 6 | 29 | Sanacharib. | 4 | | | |
| 10 | Ioseph Somniator. | 7 | 30 | Reges Persarum. | 10 | | | |
| 11 | Moises & Pharao. | 8 | 31 | Hester. | 4 | | | |
| 12 | Desertum. | 6 | 32 | Iob. | 4 | | | |
| 13 | Balaam. | 4 | 33 | Esdre. | 4 | | | |
| 14 | Iosue. | 10 | 34 | Tobias. | 6 | | | |
| 15 | Duodeci Iudices Israel | 6 | 35 | Holofernes & Iudit | 4 | | | |
| 16 | Gedeon. | 4 | 36 | Ieremias. | 4 | | | |
| 17 | Iepthe. | 4 | 37 | Susanna. | 4 | | | |
| 18 | Sampson. | 7 | 38 | Daniel. | 6 | | | |
| 19 | Ruth et booz. | 4 | 39 | Reges Iudæ. | 8 | | | |
| 20 | Dauid et Saul. | 4 | 40 | Iudas Machabeus | 8 | | | |

Continens in somma 215 fol.

*Præsenter Figuræ Biblicæ seu Historiæ sunt excusæ ANTVERPIÆ apud GERARDVM de IODE sub signo floreni aurei in Platia vulgariter dicta Catsijne veste.*

**41.** Holl. XLIV, pp. 21-22, nos 68-71. *Cf.* Mielke 1975, p. 78, no. 7.
**42.** See the recently published volumes Holl. XLIV-XLVI, compiled by Christiaan Schuckman, in which for the first time a full catalogue is offered of prints after the designs of De Vos.

For the quote from Van Mander: Van Mander/ Miedema 1994-95, Vol. 1, p. 318.
**43.** Holl. XLIV, nos 1-242.
**44.** Holl. XLIV, nos 1-36, 41-55.

11a-d. Unknown engraver after Maarten de Vos, *The History of Jacob and Esau* (a. Esau Selling his Birthright to Jacob for a Pottage of Lentils, b. Blind Isaac Blessing Jacob Disguised as Esau, c. Jacob's Dream, d. The Meeting of Jacob and Rachel), c. 1579, engravings, c. 21.2 x 26.8 cm, in: *Thesaurus...*, Antwerp (Gerard de Jode) 1585. Rijksprentenkabinet, Amsterdam

observe, however, the size of the series and take into account all the independent sheets, then it is clear that De Vos, like almost all the other major printmakers, undoubtedly also focuses more on the New Testament.[45]

De Vos' drawing style was exceptionally influential, being imitated by *Thesaurus* artists such as Jan Snellinck and Ambrosius Francken. Partly for this reason De Jode's picture Bible displays a certain unity. Typical on the one hand are the monumental groups of figures clearly influenced by Italian art and on the other, the strong emphasis on the landscape that is undoubtedly the influence of Pieter Bruegel. The engravings have a horizontal format

and measure on average some 21 x 26 cm. They include engraved captions in Latin, consisting mostly of a distich identifying the biblical passage illustrated.

In publishing his *Thesaurus* De Jode must have been inspired by the example of Christophe Plantin. It was this renowned printer and publisher who was the first to use copper plates extensively for book illustrations. Plantin was also a publisher of picture Bibles and as early as 1575 he collaborated with Philips Galle to put a small picture book on the market about the life of David (*cf.* cat. no. 56). In the early 1580s, moreover, Plantin commissioned Pieter van der Borcht, the foremost illustrator who was employed

**45.** De Vos' *New Testament* series (including the *Apostles* and the *Evangelists*): Holl. XLIV, nos 256-522, 545-566, 570-79, 581-604. 607-610, 613-628, 777-882, 892-903.

by his studio to produce two extensive series of biblical prints (cf. cat. nos 55 en 60). It was his intention that these should also be published as picture books - something that did not take place for a long time, however, and then not by Plantin himself, but by his son-in-law, Frans van Raphelingen in Leiden (c. 1592-93).[46]

The fate of this venture was to an extent typical of Old Testament printmaking in Antwerp. The year 1585 marked a turning point in the history of the Netherlands. Antwerp fell to the Spanish and from then on the Northern and Southern Netherlands would go separate ways, with religious, political and cultural differences becoming increasingly sharp. 1585 - coincidentally the year in which the definitive version of the *Thesaurus* was published - was also crucial for the history of Netherlandish art. The influence of the Counter Reformation meant that devotional features began to dominate in the art of the South. Antwerp, with the workshops of Galle, Collaert and Wierix, became the centre of Catholic devotional prints whose main subjects were Christ's Passion and the martyrdom of various saints. This development can already be seen in the oeuvre of De Vos, who though he was known as a Lutheran, managed to adapt successfully to the new situation after 1585.[47]

Many other artists, among them engravers and printsellers, however, left Antwerp after this date for religious and/or economic reasons. The Mennonite Crispijn de Passe, for instance, went to Aachen and later to Cologne while the brothers Johannes and Raphael Sadeler found employment at the court in Munich. All this was to have serious consequences for Flemish printmaking, certainly as far as the role of the Old Testament is concerned. With the exception of reproductive prints after Rubens, the illustration of the Old Testament in the South would cease to be a field for innovation. Many Flemish emigrés, however, were to make an important contribution to the artistic renewal that was occurring in the North. Henceforth it would be here that Old Testament printmaking would continue to develop, particularly in Haarlem and Amsterdam.

## Hendrick Goltzius and his School

The achievements of the Flemish printmakers lay behind the Golden Age in Dutch printmaking. The period 1585-1610 witnessed the apex of the 'Goltzius style' that originated in Netherlandish Mannerism. Hendrick Goltzius, Karel van Mander, Cornelis Cornelisz. van Haarlem, Abraham Bloemaert and their engravers took copper engraving to new artistic heights.

Besides mythological and allegorical themes, this group of artists also illustrated Old Testament subjects. However, their work lacks the systematic or encyclopaedic approach that we find in Van Heemskerck and De Vos. With the *Thesaurus* - and to a slightly lesser extent Van der Borcht's series - this domain had effectively been covered. The whole terrain of the Bible had been explored visually; from now on the market would be supplied instead with numerous reprints of these works (cat. nos 55, 58 and 60). Crispijn de Passe the Elder, who moved to Utrecht in 1612 after a stay in Cologne, still conceived of the ambitious plan of depicting the entire Bible in prints, thus surpassing even the *Thesaurus*; his project, however, foundered after the first attempt, the *Liber Genesis* (cat. no. 54). After the explosive development that had taken place, particularly during the third quarter of the sixteenth century, the domain of biblical illustration became somewhat more tranquil. It was a good century before Netherlandish print designers once more applied themselves to illustrating the Old Testament stories on such a scale. For the time being the tendency was to stick to a small number of specific themes, with the choice to a not unimportant extent being determined by formal artistic reasons.

Hendrick Goltzius (Mühlbracht 1558 - Haarlem 1617) was the first great Netherlandish *peintre-graveur* since Lucas van Leyden. In contrast with Van Heemskerck and De Vos he was trained as an engraver, executing a significant number of his prints himself. He also engraved designs by others.[48] In one of his earliest works, the four-part *History of Ruth* of 1576-78 (cat. no. 29), Goltzius still adhered in content and style to the tradition of Van Heemskerck and the Flemish reproductive engravers. In the 1580s, however, his compositions would pursue a totally new direction. This was above all due to the influence of Bartholomeus Spranger, whose work he became acquainted with in about 1583. Goltzius engraved a number of designs by this Prague court artist; his own compositions, moreover, were influenced by Spranger's elegant and mannered style, with its lively, markedly elongated figures with their complex twisted poses. Influenced by Spranger's formal idiom, Goltzius developed a new style of engraving that differed significantly from the Antwerp tradition. Typical are the lines drawn parallel and equidistant, while the hatching flows over into the forms of the bodies. Goltzius' technical virtuosity with its 'flowing play of swelling and tapering lines',[49] would have an impact on an entire generation of Dutch engravers, and in the first instance, on his own pupils and assistants such as Jacques de Gheyn II, Jan Muller, Jacob Matham and Jan Saenredam.

Goltzius began his Ruth series (cat. no. 29) while he was still living in Germany where he had been taught engraving by Coornhert in Xanten. He completed the series in Haarlem, however, where he settled in 1577. After some five years of activity in this city for Antwerp printsellers, Goltzius established his own publishing house in 1582. His career as a publisher continued for two decades. Up to 1601 he published some 440 prints, the majority of which he designed himself. A large number were also engraved by him, but most of this work was carried out by his pupils and assistants. Goltzius was the first publisher in the Northern Netherlands to build up a stock that was comparable in

---

**46.** *Cf.* for Plantin's biblical picture books: Van der Coelen 1994-95, pp. 107-110 and the literature on the subject listed there.

**47.** *Cf.* for the change that took place in printmaking in Antwerp after 1585: Savelsberg 1992, esp. p. 228; Thijs 1993, p. 6. For the change in Galle's output: Sellink 1992.

**48.** For Goltzius' work as a printmaker: Filedt Kok 1993. *Cf.* also: Evanston 1993, pp. 71-99, 112-114; Amsterdam 1993-94A, pp. 177-183. For Mannerist graphic art in the Netherlands:

Mielke 1979; Hamburg 1992.

**49.** Filedt Kok 1993, p. 167.

12a-c Goltzius workshop after Hendrick Goltzius, *Old and New Testament Prophetesses* (a. Deborah, b. Huldah, c. Anna), 1588, engravings, each c. 25 x 16.1 cm, Rijksprentenkabinet, Amsterdam

range and content with that of the great Antwerp printsellers such as Cock and Galle. Classical, mythological, allegorical and religious subjects were all covered.[50]

Biblical themes do not dominate in Goltzius' stock; nevertheless, with roughly 130 sheets, they do occupy an important place. The Old Testament with 36 sheets was clearly in a minority even if we add the eight prints Goltzius engraved for other publishers and the five prints based on his own designs that were commissioned by others.[51] Among Goltzius' earliest own publications are *Moses with the Tablets of the Law* (cat. no. 24) and *Susanna Penitent* (fig. 43.1), both dating from 1583. Besides these 'portrait-like' depictions of Old Testament figures Goltzius also designed a number of separate sheets with narrative scenes. We see, for instance, three prints with 'The Fall', one of 'Lot and his Daughters' and one of 'Susanna and the Elders'. The chance to portray the nude would seem to have been an important reason for his choice of subject matter. This is certainly the case with the series on *The Creation*, engraved by Jan Muller in 1589 after designs by Goltzius. Each of the seven sheets of this series contains one or more nude figures with an exceptional variety of postures.[52]

Apart from Muller's *The Creation* there are no series in Goltzius' stock where an Old Testament history is treated scene by scene. The series that he designed do not usually tell the main events

in the life of a biblical protagonist, but focus rather on specific themes. In *The Annunciations of the Bible* of 1586 (cat. no. 26), for instance, there are six sheets with as many moments from the Old and New Testaments in which the annunciation of the birth of a child occurs. Most typical of Goltzius' work, however, are six series he designed between 1587 and 1597 where on each sheet a single biblical protagonist is portrayed. Two of them show the heroes and heroines Jael, Samson, David and Judith (cat. no. 51) while one only shows Judith and Jael. The same basic scheme can be seen in *The Old and New Testament Prophetesses*, with Deborah, Huldah and Anna, and *The Old Testament Prophets*, with David, Isaiah, Jeremiah, Ezekiel and Daniel. Finally there is the *The Wives of the Patriarchs*, with Sarah, Rebecca, Leah and Rachel.[53]

All these series were produced in a vertical format - oval or rectangular - with the figures usually depicted in the foreground on an elevation. This means that they occupy a large part of the picture plane, while allowing us a glimpse of a distant horizon. Usually, small scenes are illustrated there with typical events from the life of the subject portrayed, serving to identify him or her. In the left hand background of *David* (fig. 51.4), for instance, we see the moment when the hero beheads Goliath. The women in *The Old and New Testament Prophetesses* (fig. 12), engraved in the Goltzius workshop in 1588, are all identifiable as prophetesses

**50.** For Goltzius' stock see: Filedt Kok 1993, pp. 198-201.
**51.** Old Testament prints in Goltzius' stock: Filedt Kok 1993, nos 1, 7, 8, 17, 25, 30, 39, 51, 61, 67, 87a, 93, 130, 137, 149, 150, 153. Prints with Old Testament subjects engraved by Goltzius for others: Holl. VIII, nos 3-6, 8, 75, 76, 363a. Old Testament prints after Goltzius' designs published by

others: Filedt Kok 1993, p. 217, no. A7; Widerkehr 1993, p. 259, no. M. 19.
**52.** Filedt Kok 1993, nos. 17, 61, 130, 149, 150; Widerkehr 1993, no. M. 19.
**53.** Filedt Kok 1993, nos 39, 51, 67, 137, 153, A7.

only because of the book they carry as an attribute.[54] Deborah, the wife of Lapidoth, was a prophetess who urged Barak to take up the struggle against the Canaanites under Sisera (Judges 4:4-14; 15). Huldah was a prophetess during the reign of Josiah who foretold the evil that would be brought upon Judah (2 Kings 22:14-20; 2 Chronicles 34:22-28). Anna was a widow 'of a great age' who as a prophetess in the Temple foresaw the redemption of Jerusalem (Luke 2:36-38). In these series instead of nudes it is fully clothed figures that predominate, with a variety of poses and portrayed from different angles. The voluminous costume that we see in *Deborah*, however, does not disguise her graceful, tall and slender appearance.

Portrait-like series of this sort had occurred earlier in Netherlandish printmaking. An important instance is Maarten van Heemkerck's series, *Exemplary Women from the Old and New Testament* of *c.* 1560, that are similar in conception and in terms of its iconography must have influenced Goltzius. De Vos' *Celebrated Women of the Old Testament* should also be mentioned in this context. Series like this, however, were marginal for Van Heemskerck and De Vos, while for Goltzius and his school they are typical. An important reason for the choice of this sort of subject matter must have been the opportunity it gave artists of depicting the human body from different viewpoints and with a wide range of postures.[55]

Like Goltzius, the four most important engravers of his school, Jacques de Gheyn II, Jan Muller, Jacob Matham and Jan Saenredam, were all active as *peintre-graveurs* thus producing prints after their own designs as well. The Old Testament rarely appears in their work, even if the quality is sometimes truly remarkable as with Muller's *Belshazzar's Feast* and Saenredam's *Susanna and the Elders* (cat. nos 42-43). Their significance for Old Testament printmaking is largely confined to their work as reproductive engravers - work that they did not only after Goltzius but also after designs by Cornelis Cornelisz. van Haarlem, Karel van Mander and Abraham Bloemaert. Jacob Matham, who took over the publishing house from his stepfather Goltzius in around 1600 when the latter decided to dedicate himself almost entirely to painting also produced an important print after a design by Rubens.[56]

The Catholic artist Cornelis Cornelisz. van Haarlem (Haarlem 1562 - Haarlem 1638) worked mainly as a painter. Due to his close contacts with his fellow townsman Goltzius, 28 engravings were made after his designs between 1588 and 1605. Only four of them, engraved by Muller, Matham and Saenredam, have Old Testament or Apocryphal subjects: *The Fall*, *Cain Killing Abel* and *Susanna and the Elders* (twice).[57] Like the separate sheets with Old Testament histories in Goltzius' stock, the important feature here is the nudity. The most spectacular is unquestionably *Cain Killing Abel* of *c.* 1589 (fig. 13, p. 22), engraved by Jan Muller and published in

Amsterdam by his father, Herman Jansz. Muller. The complex poses and vigorous movements of the muscular figures combined with a pronounced foreshortening make it a textbook example of a Mannerist composition.[58]

Many more designs for Old Testament prints were made by Karel van Mander (Meulebeke 1548 - Amsterdam 1606), who, with Goltzius and Cornelis, formed the Haarlem triumvirate. The versatile Van Mander - painter, poet, theoretician and artists' biographer - was, like Goltzius, one of the most productive Northern Netherlandish print designers of his age. We know of more than 160 prints after his designs produced in the period after *c.* 1588, a great many of which were engraved and published in Amsterdam by Jacques de Gheyn II. They include 39 prints with Old Testament or Apocryphal themes, engraved among others by De Gheyn and his apprentice, Zacharias Dolendo, by Matham and Saenredam.[59] The number is somewhat misleading, however, since about two thirds of them are contained in four extensive series. These were two narrative series (*The History of Tobit* and *The Powers that Rule the World*; based on 1 Esdras 3 and 4) and two series of 'portraits' of biblical protagonists: *Repentant Sinners from the Old and New Testament* and *The Twelve Sons of Jacob*. The two latter series are clearly in keeping with the work produced in Goltzius' workshop. For *The Twelve Sons of Jacob* (cat. no. 22), engraved by De Gheyn in around 1590, Van Mander, who, as we have seen previously, had a thorough knowledge of the history of printmaking, took his inspiration mainly from Van Heemskerck's *The Twelve Patriarchs* of 1550 (fig. 22.13). The separate prints after Van Mander's design mainly cover themes from Genesis and Exodus.

The Mennonite Van Mander was enthusiastic about the prints after the designs of the Catholic painter Abraham Bloemaert (Gorinchem 1566 - Utrecht 1651): 'Various things - designs and figures drawn by him with the pen [...] - are cut in copper by the artistic Joan Muller, and yet others by the celebrated Saenredam, who, very interested in his manner of drawing, does his best to reproduce them well and authentically with the burin'.[60] Bloemaert, who lived in Utrecht, cannot strictly speaking be included in the school of Goltzius, even though his compositions also have late Mannerist features. Many prints after his design, however, were engraved by printmakers of this school, including thirteen with Old Testament subjects, namely two series (*The History of Adam and Eve*, *The History of Ahijah and Elijah*; cat. no. 35) and three separate sheets (*The Banishment of Hagar and Ishmael*, *Elijah and the Widow of Zarephath*, *Judit and Tamar*; cat. nos 8 and 36). They were engraved and published by Matham and Saenredam between 1603 and 1605.[61]

All these prints have a vertical format and a narrative character. The elegant, elongated figures suggest those of the school of

**54.** For this series that was previously attributed to Matham (TIB IV, pp. 222-224, nos 245-247; Holl. XI, p. 217, nos 17-19) see: Filedt Kok 1993, pp. 175, 210, no. 51. Traditionally the series is known as *Old Testament Prophetesses*; Anna, however, occurs in the New Testament.
**55.** A similar series was engraved by Nicolaus Braeu after designs by Jacob Matham: TIB IV,

pp. 294-297, nos 1-4. Van Heemskerck: New Hollstein, Heemskerck, nos 265-272. De Vos: Holl. XLIV, pp. 57-60, nos 223-242. For series with exemplary women from the Bible see: Veldman 1991-92, pp. 37-39.
**56.** Matham also engraved Old Testament subjects after Italian designs (TIB IV, nos 81, 85-86), as Goltzius had done before him

(Filedt Kok 1993, no. 93). For the prints of De Gheyn, Muller, Matham and Saenredam respectively: Filedt Kok 1990, Filedt Kok 1994-95, Widerkehr 1993 and Boccazzi 1974.
**57.** McGee 1991, pp. 326, 331-332, 335-336. For the prints after designs by Cornelis: ibid., pp. 269-342.
**58.** *Cf.* Filedt Kok 1994-95, part III,

p. 11, no. B. 29; McGee 1991, pp. 277, 278; Hamburg 1992, p. 51, no. 64.
**59.** Van Mander/ Miedema 1994-95, Vol. 2, pp. 141-147, nos E2, E4, E6-8, E14-47. *Cf.* Valentiner 1930, pp. 98-110; Filedt Kok 1990, pp. 254-255, 268-269.
**60.** Van Mander/ Miedema 1994-95, Vol. 1, p. 40.
**61.** Roethlisberger 1993, pp. 114-

115, 120-129, 134-135, nos. 69, 72-77, 78, 79-82, 87. *Cf.* for Bloemaert's prints: Groningen/ Leeuwarden 1988. For Old Testament prints after designs by a fellow-townsman of Bloemaert, Joachim Wtewael, see: cat. no. 74.

Cor. Cornely Hardemant inuentor. /Johan Muller sculpsit.
Impius, ecce, Cain fratrem iugulauit Abelem, Innocuo hunc Fons sanguine primus humum.
Prò dolor! ex illo quot in orbe fuere Tyranni, Queis terra innocuo tota cruore madet.
Hermannus Muller excudebat postliminiò

13. Jan Muller after Cornelis Cornelisz. van Haarlem, *Cain Killing Abel*, c. 1589, engraving, 35.3 x 41.5 cm, Rijksprentenkabinet, Amsterdam

Goltzius. Their poses, however, are less complex and more 'classical', even when they are portrayed in movement, as in the two scenes with Elijah in the *Ahijah and Elijah* series (cat. no. 35), that, with their emphasis on diagonal lines, are done rather in a Baroque style. In *The Banishment of Hagar and Ishmael* and *Elijah and the Widow of Zarephath* (cat. nos 8 and 36) it is the vertical lines in the composition that strike one. Most of the picture plane is occupied not by the figures but by their surroundings. Dominant in these landscapes, that are rendered with tremendous virtuosity, are the ruined buildings, but they also contain countless other picturesque details. The overall painterly quality is achieved not least by variations in tonality that are the product of sophisticated engraving; it was with good reason that Van Mander praised it so highly.

The engravers of the school of Goltzius were held in high esteem not only in the Northern Netherlands. Their work enjoyed an international reputation and to some extent even served as a model for the graphic work of the Rubens school. During the second decade of the seventeenth century the famous Flemish painter, Peter Paul Rubens (Siegen 1577 - Antwerp 1640) conceived of the idea of having his most important paintings reproduced as prints in his own studio. *Judith and Holofernes*, engraved by Cornelis

I Galle of Antwerp, is thought to be the first reproductive print produced under his immediate supervision. Initially, however, the work of reproducing Rubens' paintings in print, was carried out by a group of engravers who had been trained in the Goltzius school, even though they presumably worked independently of the Flemish master. The Old Testament played a special role here.[62]

It is likely that Rubens was not satisfied with the engravers he could get in Antwerp and that he considered the engraving style of the Goltzius school as more appropriate for rendering the dynamic and painterly qualities of his work, with its distinctive palette. It was an apprentice of Jan Saenredam, the Leiden engraver Willem van Swanenburgh, who, in 1611-12, made the two earliest prints after paintings by Rubens; one of them was of *Lot and his Daughters*. Rubens may have been impressed by Van Swanenburgh's work, since, shortly before the latter's death in 1612 he travelled in person to the North, maybe in search of skilled engravers. He probably visited Haarlem, then the centre of Dutch reproductive printmaking. Around this time a number of engravers who were active there, were making prints after Old Testament paintings of the Flemish master, among them were Jacob Matham (cat. no. 28) and Willem Buytewech, who may have

62. Galle: Voorhelm Schneevoogt 1873, no. 79. For a brief summary of prints after Rubens see: Antwerp 1993. *Cf.* also: Göttingen/ Hanover/ Nuremberg 1977; Pohlen 1985.

been Matham's apprentice. In 1614, moreover, a print appeared after Rubens' *Sacrifice of Isaac* by Andries Stock, presumably an apprentice of Jacques de Gheyn II.[63]

Initially, however, no Dutch engraver worked for Rubens on anything like a regular basis, let alone under his direct supervision. This state of affairs would only change in around 1618. Lucas Vorsterman, an engraver from Zaltbommel, took up residence in Antwerp and was thus able to collaborate directly with Rubens. This development gave Antwerp printmaking a new lease of life. In 1619/20 Rubens managed to obtain privileges in France and in both the Northern and Southern Netherlands for his prints with the result that his studio became an internationally famous centre of reproductive printmaking. In fact the production of prints after Rubens' paintings continued long after the artist's death in 1640.

The Old Testament prints after Rubens were not published in series. Usually they are large-format prints with one of the master's paintings, meticulously reproduced. In seventeenth-century prints after Rubens a good twenty Old Testament themes are represented, some of which recur in more than one composition. Most of these scenes deal with the stories of the patriarchs and the kings. Among them are some that may have been chosen for their typological importance - for instance *Abraham and Melchizedek*. Other criteria for the selection, however, must have been the sensual or erotic possibilities of a theme, as with 'Lot and his Daughters', 'Judith and Holofernes' and especially 'Susanna and the Elders'.[64]

Apart from its moral - the bad influence of women and drink - the aim of the print engraved by Jacob Matham, *Samson and Delilah* (Judges 16:19) of c. 1612 must also have been to arouse the senses (cat. no. 28). When we compare this composition with that of Maarten de Vos (see ill. cat. no. 58), Rubens' own intentions and the innovatory character of his concept and composition can clearly be seen. The focus is on the protagonists and their physical energy is powerfully conveyed, not only because their bodies, with the muscular arms of the one and the heaving bosom of the other, are illustrated so forcefully, but also because of the calculated effects of light. The youth and beauty of Samson and Delilah are emphasized by the contrast with the figure of an old procuress. The wealth of the clothing and the carpet contributes to the overall sensual character. This is partly due to the engraver's success in rendering textures. In contrast with the linear style of Anton Wierix who engraved De Vos' composition, Matham's approach was a tonal one with subtle variations between light parts and darker ones.

Voorhelm Schneevoogt, who compiled a catalogue in 1873 of graphic work after Rubens, described almost a hundred prints with Old Testament themes, more than half of which were made in the seventeenth century. The Old Testament played a major role

in the development of reproductive printmaking after Rubens. In terms of number, however, it was completely outstripped by New Testament subjects, and scenes with saints and religious allegories. The prints reflect Rubens' work as a painter, many of which were commissions, often directly in the service of the Counter Reformation.[65]

## Landscapes with scenes from the Old Testament

Even before Rubens, printmaking in Holland had received another major stimulus from Flanders, namely in the domain of the 'biblical landscape'. We have already seen that Bloemaert's choice of subject matter was clearly influenced by the possibility of placing his Old Testament protagonists in a landscape context, thus being able to display his virtuosity and imaginative powers. Bloemaert was not alone in this. The popularity of a number of subjects, such as 'Hagar in the Wilderness', 'The Journey of Tobias and the Angel' and 'Elias Fed by the Ravens', is intimately linked to the required setting. While artists such as Bloemaert treated the landscape as an impressive and elaborate context for what was happening in the foreground, with others the reverse is the case: the Old Testament protagonists seem to serve merely as staffage in an all-embracing landscape.

This can already be seen in a number of prints and series published from the 1550s on by Hieronymus Cock after designs by Hans Bol, Matthys Cock, Lucas van Gassel and others. It is no surprise that Cock, the great publisher of the prints after Pieter Bruegel, showed such an interest in the landscape. Especially in series that present not just biblical episodes but other subjects as well, such as the thirteen *Landscapes with Biblical and Mythological Scenes* (see fig. 47.1), etched in 1558 by Hieronymus Cock after the designs of his brother Matthys, the central theme is clearly the landscape while the episodes themselves serve effectively only as staffage.[66] In other instances, such as the two series by Pieter van der Borcht, commissioned by Plantin in the 1580s (cf. cat. nos 55 and 60), the landscape was equally decisive for the composition. Even so the subject matter still remains the central motif here. The series were after all intended to be published as picture Bibles.

In the second half of the sixteenth century a specific Flemish landscape style was developed in the tradition of Bruegel. Typical features are the large number of motifs that are observed from nature and realistically depicted but which combine to form a 'constructed' imaginary landscape. This Flemish landscape style was brought to the North by a number of emigrés in around 1600 - particularly Gillis van Coninxloo. Working in Amsterdam around the turn of the century, he designed many landscapes, often woodland scenes with vistas, that were highly influential. Karel van Mander spotted Van Coninxloo's importance as early as 1604: 'In order to keep it brief and to express my opinion regarding his artistic works, I know of no better landscape painter in

**63.** Voorhelm Schneevoogt 1873, nos 12 (Van Swanenburgh), 41 (Matham), 7 (Buytewech), 25 (Stock). For Rubens' journey and the Dutch engravers after his work: Van Gelder 1950-51, pp. 118-130; Haverkamp Begemann 1959, pp. 7-8; De Smet 1977.

**64.** Old Testament prints after Rubens: Voorhelm Schneevoogt 1873, pp. 1-12, nos 1-97. For the role of the Old Testament in Rubens' paintings see: D'Hulst/ Vandenven 1989, pp. 19-29.
**65.** Voorhelm Schneevoogt (1873) catalogued reproductive prints

after Rubens from the seventeenth to the nineteenth centuries. Besides the 97 Old Testament prints he lists 473 from the New Testament, 85 with sacred histories, allegories and devotional subjects, 171 with Mary, 144 with male saints, 73 with female saints

and another 14 series with religious subjects. Cf. For the sheets that appeared in the seventeenth century: Van den Wijngaert 1940.
**66.** Cf. Riggs 1977, pp. 184-185. For the prints in question see: ibid., pp. 313, 326, 335-336, nos 7, 59, 60, 103.

these times; I see that in Holland his manner of working is beginning to be followed a great deal; the trees which stood here somewhat withered begin to grow like his, as far as is possible, even though some husbandmen or planters would only grudgingly admit it'. A number of Van Coninxloo's landscapes, and also those of David Vinckboons, include staffage (Van Mander talks of 'landscapes with contemporary figures'), sometimes with an Old Testament subject.[67] Typical here is the *Mountain Landscape with Tobias and the Angel* that Claes Jansz. Visscher etched in 1608 after a design by Van Coninxloo (cat. no. 47), where the action occurs in the centre of a picture plane that is dominated by the landscape.

Apart from Visscher, prints after the work of Van Coninxloo and Vinckboons were engraved by other artists, and in particular by Nicolaes de Bruyn and Jan van Londerseel, two engravers who started their careers in Antwerp but who moved later to Rotterdam. A typical feature is the large format of their plates. They are often printed on royal-sized paper and measure some 40 x 50 cm. Some of these prints were also provided with biblical staffage.[68] With regard to Old Testament themes, De Bruyn also produced several prints after his own designs, while Van Londerseel mainly worked after designs by others, particularly Gillis Claesz. de Hondecoutre. An example of an engraving after a design by the latter, himself a Flemish emigré, is the *Landscape with*

*Abraham and the Three Angels* of 1614 (fig. 14). The spacious landscape with woodlands on the left and a distant view on the right was influenced by the work of Van Coninxloo. The biblical episode takes place in the left foreground under a mighty tree with luxuriant foliage. The landscape is engraved in detail with an alternation of light and dark passages giving the whole an atmospheric quality.[69]

The Flemish landscape tradition also had an impact on the biblical prints of the Swiss-German artist Matthaeus Merian the Elder. Merian's series of 233 etchings that are characterized by a strong emphasis on landscape first appeared in Frankfurt in 1625-27 in the form of a picture Bible. Shortly afterwards copies were issued by various Amsterdam firms (cat. nos 61, 70, 77). Biblical staffage groups can not only be found in landscapes in the Flemish style, but also in realistic Dutch landscapes, made 'according to life', for instance in the work of Jan van de Velde II and Anthonie Waterloo. In the 1650s the latter even etched a series of six landscapes including scenes taken solely from the Old Testament (cat. no. 34).[70]

### Dutch printmakers before Rembrandt, c. 1610-30

The biblical landscapes of Visscher and Waterloo were etched rather than engraved. In the 1590s while the Goltzius style was still flourishing artists such as Gerrit Pietersz. began to turn to the

14. Jan van Londerseel after Gillis Claesz. de Hondecoutre, *Landscape with Abraham and the Three Angels*, 1614, engraving, 35.2 x 46.3 cm, Rijksprenten-kabinet, Amsterdam

**67.** Van Coninxloo: Van Mander/ Miedema 1994-95, Vol. 1, p. 330. Vinckboons: ibid., p. 457. For prints after Van Coninxloo see: Frankenthal 1995, pp. 132-137, 248-253. For prints after Vinckboons: Amsterdam 1989, pp. 23-26.

**68.** For these prints on royal-sized paper with biblical subject matter see: Van der Waals 1997. For De Bruyn and Van Londerseel: Holl. IV, pp. 11; XI, pp. 100-101 (the information is in part unreliable, since later states are sometimes referred to as though they were

separate prints; cf. Schapelhouman 1987, p. 152); Bredius 1915-22, Vol. 5, pp. 1594-1603.

**69.** Holl. IX, p. 80 (De Hondecoutre); Holl. XI, p. 100, no. 3 (Van Londerseel). The group of figures bears a strong resemblance to those of Salomon (and Bos) from

the 1550s (see ill. in: Van der Coelen 1995, p. 143). Cf. for De Hondecoutre: Amsterdam/ Boston/ Philadelphia 1987-88, pp. 354-355; for prints by Van Londerseel after his work see: Thieme/ Becker 1907-50, Vol. 17, p. 432.

**70.** Van de Velde: Holl. XXXIII, pp. 84, 86, nos 262, 266. Cf. also the series by Herman van Swanevelt (Holl. XXIX, pp. 50-51, nos 1-4) and the landscapes by Gilles Neyts (Holl. XIV, pp. 149-150, nos 3-4).

technique of etching. This technique reached its first height in Holland during the second decade of the seventeenth century and even replaced engraving as an artistic medium in around 1630.[71]

Etching was the ideal form for the *peintre-graveur*. Unlike engraving this technique did not require too high a level of specialization or years of training, thus allowing artists a certain freedom to experiment. It gave them the possibility of working more swiftly and they could also introduce changes in the composition if need be, while with engravings one had to take account of the wishes and possibilities of the reproductive engraver. Typical of the period from 1610-30 is the painter who besides his own paintings also made prints, even if only a limited number. In contrast with the situation in Antwerp with De Vos and in Haarlem with Goltzius, there were no longer any definite 'schools' with one or more leading designers. We are dealing now with artists operating as individuals in the major cities of the Republic: Haarlem, Amsterdam, Rotterdam, The Hague and Leiden.

In terms of subject matter, history scenes did not have pride of place in Dutch etching in this period; instead, new subjects prevailed such as landscapes, townscapes and genre scenes. In view of these preferences and given the often modest quantity of prints made by the masters of this period, it is not surprising that Old Testament subject matter is rarely found in the work of these pioneer etchers. Nonetheless, there were some striking achievements in this domain too.

Among the earliest examples in this category is *Susanna and the Elders* (fig. 15) by the painter and printmaker from The Hague, Werner van den Valckert - an etching of extremely small format of 1612. By placing the emphasis on the contrast between light and dark areas, by introducing variation in the treatment of the lines and the use of the *pointillé*, the artist attempted to achieve an effect of tonality. One influence on Van den Valckert's etching style was perhaps the work of the famous Italian artist Annibale Carracci, who in his etchings had already made a transition in around 1585 from a linear approach to one that was more painterly with plenty of contrasting effects of light.[72]

Similar features can be seen in the work of Willem Buytewech (Rotterdam 1591/92 -Rotterdam 1624), for instance in his three etchings on the theme (2 Sam. 11:2-4) of Bathsheba.[73] They date from 1615-16 when Buytewech was still active in Haarlem and are a good illustration of the way that an artist can produce variations on a theme both formally and in content. The first etching (cat. no. 30) shows a peaceful moment. Bathsheba is bathing, unaware she is being spied on by David from the roof of his palace on the right. Due to its focus on Bathsheba (depicted plastically and occupying the vertical compositional axis) the composition displays a relative repose, despite the variety in effect created by an alternation of light and dark passages, the use of stippling, and the contrast between forceful and more delicately etched lines.

15. Werner van den Valckert, *Susanna and the Elders*, 1612, etching, 7-8 x 6-7.3 cm, Print Room, British Museum, London

With the use of diagonal lines, the composition of the second etching (cat. no. 31) has a more dynamic character. This fits in perfectly with the nature of the subject: Bathsheba's peace of mind is disturbed by a messenger who arrives with a letter from David.

The third etching (fig. 16, p. 26) shows the moment when Bathsheba starts reading the letter.[74] A sparkling handling of lines, with movement in all directions, and a wide variation in light and dark passages ensures an extremely dynamic effect. Many forms have an angular expressive character. No longer is plasticity the aim; instead a free play of lines covers the whole picture plane. The formal excitement that is thus created, undoubtedly has to do with the psychology of the moment depicted: Bathsheba receives the disquieting invitation to an adultery that she may not refuse. With this combination of artistic experiment and psychological depth Buytewech's Old Testament graphic work anticipates that of Rembrandt.

Buytewech, who, in addition to his paintings and drawings, made some 35 prints that we know of, also produced another print on an Old Testament theme, namely a reproduction of Rubens' *Cain Killing Abel* (c. 1613). Later, Old Testament scenes designed by Buytewech were made into prints by Jan van de Velde II - *Tobit and Anna with the Kid* and *The History of Jonah*, a series in four parts.[75] The latter series of c. 1621 (cat. no. 38), in which apart

71. *Cf.* Burchard 1917, p. 7. Engravers, however, remained active throughout the century. Crispijn de Passe, for instance, worked in Utrecht from 1612 to 1637, presumably making engravings with Old Testament subject matter in this period too -

as did Van Londerseel and De Bruyn mentioned in the preceding paragraph. For an overview of Dutch printmaking in the seventeenth century see: Ackley 1981; Munich 1982. *Cf.* for the development of Old Testament painting in the Northern

Netherlands in the seventeenth century: Tümpel 1991 & 1994.
72. Van den Valckert: Holl. XXXII, p. 14, no. 1. *Cf.* Burchard 1917, pp. 36-38; Van Thiel 1983, pp. 132, 134, 136, 185, no. E1. For Carracci's influence on Dutch etchers see: Haverkamp

Begemann 1959, pp. 8-10.
73. *Cf.* for Buytewech's etchings: Haverkamp Begemann 1962. For religious subjects in his work see: Haverkamp Begemann 1959, pp. 6-12.
74. Holl. IV, p. 56, no. 4. *Cf.* Ackley 1981, pp. 81-82, no. 48.

75. Holl. XXXIII, pp. 8-10, nos 2-6. *Cf.* cat. no. 69.

from the etching needle a burin was used, is interesting not only because of Buytewech's Baroque composition that is full of tension, but also for its tonal effects, with many dark passages, that is probably largely Van de Velde's work. A 'desire to achieve profoundly dark tonalities' can be seen as a typical feature of Dutch printmaking. It can be found already in the work of Jan Muller (cat. no. 42), was taken a step further by Van de Velde and would come to its finest flowering in Rembrandt's deep chiaroscuro, and in the mezzotints of the late seventeenth century.[76]

Van de Velde's interest in tonal effects was considerably influenced by the night scenes after the designs of the German painter Adam Elsheimer. In the Netherlands he was known mainly through the reproductive prints of the engraver Hendrick Goudt, among them his *Tobias and the Angel* of 1613 (fig. 17, p. 27).[77] Apart from the chiaroscuro effect achieved by a regular dense pattern of engraved lines, Goudt's prints were also important because they popularized Elsheimer's poetic concept of landscape. Typical here are groups of trees with irregular silhouettes and the subdued lighting, with sun or moonlight reflected in the water. The landscapes often serve as a background for a lively and detailed group of figures situated in the immediate foreground.

Elsheimer's influence is clearly evident in two Tobias series after designs by Moyses van Uyttenbroeck (The Hague 1595/1600 - The Hague 1645/46). One of them was etched in 1620-21 by the artist himself (cat. no. 46); the other - once again with plenty of chiaroscuro -was executed by Jan van de Velde II.[78] Van Uyttenbroeck's choice of Old Testament and Aprocryphal themes - there are 24 prints by him with this subject matter - was clearly determined by his liking for Elsheimer's landscapes with their desolate atmosphere. Apart from the two Tobias series that are mainly concerned with a journey through inhospitable regions, it can be seen in the eight prints that he devoted to the theme of the banishment of Hagar. No less than six of them show the loneliness of the young woman with her child on their journey through the wilderness (cf. cat. no. 10). Just as Buytewech delighted in producing variations on the theme of Bathsheba, Van Uyttenbroeck was fascinated by the story of Hagar.[79]

A comparable concept of landscape with similar groups of figures can be seen in the work of Claes Cornelisz. Moeyaert (Durgerdam 1590/91 - Amsterdam 1655); this is clear not only in his Tobit series, but also in his other Old Testament etchings. There are a relatively large number of these - nineteen, compared with only one on a New Testament subject. They were all produced in the 1620s and 1630s and have a fairly small format (usually *c.* 12 x 20 cm). The composition is simple and the etching style somewhat crude and schematic, with a complex tangle of cross-hatching and a wealth of contrasts between light and dark passages.

Moeyaert treated this subject matter exclusively in series. Apart from *The History of Tobit*, all these series deal with Genesis:

16. Willem Buytewech, *Bathsheba Reading David's Letter, c.* 1615/16, etching, 16.2 x 15.2 cm, Rijksprentenkabinet, Amsterdam

*The History of Abraham* (cat. no. 14), *The History of Lot* (cat. no. 5) and *The History of Jacob*.[80] Arcadian landscapes with precipices, trees and 'classical' ruins comprise a background for groups of figures in the immediate foreground. Moeyaert was interested in the emotional events in the lives of the patriarchs, whom he portrayed without idealizing them in any way, looking sometimes rather awkward in their simplicity and with all their human failings. Their facial expressions and gestures indicate the state of mind of the protagonists, revealing their mutual relationships.

Moeyaert was the only one of the Amsterdam history painters from the period prior to Rembrandt who treated Old Testament subjects not only in paint but also in a fairly extensive graphic oeuvre. Pieter Lastman, the foremost artist of all these Pre-Rembrandtists, whose role in the evolution of Old Testament painting was unrivalled (figs 20.1 and 41.1), was an influence on Moeyaert but did not make any prints himself. Of Jan Pynas, another figure from this group of artists, only one print is known; this is a highly experimental etching showing Jacob dreaming with a landscape in the background that is clearly influenced by Elsheimer (cat. no. 15). Besides the genuine Pre-Rembrandtists there were some artists who worked in this tradition at a later stage and others whose work shows some kinship with theirs. Some of them, such as Gerrit Claesz. Bleker en Bartholomeus

**76.** Ackley 1981, pp. xxiii-xxv.
**77.** Holl. VIII, p. 152, no. 2. *Cf.* for Goudt: Andrews 1977, pp. 32, 38-40.
**78.** Holl. XXXIII, pp. 10-11, nos 7-10.
**79.** TIB VI (Commentary), nos 002-008, 071. For Van

Uyttenbroeck's prints see: Weisner 1963, pp. 169-183; Van Thiel 1978, pp. 22-32; Ackley 1981, pp. 195-196.
**80.** Holl. XIV, pp. 53-56, nos 1-15, 17-20. For the etching formerly atttributed to Moeyaert, Holl. 16 see: cat. no. 75. *Cf.* for Moeyaert's

etchings: Burchard 1917, pp. 92-93; Ackley 1981, pp. 112-113, 126-127; Munich 1982, p. 59. For the Jacob series see: Münster 1994, p. 306, no. 78.

Breenbergh, also produced a limited number of etchings with Old Testament subjects (cat. nos 20, 23 and 27).

Related to the work of this group of artists is the only Old Testament etching by Hercules Segers that we know of, namely his *Tobias and the Angel* of the 1620s (cat. no. 48). The relationship is, however, mainly due to the common example of Elsheimer. Segers was not only inspired by the German master's preferred type of landscape; he also derived his figures from Elsheimer's composition with the same theme. He must have known it from the print by Goudt (fig. 17). Like Goudt, Segers aimed for tonal effects. He achieved them, however, in an entirely different manner, through a new experimental technique of etching and an unorthodox use of colour. With his passion for experiment, Segers was the only genuine precursor of Rembrandt who, as is well known, admired his work greatly.[81]

## Rembrandt and after
Curiously, the real Golden Age of Dutch art, the second and third quarters of the seventeenth century, the years in which Rembrandt was active, does not on the whole coincide with the heyday of Old Testament printmaking. In this respect it was the preceding century that had the most to offer, together with a later period in the years around 1700. Due to their highly innovatory and extremely personal style, however, Rembrandt's Old Testament etchings, though few in number, did form an unsurpassed climax in the Golden Age.

Between 1629 and 1656 Rembrandt (Leiden 1606 - Amsterdam 1669) made eighteen etchings with Old Testament scenes, most of them small in format.[82] Four were intended as book illustra-

17. Hendrick Goudt after Adam Elsheimer, *Tobias and the Angel* ('The Large Tobias'), 1613, engraving, 25.6 x 26.9 cm, Rijksprentenkabinet, Amsterdam

tions and can be viewed as a series (cat. nos 52 and 76). As for the rest they were all made as independent sheets, usually with narrative scenes. Rembrandt had a definite preference for certain parts of the Old Testament. We find no less than ten subjects from Genesis (Adam and Eve, Abraham, Jacob and Joseph) and three scenes from the apocryphal Book of Tobit. In the case of *Jacob and Benjamin* (cat. no. 21) Rembrandt did not show the Old Testament characters in a narrative context, but portrayed them separately. This work differed from the series of biblical protagonists by the Goltzius school, in that he was not concerned with a heroic 'state portrait' but with making a 'snapshot' record of an intimate moment in the relation between a father and his young son. Rembrandt's originality, however, did not mean that he worked completely independently of the visual tradition and the work of his predecessors. His Old Testament etchings, such as *The Triumph of Mardocai* (cat. no. 41), show that it was precisely by engaging in a 'dialogue' with his major precursors and making a thorough study of their work that he achieved his own unique masterpieces.[83]

Although Rembrandt's graphic oeuvre was held in high esteem and enjoyed an international market, his Old Testament prints - unlike his history paintings - had few imitators. The collaboration that Rembrandt entered on in around 1631 with Jan van Vliet in order - in emulation of Rubens - to reproduce his paintings in print form, included only one print with an Old Testament theme (cat. no. 6). In around 1633 Van Vliet also made two prints that reproduce Old Testament works of Rembrandt's colleague from Leiden, Jan Lievens.[84]

A further handful of prints with Old Testament themes can be attributed to Lievens himself; most of these are extremely modest etchings but there is also an impressive woodcut (cat. nos 3 and 33). As for Rembrandt's actual pupils, only a few of them made prints with Old Testament subjects and none of them produced very many. Worth mentioning here are a couple of etchings attributed to Ferdinand Bol (cat. nos 13 and 25), one by Hendrick Heerschop and two by Constantijn van Renesse (cat. no. 37). Finally there are various artists who were influenced to a greater or lesser extent by Rembrandt's style; among them are Pieter de Grebber (cat. no. 44) and Pieter Rodermondt, each of whom produced three Old Testament etchings.[85]

After 1656 Rembrandt made no more prints with Old Testament scenes. The examples by his school mentioned here were also made before this date. From the late 1650s there was virtually no activity in this field. Not one *peintre-graveur* was still working in any serious fashion with Old Testament material. There was not even any reproductive printmaking of any outstanding quality during these years. The situation only changed after the 1660s, with the appearance of the mezzotint. This new graphic technique that was initially used mainly in the Northern Netherlands

**81.** For Segers see: Haverkamp Begemann 1973; Ackley 1981, p. 55.
**82.** See: cat. nos 2, 4, 9, 11-12, 17-19, 21, 41, 49-50, 52. Cf. for Rembrandt's biblical prints: Tümpel 1970. For a summary of his work as an etcher see: Berlin/ Amsterdam/ London 1991-92A, pp. 160-169.
**83.** See the essay by Christian Tümpel below.
**84.** Van Vliet: Amsterdam 1996, pp. 40-41, 89-92, nos 1a, 34, 35. Willem de Leeuw of Antwerp also made a reproductive print of an Old Testament composition by Rembrandt (before 1638): Bruyn 1982, pp. 47-50.
**85.** Lievens: Holl. XI, pp. 5-6, 70, nos 1-4, 99 (cf. for his etchings: Amsterdam 1988-89). Bol: Holl. III, pp. 15-16, nos 1-2 (cf. for his etchings: Tsuritani 1975-76). Van Renesse: Holl. XX, pp. 8-9, nos 1-2. Heerschop: Holl. IX, p. 4, no. 2. De Grebber: Holl. VIII, pp. 166-167, nos 1-3. Rodermondt: Holl. XX, pp. 36-37, 39, nos 1-2, 4. For printmaking by the Rembrandt school: Zilkens 1982.

and which achieved a peak there in the 1680s, made it possible to reproduce art works in a way that had not previously been possible - with a wide variety of transitions from light to dark. Due to its range of 'half tones', this 'black art' was capable of rendering the tonality of drawings and particularly of paintings to great effect.[86]

Wallerant Vaillant (Lille 1623 - Amsterdam 1677), who qualifies as the first professional mezzotint artist, made more than 200 mezzotints. Nine of them reproduce Old Testament history paintings, older and more recent, by Italians (Caravaggio, Guido Reni, Domenichino, Palma il Giovane) and by Dutch artists (Pieter Lastman, Jan Jansz. van Bronckhorst, Gerard de Lairesse). Typical of Vaillant's work are his *Jael and Sisera* and *Judith and Holofernes* where he made a pair of prints out of a somewhat older painting by Guido Reni (c. 1625/26) and a recent composition by De Lairesse (c. 1675; figs 18a-b, p. 29). Central in both is an Old Testament heroine, each portrayed with her male victim.[87]

Other Dutch mezzotint artists in this period such as Abraham Blooteling and Joannes and Paulus II van Somer, made similar prints of Old Testament compositions of artists of Italian, Dutch and French origin. Some original work was also produced by them, although sporadically. Only in the late seventeenth and in the first quarter of the eighteenth centuries would Old Testament printmaking flourish again in Holland, both numerically and in quality. Romeyn de Hooghe, Jan Luyken and Bernard Picart became active then, once more illustrating the Old Testament in systematic fashion, partly after their own designs. Their works were published as picture Bibles (cat. nos. 63-66), all of them

being made for commissions. The revival of Old Testament printmaking in around 1700 clearly coincided with the rise of a new generation of publishers, with Pieter Mortier prominent among them, who were prepared to risk investing in the production of fairly sizeable biblical picture series.[88]

The fact that, apart from a few exceptions, the Old Testament only formed a small part of the production of Dutch *peintre-graveurs* during the Golden Age, should not lead us to conclude that there was any lack of interest in this subject matter. Throughout the century countless Old Testament prints were published, often in series or in picture books. In terms of quantity Old Testament printmaking flourished as never before. What was involved, however, was mainly reprints and copies of older plates.

This is particularly clear when we look at the picture Bibles of the Golden Age. In contrast with the book illustrations of De Hooghe, Luyken and Picart in most cases here we are dealing with reprints, not original work. The Amsterdam publisher Claes Jansz. Visscher in particular specialized in reprints and pirated copies of older biblical picture books (cat. nos 55-58, 60-61).[89] One could perhaps criticize him and his fellow publishers that they aimed for big sales without taking risks, not offering any commissions for original series. On the other hand one could argue that by building up a sizeable stock of reprints and copies they helped to make the older masterpieces more generally known. In this way, they contributed to the popularity of the biblical picture, anticipating the flowering of catchpenny prints and prints for children in the eighteenth century (cat. no. 53).

**86.** For Dutch mezzotints see: Wuestman 1995.
**87.** Holl. XXXI, pp. 69-70, nos 16-17. Reni's painting: Pepper 1984, pp. 252-253, no. 104. For De Lairesse's painting, a 'modello' especially made for Vaillant, see: Roy 1992, pp. 261-262, no. P. 90.

*Cf.* for Vaillant: Ackley 1981, pp. 272-273; Wuestman 1995, pp. 66-70. For De Lairesse, one of the few *peintre-graveurs* in this period of whom a number of Old Testament prints are known, see: Roy 1992, nos G. 2-G. 8, G. 16, G. 18, G. 53 (c. 1665 - c. 1675).

**88.** *Cf.* for Dutch printmaking in the late seventeenth century: Schuckman 1989. For book illustration in the decades round 1700 see: De la Fontaine Verwey 1934, pp. 17-52.
**89.** *Cf.* below 'Something for Everyone...' by the present author.

18a-b  (companion pieces)
a. Wallerant Vaillant after Gerard de Lairesse, *Jael and Sisera*, c. 1675, mezzotint, 40.4 x 25.5 cm, Rijksprentenkabinet, Amsterdam
b. Wallerant Vaillant after Guido Reni, *Judith and Holofernes*, c. 1675, mezzotint, 40.3 x 25 cm, Rijksprentenkabinet, Amsterdam

Cat. no. 2

# Rembrandt's Old Testament Etchings

*Christian Tümpel*

In Rembrandt's etchings, as in the works of most master print-makers, biblical stories and, among these, scenes from the New Testament (especially the Childhood of Jesus and the Passion) are central themes.[1] Nevertheless, his Old Testament etchings, just eighteen in all, make an extraordinary appearance in the flat landscape of the biblical graphic art of the second third of the seventeenth century. In this genre too, Rembrandt refined the artistic potential of etching, expanded its range of interpretation, adding greatly to its power of expression in a sketch-like as well as in a painterly etching style.[2]

It was by no means Rembrandt's intention to open up new ground in the rich field of Old Testament themes with his etchings in extensive print series - other artists had done this work before him. His aim rather was to create small, individual masterpieces which would stand on their own as works of art whose content, owing to a long pictorial tradition, would be understood without long explanatory or interpretative captions. They were meant for collectors at home and abroad who, recognizing the references, would classify them in their collections mostly according to theme. Rembrandt took artistic licence in embellishing scenes (cat. no. 21), removing one or more of the main figures from the narrative context (cat. nos 21, 49, fig. 49.1) and quoting from famous works that he knew from his own collection (cat. no. 2). As he was aiming at collectors, he himself determined what pictorial vocabulary he would employ and - depending on the collector's taste - whether to execute his scenes in an edifying, narrative or genre-like way.

## The choice of subject matter

When Rembrandt first started working in the field of etching he did not know all the Old Testament stories, nor was he familiar with how they had been treated iconographically. He did not set about exploring the Old Testament themes systematically beginning, like an illustrator, with Adam and Eve and ending with the Apocrypha. Rather the encounter with other artists and works of art, the examination of various artistic problems and the preoccupation with certain background themes led to Rembrandt's interest in producing etchings with this subject matter. Other matters that influenced his choice were the fact that some of these works were executed as commissions and the problems of teaching certain themes, groups of themes or books of the Old Testament.

Almost all Rembrandt's Old Testament etchings were executed in Amsterdam. It was there that Rembrandt turned more intensely to the first part of the Bible. Of these seventeen etchings with Old Testament scenes, ten are devoted to Genesis. The fact that Rembrandt turned to Genesis is clearly connected with his own acquisition of prints of great masters as well as with the preferences of the Pre-Rembrandtists, whose paintings he re-examined. The first book of the Bible also played a central part in their work.[3] Rembrandt deliberately created his etchings in dialogue with famous engravers and woodcut artists. Instead of trying to imitate his predecessors, however, he tried to vary their compositions to suit his own style, thereby surpassing them in form and content. For his etchings, he was inspired above all by important Dutch, German, Italian and French printmakers such as Lucas van Leyden, Heinrich Aldegrever, Tobias Stimmer, Antonio Tempesta, Maarten van Heemskerck, Bernard Salomon, Matthaeus Merian, to name the more prominent ones. Irrespective of all the differences, Rembrandt's choice of Old Testament subject matter still shows most affinity with Lucas van Leyden's graphic work.[4] Regardless of whether he used masterworks (cat. nos 16a, 40, fig. 41.1) or more modest work by minor engravers (figs 19.1, 21.1) as a model, Rembrandt always transformed the ideas stylistically. His models may not always have been of outstanding quality, but it was his genius to transform pictorial solutions into unprecedented compositions.

In the only etching done in Leiden (c. 1629), the old blind man Tobit hurries to the door as his son returns home (fig. 49.1). This subject provided Rembrandt with the opportunity of treating several themes that would preoccupy him for almost his entire life: the blind man's inner vision and the wisdom of pious age.

1. Of the approximately 290 etchings Rembrandt made, the depictions of biblical themes make up the largest group by far. Of these, at least eighteen can be assigned to the Old Testament (see note 2) and 55 to the New Testament. On Rembrandt's biblical etchings see: Amsterdam 1964-65; Tümpel 1970; Dierker 1983; Raupp 1994.
2. Regarding Rembrandt's Old Testament etchings, see cat. nos 2, 4, 9, 11, 12, 17-19, 21, 32, 41, 49, 50, 52; Tümpel 1970, nos 1, 5, 8, 9, 14, 16, 18, 20, 25, 27, 30, 32, 34, 39; Münster 1994, nos 66, 68, 72, 75, 76, 80-83, 93, 98, 102, 103, 111. See also the references in the catalogue entries below. A few etchings are presumed to be representations of Old Testament narratives, but their interpretation is still disputed: B. 118 (interpreted as *Jacob and Laban*; Blanc 1854-89, no. 7), B. 120 (*Ruth and Naomi*; Tümpel 1978, pp. 96-

97, fig. 15), B. 340 (*Esther*; Kahr 1966, p. 241). On the subject of Rembrandt's etchings see also Tümpel 1986, pp. 70-75, 145, 147, 254-259, 272, 278, 279, 282, 284, and the essay by Holm Bevers in Berlin/ Amsterdam/ London 1991-92A, pp. 160-169.
3. On the Pre-Rembrandtists' choice of subjects, see Tümpel 1974A and Tümpel 1974B, pp. 35-69
4. Of the fourteen Old Testament

narratives which Rembrandt probably chose as themes himself, eight had already been employed in prints by Lucas van Leyden: *The Fall of Man*, *The Banishment of Hagar and Ishmael*, *Abraham and Isaac before the Sacrifice*, *Joseph's Coat Shown to Jacob*, *Joseph and Potiphar's Wife*, *Joseph Telling His Dreams*, *David in Prayer*, *The Triumph of Mordecai*. Unlike Lucas van Leyden, Rembrandt devoted much attention to the Book of Tobit, for

which he created three etchings: *The Blindness of Tobit* (twice), and *The Angel Departing From Tobit's Family*. The four illustrations to the *Piedra gloriosa* were commisioned works and are therefore not included in this list. For Lucas' influence on Rembrandt's etchings, see Wheelock 1983.

The Old Testament etchings that Rembrandt made in the 1630s in Amsterdam deal with 'The Fall of Man', 'The Banishment of Hagar and Ishmael' and four episodes from the story of Joseph (cat. nos 1, 9, 17-19, 21). While scenes of the Fall were not an obligatory subject for paintings, they were a must in European graphic art and Rembrandt was no exception (cat. no. 2). Amongst other great engravers, Albrecht Dürer and Lucas van Leyden (cat. no. 1) had already created masterpieces with this subject. It is not therefore surprising that Rembrandt sought and found a way of expressing the inner meaning that bore his own imprint.

The story of Abraham, to which Rembrandt first turned in his etching *The Banishment of Hagar and Ishmael* of 1637 (cat. no. 9), was a major theme both in the work of the sixteenth-century printmakers and in that of the Pre-Rembrandtists. Rembrandt took it up again in the 1640s and 1650s. By contrast, he had already dealt with the history of Joseph in the 1630s. Many prominent engravers had treated this story in print series. Inspired by them, Rembrandt dedicated four independent single etchings to this narrative (cat. nos 17-19, 21).[5] The etching *Joseph Telling His Dreams* (cat. no. 17) treats the subject of his brothers' envy: Joseph's father, the patriarch Jacob, follows the story with intense interest. The sneering reactions of the brothers betray the drama that is about to take place. Rembrandt originally intended to make a large-scale etching with the help of an assistant and had already made a grisaille on paper of the composition as he had also done with the large *Ecce Homo* (B. 77). The project fell through, however, and Rembrandt then etched the episode himself on a smaller scale.[6]

At the beginning of the 1640s, Rembrandt produced a large etching after all, a milestone in his Baroque works. It shows how the humiliated viceroy Haman, on the order of King Ahasuerus, has to lead his adversary Mordecai, the Jew whom he had condemned to death, through the city in triumph (cat. no. 41). Rembrandt's etching was inspired by Lucas van Leyden (cat. no. 40). However, in some respects it is superior to its model, for Rembrandt had learned from Lastman (fig. 41.1) how to stage scenes of large groups of people. This subject therefore provided him the opportunity to prove his ability as a director of crowd scenes.

A quick glance at the other Old Testament etchings from the 1640s reveals that - apart from the narrative of the patriarch Abraham that Rembrandt treated once more in the etching *Abraham and Isaac before the Sacrifice* (cat. no. 11) - the fate of Tobit was also a subject that preoccupied him as well. Inspired by Maarten van Heemskerck (fig. 50.2), he etched *The Angel Departing From Tobit's Family* (cat. no. 50). In the 1650s, Rembrandt again took up the subject of *The Blindness of Tobit* (cat. no. 49) which he had already dealt with in his Leiden period (fig. 49.1). It is the third etching that he devoted to this minor book of the Old Testament Apocrypha. Rembrandt was also preoccupied with scenes of recognition from the story of Abraham, where everything is transformed through heavenly intervention (cf. cat. nos 4 and 12). In addition to this, there is a moving print portraying *David in Prayer* (cat. no. 32) - again inspired by Lucas van Leyden (fig. 32.1). Here human failings and the repentance of a great hero are the central themes.

Apart from his brilliant later works, Rembrandt created four illustrations, in 1655, for Menasseh ben Israel's *Piedra gloriosa*, which were bound in the book but also circulated as single prints (cat. nos 52 and 76). Here the choice of Old Testament episodes was predetermined by the author, and was therefore not a typical. Above all Rembrandt used Bible illustrations as iconographic models for these four prints (see cat. no. 52).

## The Bible and Flavius Josephus

Since the pictorial tradition often offered him a choice of various iconographic solutions, Rembrandt was obliged to study the biblical texts again, in order to find the precise passage that corresponded best to his vision of the scene. In addition to the pictorial tradition, he also drew directly on the biblical text for his Old Testament etchings, using it as a source of inspiration to arrive at new pictorial solutions. For his late work he made use of an old Dutch Bible whose translation of the Apocrypha was based on the Vulgate translation of the Bible by St Jerome. Rembrandt apparently also read the States Bible (cat. no. 67), whose translation of the canonical books of the Old Testament was based on the original Hebrew text, that of the aprocryphal books on the Greek translation of the Bible (cat. no. 49).

Another important source of inspiration was the *Jewish Antiquities* (cat. nos 70 and 71), a recountal of the narrative parts of the Old Testament by Flavius Josephus. It not only included Jewish legends, but also frequently embellished biblical stories with moving details of psychological impact which Rembrandt gladly made use of (cf. cat. nos 11 and 12).[7]

## Iconography

Rembrandt did not simply take over the iconography of his Old Testament etchings from the models of other artists; instead he reshaped them and amplified the motifs from the narratives and their context as it was depicted in the pictorial tradition. Rembrandt wanted to illuminate the human, fateful background and make it visible. The motifs that he used to do this were often drawn from the tradition or directly inspired by a previous model, and his pictorial language also often keeps to the conventions. The way that he quoted, transformed, reinforced, omitted or condensed motifs, however, shows that what concerned him was to reveal the inner meaning. To do this effectively, he felt free to omit details that belonged to the 'history' as it was normally told, introducing unhistoric motifs instead.

---

**5.** *Joseph and Potiphar's Wife* and, *Joseph's Coat Shown to Jacob, Jacob Caressing Benjamin* and *Joseph Telling His Dreams*.
**6.** Rembrandt, with the help of an assistant, already had portrayed a later moment of the drama in the etching *Joseph's Coat Shown to Jacob*

(cat. no. 18). *Cf.* for the *Ecce Homo*: Amsterdam 1996, pp. 68-72.
**7.** See Tümpel 1984, pp. 185-192.

In some of his etchings Rembrandt quoted from the work of other artists using these erudite references to add an extra level of interpretation, thus making soteriological connections visible and sequences recognizable. In his etching *The Fall of Man* (cat. no. 2), he 'quotes' the dragon in *The Descent into Hell* (fig. 2.3) from Dürer's *Engraved Passion* series (B. 16). With this reference, Rembrandt was commenting on the pictorial tradition in which the Old Testament prefigured New Testament events. In 1638 he acquired a 'Passion' series by Dürer. This was probably Dürer's *Engraved Passion*, since Rembrandt already owned a copy of the *Small Woodcut Passion* (B. 17-52) in 1635.[8] This series, in which the Fall and Salvation are typologically juxtaposed, begins with *The Fall of Man*. In *The Descent into Hell* (fig. 2.3), Adam, who had fallen prey to sin, is freed by Christ from Satan's power. Rembrandt, like Dürer, depicts the tempter not as a snake, but as a dragon, thus emphasizing that Satan who tempted Adam and Eve was himself conquered by Christ.[9] In this respect Rembrandt was actually also keeping more faithfully to the biblical text than many of his predecessors had done. According to Genesis (3:14) the snake was condemned to crawl on its belly only after the Fall and it must therefore have had another form before then.

## The treatment of the narrative context

Poets can tell their tale from beginning to end; painters however can depict only one moment. Nevertheless, through allusions to previous events or by hinting at what is to come, they too can suggest the total story. This feature is also typical for Rembrandt's art.[10] It played a central role in French art theory of the seventeenth century. Artists had already thought about this issue long before then. Fifteenth and sixteenth century artists had shown the context by means of simultaneous scenes (see eg, cat. nos 39 and 45). By contrast, a Baroque artist like Rembrandt observed the rule of the unity of time, place and action. For that reason he no longer incorporated simultaneous scenes as the artists of the sixteenth century, whose prints served him as models, had done. Instead, to give the viewer a sense of the overall course of the narrative, Rembrandt added figures or motifs in almost all of his Old Testament etchings which evoke the preceding episode or refer to the denouement of the story. He thereby developed a model for solving this problem that was fully in conformity with the requirements of French theoreticians.

A good example is the depiction of *The Banishment of Hagar and Ishmael* (cat. no. 9).[11] God had promised the aged couple Abraham and Sarah offspring in abundance, but so far they had waited in vain. Doubting God's promise Sarah had given up hope of any children. She therefore offered Abraham her maidservant Hagar, so that she could give him an heir instead. This 'human solution' turned out to be the cause of the whole problem. Hagar, who bore

Ishmael, became arrogant towards Sarah who responded with jealousy. When Sarah herself gave birth to Isaac, she complained to Abraham, demanding that he would banish Hagar and Ishmael so that Ishmael would not share her son's inheritance. Despite his reluctance due to his feelings for Ishmael, Abraham complied with Sarah's request since that was God's will.

In his painting *The Banishment of Hagar and Ishmael* (fig. 9.1) Pieter Lastman presented an overall view of the narrative with Abraham accompanying his cherished concubine part of the way before blessing his son Ishmael and bidding her farewell with a heavy heart. Standing near the farmhouse, the aged Sarah, with Isaac on her arm, follows what is happening. Rembrandt evokes the preceding episode and the one that follows with even more vivid imagery (cat. no. 9). He has the departure take place in front of the house. Sarah, old and gaunt, watches in triumph from the window as Hagar who has been turned out of doors goes on her way. Little Isaac, the cause of the whole quarrel, peeps at them through the door. The figure of Abraham as portrayed here epitomizes the conflict between the past and the future. He stands between the two women, blessing Ishmael, who sets off with his mother into an uncertain future. The patriarch looks longingly after Hagar while at the same time, he is returning to the house, right foot first.

In the etching *Abraham Serving the Lord and Two Angels* (cat. no. 4), Rembrandt uses the figure of Ishmael, shooting the arrow at a distant target, to recall both the doubt of the aged couple in the past as well as Ishmael's banishment later, since Ishmael, the ancestor of the Ishmaelites, became an archer in the wilderness. Apart from depictions of climaxes, Rembrandt frequently showed scenes where the future event is first implied or where the memory of the decisive episode lingers on, for example, in scenes of conversation (cat. no. 11). In that way he achieved a maximum amount of inner tension with the least amount of action.

## Extraction

To capture the psychological content of a scene, artists of the sixteenth and seventeenth centuries used a type of imagery established in the Middle Ages which I have called 'Herauslösung' or extraction.[12] Rembrandt, too, applied it in three of his Old Testament etchings. Before I go into further detail on this subject, however, a brief historical survey of this pictorial solution is necessary. It is generally known that at the beginning of the fourteenth century, individual biblical figures or groups of figures were taken out of their scenic context and developed as independent representations. 'The achievement of the fourteenth century lies in the extraction of the emotional content from the scenic context [...] by isolating the main figures', as Wilhelm Pinder has pointed out. 'Each moment is a conquest of the poetical [...] The only essential feature is really the extraction of emotional content

**8.** Hofstede de Groot 1906, no. 422; Strauss/ Van der Meulen 1979, doc. 1638/2. Rembrandt's etching *Christ Chasing the Money-changers from the Temple* (B. 69) of 1635 was influenced by a print with the same subject in Dürer's *Small Woodcut Passion*; see Münz

1952, Vol. 2, pp. 96-97, no. 206.
**9.** Just how familiar Rembrandt was with typology is also proven in the etching *The Holy Family* (B. 63), where Mary steps on the snake. This gesture was a symbol of the Redemption, which, according to Medieval exegesis, was prophesied

in the divine judgement in Gen. 3:15. See Tümpel 1970, nos 1 and 64.
**10.** Tümpel 1968A, pp. 137-160; Tümpel 1969, pp. 138-153; Tümpel 1986, pp. 255-259.
**11.** See for this subject: Hamann 1936.

**12.** Cf. Tümpel 1968B, pp. 113-126; Tümpel 1969, pp. 160-187.

from the internally experienced scenic context [...]'.[13] Images of this sort were also adopted by artists of the sixteenth and seventeenth centuries - often with traditional subjects, however.[14] The same applies to Rembrandt, but he, like a number of other artists, went beyond the tradition by also employing this pictorial form for subjects which to my knowledge had not yet been used in painting and graphic art.

Rembrandt produced three Old Testament etchings in which extraction plays an important role. In the etching *Jacob Caressing Benjamin* (cat. no. 21), the love of the aged patriarch - who bestows affection on his youngest son, believing that Joseph is dead, is expressed in concentrated form. In French woodcuts on the subject *Joseph's Brothers Asking their Father to Allow Benjamin to Accompany them to Egypt* (fig. 21.1), the love which the father has transferred to Benjamin after the supposed death of his favourite son Joseph is expressed in a striking visual manner. The aged Jacob sits in a chair, the youngest son is leaning against him, or sitting in his lap while Jacob has his arm around his shoulders.

Rembrandt extracted this group from its scenic context and heightened the spontaneity and intimacy even more. Benjamin, standing between the legs of his father, leans back full of trust with a sunny smile. His father is clasping his head and gazing out as if at the viewer. With this device of extraction, the love of the proud, aged father for his son becomes the actual subject, and the narrative context recedes.

In two other etchings, however, both showing 'The Blindness of Tobit' (cat. no. 49 and fig. 49.1), the context is still indicated and the message of the scene has been further reinforced. In the moving later etching (cat. no. 49), the blind and aged Tobit, hurrying towards his returning son, misses the door entrance and stumbles over a spinning wheel. His helplessness is emphasized in particular by the fact that, unlike the models that Rembrandt used as his inspiration, the young Tobias and the angel are not depicted. Nonetheless, Rembrandt, while remaining completely faithful to the text, has managed to suggest the scene he omitted. The dog for instance that accompanied Tobias and the angel on their journey can be see heralding the return of the group: 'For he ran ahead, wagged his tail, leapt and appeared frolicsome' (Tobit 11: 9, Vulgate).

In concentrating on a few motifs, Rembrandt achieved a lucid condensation of the narrative which was especially characteristic of Baroque art. In that respect his work differs sharply from that of the Mannerists. Van Mander, for example, showed a preference for mass scenes in his own work. However, he also saw that great masters can achieve a maximum in quality with a minimum of figures and motifs.[15] Among other methods Rembrandt accomplished this with the device of extraction.

## Body Language

Body language has always been an important means of artistic expression. Convincing formulas had already been devised for many emotions and mental states that were reused in varied forms. Rembrandt, too, made use of this treasure trove of visual conventions, reinforcing them by depicting postures from preceding or succeeding events. Body language was thus employed to make the meaning of a scene clearer.[16] For instance, bewildered by the temptation with which they are confronted, Adam and Eve draw in their heads (cat. no. 2). This pose was inspired by representations of 'The Expulsion from the Garden of Eden', in which Adam and Eve shrink from the angel's flaming sword (cf. cat. no. 1d). The bitter end is foreshadowed in their crouching pose. Rembrandt's striking pictorial solutions are often achieved by intensifying the formulas of his predecessors.

In Rembrandt's etching *Joseph and Potiphar's Wife* (cat. no. 19), exposure turns into exposing. The woman's body bulges in the direction of the viewer. In *The Blindness of Tobit* (cat. no. 49), the old man hurrying towards his son is not led by a servant, as the Vulgate and pictorial tradition has it, but is stumbling and groping seeking his way with outstretched arms. Rembrandt borrowed this pose from Raphael's famous depiction of the blind Elymas (fig. 49.2). Even when Rembrandt quotes from scenes with rulers in which the iconography is traditionally strongly predetermined by convention and formulas, he manages to insert his borrowings harmonously in the total design. Many expressions of veneration in *The Triumph of Mordecai* (cat. no. 41), for instance, are conveyed by means of established visual formulas. Nonetheless, Rembrandt represents in a marvellous way the movement of the jostling crowd and the father rescuing his son from the rearing horse.

## Pictorial Language

Rembrandt's etching *The Angel Departing from Tobit's Family* (cat. no. 50) does not keep faithfully to the text of the Apocrypha. Lastman, who holds correctly to the text, depicts the angel at a distance from the house, while Rembrandt places him at the entrance of the house as was done in the older pictorial tradition. Witnesses standing in the doorway look on in fear as the heavens open up and the angel disappears in the divine light. In depicting the whole family with all the servants, and even the animals, Rembrandt arranged a number of figures of different ages in very divergent poses, expressing alarm, astonishment or prayer. Many of the motifs, like the astonished female lodger who leans out the window to catch a glimpse of the vanishing angel, belong to the convention of farewell scenes. But Rembrandt also included motifs which were part of his own repertoire to reinforce his interpretation. The aged Sarah, dazzled by the sight of the angel, has dropped the cane she was leaning on and reaches out towards this vision, deeply moved.

**13.** Pinder 1929, pp. 93 and 95.
**14.** For example the 'lonely crucified Christ' type (cf. Knipping 1974, Vol. I, p. 216).
**15.** Van Mander/ Miedema 1973, Vol. I, pp. 136, 137 (fol. 17v) gives a detailed description of 'sober history scenes'. According to him, great masters know how to attain high quality with only a few figures. They equal great lords who say little, but what they say is well-thought out.
**16.** See Tümpel 1986, pp. 52-54.

## Etching Technique

In his Old Testament etchings Rembrandt succeeded in achieving the monumentality of paintings. He developed an irregular etching technique which contributes to the liveliness of the scenes, thereby expanding the painterly as well as the graphical potentialities of the medium of etching and making the total impression more true to life. By employing an extremely varied network of lines he achieved a painterly chiaroscuro, breaking drastically with contemporary engraving with its regular contours and monotonous parallel hatching.

In his early work (cat. nos 2, 19, fig. 49.1 ) Rembrandt worked mainly with the etching needle, but from the 1630s onwards he used drypoint more and more often (cat. nos 4, 11, 12, 41). In the 1650s he sometimes even worked directly on the plate with drypoint and burin, without employing any chemical treatment (B. 78). He achieved gradations from the strongest to the most delicate lines with utmost assurance. The burr on either side of the drypoint lines produces a patchy effect on printing, resulting in a deep tonal unity.

Most of the etchings were conceived in a painterly way (cf. cat. nos 2, 9, 17). Only in a few works did Rembrandt use an etching style which could be described as loose and sketchy, giving them the appearance of drawings and sometimes even of silverpoint drawings (B. 58, 96 and 147). He soon integrated this style, however, into the painterly one, for instance by partly depicting the protagonists in this graphical conception. In this way the main figures of The Sacrifice of Isaac (cat. no. 12) stand out radiantly against the darker background.

Rembrandt used chiaroscuro to illuminate and to obscure, as a phenomenon which lights up and darkens. Due to this the figures can be seen as visual conveyers of hope or despair, lust for life or distrust or else as suggesting a foreboding of what is still hidden, depending on whether they are situated in the light or in the shadow. In a preliminary drawing of The Fall of Man (fig. 2.1) the arousal of carnal lust is shown by the movement of Eve's arm in the direction of Adam's sex. Rembrandt omitted the extreme gesture in the final etching but retained the idea (cat. no. 2). He did not conceal the genitals of the first couple, but portrayed them in shadow. Despite their apparently random placing, low highlights subtly draw attention to the importance of the driving force of sexuality which, according to the Fathers of the Church, led to the Fall.

Rembrandt sketched the scenes on the copper plate and then executed the darker sections. At intervals he made trial proofs. He used the opportunity to document the different stages of a composition by making impressions of the various states in between, much less in the Old Testament than in the New Testament etchings. Here his corrections were aimed more at the removal of minor flaws like slips of the etching needle (cat. no. 21), smudges caused by the acid solution (cat. no. 50), or small white spots (cat. no. 32).

In his New Testament etchings (eg, B. 46, 49, 53, 54, 56, 76, 77, 78, 81, 99) where he competed with master printmakers, the pleasure in altering and experimenting is manifestly greater than in those he did of Old Testament subjects. One reason for this is that he illustrated more New Testament stories as nocturnal scenes, thereby constantly recording the progress of the work by pulling trial proofs from the beginning on (B. 46, 53, 54, 56, 73, 83, 86, 50). There are admittedly just as many proofs among the Old Testament illustrations for the Piedra gloriosa (cat. no. 52), but these were not determined by artistic considerations. Rembrandt was rather taking into account the ideas and expectations of the person who commissioned the work, thus correcting the iconography of the subjects of his etchings several times.

Rembrandt deliberately made use of the fact that a single state of an etching can be printed in various ways, using different manners of application, like wiping the ink, or choosing several types of paper. He took counterproofs from fresh impressions so that he could control and, where necessary, correct the representation on the etching plate, as was the case with The Sacrifice of Abraham (see cat. no. 12). At the same time he used the counterproofs as teaching aids. Rembrandt's etchings, besides copies after his paintings and drawings, were present as study material in the studio's of his pupils and followers, as well as in those of European artists in general.

Even before Rembrandt, artist-theoreticians like Vasari and Van Mander had begun to develop criteria for the evaluation of graphic art and to establish artistic rules for this medium.[17] Much of what they called for in terms of content and form was realized by Rembrandt - although in his own style - and even surpassed by him with respect to opulence, variety, composition and intensity. Thus, for instance, he placed the protagonists mostly full-length in the centre of the composition but not only highlighted them in terms of where he placed them; he also accentuated them by literally shedding light on them and by the use of intensified hatchings.

## Reception

Already during his lifetime, Rembrandt's pupils and followers painted variations on the master's Old Testament etchings. The master's graphic art provided them with strong impulses. For example, Jan Victors was inspired by Joseph Telling his Dreams (cat. no. 17) and in an extraction Arent de Gelder elevated the etching Abraham Serving the Lord and Two Angels (cat. no. 4) to a magnificent, luminous vision.[18]

Rembrandt's etchings made him world famous not only among painters and printmakers, but also among art dealers and collectors. His prints fetched high prices at auctions in Paris and

**17.** Van Mander/ Floerke 1906, Vol. I, pp. 110ff.
**18.** For Victors, see: Sumowski IV, p. 2604, no. 1753; De Gelder: Sumowski II, p. 1168, no. 759. Cf. Münster 1994, pp. 116-117, 229, no. 8.

elsewhere. At the end of his life they were represented in the most important print collections of Europe.[19]

Thus, for Rembrandt, etchings were the medium in which he communicated with the world of art. His graphic art in particular gave him national and international fame. Apart from the many biographies on the artist, the medium also guaranteed the permanent presence of his art in public debate until other media (reproductive prints and phototype, for example) took the place of the 'musée imaginaire'.

**19.** In 1666, Michel de Marolles owned 224 etchings by Rembrandt. In 1667, the inventory of the estate of the Flemish painter and art dealer Cornelis de Wael, who had lived in Italy for over 50 years, listed 70 Rembrandt etchings (Münz 1952, Vol. 2, p. 209). The Sicilian nobleman Don Antonio Ruffo, whose attention was drawn to Rembrandt's etchings by Guercino (Strauss/ Van der Meulen 1979, doc. 1660/7), bought etchings by the artist in the year that Rembrandt died: 'Si è già accennanato alle stampe del Rembrandt che don Antonio Ruffo teneva nella galleria, e queste in numero di 189 furono spedite dal Rembrandt stesso da Amsterdam, giungendo in Messina nel dicembre 1669, come dal notamento del Ruffo. Le stampe del Rembrandt sone ricercate anche oggi essendo bellissime' (Ruffo 1916, p. 313).

# Something for Everyone? The Marketing of Old Testament Prints in Holland's Golden Age

*Peter van der Coelen*

In present-day perceptions of the visual culture of Holland's Golden Age a prominent role is played by the Old Testament history pieces of Rembrandt. In our own times, masterpieces such as *Bathsheba with the Letter from David* in the Louvre or *Jacob Blesses the Sons of Joseph* in the museum of Brunswick, Germany, have been reproduced countless times, on postcards, posters and calendars. In Rembrandt's day they were top works for the enjoyment of an élite. For a broader circle of viewers their visual image of the Old Testament was determined by prints. With their comparative cheapness and greater ease of distribution they had a much larger reach than paintings. As far as Old Testament prints are concerned, Rembrandt's etchings - now held by many to be the absolute summit of the genre - likewise occupy a place at the top. Even so, they represent only a fraction of what was available in this field in the seventeenth century. Not only were there contemporary prints to be had, there was also graphic art from the sixteenth century, both in early impressions and as later reprints or copies.

This essay presents an examination of what was on offer, in terms of Old Testament prints, in the Dutch Republic of the seventeenth century. What prints and print books were there in the book and printshops of the day? Moreover, how did publishers attempt to make their products known to a wider audience and how did they distribute their wares in the marketplace? Another crucial question is how the market for prints was structured. What buyers did publishers have in mind for their Old Testament prints and print books, who could afford them - and who actually bought them? And what, finally, is known about how they were used?

A reconstruction of the complete range of Old Testament prints cannot be attempted here, nor will such an enterprise ever be practical in the future. Much material has yet to be submitted to scholarly study and in the passage of time a great deal must have disappeared altogether. The focus here, therefore, is on a stock of prints and picture books about which exceptionally informative sources are available, namely that of Claes Jansz. Visscher, 'the most productive print publisher of his day',[1] and his successors. At the shop run by the Visscher family in Amsterdam it was possible to buy virtually anything that was being printed in intaglio: from maps of the world to weaving patterns and from game boards to Rembrandt etchings. Utility printing, popular prints, 'art prints' and picture books were all part of this stock, which in size and scope was one of the largest of the seventeenth century. Among this enormous volume of printed images, biblical art was one of the largest categories. Loose prints, print series, Bible maps, picture books and popular prints of Scriptural themes account for something like a third of all the works offered by the Visschers. And in all these, the Old Testament plays a particularly prominent part.

## Claes Jansz. Visscher and his successors

The foundations of the stock were laid by Claes Jansz. Visscher.[2] Visscher was born in 1586 or 1587 in Amsterdam, the city in which he was to spend his entire life. Before he turned to publishing the work of others, Visscher had himself achieved proficiency as an artist, possibly as a pupil of David Vinckboons (cf. cat. no. 47). As an etcher he began by working for other publishers, but it was not long before he started publishing his own prints. In 1611 he bought a house on Kalverstraat, strategically sited between the

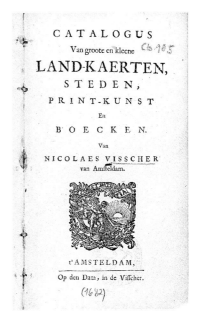

1. *Catalogus Van groote en kleene Land-Kaerten...*, Amsterdam (Nic. Visscher), c. 1680, title-page. Herzog August Bibliothek, Wolfenbüttel

**1.** Orenstein 1995, p. 242. I should like to thank Jan van der Waals, who read through an earlier version of this chapter with a critical eye, for his corrections and suggestions.
**2.** For a biography of Visscher see Simon 1958, pp. 9-19; Van Eeghen 1990; Amsterdam 1993-94A, p. 323. For Visscher's oeuvre: Holl. XXXVIII-XXXIX.

2. *Catalogus Van groote en kleene Land-Kaerten…*, Amsterdam (Nic. Visscher), c. 1680, pp. 12-13. Herzog August Bibliothek, Wolfenbüttel

Bourse and the town hall. In these surroundings, at the centre of Amsterdam's print and map trade, he built up a flourishing and wide-ranging business under the sign of 'The Fisher'. As time went by, Visscher increasingly presented himself as a publisher and gradually abandoned his artistic activities. He was a highly successful businessman and was able to invest in a number of houses.

Visscher was a member of Amsterdam's Reformed congregation, and from what is known about his life, he appears to have been strict in his beliefs. He maintained close ties with the Nieuwe Kerk, which stood not far from his shop. This was Amsterdam's principal church and the bastion of orthodox Calvinism in the city. It was in the Nieuwe Kerk that in 1608 Visscher was married by dominie Petrus Plancius, and he later maintained business and perhaps also social contacts with both the church's sexton and its precentor. Indeed, he was himself an active member of the Reformed parish. In about 1625 he became deacon, charged with tasks relating to poor-relief. As a representative of the church council the print publisher was also involved, in 1637, in the attempt to have the first performance of Joost van den Vondel's play *Gysbrecht van Aemstel* banned. Together with the ministers, he

was fiercely opposed to some scenes in the play that they held to be 'popish'.[3]

Much less is known about the religious beliefs of the later Visschers. However, it is clear that Nicolaes Visscher (1618-79) carried on his father's activities for the church. He too eventually became a deacon in about 1670.[4] It was also he who took over the running of the publishing shop on Kalverstraat following the death of Claes Jansz. in 1652. In about 1680 the shop was moved to Dam Square by his son Nicolaus (1649-1702), whose widow Elisabeth Versijl was to carry on the business until her own death in 1726.

### The Visscher catalogue

A printed catalogue bearing the title *Catalogue of great and small Maps, Towns, Prints and Books. From Nicolaes Visscher of Amsterdam* (fig. 1, p. 37) provides a well of information about what the Visscher business had to offer.[5] The catalogue lists all the printed work available from the shop: that is, all the maps, prints and books for which the Visscher business owned the plates and could therefore produce new prints whenever they were needed. Catalogues like this were not unusual in the book trade. Ever since

**3.** See Sterck 1932, pp. 35-37. For Visscher's religious convictions and their actual or supposed influence on the nature and content of his oeuvre and stock, cf. Bakker 1993; Van der Coelen 1997.
**4.** Obreen 1877-90, Vol. 3, p. 224. For Nicolaes and Nicolaus, see Kleerkooper/ Van Stockum 1914-16, pp. 887-890; Koeman 1967-85, Vol. 3, pp. 152-154; Van

Eeghen 1990, pp. 79-82.
**5.** *Catalogus Van groote en kleene Land-kaerten, Steden, Print-kunst En Boecken. Van Nicolaes Visscher van Amsteldam. t'Amsteldam, Op den Dam, in de Visscher* (Herzog August Bibliothek, Wolfenbüttel: Cb 105). Cf. for the Visscher catalogues: Nagler, Vol. 23, p. 189; Koeman 1967-85, Vol. 3, pp. 154-157; Van der Waals 1988, pp. 20, 22, 199.

**6.** Lafrery: Ehrle 1908, pp. 53-59, no. 12. Catalogue Claesz., 1609: Van Selm 1987, pp. 217-225, 258-259, no. 8. Cf. for print publishers' catalogues: Griffiths 1984; Van der Waals 1988, pp. 20-22, 198-199.
**7.** French edition: *Catalogue, de grandes & petites Cartes Geographiques, Villes, Tailles Douces, Et Livres De Cette Nature, De Nicolas Visscher,*

*D'Amsteldam. A Amsterdam, Sur le Dam, à l'enseigne du Pescheur* (Bibliothèque de l'Institut de France, Paris: 8° Duplessis 622), 24 p.. German edition: *Catalogus. Grosser und Kleiner Landkarten, Städte Druck- Kunst, Und Bücher. Bey Nicolaus Fisscher, Von Amsterdam. Zu Amsterdam in der Kalber-strasse, im Fisscher* (Bibliothèque Nationale, Paris: Q 8553bis), 20 p.

**8.** *Appendix, s.a.* (Herzog August Bibliothek, Wolfenbüttel; bound in with Cb 105), 5 p.
**9.** The Visschers themselves generally took good care to distinguish between their exceedingly similar names - Claes, Nicolaes and Nicolaus. This is a practice that deserves emulation today. The forms of the names as used in Hollstein (XXXVIII-XXXIX)

the end of the fifteenth century printers and publishers had compiled and published lists of the books they were able to supply. In the print trade, however, catalogues were not yet so common. As far as is known, the first print stock list was published in Rome in 1572 by Antonio Lafrery. The first Dutch catalogue of this kind, the *Const ende Caert-Register*, was printed in 1609 by the Amsterdam bookseller and printseller Cornelis Claesz. The catalogue brought out by Visscher is only the second known to have been published in the country and is thus an almost unique document of its day.[6]

The Visscher catalogue consists of 22 numbered pages, twenty of which describe the products. The list opens on pages 3-6 with a large section of topography and topical subjects (topographical maps, news maps, and plans and views of towns and buildings). These are followed on pages 7-22 with various sorts of prints and picture books (fig. 2, p. 38). The version in Dutch was not the only one: almost exactly the same catalogue appeared in French and German too.[7] Of the *Appendix*, which was compiled after a time to augment the main catalogue, only a Dutch version is known. This consists of five numbered pages and contains, among other things, a section devoted to work by Gerard de Lairesse.[8]

None of the three versions of the Visscher catalogue is dated. Although it was once thought that it appeared in or after 1682, it is apparent from the discussion below that a dating of *c.* 1680 would be more accurate (see Appendix, p. 61). However, more important than a precise dating may be the insight that the catalogue provides a picture of the Visscher stock as left by Nicolaes on his death in 1679. Although published by Nicolaus, the Dutch edition presents itself accordingly as *Catalogus ... Van Nicolaes Visscher*.[9]

Nicolaes himself had in turn been able to build on the work of his father. It is the plates which Claes Jansz. Visscher etched, commissioned and accumulated, the fruits of forty-five years' activity as a publisher, that constitute the core of the list. At the beginning of his career Claes Jansz. had concentrated chiefly on publishing landscape prints and town views. After the Synod of Dort these were joined by numerous topical prints attacking the Remonstrant side. Together with the news maps - with overviews of the many sieges and battles of the Eighty and Thirty Years wars - these illustrations of current affairs would certainly not have been a waste of time from the publisher's point of view. Indeed, it seems likely that they provided the financial basis for the continued expansion of the business. Visscher was now in a position to make substantial purchases at the sales of the estates of fellow publishers and printmakers. From the end of the 1630s he bought large numbers of second, third or even fourth-hand plates, particularly plates of biblical scenes. At the same time he

was commissioning new sets of plates of both Bible illustrations and popular prints.[10]

In 1652 Nicolaes Visscher carried on along the same path his father had taken. He retained the great majority of Claes Jansz.' stock, but disposed of some of the older plates. Over a period of more than a quarter of a century he also expanded the stock with new editions and by buying up stocks of old plates, including a number purchased at the auctions of the estates of Jan de Bisschop (1677) and - at the very end of Nicolaes' life - Clement de Jonghe (March 1679).[11] The catalogue, which must have appeared not long after Nicolaes' death, contains over 900 entries, together amounting to over 4,300 sheets with almost 5,000 prints. There are maps of the whole world as it was then known, views of the most important towns and cities of Europe, and plans and illustrations of both the newest and some of the oldest buildings of Amsterdam and elsewhere. Then there are a number of news maps and prints of 'Great Sieges, Land and Sea Battles', as well as other illustrations of current events. Alongside portraits of princes, kings, and secular and church leaders from present and past, prints were sold of landscapes, animals, birds, fish, genre scenes and mythological representations. Likewise in stock were drawing and architecture books, but also boards for gaming with dice.

Apart from prints from their own list, the Visscher firm also held a stock of impressions pulled from plates that they did not themselves own. These prints were purchased or bartered from colleagues; some were bought at auctions. In addition, the Visschers' shop almost certainly served, like those of their fellow printsellers and booksellers, as a stationer's. The range on offer would have included not only paper and writing materials but also frames and rods for hanging maps and prints on walls.

But the core business of the later Visscher firm was biblical prints. They account for almost one-third (approx. 31%) of the prints in the catalogue: some 350 entries with 1,519 prints, spread over 1,179 sheets. This imbalance was the effect chiefly of four picture books, but besides these there were also maps, loose prints and print series on Scriptural themes. With almost 800 prints (in 174 entries on over 600 sheets) the Old Testament accounts for more than half of these, ie, some 16% of the entire print range.

The proportion of Old Testament prints in the Visscher list was exceptionally large, compared with those of some other Netherlandish print publishers. In the second half of the sixteenth century the firm of Hieronymus Cock, the first professional print publisher in Northern Europe, published some 1,180 prints in Antwerp, of which about 22% (255) were of biblical scenes and 12% (139) depicted scenes from the Old Testament. And while

- Claes Jansz., Claes Claesz. I and Claes Claesz. II - are in my view no clearer. Besides, the last two were never even used by the Visschers themselves. In the 'Octroy' (a kind of copyright notice) in the stock catalogue the name Nicolaes is used instead of Nicolaus, although this is probably a printer's error. The printing of the catalogue must have been contracted out, since the

Visschers themselves did not have a printing press. Confusion also arises where the names are reproduced in other languages: Claes Jansz. Latinized his name as Nicolaus Ioannis Piscator, and in French he gave his first name as Nicolas. Nicolaes' name became Nicolaus in German.
**10.** For the development of the stock, *cf.* Orenstein *et al.* 1993-94,

pp. 189-195, esp. p. 194. The number given there (p. 189) and by Welzel (1996, p. 71) of 2,000 prints for the stock of Claes Jansz. is unquestionably too low. Evidently no account was taken of his picture Bibles. For Visscher's political prints on the *Bestands-twisten* - the disputes which arose during the Twelve Years' Truce between Spain and the Northern

Netherlands - see Utrecht 1994, pp. 55-81.
**11.** Van der Waals 1988, p. 178; Van Eeghen 1985, p. 61.

3. Abraham van den Broeck after Claes Jansz. Visscher, *Bible Map* (*De gelegentheyt van t'Paradys ende t'Landt Canaan*), 1643, 16.5 x 21.3 cm, University Library, Amsterdam

Hendrick Goltzius' list, built up in Haarlem between 1582 and 1601, has some 130 biblical representations out of a total of about 440 prints - as in the Visschers' case almost a third of the total - only 36 of these (ie, around 8% of the complete list) were devoted to the Old Testament. Cornelis Claesz.' Amsterdam catalogue of 1609 has a total of over 400 entries listing over 1,700 prints, excluding maps. Of these, 554 prints in 173 entries have a Scriptural theme - again, something like one-third of the total. As with Goltzius, in Claesz.' catalogue the Old Testament figures less prominently than the New: 35 entries representing some 175 prints, or about 10% of all the prints in the list.[12]

Although very few statistics on the subject are available, it may be assumed that the Visscher firm also surpassed its foreign precursors and competitors in terms of the proportion of Old Testament prints in its list. Certainly, with about 22 items Old Testament prints are greatly under-represented in the catalogue of Antonio Lafrery (Rome 1572). The vast majority of the 225 or so religious prints listed are devoted to the New Testament, Christ, the Virgin Mary and the saints. And although religious themes predominate in the 1614 catalogue of the Roman publishers Andrea and Michel'Angelo Vaccari, the Old Testament is almost wholly absent: most feature the Virgin or other saints. A

**12.** The 'Bybelsche Figueren in quarto, met schrift, 160 parcken' and 'Idem sonder schrift' have only been counted once, on the assumption that the Old Testament accounts for roughly half of the 160 representations (*Catalogue Claesz.*, 1609, fol. A2v).

The figures for Cock are based on the 'Handlist' in Riggs 1977, pp. 309-383. For Goltzius' list (Filedt Kok 1993), see Introduction, p. 20. In the substantial stock of the printseller Hendrick Hondius of The Hague (1573-1650) Old Testament prints play

only a very minor role. For Hondius' stock, cf. New Hollstein, Hondius; Orenstein 1996, pp. 171-218.

comparison of what the Visschers had to offer with the output of prints in seventeenth-century France, shows once again how exceptionally large the proportion of Old Testament prints was in their list. True, almost 30% of the French prints that survive have a religious subject, and almost half of these are devoted to biblical themes, but the Old Testament only accounts for 2% of the total.[13]

## Bible maps ('Landt-kaarten om in den Bybel te binden')

What, then, could actually be seen in all these Old Testament prints? Leafing through the Visschers' catalogue, the first section of Scriptural prints is 'Maps for binding into the Bible' ('Landt-kaarten om in den Bybel te binden'). In the seventeenth century such maps were a regular feature in the stocks of print and map publishers. It comes as no surprise that Claes Jansz. and his successors, who were among the foremost map publishers of Amsterdam, also offered them. Here two of the Visschers' hobby-horses, Bible prints and maps, come together.[14]

Of the eleven Bible maps listed, six constitute a single large-format set. As an improved version of a set first published by Claes Jansz. in 1642 they were brought out by Nicolaes Visscher in about 1657. The other five Bible maps in the list are in a smaller format and were intended for binding into octavo Bibles. They are reduced versions of Claes Jansz.'s large maps and date from 1643. For example, the map of 'The location of Paradise and the Land of Canaan, and the first inhabited Lands of the Patriarchs' (fig. 3, p. 40) is a reduction of the map of the same name in the original set, in which it measured 30.5 x 47.5 cm. Claes Jansz. Visscher is himself named as the artist and publisher, while the engraver is identified as Abraham van den Broeck. As one of the captions indicates, this map, which shows a large portion of the Near East, was intended for binding in a Bible before chapter three of Genesis, so that the reader would have an idea of where the Garden of Eden was and the places where the Old Testament patriarchs lived. At the centre right of the map there is also a small representation of the tower of Babel. Three finely drawn scenes at the top serve as a kind of introduction: to left and right the familiar scenes of the Fall and the Expulsion, and in the middle the departure of Terah, Abraham and Lot from Ur (Gen. 11:31), in which the three patriarchs dressed in the oriental style lead a caravan of asses and camels.[15]

The other maps in the catalogue that belong with the Old Testament are a 'Map of the World, showing the place of the Garden of Eden' and two others, one of which shows 'The Forty-Year Wanderings of the Children of Israel from Egypt, through the Red Sea and the Desert into the Promised Land' and 'The Holy and Famous City of Jerusalem'. Claes Jansz. probably had them cut when the States Bible appeared in 1637: it is his maps that are often bound into copies of the earliest editions of this most important of all Dutch translations of the Bible. However, Bible maps had already been around for some time: they appear with some regularity in printed Bibles from the 1520s on. Thanks to the interest that Calvin himself took in biblical geography, particularly in the correct location of Eden, their number increased all the time. Many of the Calvinist Bibles published in Geneva after 1560 contain five maps. In 1590 and 1604 the famous Amsterdam minister and cartographer Petrus Plancius attempted to improve the topographical quality of such maps and added numerous place-names. Visscher continued the work of his spiritual mentor, and his own maps were in turn imitated and copied by other publishers.

In 1549 the English printer Reyner Wolfe gave the following reason for including maps in the Bible: 'The knowledge of Cosmographie is very necessary, so that he that lacketh the same, can neither wel rede the Byble [...] nor the New Testament. [...] Therfore if a man be not seen in Cosmographie, he shall be constrained to skippe ouer many notable thinges which otherwyse shoulde do him no lytle pleasures'.[16] Bible maps were designed to increase the reader's knowledge of biblical geography - something that was considered necessary for a proper understanding of the text - but they were also supposed to enhance the pleasure of reading. To many purchasers, however, including those who bought Visscher's maps, the visual pleasure they afforded must also have been a reason for having a Bible embellished with them.

## Art Prints ('Kunst-Printen')

The major part of Visscher's catalogue consists of 'Art Prints' ('Kunst-Printen', 'Bladen', and 'Printen'), either individually or in series.[17] Here biblical subjects, which appear in some 320 prints, are certainly not in the majority. Moreover the Old Testament is only moderately represented compared with the New (about 95 prints as against 224). Even so, Old Testament prints do appear in almost every section into which the prints in the catalogue are divided.

The order of these sections is based on the size of the paper on which the prints were offered for sale. They start with the largest, imperial, measuring 55 x 72 cm ('Groote Kunst-Printen, van 1 Imperiaal-Bladt'). These are followed by royal sheets of 48 x 58 cm ('Groote Kunst-Printen, van 1 Rojaal Bladt'). The last size, which was the commonest and therefore called 'gemeen' (foolscap; literally: 'common'), was used as whole, half or quarter sheets of 32 x 42, 21 x 32 and 16 x 21 cm respectively ('Kunst-Printen, op heele Bladen [or 'halven', 'quarten'], gemeen Papier'). The Visschers used medium format of 42 x 54 cm both for their Bible maps and for prints, although the latter were always on half sheets (27 x 42 cm).

All these dimensions refer to the size of the sheets: the pictures themselves were smaller. Although publishers aimed to use paper as economically as possible - paper was their largest production cost item - the margins for prints were left fairly wide (2.5 - 5 cm

**13.** Cf. Grivel 1986, pp. 138-160. Not too many conclusions should be drawn from this comparison of stock and output: the range offered by the Visschers consisted largely of non-contemporary prints, which to some extent would also have been the case with

French publishers. Lafrery and Vaccari: Ehrle 1908, pp. 57-58, 60-66. An analysis of more contemporary stocks, such as those of the De Rossi family (cf. Consagra 1992), Danckert Danckertsz. and Clement de Jonghe, was not possible in the present context.

**14.** For map publishing in Amsterdam and the role of the Visscher firm in it, see Amsterdam 1989A, esp. p. 43. Cornelis Claesz. also sold Bible maps (Catalogue Claesz., 1609, fol. B2r). For the Visscher firm's Bible maps see Poortman/ Augusteijn 1995,

pp. 141-156, 179 ff.
**15.** The Adam-and-Eve scenes closely resemble the later prints from the set by Pieter Schut (cat. no. 62). For this map see Poortman/ Augusteijn 1995, p. 151, no. 2. Cf. Poortman 1983-86, Vol. 1, pp. 188-190. For Bible maps

see also Delano-Smith/ Ingram 1991, pp. XXI-XXIX.
**16.** Quoted from: Delano-Smith/ Ingram 1991, p. XXV.
**17.** Catalogue Visscher, pp. 7-9, 14-18, 19-22. In the French edition these were listed as 'Tailles Douces'.

or more).[18] This meant that it was possible either to bind them together in a book or to have them framed, which leads to the two most important uses to which prints were put: as documentation and information they were kept in albums, and as decoration they were hung on walls. However, it would of course be a mistake to regard these two functions as wholly separate: in either case, instruction and delight, information and aesthetic enjoyment, went together.[19]

The Old Testament 'Kunst-Printen' in the Visschers' catalogue consist largely of prints on themes from Genesis. The stories of Elijah and Tobit are also comparatively common as subject-matter. All the most important Dutch designers of Old Testament prints are represented in the list. The oldest material in this field comes from engravers of the Goltzius school. The prints on offer include *Cain Killing Abel* by Jan Muller after Cornelis Cornelisz. van Haarlem (royal paper; fig. 13, p. 22) and *Elijah and the Widow of Zarephath* (royal paper; cat. no. 36) and *The History of Ahijah and Elijah* (foolscap, whole sheets; cat. no. 35) by Jan Saenredam after Abraham Bloemaert. The first of these prints came originally from the stock of Herman Jansz. Muller. The others were published, before the plates were acquired by Claes Jansz., by Saenredam himself, Robert Willemsz. de Baudous and Joannes Janssonius.[20]

The catalogue also reveals that apart from work by members of the Goltzius school the Visscher firm owned the plates of Old Testament prints by designers originally from Flanders such as Gillis van Coninxloo, Gillis de Hondecoutre and David Vinckboons - artists who sometimes provided their 'Flemish' fantasy landscapes with biblical staffage groups. They also sold prints by designers whose landscapes and groups of figures are inspired by the work of Adam Elsheimer, such as Moyses van Uyttenbroeck.[21] Of more recent date was *Joseph Distributing Grain in Egypt*, a spectacular mass scene in imperial format drawn by Bartholomaeus Breenbergh and etched by Jan de Bisschop, the plate of which was acquired by Nicolaes Visscher in 1677 at the sale of the estate of De Bisschop's widow (cat. no. 20).

It is even possible that the Visschers owned plates of Old Testament prints by Rembrandt. The catalogue refers to 29 Rembrandt prints with the comment 'Originel'. Twenty of these are listed without mentioning their subject. Thus among the 'Quarters from foolscap sheets', the smallest format used by the Visschers, are '4 small prints by Rembrandt, original --- 4 sheets'. These were presumably four prints of the same format and on related themes, possibly a set such as the *Piedra Gloriosa* illustrations (cat. no. 52).[22]

Impressions of Old Testament prints by Rembrandt would certainly have been on sale in the Visschers' shop. In March 1679

Nicolaes spent a considerable sum buying prints from the widow of his colleague Clement de Jonghe, who had died two years earlier. According to the inventory of his estate (1679) De Jonghe's print publishing business, which from 1658 until 1679 was on Kalverstraat close to the Visschers' shop, possessed 74 copperplates of etchings by Rembrandt, including six of Old Testament scenes.[23] It is possible that Clement de Jonghe acquired these as early as 1658, when Rembrandt was obliged to sell his effects and move house. De Jonghe also sold Old Testament prints by Rembrandt's precursors and pupils, including Moeyaert, Van Vliet and Bol (cat. nos 14, 6, 13, 25).

In about 1680 it was possible to purchase from Nicolaus Visscher new impressions of single prints and series which spanned something like a century of Northern Netherlandish art. The Visscher list was not static: it was in a constant state of flux with new acquisitions and deletions. The catalogue does not yet include the most recent works: etchings by Gerard de Lairesse and mezzotints by Wallerant Vaillant. However, some Old Testament prints by De Lairesse do occur in the *Appendix* of c. 1694. No longer listed in the catalogue are various Old Testament prints that had previously been part of the stock of Claes Jansz. Thus the Old Testament oeuvre of Willem Buytewech (cat. nos 30, 38; fig. 16, p. 26), cut either by himself or by Jan II van de Velde, is completely absent. Every now and then the Visschers would sell plates. For example, part of their stock, including some plates that had been accumulated by Claes Jansz. and Nicolaes, was sold at public auction in 1684.[24]

### Prints of the Ten Commandments

Most of the Old Testament prints in the Visscher catalogue are narrative scenes. No longer in the catalogue, but like the Buytewech prints referred to above previously part of the firm's stock, are the portrait-like series by the Goltzius school, such as De Gheyn's *The Twelve Sons of Jacob* after drawings by Karel van Mander (cat. no. 22) and three series after designs by Goltzius himself (figs 12a-c, p. 20).[25] Another category within the general class of Old Testament prints is that of the so-called Ten Commandments prints. These comprise both image and text: Moses, recipient of the two tablets of stone bearing the Commandments, holds them aloft, sometimes assisted by Aaron. The text of the Commandments (Ex. 20:2-17), often in calligraphic script, appears on the tablets.

The catalogue refers to two of these Ten Commandments prints: one anonymous, 'The Ten Commandments, Dutch' ('De X Geboden, Nederduyts'), and the 'Ten Commandments, by Maria Strick' ('Tien Geboden, door Maria Strix'). This latter piece is a print made by the husband-and-wife team of Hans and Maria Strick (fig. 4, p. 43) and was made before 1609. Maria Strick was a

**18.** For paper sizes (and margins), see Jan van der Waals, in: Filedt Kok 1994-95, part II, pp. 364-371. Cf. Gaskell 1974, pp. 72-75.
**19.** For the function of prints and their collection, cf. Robinson 1981; Van der Waals 1988, pp. 13-27.
**20.** Muller after Cornelis Cornelisz.: Filedt Kok 1994-95, part III, no. B.29. Saenredam after

Bloemaert: Roethlisberger 1993, nos 78, 79-82.
**21.** Boetius à Bolswert after David Vinckboons: Holl. 3, p. 61, no. 2; Jan van de Velde II after Moyses van Uyttenbroeck: Holl. XXXIII, pp. 10-11, nos 7-10.
**22.** Cf. for the Rembrandt plates owned by the Visschers: Holl. XLI, p. 219; Hinterding 1993-94, p. 262.

In some cases, notably in the section on 'Loose prints, on whole sheets, foolscap paper', the subject is given but not the artist. Among these there are 24 with Old Testament scenes, which thematically speaking belong to the greatest successes, from 'Adam and Eve in the Garden of Eden', 'Abraham Banishing Hagar', 'The Sacrifice of

Isaac', 'David Slaying Goliath', 'Tobias and the Angel' and 'Susanna and the Elders'. These are copies of *Theatrum Biblicum* prints (cf. Holl. XLIV, nos 65a, 121a, 201b).
**23.** B. 28, 29 (?), 33, 42, 43, 153 (cat. nos 2, 9, 21, 49, 50). Cf. De Hoop Scheffer/ Boon 1971, pp. 6-17; Hinterding 1993-94, pp. 260-261. Inventory of the estate of Clement

de Jonghe: Gemeentearchief Amsterdam, NA 4528, notary J. Backer, 11-2-1679, pp. 117-146 (the Rembrandt plates on pp. 137-138). Cf. Van Eeghen 1985, pp. 61-63.
**24.** An advertisement was placed in the *Amsterdamsche Courant* of 21 October 1684. Cf. Kleerkooper/ Van Stockum 1914-16, p. 889; Van der Krogt 1985, pp. 18-19, no. 13.

4. Hans and Maria Strick, *Moses with the Tablets of the Law*, before 1609, engraving, 30.7 x 25.4 cm. University Library, Amsterdam

5. Thomas Anshelm, *Moses with the Tablets of the Law*, 1505, woodcut, 31.7 x 22.3 cm, Bayerische Staatsbibliothek, Munich

famous calligrapher. She designed the calligraphic texts which were then engraved by Hans, as here in the text of the Commandments.[26]

Comparable prints were designed by Hendrick Goltzius (cat. no. 24), Jacques II de Gheyn and Karel van Mander.[27] In the last two of these the text of the Commandments was not engraved onto the copperplate but instead the space was left open on the tablets of the law. In this way the prints could be used for a wider public, since the text, when it was subsequently added either by hand or in letterpress, could be in any language or with any numbering to suit the reader's religious denomination. This was particularly important in the light of the difference of opinion between Catholics and Protestants regarding the numbering of the individual Commandments (see cat. no. 24).

Ten Commandments prints existed even before the Reformation. The earliest known example is the woodcut by Thomas Anshelm printed at Pforzheim in 1505 (fig. 5). However, prints of this kind appear to have been particularly popular in the visual culture of Protestantism.[28] They were made in a wide variety of formats, techniques and price ranges. The Visscher firm offered

two examples in different sizes, presumably at different prices. It is mainly the best prints, in artistic terms, which have survived. This is largely because they were also collected for the artist's name. Many other less exclusive and cheaper variants must have been lost. Ten Commandments prints occur in the stocks of many print publishers. In 1609 Cornelis Claesz. was offering at least four (including those by Strick and De Gheyn), in various formats and at prices which ranged from 3/4 to 6 stivers each.[29]

In view of their size, it may be assumed that prints like those by Strick and Goltzius were often used as wall decorations. Apart from an artistic and decorative function they would certainly also have served a religious and educational purpose. Memorizing the Ten Commandments was a core component of education, not only in catechism or confirmation classes but also as part of learning to read. Along with their painted counterparts, Ten Commandments prints must have been a common feature of the Dutch interior of the sixteenth and seventeenth centuries. 'Boards' with the Ten Commandments occur frequently in the inventories of private homes. Painted wooden boards with

Buytewech plates in the catalogue of Claes Jansz.: Haverkamp Begeman 1959, nos vG 19, vG 35, CP 23, CP 24-27. Cf. Orenstein et al. 1993-94, p. 194.
25. Goltzius: Filedt Kok 1993, nos 39, 51, 67. De Gheyn after Van Mander: Filedt Kok 1990, nos 366-377.
26. Holl. XXVIII, p. 154, no. 1.

No states published by the Visschers are known, but neither are any known by Cornelis Claesz., in whose catalogue the 'Thien gheboden Maria strick' also appear, at 3/4 of a stiver (*Catalogue Claesz.*, 1609, fol. A4r). For the Stricks see Haverkorn van Uchelen 1976, pp. 340-343;

Worthen 1993, pp. 271-272.
27. De Gheyn (1595-1600): Holl. VII, p. 109, no. 1; Filedt Kok 1990, pp. 268-269, 373, no. 1. Matham after Van Mander (1630): Holl. XI, p. 216, no. 5. Cf. Veldman 1995, p. 230.
28. Anshelm: Geisberg/ Strauss 1974, Vol. 1, p. 47. The earliest known Netherlandish Ten

Commandments print is the woodcut by Cornelis Anthonisz. (Holl. XXX, p.11, no. 4; c. 1545). Later Dutch examples (both with Reformed numbering) are the prints by Hendrick Hondius of 1598 (New Hollstein, Hondius, no. 1) and Simon Frisius (Holl. VII, p. 13, no. 1).
29. *Catalogue Claesz.*, 1609, fol. A2v,

A3r, A4r. Such prints also appear in the inventory of Clement de Jonghe ('groote franse 10 gebooden'; Van Eeghen 1985, p. 62). Cf. for Ten Commandments prints Van der Waals 1997.

43

virtually the same representations were typical of the decoration of the Protestant church interior.[30]

## Picture Bibles ('Bybelsche Figuren')

Besides individual Bible prints and Bible maps, Claes Jansz. and his successors also published a large number of picture Bibles. These were not illustrated Bibles (which the Visschers did not publish), but rather books of prints without the actual text of the Bible. Picture Bibles present the Scripture in pictorial form, although they tend to confine themselves largely to miraculous events, battles and moments of exceptional pathos.[31]

Loose prints of Old Testament themes and Bible maps account for only a fraction of the print and map sections of the catalogue. It is the picture books that account for the vast majority of the Bible prints and thus, as already observed, are the reason for the biblical bias in the stock as a whole. The list refers to four picture Bibles (fig. 2, p. 38), all of them identified as 'Bybelsche Figuren'. Arranged according to paper size, the books together contain 1,201 prints, of which about 704 (on approx. 536 sheets) are devoted to the Old Testament. The equal representation of the Old Testament in the catalogue as a whole thus has to do with its over-representation in the picture Bibles.

Claes Jansz. published his first biblical picture book as early as 1616, at the beginning of his publishing career. Not long after setting up shop on Kalverstraat he seems to have managed to lay his hands on a collection of old German wood-blocks, namely a number of scenes of the Passion of Christ by Lucas Cranach. This set had first been published in 1509 at Wittenberg, so that Visscher's Amsterdam reissue dates from over a century later. However, it was not until 1637, when he was about fifty, that Claes Jansz. started to apply himself to the publishing of picture Bibles. In that year he published his *David*, a reissue of a small Antwerp picture book of 1575 on the life of David, with engravings by Johannes I Sadeler (cat. no. 56). In 1638 he seized his opportunity at the sale of the estate of his deceased Amsterdam colleague Michiel Colijn, where he purchased three sets of plates. These are the plates of two picture Bibles with etchings by the Flemish artist Pieter van der Borcht (cf. cat. nos 55 and 60) and those of the *Historia Del Testamento Vecchio* (cat. no. 57).[32]

It must have been shortly after this that Claes Jansz. made the largest purchase of his career: the plates of the *Thesaurus veteris et novi testamenti*. This picture Bible, originally published in 1579 and 1585 by Gerard de Jode in Antwerp, contains prints most of which were made after the design or in the style of Maarten de Vos (fig. 11, p. 18). In 1639 Visscher reprinted the old plates, added a couple of other series and gave the whole thing a new title: *Theatrum Biblicum* (fig. 6; cat. no. 58). From the stock list (fig. 2, p. 38) it is clear that the work was still on sale forty years later. In all the catalogue names 82 series totalling 472 sheets. Of these, 272, belonging to

58 series, show Old Testament scenes. In commercial terms the *Theatrum Biblicum* was the Visscher firm's most successful picture Bible. Editions of the book were published in 1639, 1643, 1650 and 1674. In addition, impressions of plates from the *Theatrum Biblicum* supplied by Visscher were the basis for the *Figuer-Bibel*, a biblical picture book published in 1646 by Jan Philipsz. Schabaelje.[33]

After acquiring this impressive quantity of old plates, Claes Jansz. commissioned the making of three new sets of biblical prints. In the event, these were completed or published in book form by his son Nicolaes. Foremost among them was the so-called *Royal-Size Bible*, listed in the stock catalogue as 'Biblical Figures, on Sheets of Royal' ('Bybelsche Figuren, op Royaal-bladen'). It consists of engravings averaging 40 x 51 cm, printed on royal size paper. On the subject of the identities of the artists responsible the catalogue is silent. However, it does list the subjects, numbered from 1 to 130. Of these, the Old Testament accounts for numbers 2 to 65.[34]

The *Royal-Size Bible* too was partly composed of bought-up old plates, including some engraved by Jan van Londerseel. It is possible that Claes Jansz. had already acquired these shortly after the engraver's death in 1625.[35] Some of them were reprinted in a virtually unaltered state (fig. 14, p. 24), with only Visscher's address added. Others were modified by the addition of new groups of figures in the previously often unpopulated landscapes. In the Van Londerseel plates these groups are frequently based on examples by Matthaeus Merian the Elder, in other cases on prints in the

6. *Theatrum Biblicum...*, Amsterdam (Claes Jansz. Visscher), 1639, title-page. Library of the Faculty of Theology, Tilburg

30. Veldman 1995, pp. 230-231. Cf. Van Swigchem/ Brouwer/ Van Os 1984, pp. 279-281. For the role of the Ten Commandments in education: De Booy 1977, pp. 37-65.
31. For the picture Bible as a genre, see Engammare 1994. For the biblical picture books

published by the Visschers, see Van der Coelen 1994-95. Cf. Van der Coelen 1991 & 1994, pp. 174-177.
32. On his death in 1637 Colijn's estate fell to the Orphans Court (Weeskamer). The report of its sale makes no mention of the copperplates for picture Bibles

(Register verkopingen Weeskamer, Daniel Jansz. van Beuningen erfhuizen: Gemeentearchief Amsterdam 5073, no. 963, 15-30 March 1638). For the auction cf. Enschedé 1904, pp. 48-56; Van Eeghen 1969, pp. 98-99. The sale of the plates was announced in an advertisement in the *Tijdinghen* of

20 March 1638 (Van der Krogt 1985, no. A39).
33. For the *Figuer-Bibel* see Visser 1988, Vol. 1, pp. 390-409; Schuckman 1990; Van der Coelen 1991 & 1994, pp. 174-175. For the *Thesaurus*, Introduction, pp. 16-19.
34. For the *Royal-Size Bible* see Van der Waals 1997.

35. The inventory of the Van Londerseel estate (Rotterdam, 7 January 1625) refers to '20 plaeten van één pryse, daervan de druck gelt 5 stuyvers' (Bredius 1915-22, Vol. 5, pp. 1594-1598). These may be the royal-size plates.

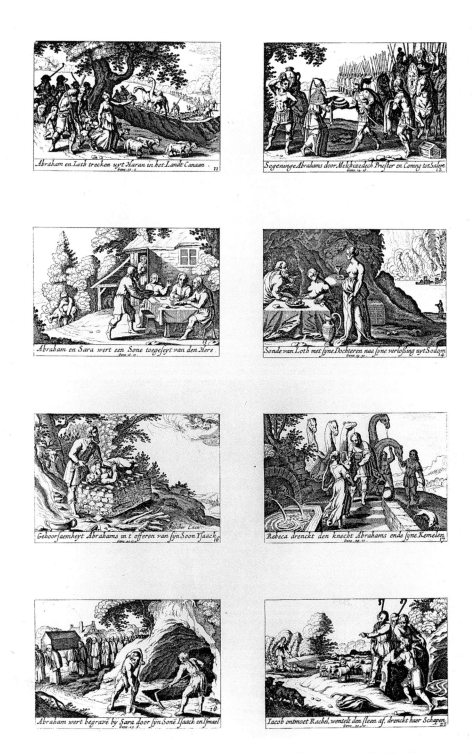

7. Pieter Hendricksz. Schut, *Print Sheet with Eight Scenes from Genesis* (numbered 11-22), c. 1650, 8 etchings on one plate, each 6.5 x 9.7 cm, Bijbels Museum, Amsterdam

*Theatrum Biblicum.* Many compositions from that book were also copied in their entirety and transferred to the royal format, as were inventions of artists such as Rubens, Breenbergh and Potter.

The Visscher firm was far from being the only one to publish royal-size biblical history prints. Many of their competitors, including Clement de Jonghe, offered related prints. However, Nicolaes Visscher managed to buy up many of their plates, so that he had a more complete range than any of his colleagues. In 1667, for example, he was able to acquire the plate of Jan Muller's *Belshazzar's Feast* (cat. no. 42) at the auction of the estate of Danckert Danckertsz., a scion of a great print publishing family whose firm was likewise established on Kalverstraat, in premises called 'de Danckbaerheijdt' (literally, 'Gratitude').[36] It seems likely that in this way the total of 130 biblical prints mentioned in the catalogue was achieved by Nicolaes. Rather than being bound together in complete picture Bibles, these prints would more often have been sold loose for the purpose of being bound into large-format States Bible editions or, as a cheap alternative to paintings, to decorate the walls.[37]

There is another biblical set which Claes Jansz. probably never planned to publish as a separate book, namely that by Pieter Hendricksz. Schut. As the description in the catalogue says, the set was conceived as '42 whole sheets, with 8 stories to a sheet, making a total of 336 figures, in octavo' (fig. 2, p. 38). Each of these 336 scenes, of which 192 come from the Old Testament, measures no more than approx. 6.5 x 9.7 cm. They were etched in groups of eight on 42 copperplates, each of which was printed on a whole sheet of foolscap paper of approx. 42 x 32 cm (*octavo*).

8. Copy after Matthaeus Merian the Elder, *Abraham and Melchizedek, c.* 1650, etching, *c.* 11.5 x 15 cm, in: *Bybel Printen...*, Amsterdam (Nicolaes Visscher), *s.a.* University Library, Amsterdam

9. Hieronymus Wierix after Maarten de Vos, *Jonah Cast into the Sea*, engraving, 18.8 x 24.6 cm, in: *Thesaurus...*, Antwerp (Gerard de Jode) 1585 (reprinted in: *Theatrum Biblicum*, Amsterdam (Visscher) 1639ff). Rijksprentenkabinet, Amsterdam

Schut's own print sheets, each of which thus contains eight illustrations in four pairs, were also bound into States Bibles (fig. 7, p. 45). That the whole set was completed in the lifetime of Claes Jansz. is evidenced by the fact that on each of the sheets there is one print bearing his address. After his father's death Nicolaes also issued the prints, with a special title-page, in book form (from 1659).[38] Nicolaus Visscher later reprinted this little picture Bible (*cf.* cat. no. 62).

Most of Schut's Old Testament compositions are reduced copies after Flemish examples in the *Theatrum Biblicum* and the *Royal-Size Bible.* A second source of inspiration was the famous picture Bible of Matthaeus Merian the Elder (Frankfurt am Main, 1625-27).[39] Visscher's competitor Cornelis Danckertsz. had already been bringing out Merian's work in pirated form since 1648, and Claes Jansz. too planned to publish a copy of the entire picture Bible. However, at the time of his death this project had yet to be completed, and it seems probable that it was first published by Nicolaes not long after his father's death in 1652 (fig. 8; cat. no. 61). After that there were to be several enlarged and improved editions. By the time the stock catalogue appeared (fig. 2, p. 38) the Visscher firm's plagiarized Merian Bible consisted of 263 etchings: copies after Merian supplemented with new prints by Schut. The Old Testament is represented in some 175 prints.[40]

The most important feature of the picture Bibles from the Visscher catalogue is their predominantly 'Flemish' character. This is apparent both in the groups of figures and in the landscapes in

**36.** The inventory of his estate (Gemeentearchief Amsterdam, NA 2852, notary Dirck Danckerts, 7 February 1667 - 1 September 1668, pp. 691-708) gives an idea of the Danckertsz. firm's stock (the plates on pp. 691-698). *Cf.* Amsterdam 1993-94B, p. 38.
**37.** A complete copy of the *Royal-Size Bible* as a picture Bible is now in

London (Print Room, British Museum: 157*.b.25): *Historiae Sacrae Veteris et Novi Testamenti... Bybelsche Figuren... Figures of the Bible...*, Amsterdam (Nic. Visscher), *s.a.* This copy contains only two prints (nos 10 and 68) on which Nicolaus' address is expressly stated.
**38.** *Toneel ofte Vertooch der Bybelsche*

*Historien, Cierlyck in 't koper gemaeckt door Pieter H. Schut*, Amsterdam (Nicolaes Visscher) 1659. See the reprint (s.l.e.a.) in the 'Zwarte Beertjes' series, no. 720. *Cf.* Van der Coelen 1994-95, pp. 112-113. For the printing of prints in *octavo* and other formats, see Van der Waals in: Filedt Kok 1994-95, part II, pp. 364-365.

**39.** For Schut's sources see Pluis 1994, pp. 70-71, 914-925.
**40.** For pirated copies of Merian in the Dutch Republic see Van der Coelen 1991 & 1994, pp. 175-177; Pluis 1994, pp. 63-68.

10. Anonymous copy after Maarten de Vos, *Jonah and the Fish*, engraving, 40 x 51.4 cm, in: *Historiae Sacrae Veteris et Novi Testamenti...* ('Royal-Size Bible'), Amsterdam (Nic. Visscher), c. 1680. Print Room, British Museum, London

11. Pieter Hendricksz. Schut, *Jonah Vomited onto Dry Land*, etching, 6.5 x 9.7 cm, in: *Toneel ofte vertooch...*, Amsterdam (Nicolaes Visscher) 1659. University Library, Amsterdam

EVOMIT ABSORPTUM CÆCO DE GUTTURE CŒTUS,

Wât is helaes de mens wanneer hy wil onthaelde
Syn Schepper, die hem doch gedurich is omtrent.
Syn wech is vol gevaer, beklaet met enckel fuchten,
En Godts is al fyn doen volkomelyck bekent.

Of Ionas hem ter Zee al gaet int Schip verstecchde,
En lqyt gerufft en flaept, verborgen is hy niet.
De Winds en waeffe Zee ontdecken fyn gebreechde,
En hy (gedwongen) fqrt hoe hy fyn Godts onerliet.

Ionas. 2.

REDDITUR ET TERRÆ QUI MODO PRÆDA FUIT Ionas. 2.

T'Verbaefde volck en weet geen beter raet te vinde,
Als dat een yder roejft nae Lande met alle macht.
Doch alles te vergeefs, de Zee moet haer verflinde,
Off Ionas overboort en proeuen Godes kracht.

Dit dan alfoo vollbracht, bewnft oock Godts genade,
Een Vis is daer gerect en helpt hem uyt gevaer,
Sy werpt hem op het Lande, en foo bevrijt van schade,
Volbrengt hy Godts bevel tot Ninive daer naer.

Iona van een Vifch ingeflockt, wert na 3 dagen weder van hem gefpogen op het drooge.
Iona 2. 10.
162

which they are placed. In the case of the figural compositions the chief name to mention here is that of Maarten de Vos. His series provided the main component of the *Thesaurus* of Gerard de Jode and hence also of the *Theatrum Biblicum*. Various prints from that book were copied in royal format for use in the

Royal-Size Bible. One example is *Jonah being Cast into the Sea* (Jonah 1:15) from De Vos' Jonah series (fig. 9, p. 46). This composition returns in the right background of the engraving (four times as large) in the *Royal-Size Bible* (fig. 10). The scene in the foreground, in which Jonah is vomited out onto dry land (Jonah 2:11) is similarly based on the example by De Vos in the *Theatrum Biblicum*. However, whereas the Flemish artist depicted the two scenes on two separate sheets, the copyist has combined them into a single engraving. Apart from this copy in royal format Claes Jansz. also had De Vos' composition reduced to 1/7 of the original format. The etching, from the set by Pieter Schut (fig. 11), shows only the scene in which Jonah is cast up onto the shore.[41]

Some of De Vos' figural groups were used in the *Royal-Size Bible* as staffage added to earlier landscapes by Gillis van Coninxloo, Jacob Saverij and Nicolaes de Bruyn. Landscapes in the Flemish style, found repeatedly in this work (fig. 14, p. 24), are also characteristic of a number of other picture Bibles in the Visscher stock. Chief among these are the two sets by the Antwerp artist Pieter van der Borcht (cf. cat. nos 55, 60). But in Merian's compositions too, the landscape - inspired by Flemish examples -

**41.** De Vos' Jonah illustrations: Holl. XLIV, pp. 43-44, nos 159-160. Of the 64 Old Testament prints in the *Royal-Size Bible*, 14 are related to designs in the *Theatrum Biblicum* and/or *Figuer-Bibel* (nos 7, 11, 15, 17, 19, 23, 26, 28-32, 36, 42, 63), mainly by De Vos. The inventions of other Old Testament *Royal-Size Bible* prints are also from De Vos

(nos 5, 20, 24, 38). The Visscher firm owned the following Old Testament series and prints after designs by De Vos: Holl. XLIV, nos 11-18 (copies), 53 (copy), 62-67, 64 (copy), 65 (two copies), 68-71, 70 (copy), 71 (copy), 83-86, 83 (copy), 84 (copy), 86 (copy), 87-90, 89 (copy), 91-97, 92 (copy), 96 (copy), 101 (copy), 105-106

(copies), 111-113 (copies), 114-117, 118-121, 121 (two copies), 122-127, 128-131, 132-137 (copies), 138-141, 158-161, 159-160 (copy), 162-165, 166-171, 172-174, 185-186, 200 (copy), and 201 (two copies). In all, then, there were 104 prints: 15 original series (of which 14 from the *Thesaurus*), 2 series in the form of copies and 24 copies of

individual prints from series by De Vos. These numbers do not include the simplified copies in the set by Schut.

12. Sisto Badalocchio after Raphael, *The Third Day of Creation: The Separation of Land and Water*, etching, 13.3 x 17.8, in: *Historia Del Testamento Vecchio*, Amsterdam (Claes Jansz. Visscher), 1638. Stuttgart, Württembergische Landesbibliothek

plays an important part (fig. 8, p. 46). Biblical scenes with extensive landscape backgrounds must have been highly popular in Holland. As Constantijn Huygens' testimony of 1629-31 bears out, Claes Jansz. Visscher must already have had a predilection for them: 'I once heard Claes Visscher of Amsterdam [...] claim that he owed his own skill purely to an early work by De Gheyn senior. This showed the disciples on the way to Emmaus, together with Christ, whom they did not recognize, against the background of a really most attractive landscape'. Prints of related compositions were made by Claes Jansz. himself (cat. no. 47). By reprinting the plates of Van der Borcht and Van Londerseel and by having those of Merian copied, he and his successors ensured that biblical prints with 'Flemish' fantasy landscapes remained on sale throughout the Golden Age. They constitute a pendant to the unhistoricized, substantive landscapes found in so many series, particularly in the Visscher catalogue.[42]

The so-called *Little Raphael Bible* has a special place among the picture Bibles offered by the Visscher firm (fig. 12; cat. no. 57). The etchings in this work reproduce the famous biblical frescoes by Raphael in the Vatican *Loggia*. They were made by Giovanni Lanfranco and Sisto Badalocchio and were first published in 1607 in Rome, under the title *Historia Del Testamento Vecchio*. As pupils of Annibale Carracci, Lanfranco and Badalocchio wanted to breathe new life into the 'classicità raffaellesca'. However, rather than producing an exact copy of the Vatican frescoes they reproduced them with considerable freedom, with vivacity and pace, thus investing their Renaissance models with a Baroque spirit. Because the prints are relatively small (approx. 13.3 x 18 cm), and because

several large-format reproductions of Raphael's *Loggia* frescoes were made later, in the seventeenth and eighteenth centuries the *Historia Del Testamento Vecchio* was often called the 'Little Raphael Bible ('Bijbeltje van Raphael').[43]

Quite soon after they were made, the copper plates of the *Historia Del Testamento Vecchio* came to Amsterdam, where from 1614 on they were used for printing reissues, first by Michiel Colijn and then by Claes Jansz. Visscher (cat. no. 57). Doubtless it was the Raphael compositions that attracted attention most, but the fact that they had been executed in a modern, free style of etching also made the book attractive. The etchings of Lanfranco and Badalocchio are characterized by an easy, sketchy style, strong contrasts of light and dark - especially in the folds of the clothing - and the use of the *pointillé* technique - all features which were also being developed in the work of Dutch printmakers at this time. There is a remarkable similarity, for example, in the handling of line in Jan Pynas' *Jacob's Dream* and Lanfranco's etching on the same theme (see cat. no. 15).

The *Little Raphael Bible* does not occur again in the catalogue, nor do Cranach's *Passion*, Sadeler's *David* or the two picture Bibles by Van der Borcht. These five works had already been deleted by 1680, presumably because the plates had finally worn out.[44]

Although the picture Bibles published by the Visschers, with their many copies and reprints of older Flemish, German and Italian works, can hardly be termed very original, they would certainly have earned their keep. Despite their lack of originality and the fact that comparable works were being published by Cornelis Claesz., Michiel Colijn (cat. no. 55), Jan Philipsz. Schabaelje (cat. no. 58), Pieter Jacobsz. Paets (cat. no. 59) and the Danckertsz. firm, it is these picture Bibles that best characterize the face of biblical illustration in the Golden Age, and it was the Visschers who dominated the market for them.[45] It was Visscher publications which ensured that the compositions of the Fleming Maarten de Vos, the German Matthaeus Merian and the Italian Raphael came to be typical of the pictorial culture of the Old Testament in the century of Rembrandt.

## Clientele

At the time of its appearance, the Visschers' stock catalogue, which provides such a superb insight into what a print publishing business had to offer in the seventeenth century, was intended as a source of information for use both by other printsellers and by customers. By this time there were also other ways of publicizing one's wares. The Visschers for example, used to advertise their new editions or acquisitions in the press. On 6 June 1643 Claes Jansz. advertised his Bible maps in the *Tijdinghen uyt verscheyde Quartieren*, one of the earliest Dutch newspapers: 'Claes Jansz. Visscher has published five different maps, highly suitable for

42. *Cf.* Amsterdam 1993-94B, pp. 36-37, 38-39. For 'Flemish' landscapes with biblical staffage, see: Introduction, pp. 23-24. Huygens' remark: Huygens/ Heesakkers 1987, p. 75.
43. *Cf.* the reproductions after the *Loggia* frescoes see Rome 1985, pp. 77-112, esp. pp. 77-80 (Lanfranco/ Badalocchio); for the frescoes: Davidson 1985.
44. One of Van der Borcht's sets, however, was still being reprinted by other publishers as late as 1717. See Hamilton 1981.
45. For the Dutch picture Bibles of the seventeenth century, see Poortman 1983-86, Vol. 2, pp. 26-97; Van der Coelen 1991 & 1994, pp. 174-179.

46. 'By Claes Iansz Visscher werdt uytghegheven vijf differente Kaertjes, seer bequaem om in alle octavo Bybelkens gebonden te werden; te weten, de ghelegentheydt van 't Paradijs, Israëls reyse in 't Landt Canaan, de Stadt Jerusalem, de wandelinge Christi, ende de reysen der Apostelen'. On the same day an advertisement also appeared in the *Courante uyt Italien ende Duytschlandt*. See Van der Krogt 1985, nos A67-A68. *Cf.* for advertising for prints Van der Waals 1988, pp. 16-17, 20-21.
47. ''t Amsterdam bij Nicolaus Visscher, op den Dam, in de Visscher, werden uijtgegeven so Konst-Printen, seer konstig in Italien getekent, en op 't koper

gebracht, na de uijtstekenste Schilderijen van Titiano Vecellio de Cadore en Paolo Caliari Veronese'. Quoted from Kleerkooper/ Van Stockum 1914-16, p. 889.
48. 'De dansen van Aldegreef sijn 12 int getal ende werden, schoen sijnde, elcx tot 2 schellingen geacht bij Visscher. Deselve hout de goden van Binck voor 6

binding in all octavo Bibles: to wit, the location of Paradise, Israel's journey into the Land of Canaan, the City of Jerusalem, the journeys of Christ, and the travels of the Apostles'.[46] The later Visschers also used advertisements, not only to sell maps but for 'art prints' as well. Thus in the *Oprechte Haerlemse Courant* of 14 September 1683 Nicolaus announced that he had for sale fifty new prints after paintings by Titian and Veronese: 'Nicolaus Visscher, at the sign of the Fisher on Dam Square, Amsterdam, has published 50 Art-Prints, very artistically drawn in Italy and transferred to copper, after the excellent Paintings of Titiano Vecellio de Cadore and Paolo Caliari Veronese'.[47]

Thanks in part to advertising of this sort, the shop 'at the sign of the Fisher' on Kalverstraat and subsequently on Dam Square would have been a familiar address to Dutch art-lovers for over a century. One of the earliest customers must have been Aernout van Buchell (or Buchelius). According to his *Res pictoriae*, in 1619 he went to Claes Jansz. for information about the earlier German printmakers (Heinrich Aldegrever, Jacob Binck, Israhel van Meckenem) and their Italian counterparts (such as Marcantonio Raimondi).[48] Constantijn Huygens probably also visited the shop (before 1631) and spoke to the proprietor, to whom he refers as 'an eminent etcher'. The 'Art and Map Shop' was also attractive to visitors from abroad. On 17 February 1711, by which time Nicolaus' widow was in charge, the German traveller Konrad von Uffenbach purchased, as he himself records, 'some maps by Blaeu to complete my atlases'.[49]

An impression of how such a visit might have gone is offered by a print after a design by Gerbrand van den Eeckhout of *c.* 1665 (fig. 13). This is a printer's device cum address print for Nicolaes Visscher's colleague Clement de Jonghe, with a representation that provides a glimpse of 'De Gekroonde Konst en Kaart Winckel': his shop on Kalverstraat. It may even be De Jonghe himself who is depicted in the right of the print, showing his wares to a number of customers. He is holding a map of Batavia (now Jakarta) at which one of the customers points. Another is examining a print which appears to be an illustration of the Annunciation. On the table between these two customers lie two heavy folio volumes, perhaps picture books. Doubtless the address print presents an idealized picture: not all De Jonghe's visitors - nor all the Visschers' customers, come to that - can have been quite as richly and elegantly dressed as these.[50]

The Visschers' own shop was the backbone for the sale of their prints and picture books, but they also had a number of agents working for them such as the painter Gillis Gerritsz. Dancker of Gouda. In 1653 he owed Nicolaes Visscher no less than 250 guilders. Important customers were other printsellers scattered about the country. Among these was the engraver and printseller Jan van Londerseel, who at the time of his death in 1625 owed Claes

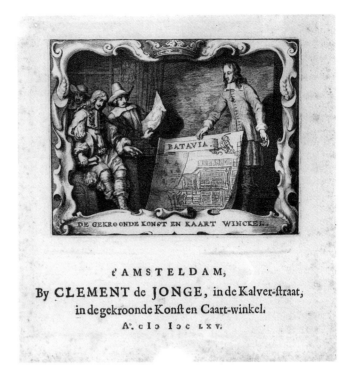

13. (After?) Gerbrandt van den Eeckhout, *Adress Print of Clement de Jonghe*, c. 1665, engraving and etching, 11.2 x 14.5 cm, Museum het Rembrandthuis, Amsterdam

Jansz. a small amount. The items in the Visscher catalogue would therefore have been available from the better bookshops and printshops of Holland as well as the Visschers' own shop in Amsterdam. In 1665 the 'bound books in the shop' of the 'art and bookseller' Jacob Saverij of Dordrecht included not only works published by himself but also publications of others. The picture Bibles on offer included the *Grooten Emblemata Sacra* of Jan Philipsz. Schabaelje, which was based on impressions of prints supplied by the Visschers (cat. no. 60).[51]

What clientele would the Visschers have had chiefly in mind for the Old Testament prints in general and for the picture Bibles in particular, their most important products in this field? One clue is provided by the books themselves. Although the source of the prints was clearly unimportant to the Visschers, they still occasionally thought it necessary to make slight alterations to the original copperplates. Thus anthropomorphic representations of God, in the person of an elderly bearded man with long hair, were burnished out and replaced by the Tetragrammaton surrounded by a halo (see cat. no. 60). In other cases Claes Jansz. Visscher retained the old God-the-Father types but gave them a new identity with an inscription. Thus by merely adding a name and a place the scene of the third day of creation (Gen. 1:9-13) in the *Little*

stuyvers. De dingen van Israël insgelijcx' (Aldegrever's dances are 12 in number and in fine condition are estimated at 2 shillings [a shilling was worth six stivers] each by Visscher. He thinks Binck's gods would be 6 stivers. Pieces by Israhel ditto). And: 'De stucken van Marc Antoon gesneden, van Raphael d'Urbijn als [...] Juditium

Paridis hielt Visscher elcx op 3 stuyver' (Visscher put the pieces cut by Marcantonio, after Raphael of Urbino as [...] the Judgement of Paris at 3 stivers each). Quoted from: Buchelius/ Hoogewerff/ Van Regteren Altena 1928, pp. 46, 47.
**49.** Von Uffenbach: quoted from Koeman 1961, p. 61 ('einige Blauische Landcharten um

meinem Atlanten zu completiren'). Huygens: Huygens/ Heesakkers 1987, p. 75.
**50.** For the address print see Van Eeghen 1985, p. 58; Amsterdam 1986-87, pp. 60-61, no. 43; Hinterding 1993-94, p. 263.
**51.** Gemeentearchief Dordrecht, ONA 248, notary A. Meynaert, 23 April 1665, fol. 229-246:

'Bibelsche Figuren oft Emblemata sacra by Jan philipsz. Schabaelie, 1654' (fol. 229v). Cf. for the inventory of Saverij: Van der Coelen 1991 & 1994, pp. 177-178. Dancker: Bredius 1915-22, Vol. 4, p. 1134. The information that Dancker was Visscher's agent was passed on to me by Jan van der Waals. Van Londerseel: 'Claes

Jansz. wt gel. saecke...f 2:10:0' (Bredius 1915-22, Vol. 5, pp. 1594-1598).

*Raphael Bible*, in which God can be seen floating over the earth, is transformed into the scene in which Enoch is taken by God (Gen. 5:24; fig. 12, p. 48). Just as in 1637 Visscher wanted to eliminate the 'popish' passages from Vondel's *Gysbreght*, so he erased the traditional personifications from his picture Bibles. Perhaps Claes Jansz. had some personal objection to these particular motifs. For Calvinists, certainly, depicting God in human form was prohibited. The Heidelberg Catechism, one of the three confessional texts adhered to by Calvinists in Holland, makes no objection to depicting 'creatures', provided this was not done with the object of venerating them, but, it reads literally: 'God neither can nor may be portrayed in any way whatsoever'.[52]

Even so, commercial considerations must also have played a part in the way these plates were altered. Some changes would have been essential in order to avoid giving offence to potential purchasers of the Calvinist persuasion, and it seems likely that it was in the first instance a Calvinist audience that Claes Jansz. Visscher hoped to reach with his reprints. It was certainly no coincidence that he brought out five of his picture Bibles precisely in the period 1637-39: the States Bible had been first published in 1637 (cat. no. 67). This long-awaited translation of the Bible into Dutch was an instant success with the Calvinist book-buying public, but it was not provided with illustrations to the text and this would have been a disappointment to many buyers. Enterprising booksellers supplied the answer, however. By offering biblical illustrations printed on loose sheets they created the possibility of embellishing the States Bible later. These sheets could be bound into copies of the Bible in the same way that maps could. As has been mentioned, Visscher also sold loose biblical prints, but there was yet another way in which he served visually oriented Bible-readers. As a kind of supplement to the States Bible from 1637 on he offered a variety of picture Bibles.[53]

Does all this mean that Claes Jansz. was aiming exclusively at a specific part of the local market, ie, the Calvinists of Holland? The answer is that he certainly was not. Visscher's picture Bibles were not intended only for those of his own religious persuasion. The form in which the publisher put these works on the market, far from restricting the potential buying public, more probably extended it. Removing the controversial representations of God did not make the prints exclusively Calvinist. On the contrary, this way Visscher could appeal to the broadest possible audience, including the Calvinists.

## Collectors and users of picture Bibles
The Visschers avoided including polemical or offensive illustrations or text in their picture Bibles. The title-pages and the prefaces of these books address no particular section of the public. No purchaser of any kind was to be excluded in advance. It is hardly surprising, then, to find that the actual purchasers of Visscher picture Bibles belonged to a variety of denominations. They are, however, difficult to trace, and not many have been identified at all.

Only two seventeenth-century Dutch private collections of prints have stayed more or less intact up to the present day. The older of these is that of Johan Thijs (1621-1653). Between 1649 and 1653 Thijs, an Amsterdam merchant's son who took a doctorate in law at Leiden, put together the *Bibliotheca Thysiana*, which he left in its entirety to Leiden University. The collection included a number of print albums, now in Leiden's print room. One of these consists almost entirely of prints from the stock of Claes Jansz. According to Thijs' cash-book, the parcel cost him the respectable sum of sixteen guilders. The main feature is Pieter van der Borcht's *Emblemata sacra* in the Visscher edition of 1639 (cf. cat. no. 60).[54]

The print collection of Michiel Hinloopen (1619-1708), scion of a prominent and wealthy Amsterdam family, has also largely been preserved; it is now in the print room of the Rijksmuseum. Hinloopen possessed over 7,000 sheets of prints, including some picture Bibles. Among these is 'The Little Bible of Raphael by Giovanni Lanfranco'.[55] Although Hinloopen's copy has not survived, and it is only known from an old inventory of his collection, this would not have been the Visscher reprint of 1638 (cat. no. 57) but the original Rome edition.

Inventories such as Hinloopen's provide a way of reconstructing libraries and collections which were dispersed following the death of their owners. The chief source of information in this area, however, is printed auction catalogues. These were drawn up whenever a collector died and the library and/or art collection had to be sold, either to settle the debts or to enable the proceeds of the estate to be distributed among the heirs according to entitlement.[56] It is clear from these catalogues that the *Little Raphael Bible* enjoyed considerable popularity. It appears in the sale catalogues of the collections of Dirk van Beeresteyn (Delft, 16 April 1695), Christiaan Huygens (The Hague, 24 October 1695), Petrus Deynoot (Rotterdam, 18 April 1724), Simon Schijnvoet (Amsterdam, 18 February 1728), Lambert Hermansz. ten Kate (Amsterdam, 16 June 1732) and Samuel van Huls (The Hague, 26 September 1735). Generally the precise edition is not given: instead, there is merely a description such as 'The Little Bible of Raphael', as in the catalogue of Samuel van Huls, former burgomaster of The Hague. It is certain, however, that Christiaan Huygens owned a copy of the first edition of the work, printed in

**52.** *Catechismus...*, Middelburg (Richard Schilders) 1611: 'XCVII. Vraghe: Machmen dan ganschelick gheen beelden maken? Antwoorde: God en can noch en mach in geenderley wijse afgebeeldet werden. Maer de creaturen, al ist dat die connen afgebeeldet werden, soo verbiedt doch God haer beeldenisse te maken ende te hebben, om die te vereeren oft Godt daervoor te dienen'. Quoted from: Bakhuizen

van den Brink 1976, p. 207. For anthropomorphic images of God, see Krücke 1959; Manuth 1993-94, pp. 240-246. *Cf.* Van der Coelen 1994-95, pp. 114-115.
**53.** *Cf.* Van der Coelen 1994-95, p. 117. For the States Bible see De Bruin 1993, pp. 203-332. For prints that were bound into it: Poortman 1983-86, Vol. 1, pp. 172-181.
**54.** Schaeps 1994, pp. 256-258.
**55.** 'De klijne bijbel van de zelve [Raphael] door Gio. Lanfranco 54

[stucks]'. Quoted from Van der Waals 1988, p. 181 (Schijnvoet book no. 27).
**56.** For book auction catalogues see Van Selm 1987, pp. 9-173. For auction catalogues with prints: Van der Waals 1988, pp. 19-20, 196-197.

**57.** Van Beeresteyn (BSC 80; Lugt 157), p. 74, no. 21: 'Het bybeltje van Raphael, bestaande in 54 stuks'. Huygens (BSC 31), pp. 69 ff., no. 7: 'Historia del Testamento Vechio dipinta in Vaticana da Raphael Urbino, Roma 1607. fig'. Deynoot (ASC Lugt 316), p. 157, no. 37: 'De Bybelsche Historien van Raphaël Urbin, de Origineele Roomsche Druk'. Schijnvoet (prints and drawings; ASC Lugt 365), no. 94: 'Dezelve [Bybel van

Raphael d'Urbino], door Giovani Lanfranchi. In kleinder Formaat'. Ten Kate (ASC Lugt 416), p. 71, no. 3: 'De Bybel van Rafaël, door Chapron, en die van Sisto Badalocci daer tegen over'. Van Huls (ASC Lugt 454), no. 113: 'De Kleyne Bybel van Raphaël fr. band'. Caution is advised when attempting to identify these editions. As early as 1613 the Badalocchio/Lanfranco set was copied (although with the addition

14. 'Art Room' in the Doll's House of Sara Rothé, 1743, Haags Gemeentemuseum, The Hague

Rome in 1607. This must have been a highly sought-after edition even then, for the Deynoot catalogue states explicitly that the book in question is 'the Original Roman Printing' and hence not a reprint. Schijnvoet, by contrast, had a copy of the later Visscher edition (cat. no. 57).[57]

Other picture Bibles produced by the Visschers were also to be found in large private libraries and print collections of the day. Thus the *Theatrum Biblicum* is mentioned in the auction catalogues of Paulus van Uchelen (Amsterdam, 1 October 1703) and Simon Schijnvoet (Amsterdam, 2 February 1728), while Joan Huydecoper van Maarsseveen (Amsterdam, 14 April 1704) possessed a copy of Schabaelje's *Figuer Bibel* based on it. The picture Bible with the pirated Merians was represented in the collections of Constant Sennepart (Amsterdam, 27 March 1704), Simon Schijnvoet and Van der Hem (The Hague, 20 November 1730). Claes Jansz.' reprint of 1639 of Pieter van der Borcht's *Emblemata sacra*, finally, appears in the sale catalogue of the collection of Joan Huydecoper.[58]

Picture Bibles published by the Visscher firm also found their way into private libraries and collections outside the major towns and cities of the province of Holland. Research into inventories and sale catalogues has yielded information about book ownership in Friesland in the seventeenth and eighteenth centuries. Thus the inventory (Leeuwarden 1685) of Antie, sister of the Mennonite minister and bookseller Hendrik Rintjes, includes a folio edition which is referred to as 'Bybelsche printen van Visscherus' - probably a copy of the *Bybel Printen*, the Merian copy produced by the Visschers (cat. no. 61). The inventory (Joure 1715) of Hessel Vegelin van Claerbergen, who was a member of the landed nobility of Friesland, lists a 'Figuur Bybel Alcmaar 1646'. Like the 'viguur Bijbel' in the inventory (Drachten 1773) of the merchant Reid Gurbes Reiding, this is a copy of Schabaelje's *Grooten Figver-Bibel*, for which Claes Jansz. supplied the print material.[59]

Nicolaus Visscher claimed, with his commercial instinct and publisher's rhetoric, that Merian's picture Bible was for 'all those who had the use of their sight' and that 'all religious persons both

of captions) by Baldassare Aloisi Galanini, and in 1615 Orazio Borgianni made his reproductions - in a slightly larger format - of the *Loggia* frescoes (see Rome 1985, pp. 80-84). These two sets each consist of 52 sheets, whereas those of Badalacchio/ Lanfranco contain 54 in the Rome edition and 55 in the Visscher edition (Visscher added sheet no. 6). In other words, Van Beeresteyn possessed the Rome edition of Badalacchio/

Lanfranco. Paulus van Uchelen (Amsterdam, 1 October 1703; BSC 92) owned the Borgianni set (IX, no. 504 'Eadem minori forma, per H.B. 1615'). The reproductive sets in a larger format by Nicolas Chaperon (1649) and Pietro Aquila and Cesare Fantetti (1675; cf. Rome 1985, pp. 86-92) also occur frequently in Dutch auction catalogues.
**58.** Van Uchelen (BSC 92), XIV, no. 794: 'N. Piscatoris theatrum

biblicum veteris & novi testamenti. Amst. 1650. fig'. Sennepart (ASC [Lugt] 188B), p. 13, no. I: 'De Bybelse Figuren van Visser, met Byschriften in 5 taalen, gebonden in een Franse band'. Huydekoper (BSC 78), no. 66: 'Figuur Bijbel van Schabaille. Amst. 1654'; no. 27: P. van der Burcht Icones V. & N. Testament. Amst. 1639'. Schijnvoet (books; BSC 74), pp. 1 ff., no. 6: 'J. Piscatoris Theatrum Biblicum, hoc est, Historia Sacra,

of Bybelse Figuuren door verscheide Meesters, op Atlas Papier gedrukt, vergulde Band'; no. 7: 'Historia Sacra, of de heilige Historie des Ouden en Nieuwe Testament, in konstige Figuuren'. [Agaat] van der Hem (BSC 157), no. 649: 'Figures de la Bible representans les principales Histoires de la Ste. Ecriture, avec l'explication en vers François & Hollandois, Amst. 1682. fig'. A copy of the original edition of

Merian's picture Bible is mentioned in Van Uchelen's catalogue (XIV, no. 553: 'Icones Biblicae oder Biblische figuren, M. Merians. Franckf. 1625').
**59.** Cf. Visser 1988, Vol. 1, pp. 359-360; 2, pp. 266-268.

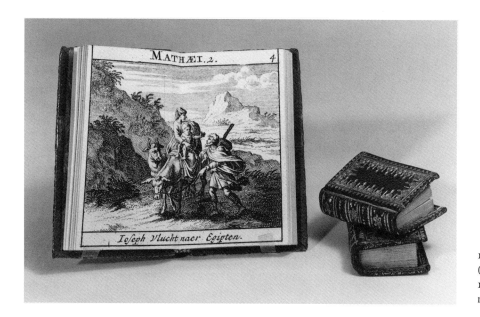

15. *Miniature Books in the Doll's House of Sara Rothé* (left: Andries van Buysen, *The Flight into Egypt*, 1736, etching, 7 x 7.5 cm), Haags Gemeente-museum, The Hague

learned and unlearned were very much taken with that work'. This is unquestionably a case of the publisher putting things in a somewhat flattering light, even if his own pirated reprint had, as he asserts, gone through a 'ready and quick sale of Copies'.[60] Handwritten notes in the margins of printed auction catalogues give an idea of the prices fetched and show that the works published by the Visschers were anything but cheap. The most expensive was the substantial *Theatrum Biblicum*, bound copies of which fetched prices at auction of between twelve (1703) and 31 (1728) guilders. In complete but unbound form the *Royal-Size Bible* must have cost something like ten guilders. In the early eighteenth century a copy of the picture Bible with the copies after Merian changed hands for seven guilders and ten stivers. Comparing price to size, the *Little Raphael Bible* was the most expensive picture Bible. Four guilders (1695), two guilders and two stivers (1702), three guilders (1728) and as much as five guilders and five stivers (1735) were paid for this little work.[61] That prices varied so widely doubtless had to do with the kind of binding and whether the edition was an early 'original' or a late reprint.[62]

But however widely prices fluctuated, it is clear that picture Bibles like these must have been beyond the reach of many, even in the prosperous Dutch Republic. People in the lower strata of society - even though together they constituted the vast majority of the population - would not have had much to do with them. True,

book ownership was not unknown here, but it was rare, and the books concerned were cheap popular literature rather than luxuriously executed books of prints. It was in the middle classes - the broad bourgeoisie - and of course also the upper echelons of society, that most books were to be found.[63]

It is hardly surprising, then, that doll's houses, as more or less accurate reflections of the dwellings of the wealthy bourgeoisie, should often have been provided with well-stocked miniature libraries. A fine example is that of the doll's house in the Gemeente Museum in The Hague (fig. 14, p. 51). This was made in 1743 to a commission from the Amsterdam merchant's wife Sara Rothé. It contains numerous miniature objects, many of which date back to the previous century. In the present context the 'art room' is particularly interesting, as it provides an idea of the kind of room in which collections were kept. The walls are decorated with imitation gilt leather hangings and tiny paintings. The collection is housed in three cabinets - one with coins and medallions, one full of curiosities (sea shells, coral etc.) and one containing books. There are two low book tables with five 'large' albums of prints and drawings. The bookcase itself stands against the rear wall and contains 28 books, bound in red leather with gold tooling. Eight of these, the 'large' volumes on the bottom shelf, contain biblical prints and together form a multivolume miniature picture Bible (fig. 15).[64]

60. Nicolaus Visscher, 'The Preface to the Reader', in: *Afbeeldingen Der voornaamste Historien...*, Amsterdam (Nicolaus Visscher), *s.a.* (University Library, Nijmegen: 754 b 2), fol. **2r, **2v.
61. *Theatrum Biblicum* ; 1703: Van Uchelen auction catalogue (BSC 92); 1728: Schijnvoet auction catalogue (BSC 74). In 1715/17 a copy of the *Figuer-Bibel* (with the prints from the *Theatrum Biblicum*) fetched eleven Carolus guilders (Visser 1988, Vol. 2, pp. 266-268). *Royal-Sized Bible*: Van der Waals 1997 (according to the inventory of Danckert Danckertsz. of 1667, in

which the royal-size prints were estimated at 1.5 stivers each). Merian copies: Schijnvoet auction catalogue, 1728 (BSC 74). *Little Raphael Bible*; 1695: Van Beresteyn auction catalogue (*cf.* Van der Waals 1988, p. 195, under no. 27); 1702: Van der Vinne auction (Bredius 1915-22, Vol. 6, p. 2210); 1728: note in copy 100 E 10 in Museum van het Boek, The Hague ('Uijt de Vercopinge van Simon Schijnvoet f 3:-'); 1735: Van Huls auction catalogue (ASC Lugt 454).
62. The prices paid for Van der Borcht's picture Bibles could also vary widely. In 1704 a copy of the

earliest impression of the large etchings fetched five guilders and ten stivers. In the same catalogue no more than twelve stivers were bid for a copy of Visscher's reprint of the smaller etchings of 1639. However, an even later reprint of this last set fetched five guilders and fifteen stivers in 1728. 1704: Huydekoper auction catalogue (BSC 78); 1728: Schijnvoet auction catalogue (BSC 74).
63. Van Selm 1992, pp. 62-76. For the social stratification of the Dutch Republic, *cf.* De Vries/ Van der Woude 1995, pp. 647-650. The 'broad bourgeoisie' and above

- those with an annual income of 600 guilders and more - accounted for only 20% of the urban population in the period 1650-1800. By contrast the two bottom strata, with an average annual income per family of 300 guilders, together made up almost half the urban population. With this kind of income it was necessary to spend 50-70% on food alone (ibid., pp. 715-716), even before paying for clothing and lodging.
64. These were prints that had been cut out of a copy of the picture Bible by Andries van Buysen: *Hondert Vijf en Vijftig*

*Bybelsche Print Verbeeldingen...*, Amsterdam (Jacob Graal) 1736 (Rijksmuseum Library, Amsterdam: 317 F 16; *cf.* Poortman 1983-86, Vol. 2, pp. 70-71). They were then bound together into miniature books which, on the scale of the doll's house, made picture Bibles in a kind of 'royal' format! For this doll's house see Pijzel-Dommisse 1988, esp. pp. 83-87. For another doll's house with a miniature picture Bible: Van der Coelen 1997, fig. 10. *Cf.* for collections of art and curiosities in Holland: Bergvelt/ Kistemaker 1992, esp. p. 81.

The owners of picture Bibles supplied by the Visschers referred to earlier, would almost certainly have kept their books in this kind of environment. Most of them possessed a substantial collection of books, prints and curiosities, and the Amsterdam merchants Paulus van Uchelen (c. 1641-1702) and Constant Sennepart (1625-1703) and the Mennonite corn-merchant Lambert Hermansz. ten Kate (1674-1731) were no exceptions; nor was Simon Schijnvoet (1652-1727), who began as a master saddler and rose to become deputy schout and chief provost of the alms-house in Amsterdam. Not all were as well-to-do as Joan Huydecoper van Maarsseveen - and certainly few were as learned as Christiaan Huygens - but without exception they were members of the uppermost strata of society.[65]

Such large collections tend to contain the more exclusive art - not just Dutch works but German and Italian ones too, and older works alongside the contemporary. They might include albums of the graphic work of Dürer, or reproductive prints after Raphael. Highly sought-after too was the work of Lucas van Leyden, an artist who had kept a very close watch on the quality of the impressions of his prints. Lucas' engravings could command exorbitant prices rising to several hundred guilders. For the rare states of Rembrandt's etchings, too, large sums were paid. Of the picture Bibles, apart from the *Little Raphael Bible* print collectors particularly liked the *Icones* of Hans Holbein the Younger and the so-called 'Little Bible by Antonio Tempesta' ('Bijbeltje van Tempeest'; fig. 19.1) - which likewise dealt only with the Old Testament.[66]

The picture Bibles sold by the Visscher firm were not brought out specially for this élite circle of collectors. Reprinted time and time again, they were considerably less exclusive than the prints of Lucas or Rembrandt. Although these books did not belong to the domain of the populace as a whole, they were nevertheless unquestionably more common than can be established on the basis of research into auction catalogues and inventories. In the case of the more modest collections no sale catalogues were printed, and in cases where an inventory was compiled it by no means always included an itemized list of the books in the collection. It is quite conceivable that someone who only wanted or could only afford one or two picture books would choose a picture Bible.[67]

The way in which they were arranged in book and art sale catalogues shows that there was something of a dual approach to picture Bibles. Sometimes they were listed under the heading of 'Prints and Drawings', where they would appear among the bound art-books and picture books, and sometimes they are treated as 'Libri theologici' and put together with Bibles and unillustrated theological works. Picture Bibles could thus be regarded either as art on a biblical theme or as Bibles in pictorial form. Some of these books, particularly the *Little Raphael Bible*, almost always appear among the art-books and would presumably therefore have been collected primarily for their aesthetic value. Others, such as many of the Visscher editions, tend rather to come under the heading of theology. In the view of many a genuine collector they would probably have been second-rate works of art, but despite that they must have been useful and pleasant possessions to many people.

'To joyn profit to pleasure' was what the Visschers, in the words of Nicolaus, aimed to do with their picture Bibles. In the English preface to his Merian copy this is explained as follows: 'This end we propos'd to our selves by the present undertaking, for what can be suppos'd more profitable than the knowledge of sacred History, and with the breasts of our mothers & nurses to suck in almost as early the two breasts of the Old & New Testament; and what can be more pleasant than to do this by pictures, which at the same time imprint the sacred story in our mind, while our sight is delighted with the contemplation of images of things which our eye hath not seen'.[68]

In the preface to his *Bybel Printen* (cat. no. 61) Nicolaes Visscher had already referred to the ancient Horatian maxim of *utile dulci*, the useful coupled with the enjoyable. He addresses himself to 'those who love virtue and art' and trusts that it will not always be a matter merely of 'viewing these biblical figures purely for entertainment', but that the reader will be spurred on to 'look up and read the contents of these figures in Holy Scripture itself'. In practice, then, to many owners their picture Bibles would have been an aid to reading the Bible and at the same time an enjoyable way of passing the time. Nicolaus Visscher also commended his picture Bible based on Merian copies as 'a means for the better instruction of [...] children and servants'.[69] Clearly, purchasers of the work would certainly have shown it to their children and would have leafed through it with them. Whether such costly editions were also made available to the servants, as Visscher suggested, is not known.

In fact, not much is known at all about how picture Bibles were used. One important question, for example, is whether only the pictures were found interesting of whether the texts were read as well. Nicolaus Visscher intended his Schut edition (cat. no. 62) 'to entertain both the adult and literate and the young and illiterate';

**65.** *Cf.* Bergvelt/ Kistemaker 1992, pp. 252, 327-328 (Schijnvoet), 322 (Ten Kate), 328 (Sennepart), 329-30 (Van Uchelen).
**66.** Holbein (90 woodcuts): Holl., German, XIVA, pp. 207-212, no. 100; Tempesta (220 etchings): TIB XXXV, nos 14-233. For prices paid for prints by Lucas van Leyden see Robinson 1981, p. xliii; for Rembrandt's etchings: Münz 1952, Vol. 2, pp. 206, 208, 213-214.
**67.** A tendency well documented in studies of book ownership is that the smaller the collection was, the larger the emphasis on theology and the Bible. *Cf.* De Kruif

1994, p. 322. It seems likely that the 'basic requirements' would also have been in the religious field when it came to prints and picture books.
**68.** Nicolaus Visscher, 'The Preface to the Reader', in: *Afbeeldingen Der voornaamste Historien...*, Amsterdam (Nicolaus Visscher), *s.a.* (University Library, Nijmegen: 754 b 2), fol. \*\*2r.
**69.** *Ibid.* (see n. 68 above).

so he at least assumed that some users would only be looking at the pictures. However, picture Bibles were not intended for teaching reading at school: there was cheaper printed matter for that purpose (cat. no. 73). Even so, these books with their simple rhymes could certainly have been useful as a teaching aid in the home. Some picture Bibles are even in several languages, including the *Royal-Size Bible* and the Merian copies published by the Visschers, which had captions in Dutch, Latin, German, French and English. In the preface to the *Bybel Printen* (cat. no. 61) Nicolaes Visscher says that this will help Dutchmen practise their languages, although whether this actually happened is difficult to determine.

The practical use to which a picture Bible was put did not, of course, have to correspond to the wishes expressed by the publisher in his foreword regarding its use and function. Nor, in essence, do the captions that were appended to the illustrations necessarily say anything about the meaning that the print actually had for the spectator, let alone the maker. In general, print designers aimed to illustrate the biblical stories in a lucid and attractive way. In particular, they had an eye for the drama of the action and its setting against the background of panoramic landscapes or imposing buildings. And they stayed well clear of particular denominational or theologically complicated interpretations.

As a sign of their own knowledge the authors of print captions or inscriptions did, however, sometimes try to add something to the image. They would then draw the reader's attention to a meaning that was not overtly expressed in the picture. Sometimes there is more than one caption, and on occasion several interpretations are found for one and the same biblical story. Nicolaes Visscher's *Bybel Printen* provides an example of this. In the captions to *The Sacrifice of Isaac* (Gen. 22:9-13), a copy of an etching by Matthaeus Merian (ill. cat. no. 61), Abraham's solid faith is emphasized. 'He was stedfast in the beliefe of Gods promises', reads the motto. In the English caption the story is concisely summarized in verse:

'God commands Abraham to slay his Son
(To trie his heart) for an oblation.
He readie was to strike, Gods Angel spak',
Hold thy hand Abra'm, spare thy Son Isaak'.

For the Dutch reader, the quatrain (by Reyer Anslo) focuses on Abraham's inner struggle: the conflict between love and duty, faith and reason. In the prose text (by Jan Philipsz. Schabaelje), by contrast, the reader's attention is drawn to 'the future Messiah, of whom Isaac was a prefiguration and shadow'.[70]

All these interpretations - narrative, moralizing, psychologizing and typologically Messianic - may have been useful to the reader, shaping his own interpretation of *The Sacrifice of Isaac*. However, he might also have simply ignored them and concentra-

ted on the beautiful landscape, the violent scene or the miraculous heavenly apparition. That the interpretation of the poet was not always accepted at face value is clear from the traces left by the book's users. Corrections, deletions or underlinings added in pen reveal the active role of the reader. Indeed in some cases the captions were actually cut out, either because of dissatisfaction with their content or simply because people were not interested in the text but only in the picture.[71]

The pictures also seem sometimes to have evoked an active response from the spectator. Here again the occasional emendation is found. In particular the frankly exposed genitals in representations of *The Fall* or *The Drunkenness of Noah* suffered in later times from such (parental?) censorship, being concealed under a thick layer of ink. However, the prints in picture Bibles also stimulated more creative action. They were cut out, coloured in or copied in the margin, often very clumsily. Constantijn Huygens, writing in 1629-31, remembers the 'congenital predilection for drawing' which he and his brother Maurits had always had: 'We never had enough of copying in our childish hand, for our own enjoyment, every engraving and woodcut that we came across'. His own children Constantijn junior and Christiaan were similarly fond of drawing at an early age. Picture books would doubtless have played a part in this. Indeed, in the summer of 1646 Christiaan Huygens made a drawing on the garden fence at his parents' house on the Plein in The Hague, based on figures in Hans Holbein's *Pictures of Death*.[72]

A related although more professional purpose to which picture Bibles were applied can be demonstrated in the case of a specific group of users: artists. Rembrandt himself drew inspiration for his own compositions from illustrations in the *Little Raphael Bible* (see cat. no. 57; fig. 57.1). Indeed, providing examples was actually one of the publishers' intended functions for such picture books. To artists they were not so much luxury items as professional utilitarian literature: reference works and model books with which they could keep themselves informed about the work of their predecessors. Thanks to two inventories it is known that Rembrandt owned a Bible, initially an earlier vernacular translation, later probably a copy of the States Bible (cat. no. 67). In order to go into Old Testament history in greater detail, he also purchased a copy of the *Jewish Antiquities* by Flavius Josephus (cat. no. 71). Also intended as documentation was the enormous collection of prints which Rembrandt assembled: the work of his famous predecessors served as a source of information and inspiration in the design of his own Old Testament representations.[73]

It is possible, then, that Rembrandt, who as evidenced by the inventory of 1656 was certainly an admirer of Raphael's work, possessed a copy of the *Little Raphael Bible*.[74] Inventories of collections show that to artists as a group, this work, together

**70.** For the interpretation of *The Sacrifice of Isaac* in picture Bibles see Van der Coelen 1991 & 1994, pp. 180-182. For the function of inscriptions on prints and the differences in the intentions of artists and authors see McGrath 1984. For the use of books, with on the one hand the intentions of

publishers and authors and on the other their reception from and 'appropriation' by readers: Chartier 1994, pp. vii-xi, 1-23.
**71.** Michiel Hinloopen excised the verses in the text margin of a royal-size biblical print after Rubens; he was interested only in the artist's invention. *Cf.* Van der Waals 1997.

For traces of wear as indications of the use to which devotional prints were put, *cf.* Frijhoff 1990, pp. 357-365.
**72.** Constantijn senior: Huygens/ Heesakkers 1987, p. 70. Christiaan: Huygens 1888-1950, Vol. 1, p. 17 (no. 10). *Cf.* Amsterdam/ Gent 1982-83, pp. 26-35.

**73.** For Rembrandt's collection see Scheller 1969. *Cf.* for artists' libraries Bialostocki 1984.
**74.** Among the 'Kunst boecken' which Rembrandt owned, four are mentioned which consisted wholly of prints after Raphael; the precise contents are not given (Strauss/ Van der Meulen 1979, no. 1656/12

[nos 196, 205, 206, 214]). *Cf.* Van der Coelen 1994-95, pp. 116-117.

with Holbein's *Icones*, was the most popular picture Bible of all. It was in the collections of several Antwerp painters. The inventory of his estate drawn up in 1628 shows that Steven II Wils, former deacon of the St Luke's Guild in Antwerp, had a copy. Presumably this was either the edition published in Rome by Orlandi or the Amsterdam reprint by Michiel Colijn. The same copy turns up again in 1642 among the possessions of his brother David van Wils. The 'Raphael Bible' in the inventory of the painter Jeremias Wildens of 1653-54, a volume which had been owned by his father Jan, another painter, may have been the Visscher reprint. The same applies to 'A small book of prints by Raphael containing the Old Testament' which was in the collection of Victor Wolfvoet (1652).[75]

But artists in the North, too, admired the work of Raphael. In 1702 the attic of the home of the Haarlem painter Vincent Lourensz. van der Vinne contained '1 painted wooden cabinet of paper art, including drawings, prints, models, art books etc'. This collection seems also to have included a copy of the *Little Raphael Bible*. It is probably the same work that also occurs in the inventory of the painter Antoni de Waardt of The Hague in 1752, and two years later in that of his Amsterdam colleague Jacob de Wit.[76]

Other biblical picture books from the Visscher list are also represented in artists' inventories. Thus in 1635 a Passion by Cranach was auctioned from the collection of the Amsterdam painter Barent van Someren. In view of the relatively low price paid (14 stivers) this would probably have been Claes Jansz.' 1616 reprint of Cranach's set.[77]

Various painters, famous and less famous, drew inspiration from the picture Bibles published by the Visschers, chiefly by the compositions in the *Theatrum Biblicum*.[78] Also very influential, particularly among minor artists and craftsmen, was the set by Pieter Schut: representations borrowed from his compositions appear on countless everyday items such as tobacco boxes, painted furniture, hearth screens and ships' transoms. Dutch tile painters in particular made grateful use of Schut's set. Indeed, almost 70% of his prints, including that of Jonah being cast up onto the shore (fig. 11, p. 47), have been shown to have been used at least once as a model for the decoration of 'Bible tiles' (fig. 16).[79]

## Picture Bibles for 'all the Christian world'

Bible tiles, which were used by those who had achieved a degree of prosperity to decorate their fireplaces or walls, are considered a typically Dutch product. Despite that, they were also exported abroad on a large scale. The picture books published by the Visscher firm were likewise by no means exclusively a part of Northern Netherlandish culture. They also spread beyond the borders of the Republic. As has been shown, a number of Antwerp artists possessed copies of the *Little Raphael Bible*, some of

16. After Pieter Hendricksz. Schut, *Jonah Vomited onto Dry Land*, tile, Amsterdam 1725-75, *c*. 13 x 13 cm, Zaanse Schans

which may have been reprints produced in Amsterdam. Despite the separation of the Northern and Southern Netherlands there were still lively trading contacts, certainly in the field of the arts. The Antwerp art dealer Herman I de Neyt, who died in Delft in 1642 while on a business trip, is a case in point. His death led to the compiling of at least three inventories: one of the goods in his home in Antwerp, the others of the stock in trade remaining in Delft and Amsterdam. From the Amsterdam inventory it may be deduced that De Neyt also purchased prints in that city - probably for sale in Antwerp. In De Neyt's Antwerp home, apart from many paintings, prints and books, there was also a copy of the *Little Raphael Bible*. In view of his trading links with Amsterdam this may well have been a copy of Claes Jansz.' reprint, which had appeared not long before (cat. no. 57).[80]

As it did for booksellers, the domestic market must have provided the main base for print publishers' sales. Only with a sound home market was it possible to do business abroad,[81] and there was certainly a healthy domestic market in Amsterdam, where both the booksellers and the major printsellers were extremely internationally oriented. The Visscher catalogue itself provides clear evidence of this in appearing not only in Dutch but also in French and German editions.

The Visschers maintained contacts with major print dealers both in Germany and France and in Italy. For example, Claes

**75.** Wils: 'Item een boecxken van LIII stucxkens wesende het Oudt Testament geëxcudeert by Sisto Baldalochi ende Joanni Lanfranci byeengebonden ende gequoteert...N˚ 33' (Duverger 639). Van Wils: 'Noch een pacxsken met printen geïntituleert Baldalochi Lanfranchi n˚ 33' (Duverger 1174).

Wildens: 'No. 38. Het Out Testament van Raephel' (Duverger 1902). 'No 545 Een boecxken printen van Raphaël inhoudende d'Oude Testament' (Duverger 1813).
**76.** Van der Vinne: 'No. 20. Bibeltje Raphel' (Bredius 1915-22, Vol. 4, pp. 1258 ff.; 6, p. 2210). De

Waardt: '[no. 188] 2 dito [Bijbelse figuurboekjes] zijnde losse prenten als een van 17 bl. en een van 12 bl. door Rafel' (ibid., Vol. 3, pp. 1023 ff.). De Wit: '[no. 35] De Bybel van Raphael d'Urbino' (ibid., Vol. 3, pp. 741 ff.).
**77.** Bredius 1915-22, Vol. 3, pp. 794 ff. ('Een Passie van Craen').

**78.** Münster 1994, esp. pp. 63, 91-95, 130-131, 162-163, 189. Cf. Van der Coelen 1994-95, pp. 115-116.
**79.** Pluis 1994, pp. 68-71, 645 (no. 1032), 926. Everyday items: Utrecht 1991-92, esp. pp. 61-63.
**80.** 'Printen van Raphaël van d'Oude Testament in een gedruct

boecxken'. See Duverger 1212. For the Amsterdam inventory, which included 'seventich verscheijden p... figueren soo van Vissch... [Visscher?] van andere meesters' and 'twee printeboeckgens', see Duverger 1210.
**81.** Berkvens-Stevelinck *et al.* 1992, pp. 251-263, 297.

Jansz. sold works published by the Hamburg bookseller Arent Pietersz. (a Dutchman) advertising them in 1645. It seems likely that Pietersz. for his part stocked Visscher publications in his shop in Hamburg. In Paris, Visscher maps were sold by the Langlois family of publishers. In Rome the great print publisher Giovanni Giacomo de Rossi could supply the Italian market with a large part of Nicolaus Visscher's list, as his stock catalogue shows. The publications of the Visscher firm were probably also available in England. One sign that this was the case is that in 1663 Tobias Flessiers, 'Painter of London', owed Nicolaes Visscher, 'Art seller on Kalverstraat, at the sign of the Fisher', over 333 guilders for goods purchased. Presumably, Flessiers did not buy them purely for his own use but also to sell them on.[82]

The Frankfurt fairs, which had been held twice annually ever since the fourteenth century, were as important for international sales in the print business as they were in the book trade. This was where one met one's foreign colleagues, with whom wares were exchanged or bought and sold. Whether the Visschers ever went to Frankfurt is not known, but it seems likely. Other Dutch print publishers such as Cornelis Claesz. and the Danckertsz. firm certainly went there, and it is known that Clement de Jonghe visited the fair in March 1659, as the council of Frankfurt declared itself willing, following a request from the emperor, to confiscate from De Jonghe 'a print insulting and belittling the emperor and the archducal house of Austria' and to impose a fine and a term in prison.[83] However, whether this sentence was actually carried out is still very much a moot point. More important is the knowledge that De Jonghe, who purchased a large number of copperplates by Rembrandt perhaps as early as 1658, a year before this accusation was made, was a visitor to the fair. It sheds new light on the rapid spread of Rembrandt's etchings in Europe.

The Visschers' international orientation is also apparent from the books themselves, most clearly in the picture Bible with the copied Merians. As already mentioned, the prints in this work were provided with commentaries in five languages (cf. cat. no. 61). One reason for this is indicated by Nicolaus Visscher himself in his foreword to the book: 'And that this light may extend its rays thrô all the Christian world, we have taught our images to speak severall languages. Not only our mother low Dutch, but likewise the manly High dutch [German], the smooth English, the Eloquent French and the learned Latine, the two last of which, are as the bridge of communication by which all the Nations of Europe can come to one another'.[84]

The Visschers' picture Bibles were indeed distributed over a large part of the Christian world. They turn up not only in

Protestant and Catholic countries but in Orthodox parts of the world too. They were being imported into Russia in the last quarter of the seventeenth century - ie, even before Tsar Peter the Great did so much to foster trade with Holland. Copies of the *Theatrum Biblicum* (cat. no. 58), the Van der Borcht reprints (cf. cat. nos 55 and 60) and the editions with the Merian copies (cat. no. 61) all found their way into Russian monasteries and into the private libraries of nobles, clerics and artists. Often the Latin inscriptions were provided with handwritten translations into Russian. The *Theatrum Biblicum* in particular was popular with the nobility and clergy. Tsar Theodore III and the patriarchs Nikon and Adrian all owned copies of this picture Bible.[85] Moreover the prints in the *Theatrum Biblicum* had a considerable influence on Russian art, as may be seen in the murals painted between 1670 and 1695 in the churches of Yaroslavl.[86]

In Russian the *Theatrum Biblicum* is called the 'Biblia Piskatora'. The Latinized version Piscator helped ensure that the Visscher family name, which was borne by three generations of publishers and would have been understood in the English and German-speaking countries too, could become a familiar one throughout the world of books and prints. Not for nothing did the map and print publisher David Funck (1642-1709) of Nuremberg refer to the founder of the Amsterdam firm as 'the *famous* Dutchman Claes Janssen Visscher'.[87]

The Visscher firm itself also did its best to promote the name. The small figure of a fisherman appears on many of its maps and print publications, becoming something of a trademark for the business. It is tempting, looking at the small figure in the bottom right corner of the Bible map (fig. 3, p. 40) to think that this might be a portrait of Claes Jansz.: the fishing-rod and net referring to his surname and the compasses to his cartographic activities. The little fisherman, who could also be seen on the signboard of the shop on Kalverstraat and was also used as a printer's device in the stock catalogues (fig. 1, p. 37), must have made a valuable contribution to the firm's international renown.[88] It can hardly have been a coincidence that in the poem that he wrote about Claes Jansz. in *Het Gulden Cabinet van de Edel Vry Schilderconst* (Antwerp, 1661-62) the biographer Cornelis de Bie talks about 'the fisher sign': 'The *fisher* sign is where honour lies. Where a man sits at the water's edge, always fishing. This sign is enough to teach and tell us whose these works are'.[89]

## Popular Prints

Clearly, the picture Bibles from the Visscher publishing house were intended for an international readership living in Protestant,

**82.** Visschers advertisement (*Courante*, 4 November 1645): Van der Krogt 1985, no. A78. Langlois: Grivel 1986, p. 179. De Rossi: Van der Waals 1988, pp. 22, 198, 199. Flessiers: Bredius 1915-22, Vol. 2, p. 624.
**83.** 'Einen der kais. Maj. und dem erzherzoglichen Hause Österreich schimpflichen und verkleinerlichen Stich' (quoted from Kapp 1886, p. 666; cf. Van Eeghen 1960-78, Vol. 5, p. 114, n. 235).

Cornelis Claesz.: Van Selm 1987, pp. 183-184. Danckertsz.: Van Eeghen 1960-78, Vol. 5, pp. 90, 120. For the Frankfurt fairs see Koch 1991. The present author is currently preparing a study of the role of the Frankfurt and Leipzig fairs in the distribution of prints in early modern times.
**84.** Nicolaus Visscher, 'The Preface to the Reader', in: *Afbeeldingen Der voornaamste Historien...*, Amsterdam (Nicolaus Visscher), s.a.

(University Library, Nijmegen: 754 b 2), fol. **2r-v.
**85.** Cf. Belobrova 1979, 1985, 1989. I am grateful to Julia Gerasimova for her summaries of these articles in Russian.
**86.** Réau 1921, pp. 303, 337 ff.
**87.** *Dreyfaches sehr nußliches Register, Dieser Accuraten Teutschländischen Land-Charten...*, Nuremberg (David Funck) s.a. (Herzog August Bibliothek, Wolfenbüttel: T 33 Helmst. 8°), fol. A2r: 'den berühmten

Holländer Claes Janssen Vischer'.
**88.** For the Visschers' signboard see Orenstein et al. 1993-94, p. 190 with fig. 33. For the angler as device: Amsterdam 1993-94B, pp. 26-27; Poortman/ Augusteijn 1995, p. 141. Cf. for printsellers' signboards Grivel 1986, pp. 235-246.
**89.** De Bie 1661-62, p. 461: 'Het Visschers teecken is (waer in de eere leyt) / Daer eenich man aen t'water sit en vist altijdt. / Dit teecken leert

ons al en gheeft ghenoch te kennen / Van wie des' wercken sijn [...]'.

Catholic and Orthodox countries: in other words, 'for all the Christian world'. The audience was geographically unbounded, nor was it linked to any particular denomination. However, this must not be allowed to blind one to the fact that there were other limitations. Picture Bibles may have been meant for the whole world, but not every citizen of the world could afford to own one.

Of course, some picture Bibles were accessible to a larger public than others, depending on their size and price. Many people, moreover, would have been able to buy, if not entire Bibles, at least individual series or prints from the books. While prices for picture Bibles started at around two guilders, in the case of loose prints - with the exception of rare impressions or very exclusive editions - they were presumably more likely to cost just a few stivers each. In 1609 Old Testament prints from the list of Cornelis Claesz. cost between 3/4 and 10 stivers apiece, depending partly on the size. At the end of the century the average price of a print, at least one from one of the major Dutch collections, was something like 3 stivers.[90]

The vast majority of people in the Low Countries, even assuming that they owned any prints at all, would have had to make do with even cheaper prints. These too were available from the Visschers, whose motto was to try to ensure that there was something in the shop for everyone. Bible maps and Ten Commandments prints could be had in various formats and thus at a range of prices. The same Old Testament compositions were available in large and small prints, as originals or copies. Typical of the Visschers' publishing strategy was the way in which Crispijn de Passe's *Liber Genesis* (cat. no. 54) was incorporated into the firm's list. Claes Jansz. had copies made of at least six of the 59 representations from this little book of 1612 devoted to Genesis. These included the one in which Jacob barters a bowl of lentil pottage for Esau's birthright (Gen. 25:29-34; fig. 17). De Passe's designs were reduced, simplified and transferred to a round picture plane (fig. 18, p. 58). In contrast to the original editions of the *Liber Genesis* the texts are brief and in Dutch. A complete copy of the *Liber Genesis* must have cost around two guilders and would thus have been too expensive for many customers. Visscher's simplified copies, which could be had on loose sheets, were unquestionably cheaper.[91]

Even in the seventeenth century, however, there were those who had misgivings about simply copying the work of others. Indeed, in a publication of 1623 Claes Jansz. himself - a question of the pot calling the kettle black, surely? - complained about pirate printers: 'The moment I had published this book, at great effort and with singular eagerness [...], it was at once copied by a shameless seeker after easy gains, full of false and clumsy plates made by an apprentice, to swindle the buyer's money from his purse'.[92] Nor,

17. Crispijn de Passe the Elder, *Jacob and Esau*, engraving, c. 8.5 x 12.7 cm, in: *Liber Genesis*, Arnhem (Jan Jansz.) 1616. University Library, Amsterdam

**90.** Van der Waals 1988, pp. 22-23 (*cf.* also pp. 119-122). For the prices of Cornelis Claesz.' prints: Van Selm 1987, pp. 217-221; Orenstein *et al.* 1993-94, pp. 172, 183.
**91.** *Cf.* Jacob Marcus auction catalogue, Amsterdam 7 September 1750, p. 60, no. 590: 'Liber Genesis, in figuris Crisp. de Pas, 1612'; with the handwritten price of f 1:18 (BSC 208). For Visscher's copies: Van der Coelen 1994-95, p. 113. Hollstein

(XXXVIII, p. 218, no. 302) identifies the set with 'B Historie van Abraham', one of the *Snylingh* sheets in the stock list. According to the statement there (*Catalogue Visscher*, p. 18), there whould then be eight prints to the sheet, which - given the diameter of 9 cm per print and the requisite margins - would seem too many for a sheet of foolscap (42 x 32 cm); moreover only two of the six prints have anything to do with Abraham; the

rest are on the theme of Jacob. Is it not more likely that these are six prints from the series 'Abrahams Offerhande, &c.' and 'Jacobs Droom, &c.' from the section headed 'Quarten, van gemeene Bladen' (ibid., p. 22)?
**92.** *Description des cinq ordres de Colomnes...*, Amsterdam (Claes Jansz. Visscher) 1623 (University Library, Amsterdam: OG 91-10), fol. *2v (*Tot Waerschouwinge van den Kooper*): 'Al so ick met groote vlijt

en sonderlinghe lust dit Boeck hadde in 't licht gebracht [...], soo is my dit selve terstont van eenen onbeschaemden Vuyl-gewinoecker naer-gedruckt, vol valsche en ondeugende Platen, van een leer-jonghen ghemaeckt, om den Kooper syn geld met bedrogh uyt de Beurs te lichten'. This is the second edition (in French and Dutch) of the prints after designs by Hans Blum (Holl. XXXVIII, pp. 159-161, nos 392-413).

18. Copy after Crispijn de Passe the Elder, *Jacob and Esau*, before 1652, etching, *c*. 9 cm (diameter), published by Claes Jansz. Visscher, Herzog Anton Ulrich Museum, Brunswick

come to that, were Visscher's own pirated and other copies all equally satisfactory from the aesthetic point of view. They did, however, ensure that prints found their way within the reach of a growing number of people.

The Visscher firm had something to offer even the smallest budget. There is no firm evidence, but there is much to suggest that Claes Jansz. was the first to publish, systematically and on a relatively large scale, a particular type of 'popular print' (fig. 19, p. 59) which was developed by others mainly in the second half of the seventeenth century (see cat. no. 53). The innovation consisted in taking a whole sheet of foolscap paper (approx. 42 x 32 cm) and covering it with several rows of scenes in the same small format. As a rule there were eight, twelve or sixteen images per sheet (*octavo*, *duodecimo*, or *sextodecimo*). These scenes, shown in a rectangular picture area, were provided with short captions in letterpress, generally rhyming. These sheets were clearly aimed at a broad public, which meant that the price could not be too high. For this reason production costs were kept low by using cheap paper and spending as little as possible on the design, for which, therefore, anonymous craftsmen were employed rather than great artists. Often, too, old blocks or copies would be used for this kind of print. The technique was usually woodcut, which could be

printed in larger numbers than engravings or etchings. Prints of this kind - the most important type of popular print - were to flourish in the Northern Netherlands particularly in the eighteenth century.[93]

The Visscher catalogue includes one section with the heading: 'Whole sheets of Cutting, or which may be cut from one, on foolscap. With A.B.C. signatures' ('Heele Bladen Snylingh, of die van een gesneden kunnen werden, op gemeen Papier. Geteeckent met A.B.C.'). The sheets in question have eight scenes of approx. 6.6 x 9.7 cm or sixteen of approx. 4.1 x 5.7 cm, printed in rows of two or four. Evidently they were meant to be cut, but doubtless they were also kept or hung as whole sheets. These sheets were conceived as sets. The numbering with letters of the alphabet made it easier to handle orders. Among the *Snylingh* sheets of eight prints four are devoted to the Old Testament. No impressions of these have survived, but sheet E ('Bybelsche Historien') is probably identical to the later reprint by Joachim Ottens (fig. 19, p. 59). The set by Pieter Schut, which was arranged in the same way (fig. 7, p. 45), clearly served as the model: both the images and the texts are the same. He may even have been the printmaker responsible.[94]

Other *Snylingh* sheets from the Visscher list, some of them etched by Schut, have themes relating to mythology, hunting, pastoral life, ships and sayings - all themes that were to become typical of popular prints. In the Visscher catalogue, however, they appear not as woodcuts with letterpress texts, but as etchings with engraved captions (some, moreover, are circular, which is also unheard-of in the popular prints of the eighteenth century). For this reason Visscher's *Snylingh* prints have been described as 'a link between the art print and the popular print proper'.[95] To what extent Claes Jansz. was really breaking new ground with these prints and thereby laying one of the foundations for the popular print is unclear. Were these really prototypes, or had this kind of popular print already developed to maturity by about 1650, when Visscher's *Snylingh* prints were made? Since so much material in this field has been lost, there is little that can be said about this with any certainty. There are certainly no comparable prints in Cornelis Claesz.' catalogue of 1609. This is not without significance, since Claesz. did have other sorts of popular printing, such as schoolbooks, in his range (*cf.* cat. no. 73).

While the Visscher firm specialized in intaglio prints, another family of artists and publishers, the Van Sichems, concentrated on woodcuts. It was they who supplied the vast number of blocks for the *Bibels Tresoor*, an Old Testament picture book that was published in 1646 by the Catholic publisher Pieter Jacobsz. Paets (*cf.* cat. nos 59 and 69). These are without exception copies and

**93.** For popular prints in the Netherlands, see De Meyer 1962; De Meyer 1970; Van Veen 1976.
**94.** Some other *Snylingh* sheets were reprinted by Ottens: Holl. XXXVIII, pp. 226-227, nos 311-312. For Joachim Ottens (1663-1719) see Van Eeghen 1960-78, Vol. 4, pp. 29-31. Sheet no. AA in the Visscher catalogue, with eight miracles of Christ (Holl. XXXVIII, p. 230, no. 350), is likewise based

on Schut's designs. Old Testament *Snylingh* sheets: 'B. Historie van Abraham', 'C. -- ditto, in 't Vierkant', 'D. Bybelsche Historien', 'E. -- als Voor' (*Catalogue Visscher*, p. 18). The sheet 'Z. Verscheyde Trappen des Ouderdoms en andere' includes a representation of the twelve patriarchs (Holl. XXXVIII, p. 229, no. 349). For the Visscher firm's popular prints see Holl. XXXVIII, pp. 217-230,

nos 302-350; De Meyer 1962, pp. 322-323.
**95.** De Meyer 1962, p. 38.

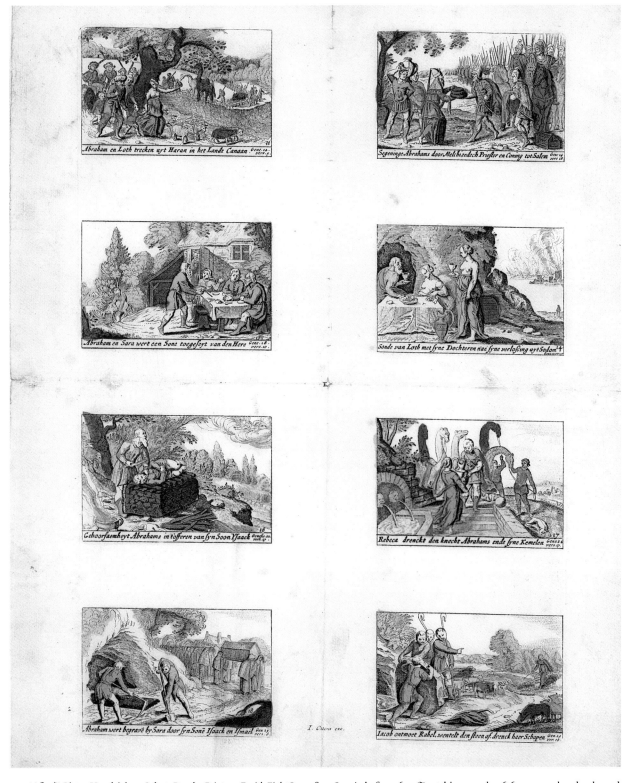

19. (After?) Pieter Hendricksz. Schut, *Popular Print no. E with Eight Scenes from Genesis*, before 1652 (?), etchings, each *c.* 6.6 x 9.7 cm, hand-coloured (reprint [?] published by Joachim Ottens), Rijksprentenkabinet, Amsterdam

compilations of earlier examples of European graphic art. Despite this lack of originality the *Bibels Tresoor* was often to be found in the libraries of the wealthy. A substantial volume of over 750 prints, its price put it beyond the reach of many,[96] but the Van Sichems' woodcuts were later to assume considerable importance for the illustration of popular printing. Copies of them appeared in biblical reading and school books (cat. no. 73) and in numerous popular prints. It was thanks to the Van Sichems' woodcuts that the imagery of sixteenth- and seventeenth-century Bible illustration lived on until well into the nineteenth century. It has been asserted that popular prints were a continuation chiefly of the medieval tradition and that their makers were averse to any kind of academic pretensions, merely wishing to express their own emotions in them.[97] In fact, it was precisely the art of the late Renaissance and early Baroque that served as their example and was copied, simplified and imitated *ad nauseam*.

With their low prices, popular prints were also known in eighteenth-century Holland as 'oortjesprenten' - an *oortje* being a quarter of a stiver; in the nineteenth century they were called 'centsprenten'. In view of the rather more exclusive etching technique and the better quality of paper that this called for, the *Snylingh* prints published by the Visschers doubtless would have been slightly more expensive. Even so, this was definitely the cheapest form of printing in their catalogue and it must have been affordable to the majority of the population.[98]

To what extent people actually bought prints is another matter. 'Prints are found in all types of households, from the humblest to the richest', Montias concluded on the basis of his study of estate inventories in seventeenth-century Delft. Similar investigations confirm that prints were to be found in all income brackets.[99] This does not, of course, mean that every member of such a group owned prints - or that, if they did, these were prints on Old Testament themes. Some - how many it is impossible to tell - would have preferred to spend their money on other things.

**96.** Simon Schijnvoet auction catalogue (books), Amsterdam 2 February 1728, p. 22, no. 11: 'Bybels Tresoor, of der zielen Lusthof, zynde Bybelsche figuren door C. Sichem, in houtsnee, fr. band' (BSC 74); with the price, 4 guilders and 5 stivers, written in by hand. Auction catalogue of [Agaat] van der Hem, The Hague 20 November 1730, p. 21, no. 255 (BSC 157): 'Chr. van Sighems Bybels-Tresoor, ofte der Zielen Lusthof Amst. 1646 met fraye platen gesneden door C. van Sighem'.
**97.** De Meyer 1962, p. 78.
**98.** Van den Berg (1995, p. 43) supposes that popular prints were already quite commonplace by about 1670 in both well-to-do and more common milieux. *Cf.* for 'cheap prints' in the early modern period in England, Watt 1991, pp. 129-253.
**99.** Montias 1982, p. 228 (Delft, 1610-80). *Cf.* Wijsenbeek-Olthuis 1987, p. 455 (Delft, 1706-30); Faber 1980, p. 152 (Amsterdam, 1701-10). *Cf.* also Schenda (1987, pp. 98-99), who suspects that the print trade only started reaching a larger section of the population in the middle of the eighteenth century, first in the towns and thereafter in rural areas.

# Appendix

*The dating of the Visscher firm's stock catalogue*

Until now it has always been supposed that the Visscher firm's stock list (figs 1-2, pp. 37, 38) did not appear until at least 1682, the year in which Nicolaus received a privilege from the States General for the making, distribution and sale of prints and maps. This 'Octroy' (7 March 1682), together with its 'Atache' from the States of Holland (15 September 1682), is bound into the surviving copies of the Dutch version of the catalogue. Close inspection, however, shows that these texts are printed on an inserted extra section which was probably not added to the catalogue until after it had been printed.[1]

That the list proper must have been compiled before 1682 is clear from the title-page of the German edition. This still bears the address 'in der Kalber-strasse, im Fisscher'. When Nicolaus Visscher took over the running of the shop after the death of his father Nicolaes in 1679 he kept it on Kalverstraat. When he registered his forthcoming marriage with the authorities on 21 November 1680 he gave that as his address. It is not clear when he moved, but it was probably quite soon after the wedding, as through his wife he now had access to the house on Dam Square that had belonged to her father.[2] Since it would not seem logical,

just when a move to a new address was imminent, to publish a new catalogue with the old address, it seems likely that Nicolaus published the list before he could have foreseen his marriage and change of address, ie, sometime between 11 September 1679 (the date of his father's funeral) and 21 November 1680 (the date of his betrothal). A perfectly plausible scenario is that drawing up an inventory of the plates was undertaken with a view to the distribution of Nicolaes' estate, and that it was while the work was in progress that the idea was conceived of issuing this inventory in print in the form of a stock catalogue.[3]

The Dutch version of the catalogue has exactly the same contents as the German, but here the address is already given as 'Op den Dam, in de Visscher', so that it must have been printed in or after 1680, like the French version (which gives the address as 'Sur le Dam, à l'enseigne du Pescheur'). The three versions cannot have been published very far apart in time, so that a provisional dating of c. 1680 for all three would appear to be the best option.[4] The *Appendix*, which is similarly undated, was probably published by Nicolaus in 1694.[5]

---

1. 'Octroy Van de Heeren Staten Generaal verleent aan Nicolaus Visscher' and 'Atache Of Octroy Van de Heeren Staten van Holland en West-vrieslandt Verleent aan Nicolaus Visscher'; text section of five leaves inserted between the title-page (fol. [A1] ie, pp. [1]-[2]) and the first page of the catalogue proper (fol. A2r ie, p. 3). This gathering, the first leaf of which bears the abnormal signature *2, was made specially for the catalogue, witness the catchword 'CATA-' on the last page, referring to the first word in the catalogue. For the usual dating, see Koeman 1967-85, Vol. 3, p. 155 (gives date as 1682); Van der Waals 1988, p. 199 (gives date as after 1682). Cf. also the recent Hollstein volumes.

2. Van Eeghen 1990, p. 80. Nicolaus certainly moved to the Dam before 14 September 1683, witness a newspaper advertisement which appeared on that day (Kleerkooper/Van Stockum 1914-16, p. 889). Betrothal of Nicolaus: *ibid.*, p. 887.

3. The winding-up of Nicolaes' estate probably took quite a while. An auction took place as late as 1684, witness an advertisement in the *Amsterdamsche Courant* (21 October 1684). Cf. Kleerkooper/Van Stockum 1914-16, p. 889. It is even possible that Nicolaes himself planned the publication of a stock list, perhaps when the States of Holland granted him a privilege for his stock in 1677. Cf. Obreen 1877-90, Vol. 1, p. 148. Jan van der Waals has suggested to me

that the acquisition of part of the stock of Clement de Jonghe (March 1679) might have given rise to the idea of compiling a catalogue: these are the most recent acquisitions in the list.

4. The French version departs slightly from the Dutch and German. It lacks the entry 'Insulae Americanae' (in the section 'Landt-kaarten van 1 Bladt', p. 4), but has a number of extra entries instead: 'Louis 14. Roy de France. / Charles 2. Roy d'Espagnes. / Charles 2. Roy d'Angleterre. / Mr. le Dauphin' (in the 'Portraits en Feuilles de Papier ordinaire' section, p. 17). The French and Dutch versions were probably printed at almost the same time: the title-pages have the same

printer's device, the books end with the same vignette, and even the initials with which the very first entry begins appear to have come from the same font. The German version, indeed, starts with the very same initial W as the Dutch, although it has a different printer's device and closes with a different vignette. Koeman (1967-85, Vol. 3, p. 155) believed that the French version might have been printed by Nicolaes even before 1677, since, in contrast to the Dutch edition, it does not include the privilege. However, the address it gives is that of Nicolaus: 'sur le Dam'. Moreover the privilege was of no significance for the French market, since it was valid only within the territory of Holland

(which is why it was also omitted from the German edition). Perhaps a precise bibliographical analysis of all the surviving copies, which in present circumstances was not possible, would provide greater certainty about the dating of the catalogue. It is to be hoped that the research of Peter Fuhring, who is in the process of compiling a bibliography of all stock lists by print publishers, will help to clarify matters.

5. Van der Waals 1988, p. 20 (caption to fig. 7).

Catalogue

# 1    The History of Adam and Eve, 1529

[GEN. 2-4]

Lucas van Leyden
*(Leiden 1494? - Leiden 1533)*

a   **The Creation of Eve**
b   **The First Prohibition**
c   **The Fall of Man**
d   **The Expulsion from Paradise**
e   **Cain Killing Abel**
f   **Adam and Eve Lamenting the Dead Abel**

Series of six engravings, 16.2 x 11.6 cm
(plate marks), state I (3)
**Inscr** 'L' (in reverse) and '1529'
Rijksprentenkabinet, Rijksmuseum,
Amsterdam (inv. nos RP-P-OB 1569, 1570,
1571, 1572, 1573 and 1574)
**Lit** Holl. X, pp. 58-59, nos 1-6; TIB XII, pp. 131-
136, nos 1(339)-6(341); New Hollstein, Lucas
van Leyden, pp. 32-37, nos 1-6; Friedländer
1963, pp. 42ff.; Amsterdam 1964-65, p. 16,
no. 1; Filedt Kok 1978, pp. 46, 148, nos B. 1-6;
Silver/ Smith 1978, pp. 240-241, 244-245, 250,
255-260; Vos 1978, pp. 27ff., 68; Washington/
Boston 1983, pp. 234-237,
nos 95-97; Amsterdam 1986, pp. 146-147,
nos 33.1-6; Nice 1992, pp. 33-35, nos 16-19;
Münster 1994, p. 299, no. 65; Dearborn 1994,
pp. 103-104, no. 12

Lucas van Leyden depicted the story of Adam and Eve in a series of six engravings. In the first print Adam lies sleeping, with Eve emerging from the right side of his body. The Creator, on their left, holds the upper part of Eve's body (Gen. 2:20-24; cat. no. 1a). In the second print, God, in the guise of an old man, addresses Himself to the first human couple, warning them not to eat from the tree of forbidden fruit (Gen. 2:16-17; cat. no. 1b).

At the centre of the print depicting the Fall (cat. no. 1c) the apple is being handed over. Eve, who is taking a pace forward, grasps the apple-tree twig proffered her by the serpent (Gen. 3:1-7). In the *Expulsion from Paradise* both Adam and Eve are fleeing, covering their sex and cringing with shame. Their faces, full of fear, are turned to the upper left-hand corner, from where a winged angel points a sword at them (Gen. 3:21-24; cat. no. 1d). The fratricide scene (cat. no. 1e) portrays Abel who, having been hurled to the ground, is trying to ward off Cain. Towering over him, the latter prepares to deliver the fatal blow with a bone. The billowing cloaks of the two men emphasize the ferocity of the struggle (Gen. 4:2-8). In the last print, Adam, lamenting the slaying of Abel, conceals his face behind his right hand while Eve, shown from the front, contorts her face in anguish and extends an arm aloft (cat. no. 1f).[1]

This series, produced late in the artist's career, typifies the influence exerted by the Italian Renaissance. As a young artist Lucas was strongly oriented towards Albrecht Dürer's prints in both his choice of motifs and composition. In turn numerous Italian artists including Marcantonio Raimondi, Andrea del Sarto and Jacopo da Pontormo drew on motifs from Lucas' prints. Later, Lucas himself was greatly inspired by Italian art - especially from the mid-1520s onwards. With regard to the series discussed here, the appearance of both Adam and Eve as well as the angel in the fourth print are clearly inspired by the work of Marcantonio Raimondi. Lucas' Eve displays a remarkable similarity to the Lucretia (1510) and Venus that Raimondi engraved after Raphael. In posture the Adam depicted in the third print of the series (cat. no. 1c) is reminiscent of Raimondi's Polyphemus in his print *Galatea Flees Polyphemus*.[2]

These borrowings stem from Lucas van Leyden's desire to convey human movement and the nude convincingly, in line with the Renaissance ideal of beauty. This quality lends these works a highly erotic character. For Lucas and his contemporaries this new focus on design largely determined their choice of subject. The broad, somewhat two-dimensional bodies of the early engravings are now superseded by figures that have a natural suppleness. A more relaxed composition, as in the third print where a seated Adam is directly juxtaposed with a standing Eve, the loosely flapping garments as in the fifth and sixth engravings, and the *contrapposto* stance of the figures - are the hallmarks of Lucas' late period that stress his marked orientation towards Italian art. Conversely, increasingly strong chiaroscuro effects indicate the lasting influence of Dürer. **GdB**

1. For the iconography of the history of Adam and Eve, see: Van de Kamp 1991 & 1994, pp. 24-26.
2. TIB XXVI, p. 10, no. 2 (after Michelangelo); p. 188, no. 192-I (after Raphael); p. 311, no. 311 (after Raphael); p. 222, no. 224-I. *Cf.* Filedt Kok 1978, pp. 46, 104 (note 48).

**a** The Creation of Eve

**b** The First Prohibition

**c** The Fall of Man

**d** The Expulsion from Paradise

**e** Cain Killing Abel

**f** Adam and Eve Lamenting the Dead Abel

## 2    The Fall of Man, 1638
[Gen. 3:6]

### Rembrandt
*(Leiden 1606 - Amsterdam 1669)*

Etching, 16.2 x 11.6 cm, state II (2)
**Inscr** 'Rembrandt. ƒ:. 1638.'
Museum het Rembrandthuis, Amsterdam
**Lit** Holl. XVIII, p. 13, no. B. 28; TIB L, p. 18,
no. 28; Münz 1952, Vol. 2, p. 87, no. 177;
Amsterdam 1964-65, p. 36, no. 21; White 1969,
pp. 41-45; Tümpel 1970, no. 1; Filedt Kok 1972,
pp. 39-40, no. B. 28; Munich 1982, pp. 73-74,
no. 49; Hamburg 1983, p. 322, no. 187;
Amsterdam 1985-86, pp. 46-47, no. 36; Smith
1987; Berlin/ Amsterdam/ London 1991-92A,
pp. 195-197, no. 11; Nice 1992, p. 41, no. 29;
Krüger 1993; Münster 1994, p. 300, no. 66;
Amsterdam 1995, p. 23, no. B. 28; Meijer 1995,
pp. 42-44

**2.1**
Rembrandt, *Study of Adam and Eve*, pen and
bistre, 11.5 x 11.5 cm, Prentenkabinet der
Rijksuniversiteit, Leiden

Rembrandt treated the story of the Fall in a series of sketches (fig. 2.1)[1] that
were to provide the basis for this highly focused composition. God created
man and woman on the sixth day of Creation. All that is forbidden to Adam
and Eve in the Garden of Eden is to eat of the tree of knowledge.
Transgression would lead to death. The serpent, the 'shrewdest' of all the
animals, persuades Eve to ignore the commandment. She, in turn, gives her
husband to eat of the forbidden fruit (Genesis 3:1-6).

The etching gives a profound and complex interpretation of this heavily
symbolic story from the book of Genesis, and differs clearly from the
pictorial tradition. Unlike Lucas van Leyden in his later series of engravings
(cat. no. 1c), Rembrandt does not idealize the first human couple. They
also lack the youthfulness of the figures in his own sketches (fig. 2.1).
By portraying their bodies as already having aged, Rembrandt seems to
emphasize their mortality. Their gestures of hesitation and admonishment
respectively allude to their knowledge of good and evil.[2] Rembrandt may
have had the idea for this interpretation from Lucas van Leyden's early

**2.2**
Lucas van Leyden, *The Fall of Man*, c. 1506,
engraving, 11.7 x 8.8 cm, Rijksprentenkabinet,
Amsterdam

**2.3**
Albrecht Dürer, *The Descent into Hell*, 1512,
engraving, 11.5 x 7.4 cm, Rijksprentenkabinet,
Amsterdam

engraving, which depicts Adam and Eve with similar gestures, already past their youthful bloom (fig. 2.2).[3]

Rembrandt's treatment of the manifestation of temptation is also unusual in that he reproduces not the serpent but a dragon, a motif that occurs in some medieval representations. Rembrandt's dragon is drawn from Dürer's *Engraved Passion* series (fig. 2.3).[4] With this erudite reference Rembrandt is commenting on the Fall, juxtaposing it typologically with the Redemption. In the *Descent into Hell*, Christ frees Adam and Eve from the power of Satan, into whose clutches they had fallen by erring. By representing the serpent - Satan - as a dragon the artist is pointing out that it is Satan himself who has led Adam and Eve astray, but that Christ has overcome him.[5]

The Leiden sketch (fig. 2.1) also depicts the Fall in terms of Eve's sexual desire. In the etching this is hinted at only in a highly sublime manner. The first man and woman are shown standing under the tree of knowledge, which frames the composition and on to which the dragon has climbed. The light falls from the upper left on to the figures, who are partly in the shadow cast by the tree's thick foliage. Rembrandt models the figures with crosshatching - the varying densities sometimes conveying the effect of dark surfaces - revealing their corporeality in all its details. He underlines the role of human sexuality by shading the genitals, yet attracting attention to them by highlighting some parts. The irregular distribution of shadow enhances the subject's dramatic effect, with the powerfully accentuated motifs in the foreground in distinct contrast to the light background. **PJ**

1. Benesch 163 and 164.
2. Tümpel 1970, no. 1.
3. B. 7; New Hollstein, Lucas van Leyden, p. 38, no. 7.
4. B. 16.
5. Tümpel 1970, no. 1.

## 3 Cain Killing Abel, *c.* 1645
[GEN. 4:1-8]

Jan Lievens
(Leiden 1607 - Amsterdam 1674)

Woodcut, 41.6 x 31.8 cm, only state
**Inscr** 'IL.'
Rijksprentenkabinet, Rijksmuseum,
Amsterdam (inv. no. RP-P-OB 12862)
**Lit** Holl. XI, p. 70, no. 99; Schneider 1932,
pp. 84, 268, no. Rov. 67; Brunswick 1979,
pp. 214-215, no. 113; Münster 1994, p. 300,
no. 67

**3.1**
Hendrick Goltzius, *Hercules Killing Cacus*,
1588, woodcut, 40.7 x 33.4 cm,
Rijksprentenkabinet, Amsterdam

The sons of the first human couple chose different occupations - Cain became a 'tiller of the ground' and Abel a shepherd. When each made an offering to God, He respected Abel's but ignored Cain's. Blind with rage, Cain then murdered his brother. Already in the aprocryphal *Wisdom of Solomon* (verse 10:3) the killing of Abel is seen as the immediate consequence of the Fall. This story of fratricide provides the first instance of a younger brother being preferred to an elder brother which, in the Bible, also occurs in the cases of Isaac, Jacob, Joseph and David.

This print by Jan Lievens, one of the eight woodcuts made by the artist, depicts Cain in the act of beating his brother to death. The work shows Rubens' influence, which might be the result of Lievens' stay in Antwerp. Of greater significance for the composition, however, is Hendrick Goltzius' woodcut *Hercules Killing Cacus* (fig. 3.1), as can be seen from the similar postures of Abel and Cacus.[1]

The Bible does not describe in detail how Cain killed Abel, nor which murder weapon he used. It reports tersely: '... and it came to pass, when they were in the field, that Cain rose up against Abel his brother, and slew him' (Gen. 4:8). Traditionally the weapon is depicted as the jawbone of an ass. The source of this motif is unclear.[2] **JK**

1. Holl. VII, p. 122, no. 373. *Cf.* Brunswick 1979, p. 214.
2. For a discussion of the murder weapon, see: Henderson 1961; Barb 1972.

## 4 Abraham Serving the Lord and Two Angels, 1656

[GEN. 18:8-15]

### Rembrandt
*(Leiden 1606 - Amsterdam 1669)*

Etching and drypoint, 15.9 x 13.1 cm, only state
**Inscr** 'Rembrandt *f*. 1656.'
Museum het Rembrandthuis, Amsterdam
**Lit** Holl. XVIII, pp. 13-14, no. B. 29; TIB L, p. 19,
no. 29; Münz 1952, Vol. 2, p. 90, no. 185;
Amsterdam 1964-65, pp. 36-37, no. 22; White
1969, pp. 93, 94; Tümpel 1970, no. 5; Filedt
Kok 1972, pp. 40-41, no. B. 29; Hamburg 1983,
p. 323, no. 188; Amsterdam 1985-86, pp. 78-
79, no. 68; Van de Kamp 1991 & 1994, pp. 29-30;
Roscam Abbing 1993; Münster 1994, p. 301,
no. 68; Amsterdam 1995, p. 24, no. B. 29

Genesis tells of three promises made by God to the childless patriarch
Abraham that he is, after all, to have numerous progeny. In Genesis 18:1-15
this promise is made for the third time. This event is the subject of the
etching. Seated in front of his home in the heat of the day, Abraham saw
three men approaching. Going to meet them, he invited them to rest under
the shadow of a tree. During the meal that Abraham offered the three
strangers, the Lord revealed to him that he and his wife Sarah, 'well stricken
in age' though they may be, would have a son within a year.

In the iconographical tradition, Abraham's guests are generally portrayed
as three similar-looking men or angels. This started to change around the
mid-seventeenth century, when artists began to emphasize one of the angels.
In Rembrandt's painting, *Abraham Serving the Angels* (fig. 4.1) dated 1646, the
emphasis is on the angel under the tree.[1] 'This visitor differs from the others
not only in format but in that he is, in all respects, the luminescent centre.
The angel is the only source of light in an otherwise dark representation, the
light that emanates from him falling onto those present. This treatment
gives the impression of a genuinely divine manifestation'.[2] The light-giving
angel is, therefore, the bringer of God's word.

It has been correctly pointed out that Rembrandt's divergent
iconographcal treatment of the subject may be attributable to Calvinist

**4.1**
Rembrandt, *Abraham Serving the Angels*, 1646,
panel, 16 x 21 cm, Aurora Trust, New York

exegesis. After all, not only does Calvin place the emphasis on one of the visitors in his own commentary on Genesis 18, but so does the Dutch States Bible, first published in 1637: 'Two angels, and the Lord Himself, appear unto Abraham in the guise of three men' (summary of Gen. 18).[3] We see this reproduced almost literally in Rembrandt's 1656 etching, in which Abraham's guests are no longer presented as three angels but as two angels accompanied by God Himself.[4]

What lends the story its vitality is the tension between God's promise to Abraham that he and Sarah shall have a son on the one hand and the advanced age of the patriarch and his wife on the other. Rembrandt gives effective expression to this contradiction - the Abraham portrayed serving his guests is old and bent by the years. Coming up the stairs, a pitcher in his left hand, he is subordinated to his heavenly guests in the compositional sense as well. God, accompanied by two angels, is making him a promise that conflicts with all the laws of nature: 'And I will certainly return unto thee according to the time of life; and, lo, Sarah thy wife shall have a son' (Gen. 18:10).

The aged Sarah, standing in the doorway in the background to the left, follows the conversation in disbelief. The young lad totally absorbed in playing with his bow and arrow is Ishmael. It is he who embodies Sarah's doubt about the promise, since it was following her failure to conceive after God's first two promises that she urged Abraham to take her maid Hagar as his concubine. Ishmael was the result of that union (Gen. 16:1-4). Later, when the third promise was indeed fulfilled and Sarah bore a son, she in her jealousy would prevail on Abraham to expel Ishmael and his mother; Ishmael then became a fine archer.

To give the scene an Oriental flavour Rembrandt drew his composition from an Indian miniature depicting four Orientals seated under a tree. He probably copied this work shortly before producing the etching.[5] He did not render the shady tree mentioned in the Bible, probably to avoid deflecting the attention from the protagonists themselves as well as in order to afford a central place in the composition to the figure of Ishmael, who embodies man's attempt to induce the fulfilment of God's promise. **PJ/CT**

1. Bredius 515; Tümpel 1986, p. 391, no. 21.
2. Van de Kamp 1991 & 1994, p. 29.
3. 'Twee engelen, ende de Heere selfs, verschijnen Abraham in de gedaente van drie mannen'. *Cf.* Van de Kamp 1991 & 1994, pp. 29-30.
4. *Ibid.* See also Roscam Abbing 1993.
5. Benesch 1187. See Royalton-Kisch 1992, pp. 141-144, no. 62.

**5**

**Lot and the Angels at the Gate of Sodom, *c.* 1615**
[GEN. 19:1]

Claes Cornelisz. Moeyaert
*(Durgerdam 1590/91 - Amsterdam 1655)*

No. 1 from a series of four: *The History of Lot*
Etching, washed in grey, only state
12.7 x 19.8 cm (plate marks)
**Inscr** (on the basement): 'CL M.*fc*'
Museum het Rembrandthuis, Amsterdam
**Lit** Holl. XIV, p. 53, no. 1; TIB LIII, p. 273, no. 6

Together with Pieter Lastman, Claes Cornelisz Moeyaert was one of the principal Pre-Rembrandtists, a group of artists in Amsterdam who represented Rembrandt's immediate predecessors. In his paintings and prints Moeyaert revealed a preference for Old Testament themes.[1] In this series, in which four etchings depict the story of Abraham's nephew Lot, the Old Testament is again the source of inspiration (Gen. 19).

One evening, when Lot was at the city gate of Sodom, two angels approached. He rose to meet them and bowed deeply (cat. no. 5). Lot insisted that the strangers lodge with him for the night and eventually they agreed. At Lot's house their feet were washed and they received a meal of unleavened bread (fig. 5.2; Gen. 19:3).

However, the people of Sodom resented the strangers and began threatening them. Lot tried in vain to calm the rabble. When they began to press towards the entrance of the house the angels suddenly struck them blind. The heavenly messengers then warned Lot that God planned to destroy the sinful city of Sodom and advised him and his family to flee. When he hesitated the angels grabbed Lot and his wife and daughters by the arm and took them out of the city (fig. 5.3; Gen. 19:16).

As they made their escape, although explicitly commanded not to, Lot's wife looked back and was immediately turned into a pillar of salt. Lot and his daughters sought refuge in a cave. Fearing that their father was the last man alive, Lot's daughters plied their father with wine and slept with him in order to bear his children (fig. 5.4; Gen. 19:31-36).

Moeyaert followed the biblical text closely, illustrating the story with vivid, gesticulating figures. The theme of the angels being welcomed in Lot's

**5.1** Lot and the Angels at the Gate of Sodom

**5.2** Lot Washing the Feet of the Angel

**5.3** Lot and his Family Leaving Sodom

**5.4** Lot and his Daughters

**5.1**
Claes Moeyaert, *Lot and the Angels at the Gate of Sodom*, etching, 12.7 x 19.8 cm, Museum het Rembrandthuis, Amsterdam

**5.2**
Claes Moeyaert, *Lot Washing the Feet of the Angels*, etching, 12.1 x 19.6 cm, Rijksprentenkabinet, Amsterdam

**5.3**
Claes Moeyaert, *Lot and his Family Leaving Sodom*, etching, 12 x 19 cm, British Museum, London

**5.4**
Claes Moeyaert, *Lot and his Daughters*, etching, 12.5 x 19.5 cm, Rijksprentenkabinet, Amsterdam

house (fig. 5.2) is an iconographic unicum. The depiction of the angels as mortals, without wings or halos, makes the identification of the scenes in the first three prints somewhat difficult. Perhaps Moeyaert was trying to suggest that Lot was unaware of their divine nature.

In the first print (cat. no. 5) Lot kneels respectfully in front of the two heavenly messengers. Two men approach with a heavy-laden mule. Lot stands out against the light background as a dark silhouette, contrasting with the two brightly-lit angels. Moeyaert borrowed the grouping of the three principal figures from an engraving on the same theme made by Cornelis Bos after Maarten van Heemskerck (fig. 5.5).[2]

With its small window and sparse furnishings, the interior in the second scene (fig. 5.2) breathes a Mediterranean atmosphere. Again, Lot is shown kneeling, this time washing the feet of one of the angels. The other one watches, together with one of Lot's daughters. His second daughter approaches with towels. Lot's wife is preparing a meal at the enormous stove. A mysterious figure wearing a high hat lurks in the doorway. Perhaps he is one of the men of Sodom who has come to complain about the strangers in Lot's house. Moeyaert skipped the blinding theme, usually a favourite among printmakers.

The third print (fig. 5.3) shows the family leaving the city. Lot and his wife appear in doubt about whether to go, and look back fearfully. One of the daughters carries food for the journey. In the background are the dilapidated walls of the city and temple-like buildings.

Again, in the final print Moeyaert tried to communicate the meaning of the story as clearly as possible. Against the background of the dark cave, with the

**5.5**
Cornelis Bos after Maarten van Heemskerck,
*Lot and the Angels at the Gate of Sodom*, c. 1551,
engraving, 25.7 x 19.7 cm, Museum Boijmans
Van Beuningen, Rotterdam

city of Sodom burning and the silhouette of Lot's
daughters seduce their father. Drunk, leaning backward, half-dressed, he
accepts the advances of his almost naked daughter while the other looks on
with a calculating glance.

The series has an endearing simplicity in the execution of details, the
composition as well as the technique employed. In each print, the somewhat
stiff figures are large and clearly outlined in the foreground, contrasting
against a light (figs 1, 3) or dark (figs. 2, 4) background - like actors against a
backdrop. By constructing the scenes along diagonal lines - a tried and
trusted method among the Pre-Rembrandtists - Moeyaert emphasized the
sense of depth. Subtle changes in tone were achieved by short, strokes of the
needle and irregular crosshatching, as well as by retouching some areas with
brush in grey ink - as in this example (cat. no. 5). These additions appear to
be the work of the artist himself.

In comparison, Moeyaert's other series, devoted to the Old Testament and
Apocryphal heroes Tobit, Jacob[3] and Abraham (cf. cat. no. 14) are densely
worked and show a greater unity and a more dynamic approach. The Jacob
series, presents a particular contrast: the etchings are characterised by
crowded compositions with regular, flowing lines. All the indications
suggest that the *History of Lot* is one of Moeyaert's earliest series, possibly
dating from before 1620. Moeyaert's typically anecdotal style and the strong
chiaroscuro effects are already plainly evident. **ME**

1. See the introduction above, p. 26.
2. New Hollstein, Heemskerck, p. 29, no. 14.
3. Tobias series: TIB VI, pp. 68-71, nos. 13 (92) - 16 (94). Jacob series: TIB LIII, pp. 277-282, nos 10-15; Münster 1994,
p. 306, no. 78. On Moeyaert's print series see also: Burchard 1917, pp. 92-93; Munich 1982, p. 59.

## 6 Lot and his Daughters, 1631

[GEN. 19:30-35]

Johannes Gillisz. van Vliet
(*Leiden 1600/10 - Leiden 1668*)
after Rembrandt
(*Leiden 1606 - Amsterdam 1669*)

Etching and burin, 27.5 x 22.3 cm, state II (5)
**Inscr** 'RH. van Rijn.jnventor. 1631. JG. van vliet
fecit.'
Museum het Rembrandthuis, Amsterdam
**Lit** B. 1; Holl. XLI, p. 146, no. 1; Tümpel 1971,
p. 24; Bruyn 1982, pp. 36-37; Zilkens 1984,
no. 33; Münster 1994, p. 301, no. 69;
Amsterdam 1996, pp. 8-9, 40-41, no. 1a.

**6.1**
Anonymous after Rembrandt, *Lot and his
Daughters*, c. 1631, red chalk, 29.2 x 23.1 cm,
British Museum, London

74

Warned by angels, Lot and his family are able to flee Sodom before their
sinful city's destruction. Initially they make for the city of Zoar. Later, Lot
moves into a cave in the mountains with his two daughters. Afraid of
remaining without progeny, the young women get their father drunk in
order to have carnal knowledge of him (Gen. 19:15-38).

Jan van Vliet's etching shows Lot's daughters plying him with drink after
the flight from their home in wicked Sodom. Visible in the background, to
the left, are the contours of Lot's wife, who has turned into a pillar of salt
after ignoring God's injunction not to look back as they flee.[1]

*Lot and his Daughters* is presumably the first of several etchings that Van Vliet
produced in 1631 after designs by Rembrandt.[2] It is fairly certain that the
work is based on a lost painting by Rembrandt dating from 1629/30. The
British Museum in London has a mirror-image drawing earlier attributed to
Van Vliet (fig. 6.1). The drawing is identical in composition apart from
various slight differences. For instance, Lot is holding a staff in the drawing
and not in the etching, which for its part depicts shoelaces that do not appear
in the drawing.[3] **JK**

1. For the iconography of the subject see: Van de Kamp 1991 & 1994, p. 34.
2. See: Amsterdam 1996, pp. 40-65, especially pp. 40-41, no. 1a.
3. For the drawing see: ibid., pp. 42-43, no. 1b.

## 7 The Banishment of Hagar and Ishmael, 1516

[GEN. 21:9-14]

Lucas van Leyden
(Leiden 1494? - Leiden 1533)

Engraving, 14.7 x 12.2 cm, only state
**Inscr** 'L 1516'
Rijksprentenkabinet, Rijksmuseum,
Amsterdam (inv. no. RP-P-OB 1589)
**Lit** Holl. X, p. 70, no. 18; TIB XII, p. 150, no. 18
(347); Hamann 1936, p. 6; New Hollstein,
Lucas van Leyden, pp. 47-48, no. 18; Filedt Kok
1978, pp. 38, 145, no. B. 18; Münster 1994,
p. 302, no. 70

Their marriage having remained childless, Sarah urged her husband Abraham to take her Egyptian maid Hagar as a concubine. Hagar became pregnant and gave birth to a son. He received the name of Ishmael. When Sarah finally gave birth to Isaac, she persuaded Abraham to banish Hagar and Ishmael in order to avoid Isaac having to share his patrimony with Ishmael later on. Following some hesitation - and after God has assuaged him as to Ishmael's fate - Abraham consented. He supplied Hagar and Ishmael with provisions and dismissed them (Gen. 16:1-4, 15; 21:1-21).

Abraham and Hagar are shown in the immediate foreground, their child Ishmael in between them. The artist depicts the moment of farewell - the very last seconds the three spend together before Hagar and Ishmael are exposed to the perils of the wilderness (Gen. 21:14). A ruin on which a tree has established itself emphasizes the three figures, directing the viewer's attention towards them. The affection they feel for each other and the closeness of their relationship is clearly evident from their gestures. Wiping tears from her eyes with her right hand, Hagar turns mournfully to the father of her child. He, for his part, is taking a step forward with his right foot as if he would wish to accompany them. His left hand is raised in what seems to be a gesture of consolation and blessing, and as if he is assuring them of his love. Hagar, however, is stepping not forward but backwards, as if still hesitating. The little boy has already turned to go, but is looking at his father. In the background Abraham's homestead is visible to the left; to the right we see a trackless wilderness that Hagar and Ishmael are now forced to enter. However salvation will not be denied to them. This is evident from a scene in the background, in which an angel shows Hagar a well, thus saving Ishmael from death by thirst. **AT**

## 8 The Banishment of Hagar and Ishmael, 1603

[GEN. 21:9-14]

Jacob Adriaensz. Matham
*(Haarlem 1571 - Haarlem 1631)*
after Abraham Bloemaert
*(Gorinchem 1566 - Utrecht 1651)*

Engraving, 43.1 x 35.4 cm, state I (2)
**Inscr** 'Cum privil. Sa. Cae.M. / Abrahamus
Bloemaert Inven. I. Maetham sculp. / et excudit
A[nn]o. 1603.'
**Caption** 'Gen. XXI. Dum petulans Dominae
non insultare veretur, / Cum nato Jussa est
vertere serva solum. / Rupert. in Gen. Sic.
Christo, Christique gregi dum illudere certant,
/ Judaeos meritò par quoque poena premit.
SSH [Simon Sovius Harlemensis].'
Museum Boijmans Van Beuningen, Rotterdam
(inv. no. BdH 7594)
**Lit** Holl. II, p. 67, no. 475; Holl. XI, p. 216,
no. 2; TIB IV, p. 53, no. 63(147); Hamann 1936,
pp. 8-9; Mielke 1979, p. 49, no. 57; Cologne
1981, pp. 91-92, no. 24; McGrath 1984, p. 78;
Evanston 1993, p. 128, no. 72; Roethlisberger
1993, pp. 114-115, no. 69; Amsterdam 1993-
94A, pp. 552-553, no. 223; Münster 1994,
p. 302, no. 71

Bloemaert presents the moment - later beloved by Rembrandt and his circle - in which Abraham, standing in front of his house, banished Hagar and their son Ishmael to the wilderness. The artist devoted particular attention to the depiction of scenic details, as is especially evident from the numerous agricultural implements in the immediate vicinity of the farmhouse.[1]

Below the scene the publisher has inserted a malicious text containing Christian, anti-Jewish prejudice. According to the traditional Christian typology, based on Paul's Epistle to the Galatians (4:21-31), Hagar, despite her youthfulness, embodies the servitude to which the Old Testament leads. The elderly Sarah, representing the freedom granted by the New Testament, usurps the dismissed Hagar's place. Hagar and Ishmael therefore symbolize the Jews, Sarah and Isaac the Christians.[2]

The print's entire artistic conception would appear to express no such intention on Bloemaert's part, however. Neither is it possible to see the figure of Hagar as an embodiment of the Jews. One also searches in vain for any clear indication that we are supposed to interpret Sarah as a triumphant representation of the new Church - all she does here is to look out of the window.[3] Bloemaert clearly did not intend to invest the work with an anti-Semitic significance. The caption was probably added later. **GdB**

1. *Cf.* for the iconography of the topic: Hamann 1936 and Van de Kamp 1991 & 1994, pp. 30-31.
2. Roethlisberger 1993, p. 115.
3. McGrath 1984, p. 78.

## The Banishment of Hagar and Ishmael, 1637
[GEN. 21:9-14]

Rembrandt
*(Leiden 1606 - Amsterdam 1669)*

Etching and drypoint, 12.5 x 9.5 cm, only state
**Inscr** 'Rembrandt / ƒ 1637'
Museum het Rembrandthuis, Amsterdam
**Lit** Holl. XVIII, p. 14, no. B. 30; TIB L, p. 20, no. 30; Hamann 1936, pp. 28-30; Münz 1952, Vol. 2, p. 86, no. 174; Amsterdam 1964-65, p. 37, no. 23; Tümpel 1970, no. 6; Filedt Kok 1972, p. 41, no. B. 30; Hamburg 1983, p. 324, no. 189; Amsterdam 1984-85, p. 85, no. 69; Amsterdam 1987-88, p. 79, no. 56; Münster 1994, pp. 30, 303, no. 72; Amsterdam 1995, p. 24, no. B. 30

**9.1**
Pieter Lastman, *The Banishment of Hagar and Ishmael*, 1612, panel, 49 x 71 cm, Hamburger Kunsthalle, Hamburg

The story of Hagar, and especially her dramatic expulsion with Ishmael, was a favourite topic of sixteenth-century artists. Lucas van Leyden devoted two masterful engravings to this theme (*cf*. cat. no. 7). Inspired by two paintings by Pieter Lastman the Pre-Rembrandtists made it a popular subject in Dutch history painting, and it was also a permanent part of Rembrandt's teaching syllabus.[1]

In his 1612 painting (fig. 9.1), Lastman emphasizes Abraham's love for Hagar and Ishmael by placing these three figures in the foreground and relegating Sarah and Isaac to the background.[2] Rembrandt, however, places Abraham between the two women, thus directing the attention to his inner conflict. The patriarch may be obeying God's will and fulfilling his obligations to Sarah and Isaac, but still it pains him to send away his concubine and a lad who is his own flesh and blood. Hagar and Ishmael have already turned to leave, which fills Sarah, looking out of the window, with visible relief. 'As he watches them depart, Abraham's only connection with them is his gesture that is simultaneously an expression of resignation and blessing for Ishmael'.[3] With his right foot he has already taken a step backwards in order to recross his doorstep, behind which the diminutive figure of Isaac is just visible in the shadows.

The house is situated to the left, with Hagar and Ishmael therefore making their way from left to right along a path that we cannot see. Rembrandt's ribbon-like composition is in the iconographical tradition. The same applies to various details, such as the motif of Hagar weeping into a handkerchief. Rembrandt's figures are based on an earlier work by Lastman, now known only from a drawn copy in Berlin.[4] **PJ/AT**

**1.** Lucas van Leyden: New Hollstein, Lucas van Leyden, pp. 46-48, nos 17-18. Pre-Rembrandtists and the Rembrandt circle: Hamann 1936; *Cf*. Münster 1994, pp. 30, 233, no. 11.
**2.** For this painting see, *inter alia*, Enklaar 1993, pp. 6-8, fig. 5; Tümpel, no. 17.
**3.** Tümpel 1970, no. 6.
**4.** *Cf*. Hamann 1936, p. 12, fig. 15.

## 10 Hagar and Ishmael in the Wilderness, c. 1630/35

[GEN. 21:14-19]

Moyses van Uyttenbroeck
*(The Hague 1595/1600 - The Hague 1645/46)*

Etching, 12.4 x 8.9 cm, state II (2)
**Inscr** 'Mo. V. Wytenbrouck *f*. /
Ma. V. Wytenbrouck ex.'
Museum Boijmans Van Beuningen, Rotterdam
(inv. no. BdH 1306)
**Lit** TIB VI, p. 63, no. 6(88), TIB VI
(Commentary), p. 64, no. 006; Burchard 1917,
p. 75; Weisner 1963, pp. 178-181; Münster
1994, p. 303, no. 73

Hagar and her son Ishmael, banished by Abraham, lost their way in the wilderness of Beersheba. When their bottle of water was finished Hagar laid Ishmael under a shrub, sitting some distance away from him so that she would not have to watch him die. An angel appeared in response to her loud weeping and comforted her. Hagar then saw a well, refilled the bottle and gave Ishmael water (Gen. 21:14-19).

Several of Van Uyttenbroeck's works are inspired by the story of Hagar, namely a series of three etchings and five separate prints.[1] He selected various scenes from the story. The Bible describes two episodes in which Hagar goes into the wilderness. The first one, in Genesis 16:5-14, recounts how the pregnant Hagar flees from her mistress after the difficult relationship between the two women has finally broken down. An angel finds Hagar beside a well in the wilderness and tells her to return home.

Clearly this etching presents the second of the episodes, related in Genesis 21. Again Hagar is wandering in the wilderness, this time with her son Ishmael. A fearful, loving mother she looks down at her visibly exhausted child who, now that the water is finished, seems not to have much longer to live. The landscape is not depicted as a wilderness since, at the time, the term *desertum* meant a deserted area rather than a desert as such. **PJ**

1. TIB VI (Commentary), nos 002-008, 071. TIB 2 and 4 are dated 1620. *Cf*. Münster 1994, pp. 3-4, no. 74.

## 11  Abraham and Isaac before the Sacrifice, 1645

[GEN. 22:6-8]

### Rembrandt
*(Leiden 1606 - Amsterdam 1669)*

Etching and drypoint, 15.7 x 13 cm, only state
**Inscr** 'Rembrandt / ƒ. 1645.'
Museum het Rembrandthuis, Amsterdam
**Lit** Holl. XVIII, p. 15, no. B. 34; TIB L, p. 23,
No. 34; Münz 1952, Vol. 2, p. 87, no. 180;
White 1969, pp. 53-55, 63, 92, 93, 168; Tümpel
1970, no. 8; Filedt Kok 1972, p. 42, no. B. 34;
Hamburg 1983, pp. 325-326, no. 191; Tümpel
1984, p. 189: Berlin/ Amsterdam/ London 1991-
92A, p. 164; Münster 1994, pp. 31, 200, 304,
no. 75; Amsterdam 1995, p. 25, no. B. 34

**11.1**
Lucas van Leyden, *Abraham and Isaac before the Sacrifice*, c. 1517, woodcut, 28.5 x 21.1 cm, Rijksprentenkabinet, Amsterdam

By commanding Abraham to make a burnt offering of his son, God put the patriarch to a severe test. Abraham did as he was ordered, travelling with his son and two of his servants to the designated mountain in the land of Moriah. When Abraham saw the place from afar he left his companions behind, and gave Isaac the wood for the burnt offering. He himself carried a pot of fire and a knife. On their way, Isaac asked: 'My father [...] behold the fire and the wood: but where is the lamb for a burnt offering?' 'My son', Abraham replied, 'God will provide himself a lamb for a burnt offering' (Gen. 22:7-8).

This is a typical Rembrandt subject. Apart from the actual climax of stories the artist frequently portrayed episodes in which the future is presaged, or depicted the aftermath of a decisive event.[1] In this case, Rembrandt's subject is the dialogue between Abraham and Isaac, just before the sacrifice.

In medieval representations in which various stages of the story are combined, the dialogue triggered by Isaac's question regarding the sacrificial lamb, is often visualized. It is also the moment Lucas van Leyden chose to depict in his woodcut (fig. 11.1).[2] Rembrandt, however, has the conversation between father and son occurring not on the way to the altar but at the altar itself. Flavius Josephus, whom Rembrandt follows here, tells of a lengthy dialogue in which Abraham explains to Isaac what God has commanded him to do.[3] Confessing that the command grieves him sorely, Abraham says that he will nevertheless obey God. This will also mean grace and honour for Isaac himself. Isaac replies that he is at peace with the decision that God and his father have made concerning his fate.

Although Rembrandt's etching is based on Josephus, he does allow ambivalent feelings between fear and faith in God to resonate. Isaac is staring ahead, his face partly covered by shadow. Nevertheless, he is composed. He holds the wood with both hands as if he has already accepted his own sacrifice. The tension is increased still further by a dark cloud that rises behind him, which Rembrandt has rendered with crosshatching.

Abraham is pointing heavenwards with his left hand while clutching his heart with his right hand in an expression of his pain and sincere obedience. **PJ/AT**

1. Tümpel 1970, no. 8.
2. B. 3; New Hollstein, Lucas van Leyden, pp. 170-171, no. 187.
3. Flavius Josephus, *Jewish Antiquities*, Book 1, ch. 13, 2ff. See: Tümpel 1970, no. 8; Tümpel 1984, p. 189.

## 12 The Sacrifice of Isaac, 1655
[GEN. 22:10-12]

### Rembrandt
*(Leiden 1606 - Amsterdam 1669)*

Etching and drypoint, 15.6 x 13.1 cm, only state
**Inscr** 'Rembrandt *f*. 1655' (d and 6 in reverse)
Museum het Rembrandthuis, Amsterdam
**Lit** Holl. XVIII, p. 15-16, no. B. 35; TIB L, p. 24, no. 35; Münz 1952, Vol. 2, p. 90, no. 184; Amsterdam 1964-65, p. 38, no. 25; Rosenberg 1968, p. 176; Boston/ New York 1969, pp. 142-144, nos 92, 93; White 1969, pp. 92-93; Tümpel 1970, no. 9; Filedt Kok 1972, pp. 42-43, no. B. 35; Munich 1982, p. 86, no. 61; Hamburg 1983, pp. 326-327, no. 192; Haak 1984, p. 261, fig. 435; Smith 1985; Amsterdam 1985-86, p. 60, no. 49; Berlin/ Amsterdam/ London 1991-92A, pp. 278-280, no. 39; Münster 1994, pp. 158-159, 305, no. 76; Amsterdam 1995, p. 25, no. B. 35; Meijer 1995, p. 81, note 14

'And they came to the place which God had told him of; and Abraham built an altar there, and laid the wood in order, and bound Isaac his son, and laid him on the altar upon the wood. And Abraham stretched forth his hand, and took the knife to slay his son. And the angel of the Lord called unto him out of heaven, and said: "Abraham, Abraham!" And he said: "Here am I". And he said: "Lay not thine hand upon the lad, neither do thou any thing unto him: for now I know that thou fearest God, seeing thou hast not withheld thy son, thine only son from me". And Abraham lifted up his eyes, and looked, and beheld behind him a ram caught in a thicket by his horns:

**12.1**
Rembrandt, *The Sacrifice of Isaac*, 1635, canvas,
193.5 x 132.8 cm, Hermitage, St Petersburg

and Abraham went and took the ram, and offered him up for a burnt offering in the stead of his son' (Gen. 22:9-13).

The dramatic and theatrical qualities that distinguish Rembrandt's 1635 painting - now in St Petersburg (fig. 12.1) - are replaced in the etching by a more psychologizing treatment.[1] Isaac is no longer the sacrificial offering who is pressed backwards over the stone by his father. Instead, he kneels devotedly beside Abraham over the altar. His father has placed a hand in front of his eyes and is clasping his head to him.

The angel who has approached Abraham from behind is holding him by the arms, thus preventing him from killing Isaac. Abraham does not actually see the angel, only hearing his voice and feeling himself being restrained. His eye sockets are dark, and his face betrays clear signs of his inner struggle between love for his son and obedience to God. He is still unable to grasp the ways in which God moves. Rembrandt emphasizes the element of mercy through the angel's outspread wings and the heavenly rays of light. The three principal figures constitute a solid group which, by virtue of the rays, are in clear contrast to the background.

Rembrandt uses the space between Isaac's cloak and the angel's wings to portray the ram caught in the thicket. [2] The animal is barely discernible beneath the dark crosshatching, however. Abraham's young assistants and the donkey they have brought with them are visible to the right and below the rock plateau upon which the sacrifice scene takes place. Spiritually blind as they are, these assistants do not perceive the divine intervention. **PJ/CT**

1. Bredius 498; Tümpel 1986, p. 389, no. 9; RRP, Vol. 3, pp. 101-113, no. A108. The painting and the etching are compared in Rosenberg 1968, p. 176. For the iconography of the subject, see: Van de Kamp 1991 & 1994, pp. 31-32.
2. Smith 1985, p. 296; Meijer 1995, p. 81, note 14.

## 13 The Sacrifice of Isaac
[GEN. 22:1-12]

Ferdinand Bol (?)
*(Dordrecht 1616 - Amsterdam 1680)*

Etching and burin, 40.5 x 32.7 cm, state 2 (II)
**Inscr** 'F Bol *f*.'
Museum Boijmans Van Beuningen, Rotterdam
(inv. no. BdH 2417)
**Lit** Holl. III, p. 15, no. 1; Blankert 1976, p. 7,
note 1; Blankert 1982, p. 91

The *Sacrifice of Isaac* is one of the most frequently portrayed Old Testament subjects in seventeenth-century Dutch art.[1] Among the artists of Rembrandt's circle it was a particular favourite. The reason is not difficult to guess: the theme - a mortal being ordered by God to slay a loved one, and then the reprieve through divine intervention - afforded a golden opportunity for drama and composition. It was an ideal theme in which to express various human emotions, such as fear, sorrow and shock. At the same time, it challenged the artist to present a vertical progression of motifs (Isaac lying on the altar, Abraham bowed over the boy and the angel hovering above) and to bring these together into a convincing composition.

Rembrandt himself devoted an etching (cat. no. 13) and two paintings to the *Sacrifice of Isaac*, one of which was probably made jointly with a pupil.[2] This last work (fig. 13.1), presently in Munich, reveals remarkable similarities with the print shown here. The composition is largely the same, although mirrored, as is the appearance and pose of both Abraham and the angel.[3] In both works the angel appears to be speeding towards the viewer, his wings spread wide and illuminated from above by a divine glow leaving the face hidden in shadow.

**13.1**
Rembrandt and pupil, *The Sacrifice of Isaac*, 1636, canvas, 195 x 132 cm, Alte Pinakothek, Munich

**13.2**
Ferdinand Bol, *The Sacrifice of Isaac, c.* 1646, canvas, measurements unknown, Mansi Coll., Lucca

On the other hand, in the foreground, the figure of Isaac reveals a different character from the defenseless, overmastered youngster of the Munich painting. Here he awaits his fate with a certain resignation, the hands loosely tied. Only his frightened glance betrays the thoughts he must be having. With his long hair and the voluptuous curves of his stomach and hips, the figure seems more like that of a young woman than a boy. And compared to Abraham and the angel, the figure of Isaac is relatively large.

On the right, in the foreground, are Isaac's clothes. The pot of burning embers is a reminder of the sacrifice Abraham is about to make. The artist has employed a delicate and varied technique in this print, ranging from loose and sketch-like etching (the sky, top right), extremely fine parallel shading (Isaac), to dense cross-hatching (the dark clouds), lending the print a wide range of tones and a lively chiaroscuro effect.

Blankert has cast some doubt on Bartsch' attribution of this etching to Rembrandt's pupil Ferdinand Bol. 'The figures,' he notes, 'seem rather dynamic for Bol, and the hands and faces appear somewhat spindly for his taste. Moreover, on all the signed impressions of this etching that I have ever seen the signature is coarsely drawn, quite different from the signatures which have been confirmed as Bol's'.[4] As far as the signature is concerned Blankert is certainly correct. However, it may be argued, that it only appears in the second state and could very well have been added by someone else at a later date. Also, the dimensions of the sheet seem to contradict an attribution to Bol. [5]

Although the limited range of Bol's graphic oeuvre[6] makes it difficult to subject the print to a thorough stylistic examination, the attribution to Bol seems to be acceptable. The rocky plateau in the foreground and the clouds, top left, are executed with a technique typical of Bol - regular, open hatching which repeatedly changes direction (*cf.* cat. no. 25).[7] Abraham and Isaac's bulging eyes are reminiscent of figures in other etchings by Bol, particularly the *Bust of an Old Man with Velvet Cap*.[8]

As far as the choice of motifs is concerned there are considerable affinities with Bol's paintings. For example, Abraham, with his short white beard, anxiously gazing upward, is remarkably similar to the same character in Bol's painting of the same episode in the Mansi collection in Lucca (fig. 13.2).[9], while the plants in the background, left, are reminiscent of the vegetation in his *Flight into Egypt* in Dresden (1644).[10] **ME**

1. For more on this theme see: Münster 1994, pp. 31-32, 157-160, 180-182.
2. Resp. Bredius 498 (fig. 12.1) and Sumowski II, p. 1018, no. 611. See: Amsterdam 1991-92B, pp. 218-219, no. 9.
3. The influence of Rembrandt's etchings is also clearly evident. For example, the execution of the illumination around the angel is highly reminiscent of the background in Rembrandt's *The Fall* (cat. no. 2) and - to a slightly lesser extent - the sky in his *Death of the Virgin* (B. 99) - both etchings dating from 1639. (Noticeably, the size of the latter [40.9 x 31.5 cm] is almost the same as that of the *Sacrifice of Isaac* which has to do with the standard sizes of paper in those times).
4. Blankert 1976, p. 7, note 1.
5. The etching by Bol that is the closest in size to the *Sacrifice of Isaac* is his *St Jerome in a Cave*, dated 1644, which is only 28.6 x 24.7 cm (Holl. III, p. 17, no. 3). On the size see also my comments in note 3.
6. Tsuritani (1974) was only able to confirm sixteen etches as definitely by Bol. On Ferdinand Bol's etchings, see also: Tsuritani 1975-76, pp. 46-47 and Munich 1982, pp. 122-123.
7. *Cf.* Holl. III, nos 3, 6, 9 and 12. This method was also employed by Rembrandt in his etching of a *Small Grey Landscape* (B. 207).
8. Holl. III, p. 24, no. 10. *Cf.* Holl. III, nos 5, 7 and 13.
9. Blankert 1982, pp. 90-91, no. 4, fig. 8 (not in Sumowski). Compare also the head of St Peter in the painting *The Release of St Peter* attributed to Bol (Sumowski I, p. 291, no. 78).
10. Sumowski I, p. 291, no. 81. George C. Kenney's book on the etchings of Ferdinand Bol, to be published in early 1997, will probably settle the question of who made *The Sacrifice of Isaac*.

**14 Abraham and Isaac Preparing to Sacrifice the Ram, before 1625**

[GEN. 22:13]

Claes Cornelisz. Moeyaert
(Durgerdam 1590/91 - Amsterdam 1655)

No. 4 from a series of five: *The History of Abraham*
Etching, 10.8 x 18.7 cm, state I (3)
Museum Boijmans Van Beuningen, Rotterdam
(inv. no. 16901)
**Lit** Holl. XIV, p. 94, no. 8; TIB LIII, p. 271, no. 004; Münster 1994, p. 305, no. 77

The Pre-Rembrandtist Claes Moeyaert produced four series of etchings featuring characters from the Old Testament: Abraham, Lot, Jacob and Tobit. The series of the *History of Abraham* comprises five sheets (figs 14.1-14.5)[1] Four of these show commonly occurring scenes: *Abraham Receiving the Angels* (Gen. 18), *The Banishment of Hagar and Ishmael* (Gen. 21:9-14), *The Sacrifice of Isaac* (Gen. 22) and *Rebecca and Eliezer at the Well* (Gen. 24:10-21). The subject of the fifth print, *Abraham and Isaac Preparing to Sacrifice the Ram*, is highly unusual.

After the angel had prevented Abraham from sacrificing his son Isaac, Abraham suddenly saw a ram caught in the thicket. He took the ram and offered it instead of his son. Moeyaert shows Abraham and Isaac preparing to sacrifice the ram. Abraham, his sleeves rolled up, is kneeling beside the animal, holding it by the horns as Isaac grabs the beast from behind. In the background is the altar. The wood on which Isaac has lain is still piled high and smoke rises from the pot of fire. Clearly, the ram is about to be sacrificed. But the viewer is also reminded of the previous episode, when Abraham was about to offer his own son. Isaac, who only moments before had been about to die, is still half-dressed. His clothes and Abraham's turban are both lying beside the altar.

Like the other prints in the series, this etching features a clear division between the foremost and rear plane. On the left the main event takes place, bordered by the motif of trees and bushes growing on a rock which was so popular among the Pre-Rembrandtists. On the right, bathed in light, is a mountainous landscape. On the road below right, as the iconographical tradition dictated, are Abraham's servants with the ass. They have

**14.1**
Claes Moeyaert, *Abraham Receiving the Angels*,
etching, 11.1 x 19.5 cm, Museum Boijmans Van
Beuningen, Rotterdam

**14.2**
Claes Moeyaert, *The Banishment of Hagar and
Ishmael*, etching, 11 x 19.5 cm, Museum
Boijmans Van Beuningen, Rotterdam

**14.3**
Claes Moeyaert, *The Sacrifice of Isaac*, etching,
11 x 19.3 cm, Museum Boijmans Van
Beuningen, Rotterdam

**14.4**
Claes Moeyaert, *Abraham and Isaac Preparing to
Sacrifice the Ram*, etching, 10.8 x 18.7 cm,
Museum Boijmans Van Beuningen, Rotterdam

**14.5**
Claes Moeyaert, *Rebecca and Eliezer at the Well*,
etching, 11.1 x 19 cm, Museum Boijmans Van
Beuningen, Rotterdam

accompanied the Patriarch and his son on their journey and will soon return
home with them. Here Moeyaert refers to the events leading up to the
sacrifice and the conclusion of the story. **MH/AT**

1. Holl. XIV, p. 54, nos 5-9; TIB LIII, pp. 267-272, nos 001-005. The second state of the series was published by Clement
de Jonghe and the third by J. de Ram. For Moeyaert's Lot series, see: cat. no. 5; for his Jacob series: Münster 1994, p. 306,
no. 78.

**14.3** The Sacrifice of Isaac

**14.1** Abraham Receiving the Angels

**14.4** Abraham and Isaac Preparing to Sacrifice the Ram

**14.2** The Banishment of Hagar and Ishmael

**14.5** Rebecca and Eliezer at the Well

## 15    Jacob's Dream, *c.* 1602

[Gen. 28:10-22]

Jan Pynas
*(Amsterdam 1583/84 - 1631 Amsterdam)*

Etching, 15.2 x 20.5 cm, only state
**Inscr.** '160[2?]'
Rijksprentenkabinet, Rijksmuseum,
Amsterdam
**Lit**. Holl. XVII, p. 116, no. 15; TIB LIII, p. 339,
no. 1; Burchard 1917, pp. 27, 28; Bauch 1935,
p. 193; Ackley 1981, pp. 37-38, no. 20

Jacob was sent by his father Isaac to his family in the land of Haran to find a bride. On the way he rested, using a stone as a cushion. He fell asleep and in his dream Jacob saw a ladder, the top of which reached to heaven, with the angels of the Lord ascending and descending. God appeared to Jacob and announced that the land on which he was sleeping would belong to him and his descendants. The following morning Jacob erected the stone as a pillar, poured oil over it and named the place Beth-el (House of God).

In Jan Pynas' etching, the foreground is entirely occupied by Jacob, asleep, holding on to his walking stick. His wide-brimmed hat has almost fallen off and encircles his head like a halo. At his feet lie a travelling bag with a lock, a calabas and a book. Pynas convincingly evokes the heaviness of Jacob's tired body as he sleeps.

Over Jacob's head looms the visionary dream, while to the right a landscape stretches out. Unlike the plastic depiction of Jacob the two angels are mainly shown in outline, providing an almost translucent effect. Their ghostlike appearance is emphasized by their frail, extremely elongated limbs.[1] Slightly further to the right is a female figure carrying a water jug, walking along the bank of a body of water. Perhaps it is a reference to Jacob's future wife Rebecca, whom the young traveller was to meet by a well not long after his dream.

Pynas' depiction clearly fits into the pictorial tradition. The position of the legs echoes the pose of the sleeping Jacob in a print of the same subject by Giovanni Lanfranco after Raphael (fig. 15.1).[2] The way in which the two artists portrayed the clouds is also similar. However, the most remarkable

similarity is the handling of line which is unusually free for the period. Unlike Pynas, Raphael placed the ladder in the centre. Lanfranco's work is a reproduction of Raphael's fresco in the Loggia of the Vatican palace, which had already been reproduced in an engraving by Jacob Bos.[3]

Pynas' composition is reflected in an etching by Moeyaert of *Jacob's Dream* made more than twenty years later .[4] Here too, the scene is divided into three parts: a foreplane showing Jacob asleep, above him a depiction of the dream and a distant landscape, separated by a diagonal column of cloud.

*Jacob's Dream* is unsigned. However, the stylistic similarity to two etchings signed with the monogram 'I.P.' in the Metropolitan Museum in New York[5] and to two drawings by Pynas' *confrère* and contemporary Pieter Lastman in the Amsterdam print room, dated 1603,[6] appear to justify the attribution to Jan Pynas.

The actual date of the print is a problem. A slip of the etching needle has left the last digit of the date, below right, unclear. It may be a 0, 1 or 2, or even a 5.[7] I consider the date 1602 to be the most likely.[8]

Only two impressions of *Jacob's Dream* are known: one in Amsterdam, shown here, and another in the British Museum. In both impressions the plate was underbitten, leaving the printed lines light grey. A mirror-image pen-and-ink drawing of the same scene forms part of the Dresden print room collection (fig. 15.2). **ME**

**15.1**
Giovanni Lanfranco after Raphael, *Jacob's Dream*, etching, 13.3 x 18 cm, in: *Historia del testamento vecchio*, Rome (Giovanni Orlandi) 1607. University Library, Amsterdam

**15.2**
Jan Pynas, *Jacob's Dream*, pen-and-ink drawing, 14 x 21 cm, Kupferstichkabinett, Dresden

1.  These elongated figures are characteristic of Pynas' later paintings, such as the *Parable of the Workers in the Vineyard* of 1612 (National Gallery, Prague; see Amsterdam 1991, p. 32, fig. 20), and can also be seen in his first known painting, the *Raising of Lazarus* of 1605 (Museum Aschaffenburg; see Amsterdam 1991, p. 28, fig. 14).
2.  Lanfranco made this print between 1605 and 1607 for his so-called 'Raphael Bible', or *Historia del testamento vecchio* (see also cat. no. 57), which he produced in conjunction with Sisto Badalocchio. *Cf.* Rome 1985, pp. 77-80.
3.  Holl. III, p. 148, no. 1. *Cf.* Rome 1985, p. 73, no. 12.
4.  Holl. XIV, p. 55, no. 10. See also: Münster 1994, p. 306, no. 78. Remarkably, Moeyaert's print is almost the same size (15.7 x 22.3 cm) as Pynas' etching of *Jacob's Dream*. For the subject, see also cat. no. 64, ill.
5.  *Jacob's Dream* and the *Annunciation*. See: Ackley 1981, p. 37, note 1 (left).
6.  Burchard 1917, p. 28. See also: Freise 1911, nos 47 and 48.
7.  Ackley argues, although not entirely convincingly, the possibility of a reversal and concludes that the date can be read alternatively as 1600, 1601, 1602, 1608, 1620, or 1621. He finds it difficult to imagine the print being executed before Pynas' journey to Italy in 1605, 'since the composition is pervaded by Elsheimer's style, or by Pieter Lastman's interpretation of that style' (Ackley 1981, p. 37). Ackley's confusion may have resulted from his use of the British Museum impression for his research. The date is clearer on the Rijksprentenkabinet example in Amsterdam.
8.  Burchard (1917, p. 27) also identified the year as '1602'.

15.1

15.2

## 16 The History of Joseph, 1512
[GEN. 37-41]

Lucas van Leyden
(Leiden 1494? - Leiden 1533)

Series of five engravings, c. 12.5 x 16.5 cm,
state I (3)
**Inscr** 'L' and '1512' (nos 16a-c); 'L' (nos 16d-e)
Museum Boijmans Van Beuningen, Rotterdam
(inv. nos BdH 11552-4; L 1969/31; BdH 9670;
BdH 12163)
**Lit** Holl. X, pp. 71-74, nos 19-23; New
Hollstein, Lucas van Leyden, pp. 48-51, nos 19-
23; TIB XII, pp. 151-155, nos 19 (348)-23 (350);
Filedt Kok 1978, pp. 36, 73, 149, nos B. 19-23;
Washington/ Boston 1983, pp. 98-101, nos 31-
32; Münster 1994, p. 306, no. 79

Joseph's brothers hated him for being his father's favourite son and for his
dreams in which - as Joseph interpreted it to them - they had to obey him.
Out of spite they threw him into a pit. Later Joseph was sold as a slave and
came to work in the household of Potiphar, an important functionary at the
court of Egypt's Pharaoh. Potiphar's wife tried to seduce Joseph. But when
she failed, she falsely accused Joseph, and he found himself in prison. There
he successfully interpreted the dreams of a cupbearer and a baker. Later, he
interpreted Pharaoh's dreams too, eventually earning an appointment as
ruler over Egypt (Gen. 37-41).

In 1512 Lucas van Leyden produced a series of engravings featuring
Joseph's astonishing story. The scenes reveal the artist's interest in the
narrative, storybook quality of the material. Lucas introduced a number of
iconographical innovations in this series which were to influence depictions
of Joseph in seventeenth century Dutch painting.

The first print shows Joseph telling his dream (cat. no. 16a). A remarkable
element is the presence of a woman next to the seated Jacob. This is probably
Rachel, Joseph's mother - although her presence is not in line with the
biblical text since by then she was no longer alive (Gen. 35:19). In his

b Joseph and Potiphar's Wife

c Potiphar's Wife Accusing Joseph

d Joseph Interpreting the Dreams in Prison

e Joseph Interpreting Pharaoh's Dreams

a  Joseph Telling his Dreams
b  Joseph and Potiphar's Wife
c  Potiphar's Wife Accusing Joseph
d  Joseph Interpreting the Dreams in Prison
e  Joseph Interpreting Pharaoh's Dreams

depictions of the same theme, in a grisaille (fig. 17.1) and etching (cat. no. 17), Rembrandt completed Jacob's family in a similar fashion by adding Rachel. There she is shown as an old woman, lying in bed. This was to influence artists who followed Rembrandt; she is rarely absent in later paintings of this theme.[1]

The second sheet shows the seduction scene in Potiphar's house (cat. no. 16b). Unusually, this episode is continued in the third print which portrays the accusation by Potiphar's wife (cat. no. 16c). Lucas treated this as a separate scene,  in contrast to the existing iconographical tradition in which it formed an additional side element in portrayals of 'Joseph and Potiphar's Wife'. In the foreground the wife of Potiphar is shown displaying Joseph's robe to her husband as proof of his servant's supposed guilt. The accusation takes place in the presence of various members of the court acting as witnesses. Joseph himself is not shown, true to the biblical text. All it says there, is that the wife spoke to her husband (Gen. 39:17) after having told her story to the household (Gen. 39:14). By including these figures Lucas recalls the preceding episode and manages to portray a wide range of human emotions and reactions.

**16.1**
Lucas van Leyden, *Potiphar's Wife Accusing Joseph*,
*c.* 1512, panel, 26.2 x 36 cm, Museum Boijmans
Van Beuningen, Rotterdam

Around the same time, Lucas was employing the accusation as a theme for a painting (fig. 16.1). In contrast to the print, one of the figures in the picture, forced into the background, on the extreme right, may be Joseph. In the seventeenth century, Joseph was to acquire a place in the iconography of this theme, especially among the Pre-Rembrandtists and Rembrandt and his circle. The text of Flavius Josephus' *Jewish Antiquities* certainly contributed to this in no small measure.[2]

Typical of Lucas' Joseph series is his selection of the rarely depicted theme of Joseph interpreting the dreams of the cupbearer and the baker (cat. no. 16d). Joseph is counting the days until the cupbearer's release and until the baker's execution on his fingers. The same motif is found in seventeenth-century painting, for example in the work of Salomon Koninck.[3]

*Joseph Interpreting Pharaoh's Dreams*, the last print in the series, is Lucas' own innovative formulation (cat. no. 16e). Pharaoh is not in bed, as often found in the traditional iconography, but is seated on his throne, at a table. Joseph kneels before him as the court officials look on. These compositional elements became standard in the later iconography and were repeated in all manner of variations.[4]

The prints in this Joseph series are typified by lively chiaroscuro effects and the careful manipulation of the space as a setting for the drama (often including a glimpse of the surrounding area or landscape). Architectural elements, such as doors, pillars and pilasters, reveal Lucas' masterly perspective skills. The expressive quality of the figures is achieved by the movement of the bodies, the turning of the heads and the animated gestures. Each motif is depicted with a confident line, the faces, hands, the folds of the cloth as well as the architectural details such as the walls, cornices and columns. The shadows are depicted with dense, remarkably even hatching. Semi-shadow is shown with more casual hatching, while lively, animated lines accurately depict the contours and shapes of the illuminated motifs.
**NvdK/AT**

**1.** *Cf.* Van de Kamp 1991 & 1994, pp. 42-43.
**2.** *Cf.* Münster 1994, pp. 45, 200, 252, cat. nos 24-25. For Lucas' painting: Rotterdam 1994, pp. 264-269, no. 57. See for Josephus: cat. nos 70 and 71.
**3.** *Cf.* Van de Kamp 1991 & 1994, p. 45.
**4.** *Ibid.*

## 17 Joseph Telling his Dreams, 1638
[GEN. 37:5-11]

### Rembrandt
*(Leiden 1606 - Amsterdam 1669)*

Etching and drypoint, 11 x 8.3 cm, state II (3)
**Inscr** 'Rembrandt.f. / 1638'
Museum het Rembrandthuis, Amsterdam
**Lit** Holl. XVIII, p. 18, no. B. 37; TIB L, p. 26,
no. 37; Münz 1952, Vol. 2, p. 86, no. 175;
Amsterdam 1964-65, pp. 39-40, no. 26;
Tümpel 1970, no. 14; Filedt Kok 1972, p. 47,
no. B. 37; Haak 1984, pp. 144, 145, fig. 225;
Berlin/ Amsterdam/ London 1991-92A, pp. 26,
28; Münster 1994, pp. 42-43, 307, no. 80;
Dearborn 1994, pp.129-130, no. 22;
Amsterdam 1995, p. 28, no. B. 37

**17.1**
Rembrandt, *Joseph Telling his Dreams,*
*c.* 1637/38, paper on panel, 51 x 39 cm,
Rijksmuseum, Amsterdam

Before etching *Joseph Telling his Dreams*, Rembrandt made a grisaille (fig. 17.1)
along with studies in red chalk of the individual figures, including Jacob.[1]
Since the oil study is on paper, Rembrandt's original plan was clearly to
collaborate with a colleague to reproduce it as a large-format master etching,
as with the *Ecce Homo* representation.[2] We do not know why he abandoned
this idea. However, he did decide later on to produce a small-scale etching on
his own, a work for which he added motifs not present in the oil study and
regrouped others that are.

Rembrandt's rendition of Joseph is impressive. Placed at the very centre of
the etching, he is describing to his father a fantastic dream he has had in
which all will bow down to him. Jacob is taken aback by what he hears while
Joseph's sister, looking up from the book she has been reading, observes
him. The brothers' individual reactions - of amazement, indignation or
ridicule - are portrayed very vividly. A few of them are already turning to each
other conspiratorially; their hatred is growing.

Rembrandt presents the scene in a bedchamber, giving it a highly intimate
character. An old lady lies in bed. If this is supposed to be Rachel then
Rembrandt is allowing himself an anachronism, since by then Joseph's
natural mother is already dead and buried (Gen. 35:18-20). The Bible
contradicts itself here because, when rebuking Joseph, Jacob asks: 'Shall I
and thy mother and thy brethren indeed come to bow down ourselves to thee

to the earth?' (Gen. 37:10). The old lady, therefore, probably represents the mother.

In his 1512 engraving, Lucas van Leyden had already depicted an old lady who is probably the mother (cat. no. 16a). The motif of a figure lying in bed also occurs in an engraving produced by Aldegrever in 1532 (see fig. 5, p. 12). This print is even more similar to Rembrandt's etching than Lucas van Leyden's composition.[3] The Aldegrever work - a simultaneous representation - shows Joseph a second time; he is now actually dreaming. If Rembrandt used Aldegrever's engraving as a model, he must have misinterpreted the sleeping figure. **PJ/CT**

**1.** Grisaille: Bredius 504; Tümpel 1986, p. 390, no. 16; RRP, Vol. 2, pp. 289-297, no. A66. Drawing: Benesch 20; Berlin/ Amsterdam/ London 1991-92A, pp. 26-28, no. 2.
**2.** For the *Ecce Homo* grisaille and etching, see: Amsterdam 1996, pp. 68-72, nos 16a-c.
**3.** Holl., German, I, p. 13, no. B.18.

## 18 Joseph's Coat Shown to Jacob, *c.* 1633
[GEN. 37:31-35]

Rembrandt
*(Leiden 1606 - Amsterdam 1669)*
*(and assistant)*

Etching and drypoint, 10.7 x 8 cm, state I (2)
**Inscr** 'Rembrant. / van.Rijn. *fc.*'
Museum het Rembrandthuis, Amsterdam
**Lit** Holl. XVIII, p. 19, no. B. 38; TIB L, p. 26, no. 38; Middleton 1878, no. 189; Rovinski 1890, no. 38; Singer 1906, p. 191; Hind 1912, p. 106; Von Seidlitz 1922, no. 38; Münz 1952, Vol. 2, pp. 85-86, no. 172; Biörklund 1968, p. 50, BB 33-I; White 1969, p. 36; Tümpel 1970, no. 16; Filedt Kok 1972, p. 47, no. B. 38; Münster 1994, p. 307, no. 81; Amsterdam 1995, p. 28, no. B. 38

**18.1**
Lucas van Leyden, *Joseph's Coat Shown to Jacob*, c. 1517, woodcut, 21.2 x 14.3 cm, Rijksprentenkabinet, Amsterdam

**18.2**
Jan Pynas, *Joseph's Coat Shown to Jacob*, 1618, panel, 90 x 119 cm, Hermitage, St Petersburg

Having sold Joseph to passing merchants in Dothan, his brothers slaughtered a goat and dipped his coat of many colours in its blood. They then brought the coat to their father, Jacob, telling him they found the garment and do not know whether it is their brother's or not. Recognizing the coat, Jacob was convinced his favourite son had been devoured by an evil beast and was plunged into mourning: 'And all his sons and all his daughters rose up to comfort him' (Gen. 37:35).

Bible illustrations usually depict the moment at which one or two brothers show Jacob the blood-stained coat. Lucas van Leyden's impressive woodcut, for instance, concentrates on the scene in which one of the sons is breaking the news to Jacob (fig. 18.1).[1] In contrast, Jan Pynas (fig. 18.2) and Claes Moeyaert devote their multi-figure history paintings to the later moment when all the children have arrived to comfort Jacob.[2]

Completely in line with the graphic tradition Rembrandt focuses on just a few figures - Jacob throwing up his hands in despair, the mother wringing her hands, and two brothers showing the coat, while indicating the place at which they claim the incident took place. To portray the individual figures Rembrandt used older studies in which he had developed stereotypes for particular age groups and emotional states.[3]

The weaknesses in this work are a sign that an assistant was also involved in its production. The contours, for instance, have an almost crude 'sketched-in' quality. Moreover, the shaded areas in the foreground and around the principal figures are extremely dark and do not flow smoothly into the light areas, which makes for overly harsh contrasts. Neither is the crosshatching - indicating the bench, for instance - as vivid and varied as in the preceding works, which Rembrandt produced entirely on his own. For these reasons Rovinski and Singer do not categorize this work as a Rembrandt while Middleton attributes it to Johannes van Vliet - a view that Von Seidlitz subscribes to with the proviso that Rembrandt did supervise the execution. Münz' assumption is that in 1632-33 Rembrandt, assisted by a pupil, reworked a version dating from around 1629.[4] The addition of 'van Rijn' to the signature only occurs in 1632/33. Jacob's intense reaction and the emphasis on gesture, giving the scene its marked dramatic quality, also tend to place this work in the 1630s. **PJ/AT**

1. B. 4; New Hollstein, Lucas van Leyden, p. 172, no. 188.
2. For the paintings of Pynas and Moeyaert (Muzeum Naradowe, Warsaw), see: Tümpel 1974B, p. 83 and p. 84, fig. 111. For the iconography of the subject see also: Van de Kamp 1991 & 1994, pp. 43-44.
3. The portrayal of the son with tousled hair is attributable to self-portraits and studies of heads by Rembrandt (cf. B. 10 and 13). He had already used this type in his etching *Peter and John at the Gate of the Temple* (B. 95; Münz 1952, Vol. 2, p. 86). The type used to portray a despairing mother is that of an old lady beginning to wring her hands (cf. the depiction of the worshipping prophetess Anna in *Simeon's Hymn of Praise* (B. 51). The pointing gesture of the son is derived from that of the angel in the last mentioned etching.
4. Hind (1912, p. 106) does not express a definite opinion while Biörklund (1968, p. 50) and White and Boon (Holl. XVIII, p. 19) accept the attribution to Rembrandt. For the problem of attribution, see also Tümpel 1970, no. 16.

## 19    Joseph and Potiphar's Wife, 1634
[GEN. 39:11-13]

Rembrandt
*(Leiden 1606 - Amsterdam 1669)*

Etching, 9 x 11.5 cm, state II (2)
**Inscr** 'Rembrandt. ƒc.1634.'
Museum het Rembrandthuis, Amsterdam
**Lit** Holl. XVIII, p. 19, no. B. 39; TIB L, p. 27,
no. 39; Münz 1952, Vol. 2, p. 86, no. 173; White
1969, p. 36; Tümpel 1970, no. 18; Filedt Kok
1972, p. 48, no. B. 39; Amsterdam 1985-86,
pp. 58-59, no. 47; Berlin/ Amsterdam/ London
1991-92A, pp. 188-189, no. 8; Münster 1994,
pp. 44, 308, no. 82; Amsterdam 1995, p. 28,
no. B. 39

**19.1**
Antonio Tempesta, *Joseph and Potiphar's Wife*,
*c.* 1600, etching, 6.7 x 6.7 cm, British Museum,
London

Joseph was a slave of the Egyptian Potiphar, an officer of Pharaoh and
captain of the guard. He gained the trust of his master. When Potiphar's wife
asked the attractive youth to lie with her he refused. One day, when they were
alone in the house, she tried to seduce him. When he again refused she
caught him by his garment but he fled, leaving the garment in her hand
(Gen. 39:1-13).

Rembrandt's composition is based largely on an etching by Antonio
Tempesta (fig. 19.1) but its realism is even starker. The treatment is, in all
respects, more naked.[1] The shameless woman's intention of seducing
Joseph is therefore all too obvious, as is Joseph's answer. Turning away in
disgust he is trying to avoid even touching her, while she is simply grabbing
him. Rembrandt uses light and shadow to provide a moral commentary -
while the chaste Joseph is portrayed against a light background, Potiphar's
wife lies in a dark, shadowy bed.[2] **PJ**

1. Tümpel 1970, no. 18. Tempesta: TIB XXXV, p. 27, no. 71 (128).
2. Berlin/ Amsterdam/ London 1991-92A, p. 188. For the iconography of the subject, see: Van de Kamp 1991 & 1994,
p. 44.

Erat fames in terra Chanàan .Et Ioseph erat Princeps in terra Aegypti, atque ad ejus nutum frumenta populis vendebantur. Genef. Cap. 42.℣. 6.
Princeps , eſt imago et exemplar Dei in terris , rerum moderator et arbiter, in cujus manu pofitæ opes , dignitas , vita . Lips . lib . de vna relig .

**20    Joseph Distributing Grain in Egypt,**
**c. 1648/57**
[GEN. 41:53-57]

Jan de Bisschop
(Amsterdam 1628 - The Hague 1671)
after Bartholomeus Breenbergh
(Deventer 1598 - Amsterdam 1657)

Etching, 49.9 x 69.7 cm, state II (3)
**Inscr** 'Barth. Breenbergh inventor et Pinxit'
**Caption** 'Erat fames in terra Chanàan. Et
Ioseph erat Princeps in terra Aegypti, atque
ad ejus nutum frumenta populis vendebantur.
Genes. Cap.42.v.6. / Princeps, est imago et
exemplar Dei in terris, rerum moderator et
arbiter, in cujus manu positae opes, dignitas,
vita. Lips. lib. de vna relig.'
Th. Laurentius Coll., Voorschoten
**Lit** Holl. II, p. 42, no. 1; Van Gelder 1972, pp. 6,
15, 63; Roethlisberger 1981, pp. 20, 81, no. 2;
Amsterdam 1992, pp. 13, 15-16, 39, 46

Having interpreted Pharaoh's dream as a prophesy of seven years of plenty
followed by seven years of famine, Joseph was appointed ruler over Egypt.
He was charged with responsibility for the kingdom's food supply, building
up massive stores in preparation for the coming shortage. Once the lean
years began, Joseph started selling the grain to the Egyptians (Gen. 41:
47-57). In the end, the famine grew so severe that they lost not just their
money, but their cattle, their land and even sold themselves as slaves to the
Pharaoh (Gen. 47:13-26).

In this majestic scene with large crowds of people, animals and buildings,
Breenbergh depicts the final phase of the famine. Standing on a dias in front
of the magnificent palace, dressed in royal garb, Joseph supervises the sale of
grain. A detailed note of the transactions is kept, both at the table to the left
of Joseph and in the foreground. Here the famished Egyptians deposit their
money in exchange for sacks of corn, dragged in from the left. The money
box in front of the table is filled to the brim. The first to arrive without money
have come on the right to barter their cattle for grain.

Breenbergh depicted Joseph distributing grain in several paintings.
In these works he continued the compositional tradition set by Lastman's
1612 painting on the same theme (fig. 20.1). Here the event was shown in
detail as a busy scene, with Joseph on a raised platform, overseeing the sale,
exchange and administration. Lastman's work influenced other painters too,
including Moeyaert and Bol.[1]

**20.1**

Pieter Lastman, *Joseph Distributing Grain in Egypt*, 1612, panel, 58.4 x 87.6 cm, National Gallery of Ireland, Dublin

One of his paintings, a now lost panel dating from 1644, was the basis for a print by Breenbergh.[2] In turn, De Bisschop, probably a pupil of Breenbergh's, produced a copy of this in which he faithfully imitated the composition and etching technique. However, some architectural details and small figures in the background are different. Like Breenbergh, he used the largest paper size (imperial) for his print.[3] Nicolaes Visscher acquired De Bisschop's copperplate in 1677. The print is mentioned in the Visscher stock catalogue under the heading 'Large Art Prints of 1 Imperial Sheet'.[4] Visscher also commissioned a smaller copy of Breenbergh's *Joseph Distributing Grain in Egypt* for his *Royal-Size Bible*. In this print several parts of the composition were left out. Furthermore the scholarly caption with the reference to Lipsius' *De una religione Liber* was replaced by a simple rhyme summarizing the story.[5] **PvdC**

1. *Cf.* Tümpel 1986, p. 19; Amsterdam 1991, pp. 73-74; Van de Kamp 1991 & 1994, pp. 46-47. For Breenbergh's paintings see: Roethlisberger 1981, nos 204, 230-231. *Cf.* Münster 1994, p. 253, no. 26.
2. Holl. III, p. 213, no. 30. *Cf.* Roethlisberger 1981, p. 81, no. 1.
3. De Bisschop produced a print of another composition by Breenbergh, namely a 1647 painting of *The Martyrdom of St. Lawrence*. This was also an imperial-size etching with a similar caption (Holl. II, p. 43, no. 3). Van Gelder (1972, pp. 6, 15) locates both prints at the end of De Bisschop's apprenticeship with Breenbergh (c. 1648), like Roethlisberger (1981, pp. 20, 81). De Bisschop may have made them at a later date, perhaps shortly after Breenbergh's death in 1657.
4. 'Joseph Koorn uytdeelende in Egypten, door Breenbergh en J. de Bisschop' (*Catalogue Visscher*, c. 1680, p. 7). For the sale of De Bisschop's plates in 1677 see: Van der Waals 1988, p. 178; Amsterdam 1992, pp. 8-9, 72.
5. *Historiae Sacrae...Bybelsche Figuren...*, Amsterdam (Nicolaus Visscher) s.a. [c. 1680] (Print Room, British Museum, London: 157*.b.25).

## 21   Jacob Caressing Benjamin, *c.* 1637

Rembrandt
*(Leiden 1606 - Amsterdam 1669)*

Etching and drypoint, 11.6 x 8.9 cm, state II (2)
**Inscr** 'Rembrandt. *f*
Museum het Rembrandthuis, Amsterdam
**Lit** Holl. XVIII, pp. 14-15, no. B. 33; TIB L, p. 22, no. 33; Jordan 1893, p. 301, note 4; Münz 1952, Vol. 2, pp. 86-87, no. 176; Tümpel 1968B, pp. 113-115; Tümpel 1970, no. 20; Filedt Kok 1972, pp. 41-42, no. B. 33; Zilkens 1984, no. 11; Münster 1994, p. 308, no. 83; Amsterdam 1995, p. 25, no. B. 33

*Als sie ir sêck nûn lârten auß,*
*Fanden sie all ir gelt zû hauß:*
*Iacob trawrt Ioseph vnd Simeon,*
*Vnd das er soll Beniamin lon.*

**21.1**
Bernard Salomon, *Jacob's Sons Return to their Father*, woodcut in: *Wol gerissnen vnd geschnidten figuren Ausz der Bibel*, Lyon (Jean de Tournes) 1554. Herzog August Bibliothek, Wolfenbüttel

**21.2**
Rembrandt, *Mother with Child*, c. 1636, pen and bistre, 18.5 x 13.3 cm, Pierpont Morgan Library, New York

The 1679 inventory of print-seller Clement de Jonghe's estate describes the subject of this etching as 'Father Abraham playing with his son'.[1] Most works of reference rep eat this designation even though Jordan had already reinterpreted the subject as 'Jacob caressing Benjamin' because the same group of figures occur in a drawing, now kept in the Albertina. This drawing clearly depicts Jacob holding Benjamin lovingly as he listens to Joseph describing his dream.[2] Tümpel points out that this interpretation can be supported not just by referring to further works by Rembrandt and his school but also by investigating the iconographic tradition. From this it appears that Rembrandt took his group of figures from representations dealing with the subject of 'Joseph's brothers asking their father to allow Benjamin to accompany them to Egypt' (Gen. 42:29-38).[3]

Rachel, Jacob's favourite wife - he had to work fourteen years to be able to marry her - bore him two sons. With Joseph, the elder, presumed dead (cf. cat. no. 18), tiny Benjamin was the only surviving child from this marriage. Hence Jacob's great love for Benjamin and his statement that he would not survive if a single hair of his were to be harmed. This is why Jacob initially refused to allow Benjamin to accompany his brothers to Egypt, even though Pharaoh's representative insisted.

This subject has been depicted only rarely. Rembrandt was presumably inspired by illustrations in sixteenth-century French picture Bibles that depict Jacob putting his arm around Benjamin, who is standing beside his chair (fig. 21.1).[4] In the late 1630s, Rembrandt produced a series of studies of mothers with small children. Several of these drawings portray a small boy who bears a resemblance to Benjamin (fig. 21.2).[5] **PJ**

1. 'Vader Abraham speelend met zijn soon'. De Hoop Scheffer/ Boon 1971, p. 8, no. 25.
2. Jordan 1893, p. 301, note 4. For the Albertina drawing, see: Benesch 526.
3. Tümpel 1968B, pp. 113-115; Tümpel 1970, no. 20.
4. Cf. Tümpel 1968B, p. 115 (with illustrations of other French examples).
5. For instance Benesch 313 and 401. Cf. Filedt Kok 1972, p. 42.

## 22 Joseph, *c.* 1590

Jacques de Gheyn II
(Antwerp 1565 - The Hague 1629)
after Karel van Mander
(Meulebeke 1548 - Amsterdam 1606)

No. 11 from a series of twelve: *The Twelve Sons of Jacob*
Engraving, 15.9 x 11.3 cm, state II (3)
**Inscr** 'KMande in / IDGeijn. sculp.'
**Caption** 'Pulcher Josepvs, foelix quoq[ue] : si modò liuor / Abfuerit : Superis deniq[ue] charus erit. 11'
Prentenkabinet der Rijksuniversiteit, Leiden (inv. no. 100.884)
**Lit** Holl. VII, p. 180, no. 376; Holl. XI, p. 164, no. 93; Valentiner 1930, pp. 35, 101, no. 24; Veldman/ De Jonge 1985, pp. 191-192; Filedt Kok 1990, pp. 255, 386, no. 376; Münster 1994, p. 309, no. 84; Van Mander/ Miedema 1994-95, Vol. 2, pp. 144-145, no. E28

Joseph, facing the viewer and portrayed here as an old man, occupies the bulk of the composition's foreground. The half-length figure is wrapped in historical apparel, the sleeves of which are draped liberally about his arms and shoulders. In his left hand Joseph clasps the handle of a stylishly curved bow; the matching arrow-filled quiver is placed immediately in front of him and to his right. Joseph's gaze is lowered, an effect enhanced by the heavily shadowed eyelids. The artist's vigorous, highly expressive rendition of the nose and eyes along with the open mouth gives the subject a reflective air as well as representing a highly characteristic type.

Van Mander's use of a bow and arrows as attributes indicates his close orientation to Genesis 49, in which Jacob blesses his twelve sons. Joseph was the second youngest and favourite son of Jacob, who promised him prowess as an archer in combat against his foes. Furthermore Joseph - later to found one of the tribes of Israel - is compared with a fruitful bough by a well (Gen. 49:22-26; *cf.* Deut. 33:16-17).[1] Van Mander incorporates this biblical symbolization into his own work in the form of two compositional references: to the left a fountain, referring to the well, to the right a tree, referring to the bough. In the light landscape section the sheaves and the stars from Joseph's dreams (Gen. 37: 5-9) are depicted.

What is special about this presentation is the way it detaches the figure of Joseph from the biblical narrative. The artist concentrates on rendering Joseph as a type, and the result is a figure with almost portrait-like features.

**21.1** Reuben  **22.2** Levi  **22.3** Simeon  **22.4** Judah

**22.5** Zebulun  **22.6** Issacher  **22.7** Dan  **22.8** Gad

**22.9** Asher  **22.10** Nephtali  **22.11** Joseph  **22.12** Benjamin

**22.1-22.12**
Jacques de Gheyn II after Karel van Mander,
*The Twelve Sons of Jacob*, c. 1590, engravings,
c. 15.9 x 11.3 cm, Prentenkabinet der
Rijksuniversiteit, Leiden

**22.13**
Dirck Volkertsz. Coornhert after Maarten van
Heemskerck, *Joseph* (from the *Twelve Patriarchs*
series, 1550), etching and engraving, 21.4 x
27.6 cm, Rijksprentenkabinet, Amsterdam

In their function as attributes, the accompanying motifs have a direct
relationship with the figure portrayed. The effect of the compositional
arrangement is to emphasize Joseph's centrality, therefore underlining his
significance still further. Van Mander and De Gheyn use strong chiaroscuro
effects to render the texture of the clothing and physiognomy, while the
highly significant background stands out unnaturally bright against the
middle distance.

This print is part of a series portraying Jacob's twelve sons, also referred to
as the twelve patriarchs (figs 22.1-22.12). Iconographically this series closely
resembles an earlier one - dating from 1550 - by Coornhert after Van
Heemskerck, depicting the same subject (fig. 22.13).[2] Most of the attributes
are found in Van Heemskerck's series as well as most of the Latin captions.
However, Van Mander did not adopt the classical statues and allegorical
animals with which Van Heemskerck provided his patriarchs. **GdB/PvdC**

1. In Genesis 49:22 the modern Dutch Willibrord translation no longer speaks of a bough but a bull.
2. For De Gheyn's and Van Mander's series, see: Filedt Kok 1990, p. 386, nos 366-377. For Van Heemskerck's series
(New Hollstein, Heemskerck, nos 52-63) and its literary and visual sources, see: Veldman/ De Jonge 1985. The series by
De Gheyn after Van Mander is mentioned in Cornelis Claesz.' 1609 stock catalogue (*Catalogue Claesz.*, fol. A3r; price: 18
stivers per quire) and was later reprinted in Schabaelje's picture Bible, *Den Grooten Emblemata Sacra* (cat. no. 60). *Cf.* Visser
1988, Vol. 2, p. 368, nos 55-66.

## 23 Moses and the Daughters of Jethro, 1638

[Ex. 2:15-17]

Gerrit Claesz. Bleker
*(Haarlem c. 1600 - Haarlem 1656)*

Etching, 29.7 x 44.3 cm, state I (2)
**Inscr** 'G Bleker *f*. 1638'
Rijksprentenkabinet, Rijksmuseum,
Amsterdam (inv. no. BI 1171)
**Lit** Holl. II, p. 47, no. 3; TIB V, p. 128, no. 3
(108); Münster 1994, p. 309, no. 85

For many years this scene was thought to represent Jacob and Rachel at the well (Gen. 29:1-10). However, Tümpel pointed this out to be a depiction of an episode in the second chapter of the Book of Exodus.[1] Fleeing from Egypt, Moses found himself in the land of Midian. There, beside a well, he encountered the seven daughters of Jethro. One of them, Zippora, he later married. Bleker, a history painter active in Haarlem, whose work was influenced by that of Lastman and Moeyaert, depicted all seven daughters. Five are shown in the foreground, where Moses is standing, talking to one of them. In the centre, standing beside the well, is the sixth, while the seventh is all the way to the left.[2]

The figures are dressed in the fantasy clothes that are typical of Dutch art of the period. Moses, usually depicted bareheaded, is wearing a turban and therefore reminiscent of depictions of the Patriarchs. Various elements refer to the Graeco-Roman world: the well is decorated with classicized festoons, and on top is a putto spitting water. Urinating pontifically in the foreground is a sheep - a specimen of unadulterated realism. **MH**

1. I am indebted to Christian Tümpel for this suggestion.
2. Another etching by Bleker also formerly wrongly identified, is discussed in cat. no. 27. For Bleker's etchings see: Ackley 1981, pp. 124-126, no. 78. *Cf.* for the artist: AKL, Vol. 11, 1995, pp. 487-488.

Right: detail of cat. no. 23

100

## 24 Moses with the Tablets of the Law, 1583

[Ex. 20:1-17; 31:18; 34:1-28; Deut. 5:1-22]

**Hendrick Goltzius**
(*Mühlbracht 1558 - Haarlem 1617*)

Engraving, 57.4 x 42.3 cm (3 plates)
state I (2)
**Inscr** 'Henricus Goltzius fecit et excudebat.
Impressum Harlemi. A[nn]o 1583'
Rijksprentenkabinet, Rijksmuseum,
Amsterdam (inv. no. RP-P-OB 10.403)
**Lit** Holl. VIII, p. 1, no. 1; TIB III, p. 10, no. 2 (11);
TIB III (Commentary), p. 9, no. 002;
Hirschmann 1921, pp. 3-4, no. 1; Filedt Kok
1993, pp. 163, 207, no. 8; Worthen 1993,
p. 280; Veldman 1995, p. 230

Moses led the Children of Israel out of Egypt through the wilderness, back to Canaan, the land of their forefathers. At Sinai he remained forty days on the mountain, where he received the laws and commandments as revealed by God. If the Children of Israel adhered to them, they could be certain of enjoying God's protection. The Ten Commandments form the basis of this covenant. They were carved into two stone tablets by the finger of God and given to Moses.

On Goltzius' print the imposing figure of Moses towers over the two Tablets of the Law. He is depicted as a powerful leader, carrying a staff and exuding self-confidence, with the attributes of a prophet, the long beard and the divine light shining over him. Two beams of light extend from his head: after having spoken with God, Moses' face shone (Ex. 34:29-30). Goltzius placed the composition in a richly ornamented portal with allegorical figures portraying Piety, Sincerity and Charity, as well as depictions of the Sacrifice of Isaac and the Good Samaritan.

Inscribed on the two tablets in a calligraphic hand are the Ten Commandments (Ex. 20:2-17). In abbreviated form they state:

1. I am the Lord thy God, who brought thee out of the land of Egypt out of the house of bondage. Thou shalt have no other gods before me.
2. Thou shalt not make unto thee any image [...].
3. Thou shalt not take the name of the Lord thy God in vain.
4. Remember the Sabbath day, to keep it holy.
5. Honour thy father and thy mother.
6. Thou shalt not kill.
7. Thou shalt not commit adultery.
8. Thou shalt not steal.
9. Thou shalt not bear false witness against thy neighbour.
10. Thou shalt not covet thy neighbour's house. Thou shalt not covet thy neighbour's wife, nor his manservant nor his maidservant, nor his ox nor his ass, nor anything that is thy neighbour's.

Although the Bible refers to *ten* commandments (Ex. 34:28), they are not actually numbered in the original text. The precise order therefore became the subject of debate. The numbering used above was supported during the Reformation by Calvin, who referred back to the Early Church. The Catholic Church (and Luther) held to a different order which the Church Father, Augustine, had argued was the correct sequence. Here, the prohibition against graven images - the second commandment in the above numbering - was presented as part of the first commandment, while the last was split into two, a ninth and tenth commandment.[1]

To judge from the order employed by Goltzius, the print would originally appear to have been intended for a Protestant audience.[2] This applies equally to the second state, published by Sadeler in Antwerp. There the Dutch text is replaced by a German translation of the Ten Commandments. This was easily arranged, since the text was engraved on a separate plate. The lines below, containing the two principal Christian commandments (Matthew 22:37-39), remained unchanged. **PvdC**

1. For a discussion of this issue see: Stirm 1977, *passim*, esp. pp. 21, 154, 161, 230.
2. Filedt Kok 1993, p. 163. *Cf.* Introduction, p. 43.

103

## 25 Gideon's Sacrifice, *c.* 1641-44

[JUDGES 6:17-20]

Ferdinand Bol
(*Dordrecht 1616 - Amsterdam 1680*)

Etching, 20.9 x 16.7 cm, state III (5)
Museum Boijmans Van Beuningen, Rotterdam
(inv. no. BdH 6714)
**Lit** Holl. III, p. 16, no. 2; Martin 1911, p. 32;
Zoege von Manteuffel 1926, p. 69; Köhne
1932A, p. 23; Köhne 1932B, p. 224; Tsuritani
1974, p. 67, no. 15; Sumowski, I, p. 291 (under
no. 79); Blankert 1982, p. 94 (under no. 11);
Amsterdam 1984-85, p. 59, no. 48

**25.1**
Ferdinand Bol, *Gideon's Sacrifice*, 1641, canvas,
83 x 71 cm, Museum het Catharijneconvent,
Utrecht

An angel informed the young Gideon that it was he who would free his people, the Israelites, from the domination of the Midianites. Gideon proceeded to prepare a kid for the angel and to bake unleavened bread. He placed the flesh on a dish and the broth in a pot. The heavenly messenger then instructed him to 'take the flesh and the unleavened cakes, and lay them upon the rock, and pour out the broth'. The angel then touched the flesh and the bread with the tip of his staff and a flame shot up out of the stone consuming the flesh and bread. Seeing this miracle, Gideon realized that he had been speaking to an angel.

The scene is set at night against the dark background of an inaccessible forest. The artist has created the suggestion of darkness with a robust and varied pattern of deeply bitten hatching. The angel, on the other hand, has been portrayed with sparse, delicate lines, giving his appearance a translucent effect. In character the angel is reminiscent of the delicate etching by Rembrandt of 1638 in which Saskia poses as St Catherine (B. 342). Beside the angel is Gideon. He turns his head in shock as the flesh and the unleavened cakes miraculously catch fire. Almost indiscernible in the darkness behind the figures, a forest giant looms.

Bol often borrowed motifs and even entire compositions (see cat. no. 13) from his teacher Rembrandt. In this case, the kneeling figure of Gideon is based directly on Tobias in Rembrandt's etching *The Angel Departing from the Family of Tobias* of 1641 (cat. no. 50).[1] However, the printing process has resulted in the mirror-image of the original. The execution of the climbing plants on the left of the print closely resembles that in Bol's *St Jerome in Penitence* of 1644 (Holl. 3).[2] The most likely date for the print shown here is between 1641 and 1644.

Bol had an apparent predilection for scenes in which angels play a prominent part. Apart from two prints, he produced seven paintings with this kind of scene (see eg, cat. no. 13 and fig. 13.2).[3] One of these paintings, *Gideon's Sacrifice*, comprises virtually the same composition as the print, although in reverse (fig. 25.1).[4] Opinions are still divided as to which of the two works came first. **ME**

1. Köhne 1932A, p. 23; Köhne 1932B, p. 224.
2. See Ackley 1981, p. 148, 149, no. 96.
3. Paintings: *Peter Released from Prison*, *c.* 1640 (Sumowski, I, no. 78), *Gideon's Sacrifice*, 1641 (Sumowski, I, no. 79); *Jacob's Dream*, *c.* 1642 (Sumowski, I, no. 80), *The Women at the Sepulchre*, 1644 (Sumowski, I, no. 83), *The Sacrifice of Isaac*, *c.* 1646 (Blankert 1982, pp. 90-91, no. 4), *Hagar and the Angel*, *c.* 1650 (Sumowski, I, no. 89), *Abraham Serving the Three Angels*, *c.* 1655 (Blankert 1982, no. 2).
4. On this painting see: Schillemans 1989, pp. 31-34

## 26 The Annunciation of Samson's Birth, 1586

[JUDGES 13:11-20]

### Hendrick Goltzius
*(Mühlbracht 1558 - Haarlem 1617)*

No. 2 from a series of six engravings:
*The Annunciations of the Bible*
20.2 x 5.5 cm, only state
**Inscr** 'HGoltzius fe'; bottom left: '2'
**Caption** 'Angelus aetherea coeli delapsus ab arce, / Samsonem in vitae venturum nunciat auras'
Rijksprentenkabinet, Rijksmuseum, Amsterdam (inv. no. RP-P-OB 10.026)
**Lit** Holl. VIII, p. 2, no. 2; TIB III, p. 11, no. 3(12); TIB III (Commentary), p. 9, no. 3 (12); Hirschmann 1921, p. 4, no. 2; Van Gent/ Pastoor 1991 & 1994, p. 70; Filedt Kok 1993, pp. 166, 208; Münster 1994, p. 311, no. 87

**26.7**
Pieter Lastman, *The Annunciation of Samson's Birth*, 1617, panel, 35.5 x 30.4 cm, Alfred Bader Coll., Milwaukee

Around 1586, Goltzius designed a series of engravings of Old and New Testament scenes in which the birth of a child is announced (figs 26.1-6). Five of the engravings were executed by Adriaen Collaert in 1586, namely the *Annunciation of Isaac's Birth* (Gen. 18:9-15), the *Annunciation of John's Birth* (Luke 1:5-20), the *Annunciation to Mary* (Luke 1:26-38), the *Annunciation to Joseph* (Matthew 1:19-25), and the *Annunciation to the Shepherds* (Luke 2:8-14).[1] The second print in the series, engraved by Goltzius himself, is the *Annunciation of Samson's Birth* (cat. no. 26). It depicts the story's two main events simultaneously: the actual announcement in the foreground and the 'Sacrifice of Manoah' in the background to the right.

After an angel had prophesied to Manoah's wife that she would bear a son, Manoah requested that the angel reappear to give him the prophesy in person. To emphasize the story's miraculous element, Goltzius reproduces Manoah and his wife as old people. The angel, leaning against a tree in a highly mannered pose, points a finger at Manoah's wife in a gesture full of significance. In his right hand the angel holds a walking stick, an attribute

**26.1** The Annunciation of Isaac's Birth

**26.2** [Hendrick Goltzius]
The Annunciation of Samson's Birth

**26.3** The Annunciation of John's Birth

**26.4** The Annunciation to Mary

**26.5** The Annunciation to Joseph

**26.6** The Annunciation to the Shepherds

**26.1-26.6**
(Adriaen Collaert after) Hendrick Goltzius,
*The Annunciations of the Bible*, 1586, engravings,
c. 20.2 x 5.5 cm, Rijksprentenkabinet,
Amsterdam

indicating that his true identity is still unknown to the couple.
Not until the burnt offering has been made and the angel ascends to heaven do they realize they have been conversing with an ambassador of God. The legend below the engraving encapsulates the Manoah episode in simple terms.

'Pieter Lastman used Goltzius's engraving as a model for his 1617 painting [fig. 26.7]. The two works display great compositional similarity with regard to the group of figures in the foreground and the organisation of the picture plane. Lastman's rendition is, however, limited to the *dramatis personae*, omitting the explanatory sacrificial scene in the background. The husband and wife have just arrived at the meeting place and are listening attentively to the angel's words.'[2] **GP**

1. Holl. IV, p. 201, no. 2; Holl. VIII, p. 130, nos 77-82; TIB III, pp. 363-367, nos 1(117)-6(118).
2. Van Gent/ Pastoor 1991 & 1994, pp. 70-71.

**27** **Manoah Offering the Angel to Prepare a Kid for him, 1638**
[JUDGES 13:15-18]

Gerrit Claesz. Bleker
*(Haarlem c. 1610 - Haarlem 1656)*

Etching, 14.2 x 21.3 cm, state I (4)
**Inscr** 'G C Bleker *f.* 1638'
Rijksprentenkabinet, Rijksmuseum,
Amsterdam (inv. no. 42:338)
**Lit** Holl. II, p. 45, no. 1; TIB V, p. 126,
no. 1(107); Münster 1994, p. 311, no. 88

Bleker's etching, formerly interpreted as 'The Angel Promises Abraham a Son' (Gen. 18:1-15), actually depicts a scene from the story of Manoah. After learning that his childless wife was to bear a son after all, Manoah offered to prepare a kid to feed the bringer of these glad tidings, whom he had not yet recognized as the angel of God.

The scene is situated in a farmyard containing goats, sheep and a horse. Seated under a tree in the foreground, to the right, is the angel. He is talking to Manoah and indicating the kid, which a farmhand has seized by the fleece. Manoah's wife is largely concealed by the two figures in the foreground. Bleker places the story in a historical setting. He may have derived his knowledge of the location from Flavius Josephus' *Jewish Antiquities*, which describes how Manoah and his wife had retired to their farmhouse when the angel appeared to them (Book V, ch. 10).

Unlike the scene of Manoah's sacrifice, this episode from the story of Manoah has received little attention from painters. One of the few exceptions we know of is a work ascribed to Lambert Jacobsz. Taking a somewhat later moment, by which time the angel has decided to sacrifice the kid to the Lord, he shows the animal being prepared in the presence of Manoah and his wife.[1] **GP**

1. Lambert Jacobsz., *The Angel Preparing a Sacrificial Kid in the Presence of Manoah and His Wife* (photo RKD, The Hague). For the iconography of 'Manoah's sacrifice', see: Van Gent/ Pastoor 1991 & 1994, pp. 71-72. For Bleker, see cat. no. 23.

## 28  Samson and Delilah, *c.* 1612

[JUDGES 16:19]

Jacob Matham
*(Haarlem 1571 - Haarlem 1631)*
after Peter Paul Rubens
*(Siegen 1577 - Antwerp 1640)*

Engraving, 35.8 x 43.2 cm, state II (2)
**Inscr** (Dedication bottom left) 'Nob. et
ampliss. V.D. NICOLAO ROCOXIO / Equiti,
pluries Antverpiae Consuli, elegantiorû
omnium / apprime studioso, Iconem hanc in
aes à se incisa, cultus et ob- / servantiae causâ,
tû quòd archetijpa tabula artifice Pet. Pauli /
Rubenij manu depicta apud ipsûm cû
admiritatione spectatur, Mathâ. / L.M.D.D.'
**Caption** (bottom left) 'Cum privil. Sa. Caes.
M.'; (bottom centre) 'Qui genus humanum
superauit robore Sampsom / Femineis tandem
vincitur insidijs. / Sic et femineâ vis Herculis
arte doloque / Occidit. ô summis sexus inique
viris!'; (bottom right) 'Pet. Pauolo Rubens
pinxit / Ja. Matham sculp. et excud.'
Teylers Museum, Haarlem (inv. no. VS I: 41)
**Lit** Holl. XI, p. 216, no. 11; TIB IV, p. 179,
no. 194(180); Voorhelm Schneevoogt 1873,
p. 6, no. 41; Stechow 1927, p. 139; Van den
Wijngaert 1940, pp. 7, 73, no. 437; Van Gelder
1950-51, pp. 120-121; Haverkamp Begemann
1959, p. 7; D'Hulst/ Vandenven 1989, pp. 108,
111; Cologne/ Vienna/ Antwerp 1992, pp. 251-
252, 594-595, no. 186.1; Van Gent/ Pastoor
1991 & 1994, p. 72; Antwerp 1993, pp. 6, 17,
no. 10.1; Münster 1994, p. 312, no. 89

Judges 16 relates how Delilah allowed herself to be bribed by the lords of the Philistines to entice Samson to tell the secret of his great strength. Prey to her seductive powers, he finally divulged that it was because his head has never been shaved. Delilah then lulled Samson to sleep in her lap, called a servant and had him shave off the seven locks of Samson's head.

The print shows Samson, his senses befuddled by drink, lying at Delilah's feet with his head in her lap. A Philistine is cutting off his hair in the light of a candle held by an old lady who, in type, is reminiscent of the brothel madams portrayed in Northern Netherlandish art. Philistine soldiers stand in the doorway, waiting for a sign that it is safe to overpower Samson.

The caption reminds us that Samson, a man whose exceptional strength places him above his fellows, is ultimately brought down by a woman's cunning - as is Hercules, whose power is also broken by female wiles and artfulness. In Rubens' innovative treatment, these powers of seduction are emphasized by Delilah's naked breasts and the brothelkeeper-type as well as the statuette of Venus and Cupid in a niche in the background.

Matham is regarded as one of the first Northern Netherlandish engravers who reproduced designs by contemporary Baroque artists such as Rubens and Moreelse.[1] In mirror-image, his work reproduces an oil sketch for a painting Rubens made around 1609 for Nicolaas Rockox, burgomaster of Antwerp. Matham's engraving presumably originates from around 1612, the year in which Rubens possibly visited Haarlem.[2] It had a profound influence on the iconography of the Samson and Delilah theme as treated in the Northern Netherlands. Rubens' invention became widely known through Matham's engraving. It was imitated by numerous artists. These included the Delft painter Christiaen van Couwenbergh, who used it as the basis for the composition he produced *c.* 1630 (fig. 28.1).[3] **PvdC/GP**

**28.1**
Christiaen van Couwenbergh, *Samson and Delilah, c.* 1630, canvas, 156 x 196 cm, Dordrechts Museum, Dordrecht

1. *Cf.* Widerkehr 1993, p. 251.
2. De Smet 1977. See also Van Gelder 1950-51, pp. 119-121 and Haverkamp Begemann 1959, p. 7. Rubens' painting was intended for the home of mayor Rockox, as Matham notes in the print's dedication. The painting is now in the National Gallery, London; the oil sketch in the Cincinnati Art Museum, Cincinnati (Ohio). See: D'Hulst/ Vandenven 1989, pp. 24, 107-115, nos 31-31b.
3. Amsterdam 1991-92, pp. 238-239, no. 23; Münster 1994, p. 266, no. 36. For the print's further influence, see: Van Gent/ Pastoor 1991 & 1994, pp. 72, 81.

## 29 The History of Ruth, 1576-78
[RUTH 1-4]

Hendrick Goltzius
(*Mühlbracht 1558 - Haarlem 1617*)

a  Orpah Leaving Ruth and Naomi
b  Ruth Gleaning Grain in the Fields of Boaz
c  Ruth and Boaz in the Threshing Shed
d  Boaz and the Elders

Series of four numbered engravings
*c.* 21.7 x 27.5 cm, state I (5)
**Inscr** (sheet 1) '1576'; (sheet 2) '1576'; (sheet 3)
'1577'; (sheet 4) 'Henricus Golssius inuent et
sculptor 1578'
**Captions** (sheet 1) 'Deserit Arpa socrum,
sequitur Ruth fortis, et inquit / Est meus et
populus, et Deus ille tuus.', 'Die Arpa ein
Moabitin, ir swigerfraw lest ziehen hin / Ruth
an Naemi helt trew vnd fest, an ir Gott
widrumb thut das best.'; (sheet 2) 'Ad quem
venisti faueat tibi Joua, Boosus. / Inquit et en
spicas sedula Ruta legit.', 'Als Ruth die ahren
laß im feldt, / sprach Boos, Gott dir alls
vergeldt. / Vnnd thu an dir Barmhertzigkeit, /
Wie du an Naemi thon hast weit.'; (sheet 3)
'Gnata (Boos inquit) felix et sancta vocaris /
Quad non es Iuuenes Ruta secuta procos.',
'Gesegnet mein Tochter (Boos sprach) dem
herren Gott der du nit gach / Gefolgt bist den
Jungen geseln, viellieber den Herrn hast
kennen woln.; (sheet 4) 'Qui fundum redimet,
Rutam quoq[ue] fumere debet. / Suscitet vt
nomen, chare propinque tuum .', 'Wer kaufft
das velt, sol sich gzimmen, das er Ruth auch
zum Weib Nemmen / Das dem verstorbnen
erweckt werd, ein saamen auff sein Grundt vnd
Erd.'
Museum Boijmans Van Beuningen, Rotterdam
(inv. nos BdH 8063, 8064, 8065, 8066)
**Lit** Holl. VIII, p. 2, nos 3-6; TIB III, pp. 12-15,
nos 4-7; TIB III (Commentary), pp. 12-16,
nos 004-007; Hirschmann 1919, pp. 32-34;
Hirschmann 1921, pp. 4-5, nos 3-6; Mielke
1979, p. 50, no. 60; Baarsen 1992, pp. 94-97;
Venlo 1993, pp. 85-88, no. 27; Münster 1994,
pp. 312-313, no. 90

This series of prints by Hendrick Goltzius summarizes the principal events of the life of Ruth in four scenes. The first print in the series shows Orpah bidding farewell to Ruth and Naomi (cat. no. 29a).[1] When Naomi left Moab following the death of her husband, Elimelech, and her two sons, both daughters-in-law decided to accompany her. Naomi insisted they remain, so Orpah returned to her parent's home; but Ruth refused to abandon her mother-in-law (Ruth 1:6-18). In the print Naomi and her faithful daughter-in-law Ruth are depicted on the left, turning towards Orpah, on the right. Simultaneously, in the background, the women are shown dividing their baggage and saying their farewells.

The theme of the second print is 'Ruth gleaning grain in the fields of Boaz' (cat. no. 29b). To ensure that they had enough to eat Ruth asked permission to glean the ears of grain dropped by the harvesters. Visiting his field, the landowner, Boaz, a kinsman of Elimelech, saw the industrious Ruth and gave her special privileges in recognition of her loyalty to Naomi (Ruth 2:3-13). In the foreground Ruth is kneeling before Boaz, holding a bundle of grain. Boaz bows slightly towards her and offers a protective gesture with his left hand.

The next episode, 'Ruth and Boaz in the Threshing Shed', is depicted in the third print of the series (cat. no. 29c). It was time for the winnowing of the barley, and Ruth lay down to sleep on the threshing floor at Boaz' feet. When he awoke she reminded him of his family responsibility towards her. As the childless wife of a deceased relative, he was obliged to marry her in order to keep the property within the family and to ensure that the family line continued (Ruth 3:14).

Finally, the fourth print depicts the episode in which Boaz redeems the property of Elimelech and his sons (cat. no. 29d). Having first given a closer relative of Ruth's the opportunity to perform this duty, he obtained permission from the ten elders of the people to marry her (Ruth 4:1-12).

The first states of the first three prints in the series are dated 1576 (cat. nos 29a and 29b) and 1577 (cat. no. 29c), thereby qualifying as Goltzius' earliest dated works. The artist therefore began the series before moving to Haarlem (summer 1577), in his German period. He drew inspiration for the depiction of the story in part from a series of engravings on the same themes designed by Adriaen de Weerdt.[2] Both series influenced the iconography of the Book of Ruth in Dutch art in the seventeenth century. Karel van Mander also appreciated De Weerdt's Ruth series, praising the prints in his *Schilder-Boeck* for their landscape backgrounds.[3] **JvG**

1. For this theme see: Tümpel 1978.
2. Attributed to Philips Galle: Holl. VII, p. 75, nos 76-79; TIB LVI, pp. 26-29, nos 008:1-4. This series is part of Gerard de Jode's *Thesaurus* (1579 and 1585) and was later reprinted in Visscher's *Theatrum Biblicum* (cat. no. 58). *Cf.* Mielke 1975, p. 79, no. 19.
3. Van Mander/ Miedema 1994-95, Vol. 1, p. 178 (fol. 230r): '...the *Story of Ruth* in which some handsome pieces of ground appear' (*cf.* Baarsen 1992, p. 94). For the influence on the Ruth iconography see: Van Gent/ Pastoor 1991 & 1994, pp. 83-85.

**a** Orpah Leaving Ruth and Naomi

**b** Ruth Gleaning Grain in the Fields of Boaz

**c** Ruth and Boaz in the Threshing Shed

**d** Boaz and the Elders

## 30 Bathsheba Combing her Hair, *c.* 1615

[2 SAM. 11:2]

Willem Buytewech
*(Rotterdam 1591/92 - Rotterdam 1624)*

Etching and drypoint, 15.5 x 10.4 cm, state II
(3)
**Inscr** 'WB; CJV [Claes Jansz. Visscher] exc.'
Museum Boijmans Van Beuningen
(inv. no. 15045)
**Lit** Holl. IV, p. 54, no. 2; TIB LIII, p. 34-35,
no. 002; Van Gelder 1931, pp. 54, 66-67, no. 19;
Haverkamp Begemann 1959, p. 8, 10ff, 46, 172,
no. vG 19; Kunstreich 1959, p. 50; Haverkamp
Begemann 1962, pp. 61, 73, no. vG 19;
Rotterdam/ Paris 1974-75, pp. 85-86, no. 111;
Münster 1994, p. 313, no. 91

The story of David and Bathsheba, an extremely popular topic among painters and engravers,[1] is narrated summarily in the second Book of Samuel: 'And it came to pass in an eveningtide, that David arose from off his bed, and walked upon the roof of the king's house: and from the roof he saw a woman washing herself; and the woman was very beautiful to look upon. And David sent and enquired after the woman, and one said, Is not this Bathsheba, the daughter of Eliam, the wife of Uriah the Hittite? And David sent messengers, and took her; and she came in unto him, and he lay with her' (2 Sam. 11:2-4). Around 1615 Buytewech produced three etchings with Bathsheba. These depict three successive scenes from the story (*cf.* cat. no. 31 and fig. 16, p. 26).

The first shows Bathsheba in profile but with her head turned to the viewer. Positioned well into the foreground, she occupies the composition's vertical axis. Behind Bathsheba and to her left we see her garden and an open landscape, to her right the king's house and David observing her from the roof. Although turned to the viewer, Bathsheba is nevertheless entirely occupied by what she is doing and her gaze is directed downwards. Like David himself we are fully aware of her beauty. He finds it irresistible although, at the particular moment depicted, the story's outcome still appears to be entirely open. **AT**

1. *Cf.* Van Gent 1991 & 1994, pp. 91, 93-94.

**Bathsheba Receiving David's Letter, 1615**

[2 SAM. 11:4]

Willem Buytewech
*(Rotterdam 1591/92 - Rotterdam 1624)*

Etching, 17.2 x 15.7 cm, only state
**Inscr** 'WB 1615'; 'BERSABE'
Rijksprentenkabinet, Rijksmuseum,
Amsterdam
**Lit** Holl. IV, p. 55, no. 3; TIB LIII, p. 36, no. 003;
Van Gelder 1931, pp. 54, 67, no. 20;
Haverkamp Begemann 1959, pp. 8, 11, 46, 172-
173, no. vG 20; Kunstreich 1959, pp. 50-51;
Haverkamp Begemann 1962, pp. 73, 74, no. vG
20; Rotterdam/ Paris 1974-75, pp. 86-87,
no. 112; Münster 1994, p. 313, no. 92

Bathsheba and the maid-servant, who is about to give her David's letter face each other across a small fountain. At this juncture the servant is still holding the letter, Bathsheba knows nothing of its contents and she is yet to transgress. Seated on a rocky plinth covered with cloth, she looks inquiringly at the servant appearing from the left. Bathsheba occupies the right of the composition, the servant - whose lower half is concealed by the fountain - the left. Bathsheba's nakedness and youth are in stark contrast to the appearance of the old lady, who is draped in a thick cloak that reaches right up to her neck. A strong chiaroscuro effect pervades the representation. Bathsheba's body is half light, half dark, with light and dark areas also alternating in the surroundings and the portrayal of the servant. The print's dark centre contrasts with light sections along the sides as well.

Beside cat. nos. 30 and 31 Buytewech devoted a third etching to the Bathsheba motif. It shows the following incident in the story - Bathsheba actually reading David's letter and apprising herself of its contents (fig. 16, p. 26). **AT**

## 32    David in Prayer, 1652
[2 SAM. 12:15-17 OR 24:16-17]

Rembrandt
(*Leiden 1606 - Amsterdam 1669*)

Etching and drypoint, 14.3 x 9.3 cm, state I (3)
**Inscr** 'Rembrandt.*f.* 1652'
Museum het Rembrandthuis, Amsterdam
**Lit** Holl. XVIII, p. 20, no. B. 41; TIB L, p. 29,
no. 41; Münz 1952, Vol. 2, p. 88, no. 182;
Rotermund 1963, p. 100; Tümpel 1970, no. 25;
Filedt Kok 1972, p. 49, no. B. 41; Hamburg
1983, pp. 330-331, no. 197; Münster 1994,
p. 314, no. 93; Amsterdam 1995, p. 30, no. B. 41

**32.1**
Lucas van Leyden, *David in Prayer*, c. 1507,
engraving, 15.8 x 11 cm, Rijksprentenkabinet,
Amsterdam

This unusual, single-figure history scene shows King David in his
bedchamber. The composition is almost entirely filled with David kneeling
before his bed, a harp on the floor and a book on a stool. His hands clasped
in fervent prayer, David gazes into the dark recesses of the bed as if they
harbour an apparition visible to him alone. His face is enlightened.

With this subject, too, Rembrandt was inspired by one of the great master
engravers, in this instance Lucas van Leyden, who, in two of his prints,
depicted a penitent David (fig. 32.1).[1] The story is that the king has
conducted a census in order to reform the army but, in doing so, has gone
against God's will. The Lord then sends a pestilence upon the people of
Israel. On seeing the angel 'that smote the people', David beseeches God to
spare them and punish him alone, since he is the only one to have sinned
(2 Samuel 24:1-17). In Lucas van Leyden's prints David is depicted praying in
a field. As a symbol of punishment, the angel of pestilence or the figure of
God bearing arrows appears. If Rembrandt intended to represent the same
scene, he transferred it to an interior, which was entirely typical of him.

The Book of Samuel also contains another instance of David doing
penance. This is when the illegitimate child he has fathered with Bathsheba
is struck down by God with an eventually fatal illness. David fasts and
beseeches God that his son may be saved, and even 'lay all night upon the
earth' (2 Samuel 12:13-17). Rotermund asserted that this is the scene that
Rembrandt is depicting.[2] In this interpretation the bed could then be an
allusion to David's adultery.[3] **PJ/AT**

1. B. 28 (see fig. 32.1) and B. 29; New Hollstein, Lucas van Leyden, pp. 57-58, nos 28-29.
2. Rotermund 1963, p. 100. *Cf.* Tümpel 1970, no. 25.
3. Hamburg 1983, pp. 330-331, no. 197.

## 33 Solomon's Idolatry, after 1652
[I KINGS 11:1-8]

Jan Lievens?
*(Leiden 1607 - Amsterdam 1674)*

Etching, 7.2 x 5.2 cm, only state
Museum het Rembrandthuis, Amsterdam
**Lit** Holl. XI, p. 6, no. 3; Ackley 1981, pp. 147-148, no. 95

King Solomon kept an enormous harem. Apart from the daughter of Pharaoh he had another seven hundred wives and three hundred concubines. Many of these were from neighbouring kingdoms. Under their influence Solomon became increasingly attracted to pagan cults as he grew older, even though God had specifically forbidden him to worship other deities.[1]

Here King Solomon is kneeling in prayer at an altar surmounted by an idol, led by one of his wives. To his left are vessels of precious wares for a sacrifice. The scene is set in a dark, curtained interior in which other women can be distinguished. Solomon's genuflection and the surrounding drapery are reminiscent of Rembrandt's etching *David in Prayer* of 1652 (cat. no. 32).

The gloomy effect is obtained by working the plate with a fanciful pattern of deeply bitten crosshatching. Only Solomon's back and the back of his head, the left arm of the foremost woman and parts of the idol have been left unworked, so that a dramatic, spotlight-effect is achieved. The illuminated parts highlight the diagonal of the composition and lead the eye from Solomon to the statue.

The small dimensions and execution of this print closely resemble etchings attributed to Lievens, namely the *Banishment of Hagar* (Holl. 1) and the *Scholar in his Study* (Holl. 85). Ackley maintains, on stylistic grounds, that these prints, together with a slightly smaller plate depicting the *Adoration of the Magi*, were probably made by a pupil of Rembrandt, and suggests Gerbrand van den Eeckhout as a candidate.[2] Nevertheless, an attribution to Lievens cannot, in my opinion, be entirely discounted. The deeply bitten lines and the manner of hatching are somewhat similar to Lievens' signed etching of *St John the Evangelist on Patmos* (Holl. 9). **ME**

1. For the subject, see: Van Gent 1991 & 1994, p. 96.
2. Ackley 1981, pp. 147, 148.

## 34 Landscape with the Unfaithful Prophet of Judah, *c.* 1660
[1 Kings 13:11-29]

Anthonie Waterloo
(Lille 1609 - Utrecht 1690)

No. 3 from a series of six: *Landscapes with Old Testament Scenes*
Etching, 29.6 x 25.3 cm, state III (3)
**Inscr** 'A.W. f. in'
Rijksprentenkabinet, Rijksmuseum, Amsterdam (inv. no. RP-P-OB 61464)
**Lit** TIB II, p. 124, no. 133 (135); TIB II (Commentary), pp. 161-163, no. 133; Ackley 1981, p. 229

**34.1**
Antonio Tempesta, *The Man of God Slain by a Lion*, *c.* 1600, etching, 6.7 x 6.7 cm, Prentenkabinet der Rijksuniversiteit, Leiden

The story of the man of God from Judah, or the 'unfaithful prophet', takes place after the division of the kingdom following Solomon's death. He had offended by ignoring God's prohibition and travelling to the city of Beth-el, eating bread there and drinking water. Continuing his journey on an ass, he was attacked by a lion, which slew him: 'And his carcass was cast in the way, and the ass stood by it, the lion also stood by the carcass' (1 Kings 13:24).

The tale of the man of God first appeared in Dutch graphic art in a four-part series by Dirck Volkertsz. Coornhert after Maarten van Heemskerck dating from *c.* 1550-52 and was subsequently painted several times by the Pre-Rembrandtists. However, the scene portrayed by Waterloo did not appear in Van Heemskerck's series, although it did occur in various sixteenth-century Bible illustrations.[1] For example, an etching by Antonio Tempesta includes a cursory depiction of the carcass, lion and ass (fig. 34.1).[2]

Waterloo placed the scene portrayed by Tempesta in a wide landscape with a city, below left. A rather unprepossessing lion guards the body of the prophet; the ass is shown a little further away, in the background. Waterloo's print was part of a six-piece series of *Landscapes with Old Testament Scenes*. Other landscape artists, such as Breenbergh, also used the man of God theme to provide staffage for landscapes.[3]

Only a few of the 128-odd landscape etchings by Waterloo are settings for history scenes. The artist, who had come to Amsterdam with his parents as a child and had later settled in Maarsseveen, travelled extensively. From the 1650s he drew particular inspiration from landscapes of the east of the country (Utrecht, Gelderland) and the Lower Rhine area.[4] **PvdC**

**1.** Van Gent 1991 & 1994, pp. 99-101. Coornhert after Van Heemskerck: New Hollstein, Heemskerck, nos 123-126.
**2.** TIB XXXV, p. 51, no. 189 (128).
**3.** Van Gent 1991 & 1994, pp. 100-101. Waterloo's series: TIB II (commentary), pp. 161-165, nos 131-136. The group of figures in the *Landscape with the Banishment of Hagar* from this series with Old Testament scenes has been copied after an etching by Pieter Holsteyn from 1659. *Cf.* Van der Coelen 1996-97, figs 7-8.
**4.** Ackley 1981, pp. 170-171, 229-230. *Cf.* Amsterdam 1993-94B, pp. 120-121, nos 61-62. For a biography of Waterloo see: Kahn-Gerzon 1992; on the publishing of his prints see: Schuckman 1993.

## 35 Elijah Fed by the Ravens, 1604
[I Kings 17:2-7]

Jan Saenredam
(Zaandam 1565 - Assendelft 1607)
after Abraham Bloemaert
(Gorinchem 1566 - Utrecht 1651)

No. 3 from a series of four engravings: *The History of Ahijah and Elijah*
25.3 x 19.3 cm, state II (2)
**Inscr** 'Abraham, Bloemaert inuen, / Joan, Saenredam sculp. et excudebat / A[nn]o 1604.'
**Caption** (by T. Schrevelius) 'Jusserat irriguas Carithi torrentis ad vndas / Thesbiten latitare Deus, volucreq[ue] ministram / Et Cererem, et pingues rostro vectare ferinas; / Cum lux alma venit, Phoeboq[ue] cadente recedit. / TSchreuelius'
Rijksprentenkabinet, Rijksmuseum, Amsterdam (inv. no. RP-P-OB 10-521)
**Lit** Holl. II, p. 68, no. 524; Holl. XXIII, p. 15, no. 14; TIB IV, p. 331, no. 22; Roethlisberger 1993, pp. 128, no. 81; Münster 1994, pp. 314-315, no. 94

**35.3** Elijah Fed by the Ravens

**35.1**
Jan Saenredam after Abraham Bloemaert, *Ahijah and Jeroboam*, 1604, engraving, c. 25.5 x 19.5 cm, Rijksprentenkabinet, Amsterdam

**35.2**
Jan Saenredam after Abraham Bloemaert, *Ahijah's Prediction*, 1604, engraving, c. 25.5 x 19.5 cm, Rijksprentenkabinet, Amsterdam

**35.3**
Jan Saenredam after Abraham Bloemaert, *Elijah Fed by the Ravens*, 1604, engraving, 25.3 x 19.3 cm, Rijksprentenkabinet, Amsterdam

**35.4**
Jan Saenredam after Abraham Bloemaert, *Elisha Taking the Robe of Elijah*, 1604, engraving, c. 25.5 x 19.5 cm, Rijksprentenkabinet, Amsterdam

Ahijah tore his cloak into twelve pieces and gave ten of them to Jeroboam. He told him to see these as symbolizing ten of the twelve tribes of Israel that God will rend from the hand of Solomon and present to Jeroboam, the apostate king's young adversary (fig. 35.1; 1 Kings 11:29-39). Sitting on a bank of earth along the way, Jeroboam is directing his attention to one of the pieces Ahijah is offering. Jeroboam already holds pieces of the coat in his right hand while, standing to his right, Ahijah has the rest of the garment slung over his left arm. Immediately behind Jeroboam is the shadowy, cleft trunk of a half-dead tree.

When Jeroboam's son fell sick he sent his wife to Ahijah to ask him what was to become of the child. Ahijah prophesied misfortune and death for Jeroboam, himself now sinful and apostate, and his family. Those members of the family who die in the city will be eaten by dogs, those dying in the country by 'fowls of the air' (fig. 35.2; 1 Kings:1-16). Ahijah, in the lower right-hand side of the composition, is seated beneath a shadowy, cleft tree-

**35.1** Ahijah and Jeroboam

**35.2** Ahijah's Prediction

**35.4** Elisha Taking the Robe of Elijah

trunk. He raises his left hand in horror at a young man's corpse being savaged by two dogs. A crown lying close to the dead man identifies him as a member of the royal house of Jeroboam. Behind the body the left side of the scene is occupied by the crumbling masonry of a mighty wall. Ahijah's raised right hand indicates the background, where three birds circle around the lifeless body of another man. A fourth bird already appears to be picking at the corpse.

In the third print an elderly, bald-headed and bearded Elijah is seated in the lower right-hand side (cat. no. 35). He has raised his right hand to take bread out of the beak of a swooping raven. A second bird, also bearing food, is approaching. A brook flows at Elijah's feet. The scene is framed by gnarled tree-trunks and leafy boughs.

The fourth print in the series (fig. 35.4) depicts a scene from the story of Elijah and Elisha. Elijah tells Elisha that God has prophesied his - Elijah's - death. Together they head towards the River Jordan, which splits and becomes fordable when Elijah beats its waters with his cloak. While 'a chariot of fire with steeds of fire' separates the two prophets from one another, with Elijah ascending to heaven in the chariot, Elijah's spirit passes into Elisha (2 Kings 1:2-14). The print shows Elijah's ascent in the chariot. At the composition's centre Elisha, half-kneeling with his arms aloft, is turned towards the heaven-bound vehicle. Sliding down between his arms is Elijah's cloak, which Elisha will later use again to cross the Jordan. In the foreground the right side is delimited by massive, soaring and partially shaded trees and tree-trunks.

All four scenes depict episodes from prophets' lives. While the subject of the first two prints is the rise of a divinely appointed king of the Israelites and his subsequent fall, the second pair deals with the divinely providential life of the prophet Elijah. Given their stylistic similarities the four prints are traditionally regarded as an integral series, which would also appear to be indicated by their format and captions.[1] Having said this however, the artistic treatment of the composition suggests two sets of pendants. The first print's compositional centre is framed by the trees and figures, the effect of which is to emphasize Jeroboam. The figure of Ahijah juxtaposed to him, coupled with the tree-trunk, yields a triangle that reinforces the stability of the composition. In the second print the motif's constituent parts are arranged at the side and aligned with the scene in the background. The figures' alignment with the crumbling masonry and tree-trunk is clearly evident, an effect that highlights the composition's severely vertical orientation. The ruined wall as well as the trees - which, to a degree, are in dark shadow - are a portent to the viewer of the fateful outcome of the scenes portrayed.

The positive nature of the scenes depicted in the third and fourth print, led to the artist's departure from the traditional symbolization in favour of a freer composition that emphasizes the diagonal elements. The surrounding scenery is depicted here for its own sake. **GdB**

---

1. The numbers '3' and '4' on the second pair were only added in state II. *Cf.* Roethlisberger 1993, pp. 128, 129.

## 36  Elijah and the Widow of Zarephath, 1604

[1 KINGS 17:8-10]

**Jan Saenredam**
(*Zaandam 1565 - Assendelft 1607*)
after **Abraham Bloemaert**
(*Gorinchem 1566 - Utrecht 1651*)

Engraving, 42.2 x 31.9 cm, state I (5)
**Inscr** 'Abraham Bloemaert / inuentor / Joan. Saenredam sculp. / et excudebat. 1604'
**Caption** (by T. Schrevelius) 'Coelitus edocta qui pastus ab alite vates / Venerat ad portas parva Sarepta tuas: / Munus ait viduae ramalia sparsa legenti / Egiguum gratus sed Cereale peto. / Cui mulier, tesler [testor] viventis conscia Jovae / Numina, et aeternum quem colis ipse Deum. / Dona laboratae Cereris non vlla supersunt / Spes oleum et vitae parca farina meae / Pone metum mulier, quin hinc abis, inquit Helias / Et mihi, mox vobis liba parata refers! / Nam Deus Abramidum nostri miseratus ab alto / Hac ait, hac certa percipe dicta fide: / Vrna rinascentis cumulo foecunda farina / Stillantisq[ue] olei vena perennis erit. / Donec pacatum laxabit nubila caelum / Et granis effusis decidet imber aquis. / TSchreuelius' Rijksprentenkabinet, Rijksmuseum, Amsterdam (inv. no. RP-P-OB 10-516)
**Lit** Holl. II, p. 68, no. 521; Holl. XXIII, p. 17, no. 16; TIB IV, p. 328, no. 19(226); Hamann 1936, pp. 24, 25; Rockville 1981, pp. 80-81, no. 54; Van Gent 1991 & 1994, p. 101; Roethlisberger 1993, pp. 126-127, no. 78; Münster 1994, p. 316, no. 95

Arriving at Zarephath, Elijah met a widow gathering sticks at the gates of the city and asked her for water and bread. Despite her poverty she helped the prophet, taking him into her house. When her son later fell seriously ill, Elijah revived him (1 Kings 17:8-24). Saenredam's print after Bloemaert shows the moment at which the prophet and widow meet. Inclined slightly forward, Elijah is addressing her. She, accompanied by her son, is kneeling to grasp the sticks from the ground. At the same time this posture expresses her attitude of humility towards the prophet.

As with the *Banishment of Hagar and Ishmael* (cat. no. 8) the artist devotes particular attention to the surrounding architecture and scenery, which is brought to life with a host of details such as parts of buildings, fencing and bushes. That Bloemaert was the son of an architect is certainly not without relevance in this connection. Lastman, Pynas and Moeyaert were later to borrow architectural motifs typical of Bloemaert's work as reproduced in cat. nos 8 and 36.[1] **GdB**

---

1. Roethlisberger 1993, p. 127. For the iconography of the subject and the influence exerted by the print, see also: Van Gent 1991 & 1994, p. 101.

## 37 The Children of Beth-el Attacked by Bears, 1653

[2 KINGS 2: 22-25]

Constantijn Daniel van Renesse
(Maarssen 1626 - Eindhoven 1680)

Etching, 17.8 x 24.2 cm, only state
**Inscr** 'C A Renesse: fe. / et inventor / 1653'
Rijksprentenkabinet, Rijksmuseum,
Amsterdam (inv. no. RP-P-OB 12819)
**Lit** Holl. XX, p. 9, no. 2; Vermeeren 1978, p. 11;
Zilkens 1982, pp. 90-92

In a delightful landscape a gruesome episode is enacted. On the right children are attacked by wild bears while on the left a bearded old man appears to walk away from the scene unmoved. It is an event in the life of the prophet Elisha. Like Elijah, his master, Elisha was able to perform miracles. On his way from the city of Jericho to Beth-el, a large group of youngsters began following him. They were making fun of him, ridiculing his baldness. Elisha turned round and cursed them. Immediately two bears came out of the woods. The children had no time to escape and the wild animals managed to maul forty-two of them. The print shows how Elisha, wrapped in Elijah's cloak, looks round just as the children are attacked. The city in the background is probably meant to be Jericho. The bears are illuminated by beams of heavenly light.

The etching is dated 1653, the last year from which prints by Van Renesse are known. This is probably due to his rather busy schedule as town secretary in Eindhoven, an appointment made on 25 August 1653.[1] Between 1649 - the year in which he was taught by Rembrandt as an amateur pupil - and 1653 Van Renesse is only known to have made seventeen prints, using etching and drypoint technique. Most are portraits or genre pieces. Only two show scenes from the Bible, both from the Old Testament.

In the seventeenth century, few Dutch print artists actually depicted the children of Beth-el. Van Renesse's choice is remarkable. The Old Testament stories about Elijah and Elisha were popular among Rembrandt's predecessors and pupils, although mainly depicted in paintings.[2] Although these artists often drew inspiration for their compositions from sixteenth-century prints, they rarely felt the need to make their own prints of the stories. While the engravings Jan Saenredam made after Abraham Bloemaert reveal a clear interest in the graphic depiction of the miraculous lives of Elijah and Elisha (cat. nos 35 and 36), the artists of Rembrandt's circle appear to have cared little for the subject.

According to Zilkens, Rembrandt contributed to this print by Van Renesse. This is unlikely, however. All the figures in the *Children of Beth-el Attacked by Bears* - even the youngsters shown in the foreground - have similar, rather rounded forms and are evenly shaded with delicate hatching, completely in the style of Van Renesse's other prints, as well as his drawings and paintings. Moreover, the landscape elements are cautiously drawn, without any particular virtuosity.[3] **AH**

1. For Van Renesse see: Vermeeren 1978; Vermeeren 1979; on his prints see: Ackley 1981, p. 215; Zilkens 1982, pp. 83-99.
2. See: Münster 1994, pp. 98-101, 162-164, 282-285.
3. A noticeable aspect is that both the appearance and position of the foremost bear are similar to that of the rather unimpressive lion in Rembrandt's etching *St Jerome Reading* of 1634 (B. 100). The figure of Elisha resembles the one in an etching of the same subject in a picture Bible by Matthaeus Merian the Elder (1625-1627).

## 38 The History of Jonah, c. 1621

[JONAH 1-4]

Jan van de Velde II
(*Rotterdam or Delft c. 1593 - 1641 Enkhuizen*)
after Willem Buytewech
(*Rotterdam 1591/92 - Rotterdam 1624*)

Four numbered prints
Etching and burin (sheet 1 and 4), engraving (sheet 2 and 3), c. 19 x 11 cm
**Inscr** (sheet 1, state I [3]) 'WB. in. J. v. velde. fec.'; (sheet 2, state II [3]) 'J. v. Velde fec. WB in'; (sheet 3, state II [2]) 'J. v. velde fec. CJV excu. WB.in.'; (sheet 4, state II [2]) 'J. v. velde fec. WB. in.'
**Captions** (sheet 1) 'Redditus at terrae Niniven terroribus implet, / Aßyriosq[ue] viros praemonet exitij.'; (sheet 2) 'Dum detrectat opus Desertor Numinis almi: / Bellua praecipitem, forte jubente, vorat.'; (sheet 3) 'Divino Niniven jussu legatur Jonas / Sontibus irati jussa referre Dei'; '3'; (sheet 4) 'Invocat hinc Lachesin, quod poenituiße videret, / Peccati Populum, supplicyq[ue] Deum'; '4' Rijksprentenkabinet, Rijksmuseum, Amsterdam (inv. nos 15293-15297)

Jan van de Velde II's series after Willem Buytewech depicts the story of the prophet Jonah in four prints. The first scene shows Jonah being instructed to go to the city of Nineveh and preach to its sinful citizens (Jonah 1:1-2; cat. no. 38a). In a barren landscape by the sea, Jonah is depicted kneeling reverently, dressed in a simple garment which, together with the book on the left in the foreground, identifies him as a prophet. He looks up and receives the divine message, symbolized by four cherubs on clouds around a shaft of light.

Jonah tried to evade the divine command, fleeing to Tarshish by boat. But the Lord caused a mighty storm which threatened to sink the ship. Jonah confessed what he had done to the crew and ordered them to throw him overboard (Jonah 1:3-16). This is the moment shown in the second print (cat. no. 38b). With consummate skill Buytewech uses conflicting diagonal movement and powerful chiaroscuro effects to depict the perilous situation. The ship seems about to break up in the tempest; one of the sails has come loose and collapsed. The six-man crew, muscular sailors desperately trying to save their ship, cast the disobedient prophet overboard. Below right is the awesome, gaping mouth of a gigantic fish, about to swallow Jonah. But this sea monster, sent by God, would be Jonah's salvation. Having spent three days and three nights in the belly of the fish he is vomited onto dry land (Jonah 2). Unusually, this moment, one of the most popular in Jonah iconography, is not included in the series.

Jonah changed his mind and decided to go to Nineveh to carry out God's command, prophesying that the city would be overturned in forty days (Jonah 3:3-4). This is the subject of the third print (cat. no. 38c). Jonah is standing in the centre. Strong and determined, he explains what awaits the

a The Calling of Jonah

b Jonah Cast into the Sea

**Lit** Holl. IV, p. 77, nos 18-21; Holl. XXXIII, pp. 8-9, nos 2-5; Franken/ Van der Kellen 1968, pp. 46-47, nos 50-53; Haverkamp Begemann 1959, pp. 8, 193-195, nos CP 24-27; Kunstreich 1959, pp. 51-52; Rotterdam/ Paris 1974-75, pp. 134-137, nos 167-170; Groningen 1994, pp. 16-17, 24, no. 7

a   The Calling of Jonah
b   Jonah Cast into the Sea
c   Jonah Preaching at Nineveh
d   Jonah Sitting under the Gourd

Ninevites and their city. Various imposing buildings are shown in the background: 'Nineveh was an exceedingly great city of three days' journey' (Jonah 3:3).

Contrary to expectations, the Ninevites repented. They did penance and God resolved to spare the city. But that made Jonah angry; he felt his life no longer had any meaning now that his prophesies of doom were to remain unfulfilled. So the seer built a shelter outside the city and sat down to watch what would happen. God decided to teach him a lesson. He prepared a tree, allowing it to grow overnight to shield Jonah from the sun. But immediately he allowed the tree to wither. When Jonah started to complain about the fate of the tree, God was able to explain that in that case, he had had every reason to spare an entire city (Jonah 4). In the fourth print Jonah is shown under his shelter (cat. no. 38d). Disgruntled and wringing his hands, he complains about his fate. In line with tradition, Buytewech has depicted the tree that shades Jonah as a gourd. The bright rays of light indicate that the plant's fast growth and its sudden huge size are the work of God.

An important contribution to the Jonah iconography came from series by Maarten van Heemskerck and Maarten de Vos. The former produced two

Divino Niniven jussu legatur Jonas
Sontibus irati jussa referro Dei.

WB.in.3

3 . J.D.Velde fec. Ŧ. excu.

Invocat sinc Lachesin, quod pœnituisse videret;
Peccati Populum, supplicyq̃ Deum.

J.v.velde.fec.

WB.in.

4

**c** Jonah Preaching at Nineveh

**d** Jonah Sitting under the Gourd

series about Jonah, the latter designed no less than four.[1] Buytewech's prints
were influenced by these series, but he gave the story his own unique vision.
The second print showing 'Jonah Cast into the Sea' (cat. no. 38b) reveals
similarities with De Vos' depiction in the 1585 *Thesaurus* (fig. 9, p. 46).
However, Buytewech shows the scene in close up, thereby increasing the
drama: the emphasis is entirely on the horrified crew and the dreadful fish.
The unusually narrow, upright format enabled Buytewech to achieve some
remarkable compositions. The first two sheets, with their use of the
diagonal, have a powerful Baroque character, while the others, with their
predominantly vertical lines, exude a sense of calm.[2] **PvdC**

**1.** Van Heemskerck: New Hollstein, Heemskerck, nos 174-177, 179-182. De Vos: Holl. XLIV, pp. 40-44, nos 142-147,
148-153, 154-157, 158-161 (*Thesaurus*). For the *Thesaurus* series see: Mielke 1975, p. 81, no. 41. For the iconography of Jonah
and the fish, see: Judson 1964; Judson 1969.
**2.** Haverkamp Begemann (1959, pp. 193, 194) noted the influence of Rubens in the first two prints. Van de Velde's series
after Buytewech was later included in Schabaelje's *Grooten Emblemata Sacra* of 1654 (cat. no. 60).

## The History of Esther, 1564

[ESTHER 2-7]

Philips Galle
(Haarlem 1537 - Antwerp 1612)
after Maarten van Heemskerck
(Heemskerk 1498 - Haarlem 1574)

a  **Esther Crowned by Ahasuerus**
b  **Mordecai Overhearing the Treason of Bigthan and Teresh**
c  **Ahasuerus Commissions to Destroy the Jewish People**
d  **Esther's Servants Telling her of Mordecai's Refusal of the Raiment**
e  **Esther before Ahasuerus, Inviting him for a Banquet**
f  **Ahasuerus Consulting the Book of Chronicles**
g  **Ahasuerus Consulting Haman**
h  **Esther Accusing Haman at the Banquet**

Series of eight numbered engravings
c. 20.5 x 25 cm, state I (4)
**Inscr** (sheet 1) 'MARTINVS HEEMSKERCK INVENTOR PGALLE / FECIT / 1564';
(sheet 2-8) 'MHEE. IN.'
**Captions** (sheet 1) 'Assuerus fuluo placitam diademate velat / Reginam, & celebri tedas epulo ornat amatae. / HADR. IVN. [Hadrianus Junius]'; (sheet 2) 'In cruce perfidae meritas dependere poenas / Par fuit Eunuchos, Regem obtruncare paratos.'; (sheet 3) 'In recutitam odium gentem Haman vt expiet atrox, / Illorum in iugulos edictum sancit acerbum.'; (sheet 4) 'Excidium Regina tuae illaetabile gentis / Dum reputas, coelum supplex in vota fatigas.'; (sheet 5) 'Ast animum recipe, en tibi Rex gemmantia tendit / Sceptra ultro, expleti prima argumenta furoris.'; (sheet 6) 'Consulit annales, fido praeeunte anagnoste, / Rex, ubi non habitum virtuti discit honorem.'; (sheet 7) 'Inuehitur cultu regali, ostro que superbus / Mardochus, inuidiam que onerat, sed in hoste cruento.'; (sheet 8) 'Extremum te epulis Haman feralibus exple, / Te tua crux manet, hanc Nemesin gula fracta moratur.'
Museum Boijmans Van Beuningen, Rotterdam
**Lit** Kerrich 1829, pp. 29-30; Holl. VII, p. 74, nos 39-46; Holl. VIII, p. 243, nos 248-255; New Hollstein, Heemskerck, nos 151-158; TIB LVI, pp. 65-72, nos 017:1-017:8; Tümpel 1968B, pp. 106-110; Van de Waal 1969, pp. 201-202; Veldman 1991-92, pp. 35-36; Utrecht 1991-92, p. 84, no. 9; Münster 1994, p. 317, no. 96

a  Esther Crowned by Ahasuerus

d  Esther's Servants Telling her of Mordecai's Refusal of the Raiment

After King Ahasuerus' queen Vashti had refused his command to display her beauty to his guests at a sumptuous feast, he banished her and took Esther as his queen. The first print in the series shows Esther's coronation (Esther 2:17-18; cat. no. 39a). The figures depicted at table, in the background to the right, are a reminder of the meal Vashti had refused to attend. The King's grandeur and might are obvious from the rich apparel worn by the persons in the foreground. By portraying the coronation scene in the first print the artist is indicating that the series concerns major events from the life of a ruler of significance.

Later, Ahasuerus heared about a plot against him that Esther's foster-father Mordecai had been able to foil (Esther 2:19-23). The second print shows Mordecai - located along the composition's central axis and emphasized by a column and a plinth - overhearing the plot being hatched (cat. no. 39b). By the first three prints of the series - the third one depicting the moment at which Ahasuerus hands Haman a ring and appoints him as his senior lieutenant (Esther 3:8-15; cat. no. 39c) - the three main personages of the Book of Esther have been introduced. For uncovering the treason against Ahasuerus, Mordecai is honoured with a triumphal march that Haman is

**b** Mordecai Overhearing the Treason of Bigthan and Teresh

**c** Ahasuerus Commissions to Destroy the Jewish People

**e** Esther before Ahasuerus, Inviting him for a Banquet

**f** Ahasuerus Consulting the Book of Chronicles

**g** Ahasuerus Consulting Haman

**h** Esther Accusing Haman at the Banquet

125

obliged to lead. The rest of the series deals with the subsequent events that culminate in Haman being hanged on the gallows for having planned to persecute the Jews, a plan that Esther, herself a Jewess, had discovered (cat. nos 39d-h).[1]

In his depiction of the story, the artist is at pains to leave no room for misunderstanding. For this reason to each principal scene a supplementary scene has been added, to which it is closely related both thematically and formally. This role is fulfilled most notably by architecture which, in the shape of pedestals, columns, ledges and apertures, is used to emphasize the figures. The typically Mannerist gestures and the faithfulness to detail yield extremely rich as well as dynamic compositions.

This series after Van Heemskerck must have enjoyed a tremendous reputation among seventeenth-century Dutch artists. Besides serving frequently as sources of inspiration for scenes from the Book of Esther, the etchings introduced subjects that had not previously been depicted. The concurrent, explanatory scenes were sometimes also selected as subjects for paintings in the seventeenth century.[2] **AT**

1. *Cf.* Esther 4:1-16 (cat. no. 39d), 5:1-4 (cat. no. 39e), 6:1-3 (cat. no. 39f), 6:6-11 (cat. no. 39g), 7:1-7 (cat. no. 39h).
2. *Cf.* Boonen 1991 & 1994, pp. 106-110.

## 40  The Triumph of Mordecai, 1515
[ESTHER 6:11]

Lucas van Leyden
*(Leiden 1494? - Leiden 1533)*

Engraving, 21 x 28.9 cm, state II (3)
**Inscr** 'L 1515'
Museum Boijmans Van Beuningen, Rotterdam
(inv. no. BdH 12167)
**Lit** Holl. X, p. 84, no. 32; TIB XII, p. 164, no. 32(355); New Hollstein, Lucas van Leyden, pp. 61, 63, no. 32; Amsterdam 1964-65, pp. 25-26, no. 12; Filedt Kok 1978, pp. 36-38, 151, no. B. 32; Washington/ Boston 1983, pp. 142-143, no. 48; Münster 1994, pp. 317-318, no. 97

Esther's foster-father Mordecai had once saved Ahasuerus' life. When, years later, the king learned that Mordecai has never been rewarded for this, he instructed Haman, his chief minister, to lead him in triumph through the city on horseback and clad in royal apparel. Haman, despite hating the Jews intensely and wishing only for them all to be killed, had no choice but to obey the king's command. This marks the start of his own downfall (Esther 6:1-11).

The print shows Mordecai mounted on the king's horse with Haman, arch-enemy of the Jews, holding the reins. The people are assembled for Mordecai's triumphal procession. In the background, on the left, we see the noblemen, on the right the citizenry while, in the foreground, peasants who have brought their wares to the city pay homage to Mordecai.[1] The gallows on the hill, in the far distance, indicates how the story will end - Haman, who has actually had the gallows built for Mordecai, is ultimately hanged from them himself. **PJ**

1. Amsterdam 1964-65, p. 26. *Cf.* Filedt Kok 1978, p. 38.

## 41  The Triumph of Mordecai, *c.* 1641

[ESTHER 6:11]

### Rembrandt
*(Leiden 1606 - Amsterdam 1669)*

Etching and drypoint, 17.4 x 21.5 cm, only state
Museum het Rembrandthuis, Amsterdam
**Lit** Holl. XVIII, p. 20, no. B. 40; TIB L, p. 28,
no. 40; Münz 1952, Vol. 2, p. 87, no. 178;
Amsterdam 1964-65, p. 40, no. 27; White 1969,
pp. 47-51; Tümpel 1970, no. 27; Filedt Kok
1972, pp. 48-49, no. B. 40; Forssman 1976;
Hamburg 1983, pp. 332-333, no. 198;
Wheelock 1983, pp. 292, 293; Zilkens 1984,
no. 17; Amsterdam 1985-86, pp. 20-21, no. 3;
Perlove 1993; Münster 1994, p. 318, no. 98;
Raupp 1994, p. 412; Amsterdam 1995, p. 29,
no. B. 40

**41.1**
Pieter Lastman, *The Triumph of Mordecai,* 1624,
panel, 52 x 71.5 cm, Museum het Rembrandthuis, Amsterdam

Rembrandt's etchings frequently deal with subjects already depicted by
earlier masters, as with this particular work. Indeed, not just the subject but
even individual figures (the kneeling man holding his hat, and the man
removing his hat) are derived from Lucas van Leyden's 1515 engraving
(cat. no. 40). This was also the model for Pieter Lastman's 1624 painting
(fig. 41.1) which, in turn, served as Rembrandt's own source of inspiration.[1]
The composition, the architecture (the arch of the city gate, the classical
domed building in the background) and the two principal figures are
obviously taken from the painting.

Unlike Lucas and Lastman, however, Rembrandt puts Haman in the
foreground. Here sustaining a severe reverse and about to be hanged, he is
really the chief protagonist. King Ahasuerus and Queen Esther look down
upon the scene from a balcony to the right. Münz regards these figures as a
self-portrait and a portrait of Rembrandt's wife Saskia respectively.[2] **PJ**

1. Tümpel 1970, no. 27. Lastman: Münster 1994, p. 287, no. 55; Tümpel, no. 88. For the iconography of the topic, see:
Boonen 1991 & 1994, p. 108.
2. Münz 1952, Vol. 2, p. 87, no. 178.

## 42 Belshazzar's Feast, *c.* 1598

[DANIEL 5:1-6]

Jan Muller
(Amsterdam 1571 - Amsterdam 1628)

Engraving, 35.9 x 40.5 cm (plate marks),
state II (3)
**Inscr** 'Joannes Muller: fecit. Harman Muller
excudebat'; (upper centre) 'MANE THETEL
PHARES.'
**Caption** 'Cernite Chaldaei viuâ sub imagine
Regis, / Horresco referens, diuini numinis
iram. / Scilicèt hac decuit plecti ratione,
superbâ, / Numine contempto, linguâ qui Idola
crepabat. / Qui simili peccare modo
praesumitis, isto / Discite ab exemplo, similis
ne poena sequatur.'
Rijksprentenkabinet, Rijksmuseum,
Amsterdam (inv. no. RP-P-OB 32094)
**Lit** Holl. XIV, p. 105, no. 11; TIB IV, p. 444, no. 1
(265); Boon 1953, p. 31; Amsterdam 1955,
p. 100, no. 154; Reznicek 1956, pp. 99-101, 111,
no. 1 (drawing); Mielke 1979, p. 51, no. 64;
Schapelhouman 1987, pp. 104-106, no. 64
(drawing); Davis 1988, pp. 304-305, no. 139;
Evanston 1993, p. 128, no. 76; Amsterdam
1993-94A, pp. 385-386, no. 42; Filedt Kok
1994-95, part I, pp. 240-241, 244, part II,
p. 361, part III, p. 5, no. B. 1

'Belshazzar the king, made a great feast to a thousand of his lords,
and drank wine before the thousand. Belshazzar, while he tasted the
wine, commanded to bring the golden and silver vessels which his
father, Nebuchadnezzar, had taken out of the temple which was in
Jerusalem [...] and the king, and his princes, his wives, and his concubines,
drank in them [...]. In the same hour came forth fingers of a man's hand
and wrote over against the lamp upon the plaster of the wall of the king's
palace; and the king saw the part of the hand that wrote. Then the king's
countenance was changed and his thoughts troubled him so that the
joints of his loins were loosed and his knees smote one against another'
(Daniel 5:1-6).

A striking similarity with Tintoretto's famous painting of the *Last Supper* in
San Giorgio Maggiore in Venice (fig. 42.1) is what today's viewer might
first notice when seeing Muller's *Belshazzar's Feast*. Both banquet scenes
feature a long table, diagonally placed, with numerous guests shown in an
'ethereal, flickering light'.[1] Other similarities include the prominent
chandelier and the vessels. Yet it remains unclear how Muller could have
been influenced by Tintoretto's masterpiece. As far as is known, there were
no contemporary reproductive prints of the painting and today, doubt is cast
on whether Muller ever undertook the journey he was once assumed to have
made to Italy.[2]

But was it necessary for the artist to have known Tintoretto's *Last Supper*?
Surely the various elements in Muller's composition were part and parcel of
an existing iconographical tradition surrounding Belshazzar's Feast. An
essential link in this argument is a small woodcut in a picture Bible of 1554
by Bernard Salomon, an artist from Lyon (fig. 42.2). It contains the diagonal
table with, at its head, seated on a throne underneath a canopy, the king,
gesticulating. The various guests are also shown in diverse positions and

**42.1**
Jacopo Tintoretto, *The Last Supper*, 1592-94, canvas, 365 x 569 cm, S. Giorgio Maggiore, Venice

**42.2**
Bernard Salomon, *Belshazzar's Feast*, woodcut, 6 x 8 cm, in: *Figure Del Vecchio Testamento*, Lyon 1554. Herzog August Bibliothek, Wolfenbüttel

**42.3**
Hans Vredeman de Vries, *Belshazzar's Feast*, engraving, c. 24 x 32.8 cm, in: *Thesaurus...*, Antwerp 1579. Rijksprentenkabinet, Amsterdam

poses. Noticeably similar motifs are the vessels on the foremost table and the musicians with their instruments on the balcony.[3]

Most of these motifs also occur in Hans Vredeman de Vries' engraving in the *Thesaurus* picture Bible of 1579 (fig. 42.3).[4] Vredeman clearly based his design on Salomon's example. New elements, however, include the chandelier, top left - completely in line with the biblical text, although absent in earlier depictions of the scene - and the dog in the central foreground. Muller adopted both dog and chandelier. Nevertheless, in other ways his portrayal has more in common with Salomon's print: the vessels in the foreground, the musicians and the gesticulating king, his hand almost echoing the mysterious hand writing on the wall.

Despite these influences, Muller's print has a completely different character than these earlier examples. This lies in the artist's decision to depict the feast as a nocturnal banquet. Although no specific time is stated in the Bible, this is certainly not a surprising choice. Muller may have hit on the idea as a result of the chandelier (which is not lit in Vredeman's print). Moreover, the depiction reflects the artist's predilection for nighttime scenes and dramatic lighting. Naturally, when depicting banquets artists would have had scenes of the Last Supper in mind. It was traditional, given the time of day of the meal, to depict this scene in semi-darkness and candlelight. Indeed, Muller had done so himself some years earlier, in an engraving of 1594.[5] By placing the traditional elements of Salomon and Vredeman's compositions in the nocturnal tradition of the Last Supper, Muller achieved an effect which closely resembled Tintoretto's masterpiece - although he probably had never actually seen the work.

There is a world of difference between Salomon's and Muller's prints, not just in format. Muller produced a highly dramatic scene, with numerous Spranger-like figures, elongated in the Mannerist style and in lively poses. With the lighting he managed to achieve a spectacular effect, as well as bringing a certain order to the numerous figures in the composition. Muller's setting was highly successful. The print, closely related to the illustrations in sixteenth-century picture Bibles, was in turn incorporated in a seventeenth-century picture Bible (Visscher's *Royal-Size Bible*) and subsequently copied for various other biblical picture books.[6] Muller's design was clearly influential. The theme of Belshazzar's Feast was henceforth depicted as a nocturnal banquet, with a particular emphasis on chiaroscuro.[7] **PvdC**

1. Schapelhouman 1987, p. 106.
2. Filedt Kok 1994-95, part I, pp. 240-241.
3. *Figure Del Vecchio Testamento, Con Versi Toscani, Per Damian Maraffi nuouamente composti, illustrate*, Lyon (Jean de Tournes) 1554, fol. Q5v (Herzog August Bibliothek, Wolfenbüttel: 110.4 Poet. (1)). Cf. Cartier 1937-38, pp. 365-366, no. 268. A diagonally-placed table - although somewhat primitive - already occurs in the simple woodcut of *Belshazzar's Feast* in *Die Vier Historien...*, Bamberg (Albrecht Pfister) 1462. See: TIB LXXX, p. 34, no. 1462/26.
4. *Thesaurus Sacrarum Historiarum Veteris Testamenti...*, Antwerp (Gerard de Jode) 1579 (Rijksprentenkabinet, Amsterdam). The print also occurs in the 1585 edition (Mielke 1975, p. 81, no. 38) as well as in the *Theatrum Biblicum* editions published by the Visscher family (cf. cat. no. 58).
5. After Gillis Coignet: TIB IV, p. 468, no. 28. For Muller's preference for dramatically lit scenes see also: Ackley 1981, pp. 16-17, no. 8. Belshazzar's Feast is also depicted as a nighttime banquet in an undated engraving by Crispijn de Passe I after Maarten de Vos (Holl. XLIV, pp. 62-63, no. 252).
6. Visscher: *Historiae Sacrae ... Bybelsche Figuren...*, Amsterdam (Nicolaus Visscher), c. 1680 (Print Room, British Museum, London: 157*.b.25). Copies are found in the 1625-27 picture Bible by Merian and the *Grooten Emblemata Sacra* published by Schabaelje in 1654 (cf. cat. no. 60). For other (drawn and painted) copies see: Möhle 1951, pp. 103-109; Reznicek 1956, p. 101.
7. As is Rembrandt's painting (c. 1635) in the National Gallery in London (Bredius 497). On this theme among Rembrandt and his circle, see: Boonen 1991 & 1994, pp. 110-111.

## 43  Susanna and the Elders, *c.* 1605

[DANIEL 13:15-27]

Jan Saenredam
(Zaandam 1565 - Assendelft 1607)

Engraving, 8.3 x 6.3 cm (oval), only state
**Inscr** 'JSaenredam / fe'
Prof. Dr L.H. van der Tweel Coll., Amsterdam
**Lit** Holl. XXIII, p. 21, no. 21; TIB IV, p. 310,
no. 1 (219); Boccazzi 1974, p. 45

**43.2**
Pierre Eskrich, *Susanna and the Elders*, woodcut
in: *Figvres De La Bible, Illvstrees De Hvictains
Francoys, Pour L'Interpretation Et Intelligence
D'Icelles*, Lyon (Guillaume Rouillé) 1564. British
Library, London

Susanna, wife of Joakim, was a 'very fair woman and one that feared the Lord'. One afternoon she went for a walk in a park nearby, as she often did, accompanied by two maids. It was a hot day, and Susanna decided to bathe. She ordered her maids to fetch oils and balsam while she remained alone. It was then that the two elders, appointed by the people as judges, seized their opportunity. They had had their eye on Susanna for some time and had become 'inflamed with love for her'. That day they were spying on her, concealed in the garden. As soon as she was alone they ran up and tried to force her to lie with them. Susanna managed to foil them by crying out loud (Daniel 13:1-27).

The scene depicted by Saenredam was probably based on the 1583 engraving by Goltzius - also an oval print in which the figure of Susanna dominates the picture plane (fig. 43.1).[1] However, Goltzius' print is more a 'portrait' of Susanna. The actual story is shown in miniature in the background, added only to identify the main subject. Goltzius' print is closely related to depictions of saints, particularly to his own print of Mary Magdalene, an engraving of 1582.[2]

Saenredam's portrayal is also related to the Mary Magdalene iconographic tradition. Like the sinner, the pious Susanna is shown half-length with long hair. Unlike Goltzius, Saenredam did not turn this into a 'portrait', but rather a history scene, although summarily. He placed all the principal elements of the story inside the oval: top left, the two elders, right - as part of the pool - a fountain and in the centre, the naked Susanna.[3]

In contrast to most artists, rather than show the moment when the elders seize the young beauty (*cf.* cat. no. 44), Saenredam elected to show a different part of the story. Not the fear of the woman threatened, but the as yet

**43.1**
Hendrick Goltzius, *Susanna Penitent*, 1583, engraving, 18.6 x 14.5 cm, Museum Boijmans Van Beuningen, Rotterdam

undisturbed moment of bathing. Susanna is clearly enjoying the refreshing water. She has no idea of the danger and makes no effort to conceal her nakedness. The atmosphere in Saenredam's print shows a particular resemblance to a woodcut in Pierre Eskrich's 1564 picture Bible (fig. 43.2): Susanna looks up to the fountain as she enjoys the flowing water, unaware of the impending danger. Here the men are shown further off and, as in Saenredam's print, Susanna cannot see them.[4]

With his dynamic style Saenredam, 'one of the most gifted of the Dutch mannerist engravers',[5] managed to depict an extremely sensual scene. The composition contains a profusion of rounded forms: the long curls of hair, the soft curves of the body, the breasts and the billowing draperies. The fountain to which Susanna turns with an ecstatic gaze contributes to the erotic character. In fact the water flows from sculpted breasts.[6] Even the elders are not depicted as entirely unpleasant. They are not the usual repulsive types, as, for example, in De Grebber's portrayal (cat. no. 44). There is hardly any explicit visual hint to the dramatic sequel, not even a moralising caption. **PvdC**

1. Holl. VIII, p. 3, no. 7.
2. Holl. VIII, p. 15, no. 52. This work was strongly influenced by Titian's *Magdalene*, which Goltzius probably knew from the print by Cornelis Cort. See: Filedt Kok 1993, p. 163.
3. Two other engravings of the history of Susanna exist by Saenredam, one after Cornelis Cornelisz. van Haarlem and one after Goltzius (Holl. XXXIII, p. 22, no. 22, p. 23, no. 23). For a discussion of this theme in Dutch art see: Boonen 1991 & 1994, pp. 112-113.
4. *Cf.* For this picture Bible (copy in British Library, London: 683.b.7.): Baudrier 1895-1921, Vol. 9, p. 296.
5. Filedt Kok (1993) p. 186. Saenredam's dated prints based on his own design are from 1596-1606 (Boccazzi 1974, p. 36).
6. This motif is also found on another print by Saenredam (after Goltzius): Holl. XXXIII, p. 23, no. 23.

## 44 Susanna and the Elders, 1653
[DANIEL 13:15-25]

Pieter Fransz. de Grebber
(*Haarlem c. 1600 - Haarlem 1653*)

Etching, 39.2 x 28 cm, only state
**Inscr** 'P DG 1653'
**Caption** 'Constans'
Rijksprentenkabinet, Rijksmuseum,
Amsterdam (inv. no. RP-P-OB 11939)
**Lit** Holl. VIII, p. 167, no. 3; Münster 1994,
p. 323, no. 105

Susanna is seated at the pool in the park belonging to her husband Joakim. Having been about to divest herself of her robe in order to bathe, she is hastily wrapping it around herself again as two old men - elders or judges - approach her from the rear. Grabbing her, they try to remove the robe.

By capturing precisely this moment, De Grebber provides a dramatic portrayal of the apocryphal story. Susanna listens in desperation to her tormentors demanding that she bow to their will. The man on the right, his index finger raised, urges her to accept their proposition: 'Behold, the garden doors are shut, that no man can see us, and we are in love with thee; therefore consent unto us, and lie with us. If thou wilt not, we will bear witness against thee, that a young man was with thee [...]' (Daniel 13:20-21). Susanna refused to submit to blackmail and replied: 'I am straightened on every side: for if I do this thing, it is death unto me: and if I do not, I cannot escape your hands. It is better for me to fall into your hands, and not to do it, than to sin in the sight of the Lord' (Daniel 13:22-23). The inscription 'Constans' is a reference to Susanna's virtuous behaviour.

Although himself a pupil of Goltzius, De Grebber preferred not to depict the theme in an erotic way, as in the prints of the Goltzius school (*cf.* cat. no. 43). He even decided not to show Susanna naked, as was traditional, rather focusing on the psychological aspect of the theme. To judge from their self-confident expressions the men clearly think that they have the young, frightened woman completely in their power. De Grebber's compelling adaptation of the subject indicates his own adherence to the second of the 'eleven rules of art' he had had printed in 1649, namely that 'it is important [for artists] to read the histories carefully (especially in the case of biblical and true stories) so that their meaning can be represented as accurately as possible'.[1]

The date on the etching should probably not, as until recently, be read as 1655 but as 1653. This would make it one of the last works by the painter De Grebber, by whom only a limited number of graphic works are known.[2]
**PvdC/PJ**

1. 'II. Is 't van noode datmen de Historien wel door-leest: (bysonder als het schriftuerlijcke ofte waerachtighe Historien zyn) om den sin soo nae als 't moghelijck is wel uyt te beelden'. Pieter Fransz. de Grebber, *Regulen...*, Haarlem (Pieter Casteleyn) 1649. Quoted from: Van Thiel 1965, p. 126.
2. Acknowledgments to Christiaan Schuckman. For De Grebber, see: Hazeleger 1979. For his prints: Amsterdam 1996, pp. 93-94, no. 37. For his Old Testament paintings: Münster 1994, p. 275, no. 44, p. 284, no. 52.

CONSTANS.

## 45 The History of Judith and Holofernes, c. 1564
[JUDITH 5-15]

Philips Galle
(Haarlem 1537 - Antwerp 1612)
after Maarten van Heemskerck
(Heemskerk 1498 - Haarlem 1574)

a  **Achior Pleading with Holofernes for the Israelites**
b  **The Israelites Finding Achior**
c  **Judith Addressing the Elders of Bethulia**
d  **Judith Preparing herself to Leave for the Enemies' Camp**
e  **Judith Presented to Holofernes**
f  **Judith Slaying Holofernes**
g  **Judith Displaying Holofernes' Head**
h  **The Discovery of Holofernes' Corpse**

Series of eight numbered engravings
c. 19.3 x 24.3 cm, state I (2)
**Inscr** (cat. no. 45 a) 'MAERTIINVS
HEEMSKERCK INVEN. / 1564 / PG';
(cat. nos 45b-h) 'MHEEM.IN.'
**Captions** (sheet 1) 'Jnfelix Achior, defensi
nvminis ergô, / Roboreo adstrictvs fert vincla
tenacia, trvnco. / HADR. IVN. [Hadrianus
Junius]'; (sheet 2) 'Sed gens Isacidvm, vatis
concvssa periclo, / Expedit insontem, nvmen
qve in vota fatigat.'; (sheet 3) 'Stvltitiae
popvlvm accvsat, praescribere coelo / Avsvm,
havrit qve Devm Ivdith svb pectore supplex';
(sheet 4) 'Instrvit Annona, fidam potv qve cibo
qve / Ancillam, et propero Ivdith pede tendit ad
hostem.'; (sheet 5) 'Assyrii pedibvs svpplex
advolvitvr hostis, / Accvmbitqve simvl, dictis et
pectora mvlcet.'; (sheet 6) 'Obtrvncat regem
somno temeto qve sepvltvm, / Hinc comite
ancilla patriam discedit ad vrbem.'; (sheet 7)
'Pvblica flammivomae testantvr gavdia taedae,
/ Qvvum capvt im[m]anis depromit bvlga
tyranni.'; (sheet 8) 'Barbara gens, celerate
fvgam, obsidione solvta, / Praecipitem, Rex
ecce iacet sine nomine trvncvs.'
Museum Boijmans Van Beuningen, Rotterdam
(inv. no. L 88/31 a-h)
**Lit** Kerrich 1829, pp. 35-36, nos 1-8; Holl. VII,
p. 74, nos 47-54; Holl. VIII, p. 243, nos 272-
279; New Hollstein, Heemskerck, pp. 178-183,
nos 207-214; TIB LVI, pp. 57-64, nos 016:1-
016:8; Veldman 1991-92, p. 35; Münster 1994,
p. 319, no. 99

a  Achior Pleading with Holofernes for the Israelites

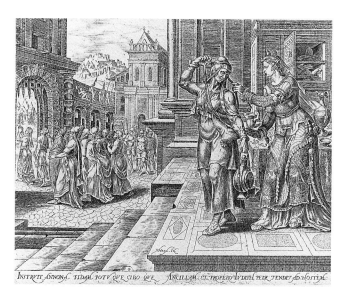
d  Judith Preparing herself to Leave for the Enemies' Camp

This series of eight engravings, arranged in chronological order, is dedicated to the story of Judith as related in the Apocrypha. In each individual print various episodes of the story are depicted. The monumentality of the figures along with the antiquarian decor reflect the general interest of sixteenth- and seventeenth-century artists in classical art - Van Heemskerck himself spent the period 1532-1535 in Rome. The series served as the basis for later treatments of the topic by artists such as Jan de Bray.[1]

The Ammonite leader Achior stands before Holofernes, his general, informing him about the military strength of the Israelites (cat. no. 45a). Out of fear of the God of Israel he advices Holofernes not to attack the Jewish city of Bethunia. In the background we see Holofernes, enraged by this advice, causing Achior to be carried off to Bethulia and be tied to a tree (Judith 5:1-25; 6:7-10). Achior is set free by the Bethulian army and, in the distance, we see his entry into Bethulia followed by the scene in which the city's elders question him (Judith 6:10-19; cat. no. 45b).

Judith, a rich widow of Bethulia, receives the elders in the presence of her maid Abra (cat. no. 45c). She tells them of her plan to prevent the city falling

134

**b** The Israelites Finding Achior

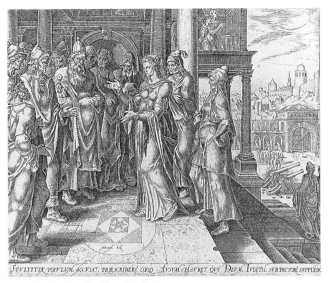

**c** Judith Addressing the Elders of Bethulia

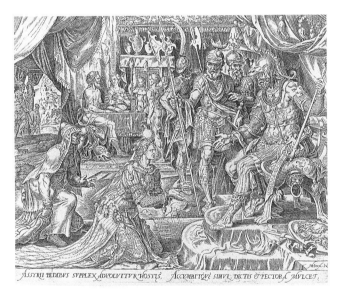

**e** Judith Presented to Holofernes

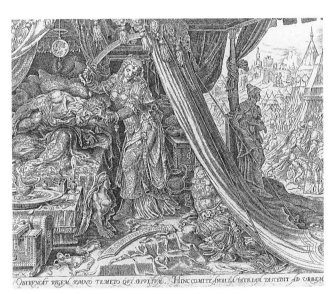

**f** Judith Slaying Holofernes

**g** Judith Displaying Holofernes's Head

**h** The Discovery of Holofernes's Corpse

into the hands of Holofernes (Judith 8 and 9). After Judith and her maid have prepared themselves for the meeting with Holofernes, they pass through the city gate on their way to the general's camp (Judith 10:5-17; cat. no. 45d). Gaining admittance, they announce to Holofernes that God will grant him victory (cat. no. 45e). Holofernes, lavishly armoured, is seated before the kneeling women on a classically inspired throne (Judith 10:17-20; 11:1-21; 12:1-4).

The act of liberation and the climax of the story, namely the slaying of Holofernes, is depicted in the sixth print of the series (cat. no. 45f). This event takes place in the evening of the fourth day of Judith's stay in the camp. Seizing the sleeping general by the hair, Judith raises the sword - gleaming menacingly - to strike the fatal blow (Judith 13:1-14). Having returned to Bethulia and standing on a dais Judith shows Holofernes' head to the city elders (cat. no. 45g). Her maid beside her is holding the sack in which it was carried out of the camp. Numerous blazing torches identify this as a nocturnal scene (Judith 13:14-21). The successful assassination is followed up by a lightning attack by the Bethulians on the Assyrians. Panicking at finding their general slain and still in a state of utter confusion, the Assyrian warriors break ranks and flee (Judith 14:8-17; 15:1-6; cat. no. 45h). **GdB**

1. *Cf.* Amsterdam 1991-92, p. 256, no. 36; Münster 1994, p. 291, no. 58. See also: Boonen 1991 & 1994, pp. 117-118.

## 46 The History of Tobias, 1620-21
[TOBIT 5-11]

Moyses van Uyttenbroeck
*(The Hague 1595/1600 - The Hague 1645/46)*

a **Tobit Delivering Tobias to the Guidance of the Angel**
b **Tobias Frightened by the Fish**
c **Tobias and the Angel**
d **Tobias Healing his Father's Blindness**

Series of four etchings, *c.* 12.8 x 18.3 cm
**Inscr** (sheet 1, state II [4]) 'M VB 1620'; (sheet 2, state II [4]) 'Mo Wtenbrouck 1620'; (sheet 3, state II [4]) '1620'; (sheet 4, state I [4]) 'MV Wtenbrouck 1621'
Rijksprentenkabinet, Rijksmuseum, Amsterdam (inv. nos A 16519, A 4190, RP-P-OB 24981, 1936:436)
**Lit** TIB VI, p. 68-71, nos 13(92)-16(94); TIB VI (Commentary), pp. 67-73, nos 013(92)-016(94); Burchard 1917, p. 74; Van de Waal 1947, p. 150; Weisner 1963, pp. 172, 175-176; Münster 1994, p. 320, no. 100

Old Tobit sent his son Tobias to collect a debt. God provided the young Tobias with the angel Raphael as a companion whom he did not, however, recognize. They departed, Tobias' dog running along with them. On Raphael's instructions Tobias caught a dangerous fish, gutted it and set its heart, liver and gall aside. Using these, he was later able not only to free his future wife from an evil spirit but also heal his father's blindness.

The first print shows the moment at which old, blind Tobit takes leave of his son, giving him Azarias - who is really the angel Raphael - as a travelling companion (Tobit 5:17; cat. no. 46a). Behind the three large figures in the foreground the broad vista of a hilly landscape receding into the distance in several planes is an indication of the long journey that lies ahead of Tobias and Raphael.

In the second print the moment is depicted at which Tobias, while washing his feet in a river, is attacked by a dangerous fish (Tobit 6:1-3; cat. no. 46b). However, in Van Uyttenbrouck's print the fish does not look particularly menacing. And even the idyllic landscape, with its cowherd and cow, seems to contradict this dramatic event.

In the third print in the series (cat. no. 46c) the gestures of the two figures indicate that they are having an animated conversation. The gutted fish in Tobias' right hand is a reference to the preceding event, which culminated in his overpowering the creature. At the same time the angel explains how he will soon be able to use the fish's organs (Tobit 6:6 ff.).

The fourth print depicts the healing of Tobit's blindness with the fish's gall which Tobias presented for the purpose, on the advice of Raphael

a  Tobit Delivering Tobias to the Guidance of the Angel

b  Tobias Frightened by the Fish

c  Tobias and the Angel

d  Tobias Healing his Father's Blindness

(Tobit 11:11-12; cat. no. 46d). This representation of the subject differs from most others in that it is not Tobias but Raphael who heals the father. Also in contrast to several examples is that Raphael is identifiable as an angel by his wings. In works by artists of the Rembrandt School portraying scenes with the same motifs the figures are in contemporary costume.[1]

Van Uyttenbroeck's spacious, Arcadian landscape and his chiaroscuro contrasts show the influence of Elsheimer, whose work was known in Holland through the engravings by Hendrick Goudt (fig. 17, p. 27).[2] The Tobias series discussed here is one of Van Uyttenbroeck's more mature and stylistically balanced works. **GdB**

1. *Cf.* Boonen 1991 & 1994, pp. 113-117.
2. Frankfurt am Main 1966-67, pp. 118-121, nos 273-279; Andrews 1977, pp. 32, 38-40.

## 47 Mountain Landscape with Tobias and the Angel, 1608

[TOBIT 6]

Claes Jansz. Visscher
(Amsterdam 1586/87 - Amsterdam 1652)
after Gillis van Coninxloo
(Antwerp 1544 - Amsterdam 1606)

Etching, 21.8 x 31.1 cm, only state
**Inscr** 'Egidius Coningslo in: CJVisscher fecit et excud. / 1608.'
**Caption** (by R.L. [R. Lubbaeus]) 'Dum chari obsequio patris comitante Tobias / Junior it Raphaële Ragas, exenterat undâ / Tigridis egressum piscem, aligeroq[ue] docente / In promptu est oculis capto medicina parenti.'
Museum Boijmans Van Beuningen, Rotterdam (inv. no. L 1977/16)
**Lit** Holl. IV, p. 221, no. 19 (Coninxloo); Holl. XXXVIII, p. 12, no. 10 (Visscher); Blok 1918-19, p. 108; Simon 1958, no. 10; Amsterdam 1993-94A, p. 170; Frankenthal 1995, p. 134

**47.1**
Hieronymus Cock after Matthys Cock, *Tobias and the Angel*, 1558, etching, 22.9 x 31.4 cm, Rijksprentenkabinet, Amsterdam

Depicted here is the journey of the young Tobias accompanied by the angel Raphael, the same theme as shown by Van Uyttenbroeck (cat. no. 46c) and Segers (cat. no. 48). In fact landscape also played a major role in their prints. In Van Coninxloo's composition, it dominates the scene. The figures of Tobias and the angel - shown as pilgrims with wide-brimmed hats and sticks, preceded by the dog - form the staffage of an extensive landscape. Left, in the background, near the house on the water, is the scene of 'Tobias and the fish', the next episode in the story.

Van Coninxloo's conception is closely related to a type of print already made by Hieronymus Cock in 1558 after a design by his brother Matthys (fig. 47.1).[1] Here too, the landscape dominates: a typical Flemish fantasy landscape with mountains, a winding river, picturesque buildings, decorative flora and human figures. Similar elements are found in Van Coninxloo's composition. It is divided into different planes, offering a panoramic view of a valley. New, compared with Cock, are the enormous trees with their thick foliage and varying chiaroscuro effects. Later in the century, the theme was depicted a number of times in comprehensive landscapes by artists such as Anthonie Waterloo.[2]

Together with David Vinckboons, Van Coninxloo introduced the Flemish landscape tradition into the Northern Netherlands. Claes Jansz. Visscher - perhaps a pupil of Vinckboons - was one of the first native Dutch artists to exploit the genre. In addition to etchings after designs by Vinckboons and Van Coninxloo, he also produced his own drawings and prints. On 3 March 1607 Visscher bought a drawing by Van Coninxloo for five guilders and five stivers at the sale of the master's estate, as well as 'various drawings'. One of these may have been the basis for this etching of Tobias and the angel of 1608.[3] **PvdC**

1. Holl. IV, p. 179, no. 19. From a series of *Landscapes with Biblical and Mythological Scenes*. Cf. Riggs 1977, pp. 273-279, nos 38-50 (no. 48).
2. TIB II, p. 125, no. 134 (136).
3. Amsterdam 1993-94A, p. 170. Cf. Briels 1976, p. 240.

## 48 Tobias and the Angel, 1620s
[TOBIT 6]

**Hercules Segers**
*(Haarlem? 1589/90 - The Hague 1633/38)*

Etching, 20.2 x 27.8 cm, only state
Rijksprentenkabinet, Rijksmuseum,
Amsterdam (inv. no. RP-P-OB 796)
**Lit** Holl. XXVI, p. 184, no. 1a; Frankfurt am
Main 1966-67, p. 126, no. 295; Amsterdam
1967, p. 19, no. 1; Haverkamp Begemann 1973,
pp. 29, 43-44, 53-55, 57, 65, no. 1a; Andrews
1977, p. 32; Van der Waals 1988, pp. 145, 206;
Münster 1994, p. 321, no. 101

**48.1**
Rembrandt, *The Flight into Egypt*, c. 1652,
etching, 21.2 x 28.4 cm, Museum het
Rembrandthuis, Amsterdam

Segers' oeuvre contains only two etchings in which figures play an important
role. *Tobias and the Angel* is one of them.[1] The subject is taken from the Book
of Tobit, popular in the circles of Elsheimer and Rembrandt. Tobias,
accompanied by Raphael, is on his way to Media. He carries the fish he has
caught on the angel's advice (Tobit 6:2-9).

The diagonal structure of the landscape is typical of Elsheimer. This
etching is a free adaption - with left and right reversed - of an engraving by
Hendrik Goudt dating from 1613 (fig. 17, p. 27) and itself based on a painting
by Elsheimer.[2] Segers borrowed Goudt's figures but changed the landscape,
depicting a low instead of a high horizon. His composition also emphasizes
the foreground, with the lake replaced by a valley.

Segers' copper plate came into the possession of Rembrandt, who
reworked its right half. By replacing the travelling Tobias and his companion
with the Holy Family he turned the subject into the *Flight into Egypt* (fig. 48.1).[3]
**PJ**

1. *The Lamentation* (Holl. 2) is the second etching.
2. Holl. VIII, p. 152, no. 2. *Cf.* Frankfurt am Main 1966-67, p. 119, no. 274.
3. B. 56. *Cf.* Ackley 1981, pp. 237-239, no. 164.

## 49 The Blindness of Tobit, 1651
[TOBIT 11:10]

### Rembrandt
*(Leiden 1606 - Amsterdam 1669)*

Etching and drypoint, 16 x 12.9 cm, state I (2)
**Inscr** 'Rembrandt *f*. 1651'
Museum het Rembrandthuis, Amsterdam
**Lit** Holl. XVIII, p. 21, no. B. 42; TIB L, p. 30,
no. 42; Münz 1952, Vol. 2, pp. 87-88, no. 181;
Amsterdam 1964-65, pp. 40-41, no. 28; Clark
1966, pp. 51, 52; Tümpel 1970, no. 32; Filedt
Kok 1972, pp. 49-50, no. B. 42; Hamburg 1983,
pp. 334-335, no. 200; Münster 1994, p. 322,
no. 103; Amsterdam 1995, p. 30, no. B. 42

**49.1**
Rembrandt, *The Blindness of Tobit*, c. 1629,
etching, 7.9 x 6.3 cm, state II (5), Teylers
Museum, Haarlem

After a long wait, Anna and Tobit experienced the happy homecoming of
their son (Tobit 11:5-11). The Latin Vulgate text and Greek Septuagint version
differ strongly in this passage.[1] In the Vulgate we read of a dog that
accompanies Tobias on his journey scampering on ahead, wagging its tail
and jumping up. Tobit immediately jumps to his feet and rushes to the door,
but stumbles. He then calls an assistant to guide him. In this version he
greets his son before his wife does. This order is reversed in the Septuagint
(whose Apocrypha translation forms the basis for the 1637 Dutch States
Bible), which has Tobit following on later - without help - after colliding with
the door. Neither a dog nor an assistant are mentioned.

Rembrandt etched this scene twice, first around 1629 and again in 1651.
The earlier work (fig. 49.1) focuses entirely on blind Tobit rushing to the
door, hand outstretched.[2] The treatment is so unusual that Bartsch did not
even recognize the subject, categorizing it alongside the artist's depictions
of beggars and everyday scenes. This illustrates the exceptional, yet
chracteristic quality of this work. Rembrandt conveys the story merely
through the physiognomy and gestures, the action itself, the setting, the
protagonist's age and the scarce references to his social status. In an early
state, which has not been preserved, the returning Tobias and his welcoming
mother are still visible through the door.[3] Rembrandt later covered this

**49.2**
Agostino Veneziano after Raphael, *The Blindness of Elymas*, 1516, engraving, 25.8 x 33.4 cm, British Museum, London

group with crosshatching in order - subsequently - to abstract his principal figure from the context of the story. The attention is now focused entirely on Tobit hurrying to the door.

In his later - 1651 - etching Rembrandt combines the motifs of both text versions. While Tobit is groping his way to the door unaided (Septuagint) the dog fawns around him (Vulgate). The old man has already collided (Vulgate) with his wife's spinning-wheel, which has toppled on the floor in front of the hearth.

Although here, too, Rembrandt shows the figure of Tobit in isolation, he also incorporates several other motifs that recall the narrative context. The interior presentation so typical of Rembrandt warrants the strong chiaroscuro effects. Tobit, illuminated from behind by the open fire, casts his shadow on the ground and the wall. Moreover, the unlit recess beside the fireplace provides a dark background against which he stands out sharply. Rembrandt derives his figure's posture from that of Elymas in a 1516 engraving by Agostino Veneziano after Raphael (fig. 49.2).[4] **PJ/AT**

1. *Cf.* Tümpel 1970, no. 32.
2. B. 153. *Cf.* Münster 1994, p. 321, no. 102.
3. Münz 1952, Vol. 2, p. 85, no. 171.
4. TIB XXVI, pp. 61-62, no. 43. *Cf.* Münz 1952, Vol. 2, pp. 87-88.

## 50 The Angel Departing from Tobit's Family, 1641

[TOBIT 12:16-22]

**Rembrandt**
*(Leiden 1606 - Amsterdam 1669)*

Etching and drypoint, 10.3 x 15.4 cm, state II
(4)
**Inscr** 'Rembrandt *f* 1641'
Museum het Rembrandthuis, Amsterdam
**Lit** Holl. XVIII, pp. 21-22, no. B. 43; TIB L,
p. 31, no. 43; Münz 1952, Vol. 2, p. 87, no. 179;
Clark 1966, pp. 80, 81; Tümpel 1970, no. 34;
Filedt Kok 1972, p. 50, no. B. 43; Hamburg
1983, pp. 334-335, no. 201; Zilkens 1984,
no. 16; Amsterdam 1984-85, pp. 58, 59;
Münster 1994, p. 322, no. 104; Raupp 1994,
pp. 408-409; Amsterdam 1995, p. 31, no. B. 43

**50.1**
Pieter Lastman, *The Angel Departing from Tobit's
Family*, 1618, panel, 63 x 91.5 cm, Statens
Museum for Kunst, Copenhagen

**50.2**
Dirck Volkertsz. Coornhert after Maarten van
Heemskerck, *The Angel Departing from Tobit's
Family, c.* 1548, woodcut, 23.9 x 18.9 cm,
Rijksprentenkabinet, Amsterdam

Following Tobias' homecoming he and his father decided to thank the angel Raphael for accompanying him by giving him half of what Tobias had brought back. At this point Raphael revealed his true identity to the father and son. Frightened out of their wits they prostrated themselves before the angel, who then departed by ascending to heaven (Tobit 12).

The etching shows Tobit and Tobias kneeling in worship. Anna and Sarah, their wives, are also illuminated by the shaft of light that shines down from heaven. So is the dog. Other figures portrayed are outside the light; the fact that they are in the shadow indicates that they remain untouched by this divine revelation.

In the foreground, to the right, Rembrandt depicts the treasure that Tobias and his father had intended for Raphael. The pack mule is a reference to the caravan with which Tobias and his wife returned home. These motifs are also present in Lastman's 1618 painting (fig. 50.1).[1]

The treatment of the ascending angel closely resembles that of a woodcut by Maarten van Heemskerck (fig. 50.2), though Rembrandt renders only half the figure.[2] Rembrandt produced a painting on the same subject in 1637.[3] Here, too, he turned to the woodcut for his angel, as well as for the other figures. **PJ**

1. For Lastman's painting (Tümpel, no. 97) and the iconography of the subject, see: Boonen 1991 & 1994, pp. 116-117.
2. New Hollstein, Heemskerck, p. 162, no. 188.
3. Bredius 503; Tümpel 1986, p. 390, no. 15; RRP, Vol. 3, pp. 232-241, no. A 121.

## 51  Jael, c. 1597

Nicolaus Braeu
(active in Haarlem in the late 1580s and
1590s)
after Hendrick Goltzius
(Mühlbracht 1558 - Haarlem 1617)

No. 1 from a series of four engravings: *Heroes
and Heroines of the Old Testament*
41.7 x 32.3 cm (oval), only state
**Inscr** 'HG Inuen. Nicolus. braeu. schulp.'
**Caption** (T. Schrevelius) 'Sisera falcatos agitans
in proelia currus Cornipedes stimulabat equos;
cum monte Barakus Protinus infestis deduxit
cornibus agmen: Tristis vbi infausto commissa
est omine pugna. Hospitio excepit fugientem
clade suorum. Infidiosa Iahel, acto per tempora
clavo. T Schrevelius.'
Rijksprentenkabinet, Rijksmuseum,
Amsterdam (inv. no. RP-P-BI 1984)
**Lit** Holl. III, p. 199, no. 1; Holl. VIII, p. 130,
no. 63; TIB III, p. 353, no. 1 (115); Spicer 1989,
*passim*; Spicer 1991, pp. 275, 280; Filedt Kok
1993, pp. 193, 217, no. A.7; Münster 1994,
p. 324, no. 107

**51.5**
Hendrick Goltzius, Jael, *c.* 1589, red chalk,
36.8 x 26.2 cm, Thomas le Claire Kunsthandel,
Hamburg

Apart from print series illustrating a particular story, sixteenth-century
artists also produced thematic series of figures selected from Old Testament
stories. For example, there are series of wives of the Patriarchs, of women's
wiles, of Old Testament heroes and Old Testament heroines. This series
combines the two latter categories.

Jael, Samson, Judith and David (figs 51.1-51.4) are all portrayed full-length,
in the foreground, with their characteristic attributes, while in the
background their heroic deed is depicted. Jael holds the hammer and peg
with which she killed Sisera (Judges 4:17-23). Samson holds the jawbone
with which he slew a thousand Philistines (Judges 15:15-20). Judith displays
the head of Holofernes and holds the sword with which she decapitated him
(Judith 13:6-10). Finally, David leans on the giant sword with which he cut off
the head of Goliath, that he carries in his left hand (1 Sam. 17:51).

Goltzius had designed a series based on the same theme and the same
figures once before, probably around 1587.[1] In this he shows the heroes and
heroines alternately from the front, back, in profile, and at an oblique angle
as a *tour de force*. In the series shown here, all the figures, except Jael, are
shown from the front. A preparatory drawing has survived for the print of

David, dating from 1589. Recently, a drawn study for the print of Jael appeared on the art market (fig. 51.5).[2]

Series such as this usually had some moralising message. Jael, Samson, Judith and David were heroes who had risked their own lives to save their people from the enemy. In the sixteenth and seventeenth centuries, their stories were associated with contemporary events during the Revolt against Spain. In poems, sermons, plays and occasionally even paintings, the leaders of the Dutch Revolt were compared to the Old Testament heroes, while the Spaniards were depicted as their biblical adversaries.[3] In this case, however, the captions around the prints are interpretations of the content of the Bible stories and make no reference to political issues. **MH**

**51.1-51.4**
Nicolaus Braeu after Hendrick Goltzius, *Heroes and Heroines of the Old Testament*, c. 1597, engravings, 41.7 x 32.3 cm, Rijksprentenkabinet, Amsterdam

1. Holl. XI, p. 217, nos 23-26; TIB IV, pp. 228-231, nos 251-254; Filedt Kok 1993, p. 209, no. 39. *Cf.* Amsterdam 1993-94A, pp. 347-348, no. 14.
2. The dating of the prints to c. 1597 is based on Filedt Kok 1993, pp. 193, 217, no. A.7. For the drawing of David see: Spicer 1989; Jael: Thomas le Claire Kunsthandel, *Women Observed. Twenty Master Drawings*, Hamburg 1996, no. 6 (acknowledgements Gerlinde de Beer).
3. *Cf.* Huiskamp 1991 & 1994, esp. pp. 146-149. See also cat. no. 75.

51.1 Jael

51.2 Samson

51.3 Judith

51.4 David

Rembrandt
(Leiden 1606 - Amsterdam 1669)

left to right
a  **Nebuchadnezzar's Dream**
b  **Daniel's Vision of the Four Beasts**
c  **Jacob's Dream**
d  **David and Goliath**

Series of four etchings in: Menasseh ben Israel,
*Piedra Gloriosa O De La Estatua De Nebuchadnesar...*,
Amsterdam (Menasseh ben Israel) 1655
[For the book, see cat. no. 76]
Etching, drypoint and burin, *c.* 25.2 x 15.9 cm
Rijksmuseum, Rijksprentenkabinet,
Amsterdam
**Lit** Holl. XVIII, pp. 16-18, no. B. 36; TIB L,
p. 25, no. 36; Münz 1952, Vol. 2, pp. 88-90,
nos 183A-183D; Van de Waal 1954-55; Tümpel
1970, no. 39; Filedt Kok 1972, pp. 44-46, nos B.
36a-36d; Tümpel 1977, pp. 77-80; Munich
1982, pp. 82-84, no. 59; Amsterdam 1987-88,
pp. 32-34, nos 15-16; Tümpel 1993, pp. 145-
147; Carstensen 1993, pp. 52-59; Münster 1994,
pp. 184, 211, 326, no. 111; Amsterdam 1995,
pp. 26-27, nos B. 36a-36d

The author of *Piedra Gloriosa*, Menasseh ben Israel (1604-1657), was the son
of a Portuguese Jew who had fled from the Inquisition and settled in
Amsterdam.[1] By the age of eighteen he had obtained a prominent position in
Amsterdam's Jewish community. He founded the city's first Hebrew
printing house. In 1655 he commissioned Rembrandt - who may already
have etched his portrait in 1636 - to make four illustrations for the book.[2]
The prints were to be purchased separately and be bound into the work, a
Spanish treatise on the Jewish faith in the coming of the Messiah. The work,

apocalyptic in tone, is focused on the 'glorious stone' (*piedra gloriosa*) that symbolizes the Messiah. In each of the first three biblical stories illustrated by Rembrandt a stone bringing benefit to Israel is mentioned. Menasseh asserts that only one stone is involved, not three different ones, and that this stone is a symbol of the Messiah.

King Nebuchadnezzar of Babylon dreamt he saw an image whose 'head was of fine gold, his breast and his arms of silver, his belly and his thighs of brass, his legs of iron, his feet part of iron and clay'. Then, 'a stone was cut out without hands, which smote the image upon his feet'. Gradually the image was 'broken to pieces' and carried away by the wind, and 'the stone that smote the image became a great mountain, and filled the whole earth'. Daniel, himself an exile, interpreted the image as symbolizing the kingdoms that would perish (Daniel 2:31-35; cat. no. 52a).

For Menasseh the stone that destroyed the image is not just a symbol of the Messiah. It is also identical to the stone that the patriarch Jacob slept on when he dreamt of a ladder leading to heaven with the angels of God ascending and descending on it (Gen. 28:11-15; cat. no. 52c). The stone that Jacob's head rested upon is, in turn, the one that David used to slay Goliath, Israel's enemy (1 Samuel 17:49; cat. no. 52d).

The stone mentioned in the first three stories is, as we have seen, the symbol of the Messiah. The fourth etching depicts one of Daniel's visions of the coming of the Messiah (cat. no. 52b). In his apocalyptic dream he saw four great beasts arise from the sea. Thereafter the 'Ancient of days' (ie, God) appeared to him in a garment as white as snow, with a head of hair like pure wool, and seated on a throne of flames. The four monsters were destroyed and 'everlasting dominion' given to 'one like the Son of man'. The beasts stand for the four empires of Babylon, Persia, Macedonia and Rome, to be followed by a fifth - Israel (Daniel 7:17-27). Despite the second commandment, which is interpreted by many as prohibiting representations of God but by others merely as precluding the worshipping of graven images, Rembrandt portrays the God that Daniel saw in his vision in human form.[3]

Rembrandt was probably not able to read the Spanish text. He based his etchings on the iconographical tradition, but made adjustments as required by Menasseh. Münz has demonstrated that, for *Nebuchadnezzar's Dream* and *Daniel's Vision*, he probably used Bible illustrations by Matthaeus Merian the Elder.[4] Rembrandt's model for David and Goliath was Tobias Stimmer's woodcut in the *Neue Künstliche Figuren Biblischer Historien* (Basel 1576).[5] In its original treatment, *Jacob's Dream*, probably the only one of the topics that he had dealt with previously (fig. 52.1),[6] probably derives from Pre-Rembrandtist works.[7]

Rembrandt obviously had difficulties in harmonizing his ideas - heavily influenced by the iconographical tradition - with those of Menasseh, whose literary expectations he could fulfil only to a degree. Hence the numerous corrections he made in *Nebuchadnezzar's Dream* and *Jacob's Dream*. In the first and second state of *Nebuchadnezzar's Dream* it is the image's legs and not its feet that are 'smote' by the stone. This is corrected in the third state. In the fifth, the image even bears the names of the four empires by way of elucidation.

The corrections in *Jacob's Dream* are even more drastic. In the first state the patriarch is asleep at the foot of the ladder, in line with the iconographical tradition and the Bible. The ladder reaches up to around the centre of the composition. In Menasseh's opinion, however, the ladder's centre signified

**52.1**
Rembrandt, *Jacob's Dream*, c. 1644, pen and bistre, 25 x 20.8 cm, Musée du Louvre, Paris

**52.2**
Salom Italia (after Rembrandt), *Daniel's Vision*, after 1655, etching, Library of the Hebrew Union College, Cincinnati

Jerusalem, the site of Jacob's resting place. This is why, in the later states, the ladder is carried through to the bottom of the composition. This solution does not succeed artistically, since Jacob is now suspended above the ground.

Rembrandt's readiness to accommodate his patron at the expense of his own artistic ideas suggests that Menasseh had discussed his innovative interpretation of the biblical text with him. But even Menasseh - a Jew and as such bound by the second commandment - generously overlooked the fact that Rembrandt emulated early Bible illustrators by rendering the God of *Daniel's Vision* in human form.[8] We do not know whether Menasseh's indulgence stemmed from his liberal attitude or his impending visit to England, undertaken to persuade Cromwell to lift the prohibition on Jews entering the country.

Later on Rembrandt's etchings were replaced by copies attributed to Salom Italia and in which the figure of God is symbolized by rays of light forming a nimbus (fig. 52.2).[9] **PJ/CT**

1. The following remarks refer to several conclusions from the seminal essay Van de Waal published in 1954-55.
2. For the portrait etching (B. 269), see: Münster 1994, pp. 210, 325, no. 109. See also Dubiez 1992 and Dudok van Heel 1993, which rebut the identification.
3. See, for instance, Venant's painting: Tümpel 1974B, p. 70, fig. 95.
4. Münz 1952, Vol. 2, pp. 89-90.
5. Tümpel 1970, no. 39.
6. Benesch 557. See also Benesch 125 and 558.
7. See note 3.
8. Cf. Van Voolen 1994, pp. 211, 218, note 27.
9. Cf. Van de Waal 1954-55, p. 56 and figs 9-12.

## 53    Biblical Figures from the Old Testament, *c.* 1720

*Bybelsche Figuren van het Oude Testament,* Amsterdam (Gysbert de Groot-Keur) s.a. [1738-56]
Series of sixteen woodcuts on a single sheet, partly handcoloured with orange, blue and yellow, *c.* 31 x 43 cm; each woodcut *c.* 5.2 x 6.5 cm
Boerma Coll., Landsmeer
**Lit** De Meyer 1962, pp. 154, 365; Boerma 1980, p. 14, no. 23

One of the principal publishers of popular prints in the second half of the seventeenth and first half of the eighteenth century was the firm of De Groot in Amsterdam. Between 1719 and 1724 the heirs of Henrina Blaeu, widow of Gysbert de Groot, were in partnership with Antony van Dam. Besides school books about biblical characters (cat. no. 73) they also published biblical prints, including the *Bybelsche Figuren van het Oude Testament.* This example is a reprint by Gysbert de Groot-Keur, the last representative of this publishing family.[1]

The sheet contains sixteen pictures: four rows of four. They are simple woodcuts with a straightforward linear style and abrupt hatching. This is all the more obvious when compared with prints from the heyday of the woodcut - the sixteenth century - on which they are partly based. For example, the depiction of Samson carrying the doors of the city gates of Gaza is derived from a woodcut in the picture Bible by Tobias Stimmer (fig. 53.1).[2] The hero's pose, lifting the heavy doors on his back, is similar. Here, however, the figure is simplified, as is the setting.

Ziet Samfon heeft door groote kracht,
Stads Deuren op een Berg gebracht.

In noot de Heer zijn hulp bewijst,
Door Ravens Elias gefpijst.

De huut van Haman tot de Jood,
Brengt door een ftrop hem tot 'er dood.

Nebucadnezars breyn ontftelt,
Eet als een beeft hier gras op 't velt.

Dit 's 't loon van Abfalon, die ftout
Doorfteeken wort aan 't Eyken hout.

De Swaluw zig in 't neft bevind,
Maakt door haar drek Tobias blind.

De dronkenfchap die 't breyn berooft,
Sterkt Judiths hand, koft Veldheers hooft.

Den Engel 't fpraaklits banden breckt,
Tot Biliam den Ezel fpreekt.

Ziet Samfon fchrikt wierbor 't gefchreeuw,
Maar fcheurt-win een, een jonge Leeuw.

De Vis die door het water vloog,
Spowt Jonas uyt hier op het droog.

De Schipliën door de Zeo verftoort,
Die werpen Jonas buyten boort.

In fchijn van vriendfchap, boos en fel,
Doorfteekt Abner Ahazael.

Bels Priefters loosheyt wert ontdekt,
Daar, Daniels afch 't bewijs verftrekt.

Noyt wankelt Job, maar looft zijn Godt,
Schoon hy wert van zijn Wijf befpot.

Men werpt hier Daniel in de kuyl
Der Leeuwen, voor der Leeuwen muyl.

Een vuur'ge Wagen opwaarts voert,
Elia, dat Eliza ontroert.

t' Amfterdam , By Gysbert de Groot Keur, Boek-verkoper op de Nieuwe-dijk/ in de Groote Bybels.

*left to right*

1 Samson with the Doors of the City Gates of Gaza [Judges 16:1-3]
2 Elijah Fed by the Ravens [1 Kings 17:1-7]
3 The Banquet of Esther, Haman and Ahasueros; The Hanging of Haman [Esther 7:1-9]
4 King Nebuchadnezzar Expelled, Dwelling with the Beasts of the Field [Dan. 4:25-30]
5 The Death of Absalom [2 Sam. 18:9-18]
6 The Blindness of Tobit [Tob. 2:7-10]
7 Judith Holding the Head of Holofernes [Judith 13:6-10]
8 Balaam and the Ass [Numbers 22:22-35]

9 Samson Killing the Lion [Judges 14:5-6]
10 Jonah Vomited onto Dry Land by the Fish [Jonah 2:1]
11 Jonah Thrown from the Ship [Jonah 1:15]
12 Abner Smites Asahel [2 Sam. 2:22-23]
13 Daniel and the Statue of Bel [Dan. 14:1-22]
14 Job Seated among the Ashes, Tormented by Satan and Berated by his Wife [Job 2:7-10]
15 Daniel in the Lions Den [Dan. 6: 4-24; 14:28-42]
16 Elijah Ascending to Heaven [2 Kings 2:1-18]

**53.1**
Tobias Stimmer, *Samson with the Doors of the City Gates of Gaza*, woodcut, c. 6 x 8.3 cm, in: *Nouae Tobiae Stimmeri Sacrorvm Bibliorvm figurae...*, Strasbourg 1590. Herzog August Bibliothek, Wolfenbüttel

This theme from the story of Samson may have been chosen for the hero's 'great strength', which is mentioned in the caption. In all sixteen pictures the themes are spectacular events, sometimes exceptionally bloodthirsty (hanging, impalement, decapitation) but more often with a miraculous or even fairytale character. A remarkable aspect is the frequent appearance of animals (2, 4, 5, 6, 8, 9, 10, 11, 15 and 16). This is typical of the popular print genre. Among the early publications of De Groot, besides the biblical prints, are prints of literary and historical heroes and particularly of animals, birds and sea-monsters. From the late seventeenth to the early nineteenth century animal prints, together with biblical prints, featured prominently in the lists of publishers of popular prints.[3]

Inscriptions below each picture provide a brief summary of the story, sometimes directly addressing the reader ('See ...'). Apart for where this is obvious from the story (eg, no. 7: dangers of intoxication), there is no moralising here and no allegorical or typological interpretation. The inscription below no. 10, for example, states simply: 'The fish that swam through the water, vomited Jonah onto dry land'. No attempt is made to teach the spectator a moral lesson or to educate the public in any way.

Who were the spectators? The copy shown here is not explicitly aimed at a particular age group or section of the population. It seems to be intended for anyone able to purchase a copy. In the eighteenth century these popular prints were known as 'oortjes' prints, after the price usually charged (1 oortje = 1/4 stiver). This impression would probably have cost more, being partly illuminated. The colour was not applied with stencils, but with a brush or thumb, providing rhythmic patches of orange, blue and yellow without regard for the contours.

Those who might require some spiritual content in a print of savages surrounded by wild animals (4) or soldiers slain in battle (12) would have had to have a sound knowledge of the Bible. After all, these stories are not the most well-known. Remarkably, the publisher left out any biblical references in the captions, as was conventional in picture Bibles. Might this mean that the print was intended for a public which would have had no access to the original stories? Either way, the print was obviously successful. After 1756 it was reprinted by Johannes Kannewet, the main publisher of popular prints in the later eighteenth century.[4] **PvdC**

1. On the De Groot stock see: De Meyer 1962, pp. 33-34, 148-158. *Cf.* For popular prints in the Netherlands: De Meyer 1970; Van Veen 1976.
2. *Nouae Tobiae Stimmeri Sacrorvm Bibliorvm figurae... Newe Biblische Figuren, durch Tobiam Stim[m]er gerissen...*, Strasbourg, Bernhard Jobin, 1590 (Herzog August Bibliothek, Wolfenbüttel: 674.10 Theol. 8˚).
3. Van Veen 1976, p. 106.
4. On Kannewet see: Van den Berg 1993, pp. 18-43.

Right: detail of cat. no. 66

Crispijn de Passe the Elder, *Liber Genesis Continens Originem Sev Creationem mundi et humani generis propagationem terraeque prioris cataclysmum tum noui orbis restaurationem et sanctae ac electae gentis vocationem. Aeneis omnia incisa Laminis operâ & cura Crisp. Passaei Zel. A[nn]o MDCXII...*, Arnhem, Jan Jansz., 1612 (quarto)

Rijksmuseum Library, Amsterdam (326 I 1)
**Lit** Franken 1881, no. 1342; Holl. XV, pp. 289-291, no. 855; Amsterdam 1934-36, Vol. 2, p. 410; Van der Coelen 1991 & 1994, pp. 168-169; Van der Coelen 1992, pp. 106-108; Münster 1994, p. 330, no. 118

**Illustrated:** Crispijn de Passe the Elder, *Isaac and Rebecca Spied upon by Abimelech*, engraving in: *Liber Genesis...*, Arnhem 1612

**54.1**
Crispijn de Passe the Elder, *Isaac and Rebecca Spied upon by Abimelech*, after 1616, engraving, state III (3), Rijksprentenkabinet, Amsterdam

In the early seventeenth century, the engraver Crispijn de Passe (1564-1637) decided to produce a complete picture Bible. His idea was not new. Already in the sixteenth century artists and printers had compiled picture books containing hundreds of biblical illustrations. These picture Bibles are products of the *pictura-poesis* literature, presenting the Scriptures in word and image. De Passe's plan was ambitious, both aesthetically, as in size: the number of prints was to surpass all previous picture Bibles.

However, the *Liber Genesis* was the only part of De Passe's project to see the light of day. It contains fifty-nine illustrations of scenes from Genesis accompanied by short Latin texts. These include popular themes such as the *Sacrifice of Isaac* as well as less well-known stories, like the scene shown here in which King Abimelech spies upon Isaac caressing Rebecca (Gen. 26:1-8). In the third state (after 1616) the Latin text was replaced by two lines of Dutch prose (fig. 54.1). According to De Passe, his *Liber Genesis* was intended as an aid to those who had difficulties reading the Bible. At the same time he recommended the book as a reference work and a source of inspiration for artists (cf. cat. no. 57). **PvdC**

Ici fçait on voir figuratiuement, comment Ruth amaf-
fe les efpies pour en viure. cap. 2. & comment Ruth s'hu-
milie. cap. 2. & comment on demande apres Ruth qui elle
eft. cap. 2. & qu'elle reçoit vn enfant en fon giron. cap. 4.
& que Boos prend les gens à la porte pour tefmoings fur
l'Heritage qu'il achapte. cap. 4. Ceci nous fert tout d'e-
xemple à ce que foyons auffi reaument refpiritualifé en
l'humilité de Ruth, & que puifsions receuoir ceft Enfant

de Ruth en noftre giron: qui eft la nouuelle-Naiffance en
Chrift, parquoi tout le Peuple qui eft en la Porte (qui font
les Sens & Penfees, qui font à l'huys & la Porte du cœur)
atteftera que la Nature diuine eft notre Heritage. Et alors
les Inconnus demanderont d'où eft venue cefte nouuelle-
Naiffance, pource qu'elle n'eft pas de leurs Lignées.
                    Prenés le à cœur.
                                                          Le

## 55  Figures

Pieter van der Borcht, *Figvres De Tovtes
Les Plvs Remarqvables Histoires, Et Avltres
Evenements Dv Vieil Et Novveav
Testament...*, Amsterdam, Michiel
Colijn, 1613 (quarto oblong)

University Library, Amsterdam (973 G 29)
**Lit** Hamilton 1981, pp. 287-289; Van der Coelen
1991 & 1994, p. 175

**Illustrated:** Pieter van der Borcht, *The History of
Ruth*, etching in: *Figures...*, Amsterdam 1613

Each of the prints in this series by Pieter van der Borcht (c. 1535/40-1608)
provides a simultaneous depiction of consecutive events in one particular
book of the Bible. In the picture reproduced here, for example, seven
episodes from the Book of Ruth are shown. From left to right the artist
portrays Ruth and Boaz on the threshing floor (3), Naomi taking leave of
her daughters (1), Ruth and Boaz meeting (2), Ruth gleaning ears of grain
on Boaz' field (2), Boaz and the elders meeting at the city gates (4), Boaz
inquiring of his servant (2) and the birth of Obed (4). The figures
accompanying the various scenes correspond with the chapters of the book
of Ruth in which the event occurs.

The eighty-eight etchings were Christophe Plantin's second commission
from Van der Borcht (cf. cat. no. 60). The series, first published at the end of
the sixteenth century by the Leiden printer Frans van Raphelingen, was
reprinted several times in the seventeenth century. This edition by Michiel
Colijn, published in 1613, contains French translations of the captions which
the Spiritualist Hendrik Jansen van Barrefelt (Hiël) had originally devised for
the series. These were not included in the version published by the Calvinist
Claes Jansz. Visscher. His edition of 1639 is purely a picture book.[1] **PvdC**

1. *Cf.* Münster 1994, p. 331, no. 121; Van der Coelen 1994-95, p. 119, no. 5.

Johannes I Sadeler after Gerard van
Groeningen, David, Hoc Est Virtutis
Exercitatissimae Probatum Deo
Spectaculum, Ex David Pastoris, Militis,
Regis, Exulis, Ac Prophetae Exemplis,
Amsterdam, Claes Jansz. Visscher,
1637 (quarto)

Prentenkabinet der Rijksuniversiteit, Leiden
(inv. no. 102.036)
**Lit** Münster 1994, p. 331, no. 122; Van der
Coelen 1994-95, p. 119, no. 2

**Illustrated:** Johannes I Sadeler after Gerard van
Groeningen, David Slaying Goliath, engraving in:
David..., Amsterdam 1637

In 1637 the Amsterdam print-, map- and bookseller Claes Jansz. Visscher
published a reprint of a picture book which had originally appeared some
sixty years earlier in Antwerp. It features the life of David and contains
forty-eight illustrations, engraved by Johannes I Sadeler (1550-c. 1600)
and designed by Gerard van Groeningen (active in Antwerp, 1570s).[1]
The engravings are accompanied by mottos and captions, each focusing on
one of David's virtues. The texts were devised by the Spanish theologian
Benito Arias Montano, a friend of Christophe Plantin who first published
the work in co-operation with Philips Galle in 1575.

Shown here is the depiction of David and Goliath in the 1637 edition
(1 Samuel 17:38-51). Visscher's reprint will certainly have contributed to the
influence which Sadeler's prints, later also included in Schabaelje's Grooten
Emblemata Sacra (cat. no. 60), exercised on the David iconography in Dutch
painting.[2]

This was the first in a series of five different biblical picture books - all
reprints of earlier works - that Visscher published between 1637 and 1639
(see also cat. nos. 57 and 58). The timing was no coincidence. Visscher's
intention was to provide the image-oriented reader with a supplement to the
- unillustrated - States Bible, the first edition of which appeared in 1637.[3]
**PvdC**

1. The engravings were formerly attributed to Philips Galle. For the new attribution see: Van der Coelen 1994-95, p. 108.
For Van Groeningen: Mielke 1967, pp. 171-173, 179-180; Mielke 1995. Cf. for the David series: Hänsel 1991, pp. 118-127.
2. Cf. Van Gent 1991 & 1994, pp. 91, 92, 94-95.
3. Cf. Van der Coelen 1994-95, p. 117.

## 57 Historia Del Testamento Vecchio

Sisto Badalocchio & Giovanni Lanfranco, *Historia Del Testamento Vecchio Dipinta In Roma Nel Vaticano Da Raffaelle Di Vrbino Et intagliata in rame da Sisto Badalocchi et Giouan[n]i Lanfranchi Parmigiani...*, Amsterdam, Claes Jansz. Visscher, 1638 (octavo oblong)

Museum van het Boek, The Hague (100 E 10)
**Lit** Nagler, Vol. 16, p. 342; Krücke 1959, p. 82; Rome 1985, p. 79; Münster 1994, pp. 331-332, no. 123; Van der Coelen 1994-95, p. 119, no. 3

**Illustrated**: Sisto Badalocchio after Raphael, *Isaac and Rebecca Spied upon by Abimelech*, etching in: *Historia Del Testamento Vecchio...*, Amsterdam 1638

**57.1**
Rembrandt, *Isaac and Rebecca Spied upon by Abimelech*, pen and bistre, 14.5 x 18.5 cm, W.H. Kramarsky Coll., New York

The Italian artists Sisto Badalocchio (1585-after 1620?) and Giovanni Lanfranco (1582-1647), pupils of the famous painter Annibale Carracci, made a series of free reproductions of the frescos in the Loggia of the Vatican Palace in Rome. Commissioned by Pope Leo X, the vaults of this colonnaded hall had been decorated in 1518/19 with scenes from the Bible after designs by Raphael: forty-eight episodes from the Old Testament and four from the New.

The etchings, mirror-images of the frescos, were printed in 1607 in book form by the Roman publisher Giovanni Orlandi under the title *Historia Del Testamento Vecchio*. Later, Orlandi sold the plates to his Amsterdam colleague Michiel Colijn, who published a reprint in 1614. In 1638 the copper plates of the etchings were acquired by the Amsterdam publisher Claes Jansz. Visscher. He probably bought the plates at the sale of Colijn's estate.

The Amsterdam reprints increased the fame of Raphael's compositions. Reproductive prints enabled artists who had never been to Italy to see the achievements of the Renaissance. Rembrandt, for example, probably owned a copy of *Historia Del Testamento Vecchio*. One of his masterpieces currently in the Rijksmuseum, known as the *Jewish Bride* but actually a portrayal of Isaac and Rebecca, was inspired by a print in this volume. A preparatory sketch for the painting (fig. 57.1)[1] clearly reveals that the artist used the etching shown here, *Isaac and Rebecca spied upon by Abimelech* (Gen. 26:8), as a visual source. Rembrandt may also have known Crispijn de Passe's depiction of the same theme in the *Liber Genesis* (cat. no. 54).[2]

The copy of *Historia del testamento vecchio* shown here was originally owned by Simon Schijnvoet (1652-1727), deputy schout and chief provost of the alms-house in Amsterdam. His large collection of prints and drawings was auctioned in Amsterdam on 18 February 1728. The book is mentioned in the auction catalogue under no. 94 among a diversity of biblical picture books and was sold for 3 guilders. **PvdC**

1. Benesch 988.
2. Tümpel 1986, pp. 355-357. *Cf.* Hoekstra 1996-97, pp. 60-61.

*Robur Vbi Samſon meretrice prodit auare, Hostibus, effosso lumine, preda fuit.    Judicum. 16. Cap.*    6

## 58    Theatrum Biblicum

Various artists, *Theatrum Biblicum Hoc Est Historiae Sacrae Veteris Et Novi Testamenti Tabulis Aeneis Expressae. Opus praestantißimorum huius ac superioris seculi pictorum atque sculptorum, summo studio conquisitum et in lucem editum per Nicolaum Iohannis Piscatorem*, Amsterdam, Claes Jansz. Visscher, 1639 (folio oblong)

Theological Faculty Library, Tilburg (TF PRE 280)
Lit Mauquoy-Hendrickx 1978-83, Vol. III. 2, p. 626; Van der Coelen 1994-95, p. 119, no. 6a

**Illustrated:** Antonie Wierix after Maarten de Vos, *Samson and Delilah*, engraving in: *Theatrum Biblicum...*, Amsterdam 1639

In addition to literary sources such as the Bible and the works of Flavius Josephus artists also based their depictions of biblical scenes on visual information. Before starting a picture an artist would often refer to compositions by predecessors. Naturally, prints would be the first examples to be examined, since these were the most readily available. The Pre-Rembrandtists, for instance, often drew their inspiration from the *Thesaurus*, a biblical picture book published in Antwerp by Gerard de Jode in 1579 and 1585.

This *Thesaurus* contains various series of engravings by a diversity of Northern and Southern Netherlandish artists, including Jan Snellinck, Maarten de Vos and Maarten van Heemskerck. Most of the series depict stories about the Patriarchs and the Kings. Characteristic of the compositions are the monumental, Italianate groups of figures and the detailed depiction of the landscape. Generally, the engravings are accompanied by a Latin distich.[1]

The copperplates of the *Thesaurus* were acquired some time in the seventeenth century by the Amsterdam publisher Claes Jansz. Visscher. He began reprinting them in 1639 for his *Theatrum Biblicum*, a new edition of the *Thesaurus* containing several new series. In the engraving shown here Samson is depicted sleeping as Delilah cuts his hair, the source of his superhuman strength (Judges 16:19-21). This scene was engraved by Antonie Wierix after a drawing by Maarten de Vos.[2] Several reprints of the *Theatrum Biblicum* appeared. In fact, the book was even being sold after 1680 by Visscher's grandson Nicolaus Visscher. Only two copies of this rare 1639 edition are known. The volume contains 355 sheets and was originally owned by a monastery.[3] **PvdC**

1. See for the *Thesaurus*: Mielke 1975. *Cf.* for the 1579 edition: Münster 1994, p. 329, no. 117.
2. Holl. XLIV, no. 96-II.
3. Capuchin Library, Handel/Den Bosch.

Christoffel II van Sichem & Christoffel III van Sichem, *Bibels Tresoor, Ofte der Zielen Lusthof, Uytgebeelt in Figueren, door verscheyden Meesters. Ende gesneden, door Christoffel Van Sichem*, Amsterdam, Pieter Jacobsz. Paets, 1646 (octavo)

University Library, Nijmegen (641 c 9)
**Lit** BCNI no. 10045; Holl. XXVII, pp. 48-49, no. 48; Lehmann-Haupt 1975, p. 289; Poortman 1983-86, Vol. 2, p. 96; Van der Coelen 1991 & 1994, pp. 178-179; Van der Coelen 1992, p. 108; Münster 1994, p. 330, no. 119

**Illustrated:** Christoffel II/III van Sichem, *The King of Assyria Orders One of the Priests Deported from Samaria to Return Hence*, woodcut in: *Bibels Tresoor...*, Amsterdam 1646

**59.1**
Giorgio Ghisi after Raphael, *The School of Athens*, 1550, engraving (2 plates), 52.6 x 82.4 cm (together), Herzog Anton Ulrich Museum, Brunswick

The *Bibels Tresoor* contains countless highlights of European graphic art, from Dürer to Rembrandt, although as copies, not originals. The woodcuts in this volume were cut by Christoffel II van Sichem (c. 1581-1658) and his son, Christoffel III (1618-1659). Pieter Jacobsz. Paets' title for the work is appropriate since the book is indeed a 'biblical treasury' with well over 750 Old Testament prints.

Apart from well-known stories, such as the 'Fall of Man', the 'Sacrifice of Isaac' and 'David and Goliath', the illustrations also include less familiar episodes from the lives of the patriarchs and the kings. Even some obscure events only hinted at in the Bible are shown. One example, incidentally revealing the Van Sichems and their publisher's casual attitude toward their models, is the *593. Figuer*. This scene is clearly based on Raphael's famous *School of Athens*. The fresco in the *Stanza della Segnatura* in the Vatican Palace was well-known from reproductive prints, among them Giorgio Ghisi's version (published by Hieronymus Cock of Antwerp in 1550, fig. 59.1).[1] Without making any changes, just adding a text, the scene was placed in an entirely new context: 'The Assyrian king orders a priest to be brought to Samaria'. Instead of Raphael's ancient philosophers and academicians grouped around Plato and Aristotle, the same figures now represent a royal court in Old Testament times: the king of Assyria commands one of the priests deported from Samaria to return to teach the new inhabitants of the land how to serve the Lord (2 Kings 17:24-28).

As an encyclopaedic reference work for the Old Testament, the *Bibels Tresoor* is far more detailed than the work planned by Crispijn de Passe (*cf.* cat. no. 54). Paets intended his book to be more than an aesthetic compilation. According to the subtitle, he wanted this to be a 'pleasure garden for the soul'. To accompany the illustrations, the Catholic bookseller selected quotations from the Bible. These were taken from the Moerentorf Bible, the translation of the Vulgate approved by the Catholic Church, an edition of which Paets was to publish in 1657 (cat. no. 69). **PvdC**

1. TIB XXXI, pp. 64-65, no. 24 (394). *Cf.* Rome 1985, pp. 38-41.

*Den Grooten Emblemata Sacra, Bestaande in meer dan Vier hondert Bybelsche Figueren, Soo des Ouden als des Nieuwen Testaments...*, Amsterdam, Tymon Houthaak for Jan Philipsz. Schabaelje, 1654 (folio)

Rijksmuseum Library, Amsterdam (329 A 12)
**Lit** Amsterdam 1934-36, Vol. 2, p. 411; Hamilton 1981, pp. 291-294; Poortman 1983-86, Vol. 2, pp. 37-39; Visser 1988, Vol. 1, pp. 424-448; Vol. 2, pp. 208-209; Münster 1994, p. 330, no. 120

**Illustrated:** Pieter van der Borcht, *The Cursing of Cain*, etching in: *Emblemata Sacra...*, Amsterdam 1654

**60.1**
Pieter van der Borcht, *The Cursing of Cain*, etching in: *Emblemata Sacra...*, Amsterdam (Michiel Colijn) 1613. Rijksmuseum Library, Amsterdam

This biblical picture book was compiled by the Mennonite minister and poet Jan Philipsz. Schabaelje. The principal feature of this compilation is a series of almost one hundred etchings which had originally been commissioned by Christophe Plantin from the Antwerp artist Pieter van der Borcht and made between 1582 and 1585. The large etchings were published in Leiden at the end of the sixteenth century by Plantin's son-in-law, Frans van Raphelingen. In the seventeenth century numerous reprints appeared, among them editions by Michiel Colijn and Claes Jansz. Visscher of Amsterdam. The emphasis on the landscape may have been one of the reasons for their popularity.

Shown here is Van der Borcht's etching of the Cursing of Cain (Gen. 4:9-16). Having slain his brother Abel, Cain is banished by God. Here he is about to go to 'the land of Nod, on the east of Eden'. Below right is the lifeless body of Abel. Cain looks up to the source of the voice of God. Van der Borcht originally portrayed God as an old man with a long beard and hair waving in the wind (fig. 60.1). In 1639, when he reprinted the series, Claes Jansz. Visscher removed the personification, replacing it with the Tetragrammaton in an oval space. Many potential buyers would have been offended by anthropomorphic representations of God.[1] **PvdC**

1. *Cf.* Van der Coelen 1994-95, pp. 114-115.

Anonymous after Matthaeus Merian the Elder, *Bybel Printen, Vertoonende de voornaemste Historien der Heylige Schrifture, konstigh afgebeelt door Matthaeus Merian, En nu met veel treffelicke Historien vermeerdert, aerdigh geteeckent en in koper gemaeckt door Pieter Hendricksz Schut...*, Amsterdam, Nicolaes Visscher, *s.a.* (folio)

University Library, Amsterdam (454 B 30)
**Lit** Beckey 1941, pp. 61-62; Poortman 1983-86, Vol. 2, pp. 74-76; Van der Coelen 1991 & 1994, pp. 175-176; Wüthrich 1993, p. 21, no. 2a; Münster 1994, p. 332, no. 124; Pluis 1994, pp. 66-68

**Illustrated**: Anonymous after Matthaeus Merian, *The Sacrifice of Isaac*, etching in: *Bybel Printen...*, Amsterdam *s.a.*

**61.1**
Matthaeus Merian the Elder, *The Sacrifice of Isaac*, etching in: *Icones Biblicae...*, Strasbourg 1629-30. University Library, Nijmegen

In the mid-seventeenth century Amsterdam print publishers Visscher and Danckertsz. began producing a series of picture Bibles with copies after the 233 biblical prints by Matthaeus Merian the Elder (1593-1650). The original etchings (*Icones Biblicae*) were first published in Frankfurt am Main (1625-27) and Strasbourg (1629-30) (fig. 61.1). Merian set most of his biblical scenes, like the *Sacrifice of Isaac* (Gen. 22:1-18), in broad landscapes. The majority depict stories from the Pentateuch, although he also had a penchant for battle scenes from the books of Kings.

To accompany the Merian copies the Amsterdam picture Bibles included captions in various languages. Most had already been written for the original German editions by the Protestant minister Johann Ludwig Gottfried. However, the Dutch (by Reyer Anslo) and English quatrains and the Dutch prose texts were new. In the text accompanying the *Sacrifice of Isaac* the emphasis is on Abraham's obedience: 'He was stedfast in the beliefe of Gods promises'.

The edition shown here was published by Claes Jansz. Visscher's son and heir Nicolaes Visscher. His son Nicolaus also published reprints of the picture Bible with extra texts and prints. Merian's compositions enjoyed a huge audience, although in the form of copies. Apart from the picture Bibles, Merian copies also appeared in editions of Flavius Josephus and a *Haggadah* (*cf.* cat. nos 62, 70, 77). **PvdC**

Pieter Hendricksz. Schut, *Afbeeldingen Van de Heilige Historien Des ouden en nieuwen Testaments. Met korte byschriften en gedigten verrykt Door Johannes Vollenhove, Dr. der H. Theologie en Predicant in 's Gravenhage. Voor dezen uytgegeven door Nicolaus Visscher,* Amsterdam, Rudolph & Gerard Wetstein, *s.a.* (quarto)

University Library, Nijmegen (223 c 87)
**Lit** Poortman 1983-86, Vol. 2, pp. 79-80; Münster 1994, p. 332, no. 125; Pluis 1994, pp. 68-71; Van der Coelen 1994-95, pp. 112-113

**Illustrated**: Pieter Hendricksz. Schut, *The Sacrifice of Isaac,* etching in: *Afbeeldingen van de Heilige Historien...,* Amsterdam *s.a.*

16    G E N E S. XXII. 1-18.

Abrahams offerhande.

*Gehoorsaemheyt Abrahams in t offeren van syn Soon Ysaack*

*Natuur door genade overweldigt.*

Wat laft ! zo ver te gaan met Ifak ? hem te binden?
Te flagten, kerven, door altaarvlam te verflinden?
'k Zie Abrams hant hier toe gereet , die 't lieffte pant
Zelf uit zyn lykafch kan herwachten van Godts hant.

It was in the middle of the seventeenth century that Claes Jansz. Visscher commissioned Pieter Hendricksz. Schut (1618/19-c. 1660) to produce 336 prints of episodes from the Bible. The etchings are all small in format. Most of Schut's compositions are reductions of Flemish originals, including engravings which had already appeared in Visscher's *Theatrum Biblicum* (cat. no. 58). A second source of inspiration was Matthaeus Merian's famous picture Bible. The etching of the *Sacrifice of Isaac* is clearly based on Merian's original (see fig. 61.1). Schut offers an abridged version of Merian's composition showing the figures but leaving out much of the landscape and sky.

Schut's series first appeared in a bound edition in 1659, published by Nicolaes Visscher (*Toneel ofte Vertooch der Bybelsche Historien*). This picture Bible was widely available and frequently reprinted. The edition shown here, with quatrains by the Reformed minister Joannes Vollenhove of The Hague, was first published by Nicolaus Visscher after 1679. Vollenhove's poems are dramatic works. The poet emphasized the violence of the sacrifice: 'What a command! To go so far with Isaac? To bind him? To beat, to cut, to consume in the altar's flames?' **PvdC**

# 63 History of the Old and New Testaments

Various artists, *Historie Des Ouden En Nieuwen Testaments, Verrykt met meer dan vierhonderd Printverbeeldingen In koper gesneeden. Met Privilegie Van de Heeren Staaten van Holland en Westfriesland. Eerste Deel*, Amsterdam, Pieter Mortier, 1700 (folio)

University Library, Nijmegen (248 A 22 [1])
**Lit** Van Eeghen/ Van der Kellen 1905, pp. 491-499, no. 351; De la Fontaine Verwey 1934, p. 38; Poortman 1983-86, Vol. 2, pp. 98-105; Utrecht 1991-92, p. 93, no. 89; Münster 1994, p. 334, no. 130

**Illustrated:** Bernard Picart, *Judith Enters the Tent of Holofernes* and *Judith Putting the Head of Holofernes in a Sack*, engravings in: *Historie des Ouden en Nieuwen Testaments...*, Amsterdam 1700

With the advent of Romeyn de Hooghe, Jan Luyken and Bernard Picart Dutch graphic art began once again to flourish towards the end of the seventeenth century. The so-called 'Large Mortier Bible', a picture Bible named after the publisher, contains prints by Luyken, Picart, Jan Goeree and Otto Elliger that reveal an originality seldom found among the earlier reprints and copies of the world of Dutch biblical illustration.[1] It is the first of a series of remarkable high-quality picture Bibles that began to appear in the first quarter of the eighteenth century.

The work was published in two volumes of which the Old Testament section contains 282 engravings. The accompanying prose text was originally written in French by David Martin and translated into Dutch by Willem Sewel. The publisher, Pieter Mortier, charged clients, who could order the work by subscription, thirty-six guilders for an unbound copy. That is, three stivers per print leaf and one stuiver per text sheet. For a copy of the book on 'large royal paper' he charged forty-seven guilders and five stivers. In his foreword the publisher praised the skill of the artists in depicting various sorts of light. This quality is indeed visible in the two scenes shown here from the Book of Judith, both by Bernard Picart. Above Judith is shown entering Holofernes' tent at night (Judith 10:17ff.) and below, having decapitated him, she puts his head in a sack (Judith 13:9-10). Not all the compositions in this picture Bible are quite as successful. Many of the figures are less well proportioned and their gestures rather wooden.

Mortier dedicated the work to the pensionary of Holland Anthonie Heinsius, whom he warns 'that even shrewd and practiced Statesmen can learn excellent and beneficial lessons from this sacred History, and can find out how superbly the tireless Moses, the heroic Joshua, the industrious Samuel, the pious David, the wise Solomon, and many other excellent men ruled God's chosen people in former times'.[2] **PvdC**

1. The painter David van der Plaes was artistic supervisor. There was a major disagreement in 1703 between Mortier and Van der Plaes about the bill. See: Van Gelder 1916; De la Fontaine Verwey 1941, pp. 3-4; Van Eeghen 1960-78, Vol. 3, p. 263.
2. The Dutch text runs: '[...] dat zelfs schrandere en dooroefende Staatkundigen, uyt deeze heylige Historie voortreffelyke en heylzaame lessen konnen haalen, en daar uyt leeren hoe loffelyk in de aalouden tyden de onvermoeide Moses, de heldhaftige Josua, de yverige Samuël, de godvruchtige David, de wyze Salomon, en veele andere voortreffelyke mannen, Gods uytverkooren volk eertyds hebben geregeerd'.

JUDITH, X, vs. 17
Judith komt des nachts inde tent van Holophernus.
JUDITH X, vs 17.
Judith vient de nuit en la tente d'Holopherne.

JUDITH, XIII
Judith houd Holophernus Hooft af en verlost Bethulien.
JUDITH XIII.
Judith coupe la tête d'Holopherne, & delivre Bethulie.

162

Romeyn de Hooghe, *Alle de Voornaamste Historien Des Ouden en Nieuwen Testaments. Verbeeld in uytsteekende Konst-Platen, Door den Wyd-beroemden Heer, en Mr. Romeyn de Hooge. Met omstandige verklaring der Stoffen, en seer beknopte Punt-Digten, Van den Eerw: Godsgel: Heer Henricus Vos…,* Amsterdam, Jacob Lindenberg, 1703 (folio)

University Library, Amsterdam (2415 A 21)
**Lit** Holl. IX, p. 118, no. 2; Van Eeghen 1960-78, Vol. 3, pp. 215-220; Landwehr 1970, p. 215, no. 100; Poortman 1980; Poortman 1983-86, Vol. 2, pp. 109-111; Münster 1994, p. 335, no. 131

**Illustrated:** Romeyn de Hooghe, *Jacob's Dream* (centre), *The Sacrifice of Isaac* (top left), *Isaac Blessing Jacob* (top right), *The Meeting of Jacob and Esau* (bottom left) and *The Death of the Shechemites* (bottom right), etching in: *Alle de voornaamste historien…*, Amsterdam 1703

Romeyn de Hooghe (1645-1708) is considered 'the most important and the most prolific Dutch etcher of the period immediately following Rembrandt'.[1] He was a man of many talents, an artist, a law graduate and a writer. The publisher Jacob Lindenberg commissioned De Hooghe to produce a series of 139 prints for a picture Bible, which first appeared in 1703. Most of the illustrations contain five scenes: a large oval in the middle surrounded by four smaller scenes in each of the corners. The illustrations are etched in a brisk, Late-Baroque style with particular attention to chiaroscuro. Shown here is *Jacob's Dream* (Gen. 28:10-16), surrounded in the corners by scenes from the Book of Genesis: the *Sacrifice of Isaac* (Gen. 22:1-18), *Isaac blessing Jacob* (Gen. 27:1-30), the *Meeting of Jacob and Esau* (Gen. 33) and the *Death of the Shechemites* (Gen. 34:25-30).

The edition, with explanatory texts by the Lutheran clergyman Henricus Vos, was dedicated to the directors of the Dutch East India Company. Lindenberg reminds them of their duty to spread the Scriptures among the 'heathens': 'They [the heathens] eagerly open their ears to witness the miracles of the various ages of the Lord: and since the ears are assisted in this Bible by the eyes, the effect on their emotions will be even greater.'[2] **PvdC**

1. Henkel 1926, p. 261.
2. 'Zy [de heidenen] openen haare ooren met gretigheid, om de wonderen der verscheide tyden des Heeren te zien: maar terwyl de ooren in dezen Bybel met de oogen geholpen worden, zal de indruk grooter zyn op hare gemoederen'.

## 65    Icones Biblicae

Jan Luyken, *Icones Biblicae Veteris et N:
Testamenti. Figures Du Vieux et du Nouveau
Testament. Inventées et Gravées Par Jan
Luyken. Print-Verbeeldingen der Historien
des Ouden en Nieuwen Testaments*,
Amsterdam, Pieter Mortier, *s.a.*
[1708], (folio)

Amsterdam Historical Museum, Amsterdam
(inv. no. A 41227)
**Lit** Van Eeghen/ Van der Kellen 1905, pp. 658-
669, no. 429; Holl. XI, p. 140, no. 429;
Poortman 1983-86, Vol. 2, p. 131; Münster
1994, p. 335, no. 132

**Illustrated:** Jan Luyken, *The Sacrifice of Elijah*,
etching in: *Icones Biblicae..*, Amsterdam 1708

Jan Luyken (1649-1712), an eminent poet as well as a talented etcher, was by
far the most productive Bible illustrator at the turn of the seventeenth and
eighteenth century. Together with his son Casper he was responsible for the
picture Bible published by Christoph Weigel in Nuremberg (1708) and the
*Schriftuurlijke Geschiedenissen* published in Amsterdam (1712). For the latter he
also contributed the text, with poems that bear witness to his pietism.

In addition, Luyken provided illustrations for three picture Bibles
published by Pieter Mortier (cf. cat. no. 63). Of these, the *Icones Biblicae* are
undoubtedly the most spectacular. With the masterly touch of a director, the
artist composed scenes, often of crowds, with a drama that presages the
work of the later Gustave Doré.[1] The book, of which the first edition is dated
1708, comprises sixty-two large etchings (c. 32 x 43 cm) with a short
description of the subject in Dutch and French. Shown here is the thirty-
second print depicting *Elijah's Sacrifice* (1 Kings 18:20-40).

From the advertisement published in the *Amsterdamse Courant* by Mortier's
widow in 1712 it is clear that the prints could also be purchased separately
and bound into Bibles. Depending on the paper size, they were 8 or 10
stuivers a piece.[2] **PvdC**

1. Cf. Veldman 1987A, p. 36.
2. Van Eeghen 1960-78, Vol. 3, pp. 264-265.

Gerard Hoet, Arnold Houbraken &
Bernard Picart, *Taferelen Der Voornaamste
Geschiedenissen Van Het Oude En Nieuwe
Testament, En Andere Boeken, By de Heilige
Schrift Gevoegt, Door De Vermaarde
Kunstenaars Hoet, Houbraken, en Picart
Getekent, En Van De Beste Meesters In Koper
Gesneden, En Met Beschryvingen Uitgebreid.
Het Eerste Deel,* The Hague, Pieter de
Hondt, 1728 (folio)

Nederlands Openluchtmuseum, Arnhem
(Tresor P-3)
**Lit** De la Fontaine Verwey 1934, pp. 31-32;
Poortman 1983-86, Vol. 2, pp. 137-145; Utrecht
1991-92, p. 94, no. 93; Münster 1994, p. 336,
no. 133; Pluis 1994, pp. 75-76; Groningen
1994, pp. 20, 25, no. 37

**Illustrated:** Andries van Buysen after Gerard
Hoet, *The Fall of Man,* engraving in: *Taferelen Der
Voornaamste Geschiedenissen...,* The Hague 1728

In 1710 Bernard Picart (1673-1733) moved from Paris to Amsterdam. In the
same year the artist, who had already contributed to the 'Large Mortier Bible'
(cat. no. 63), concluded a contract with the publisher Hendrick Adriaen van
der Marck. It was agreed that he would complete a series of biblical prints
started by Gerard Hoet (1648-1733) and Arnold Houbraken (1660-1719).
For the design and (subcontracted) engraving of each print, he would receive
100 (half-folio sheet) or 200 (plano sheet) guilders.[1] Eventually, between
1705 and 1720, a total of 214 prints were produced, of which most were by
designed by Hoet (105), Houbraken (25) and Picart (70). Some thirty Dutch
and French engravers completed the actual plates.

For the first edition of these Bible prints, which appeared in 1720, the
contract stipulated a total of 2,500 copies. The second edition was published
in 1728 in three volumes by Pieter de Hondt of The Hague. This time the
engravings were accompanied by texts by Jacques Saurin, a clergyman from
the city's Walloon church. Shown here is the *Fall of Man* (Gen. 3:1-7),
engraved by Andries van Buysen after a design by Gerard Hoet. The print is
typical of the French flavour of the entire series with its balanced
composition and the idealized figures engraved with careful accuracy.
The contrast with Rembrandt's loose and natural portrayal of the same
theme (cat. no. 2) could hardly be greater. The title is engraved below in six
languages, of which the English version reads: 'Eve gives the fruit of the Tree
of Knowlege of which she had eat to her Husband'. **PvdC**

1. Bredius 1911; Van Eeghen 1960-78, Vol. 1, pp. 104-105.

*Biblia, Dat Is De gantsche H. Schrifture,
vervattende alle de Canonijcke Boecken des
Ouden en des Nieuwen Testaments. Door last
der Hoogh-Mog: Heeren Staten Generael
vande Vereenighde Nederlanden, en volgens
het Besluyt vande Synode Nationael,
gehouden tot Dordrecht, inde Iaren 1618
ende 1619. Uyt de Oorspronckelijcke talen in
onse Nederlandtsche tale getrouwelijck over-
geset...*, Amsterdam, Widow of Paulus
Aertsz. van Ravesteyn, 1657 (folio)

University Library, Amsterdam (487 A 7)
**Lit** Poortman 1983-86, Vol. 1, pp. 148-151, 158;
De Bruin 1993, pp. 233-332; Münster 1994,
p. 328, no. 112

**Illustrated**: Engraved titlepage of *Biblia...*,
Amsterdam 1657

At the Synod of Dort (Dordrecht) of the Reformed Church in 1618-19 it was
decided to commission a new Dutch translation of the Bible based on the
original Hebrew and Greek texts. According to the resolution of the States
General, this so-called States translation of the Bible was first published in
1637. The corrected edition of 1657 became the standard version on which
all later editions were based. A majestic portico on the titlepage of this
edition frames the title. On the broken pediment is an open Bible. In
addition to the arms of the States, the cartouche at the bottom of the page
contains a depiction of the prophet Elijah being fed by ravens in the valley of
Kerith (1 Kings 17:1-7).

Apart from the titlepage, no illustrations were included in the States Bible.
However, print publishers produced separate biblical prints in various sizes.
By including these prints in their own copies individual purchasers could
assemble their own illustrated Bible.

Because of its late date and the existence of a powerful pictorial tradition,
the States Bible translation exercised little influence on the iconography of
Old Testament illustrations. Only later in the century, when the translation
had become an integral part of Protestant culture, did paintings and prints
appear with motifs dirived from the States Bible text, for example in
Rembrandt's later works and in paintings by his pupil Arent de Gelder.[1] **PvdC**

1. *Cf.* Tümpel 1991 & 1994, p. 22.

*Biblia Hebraica Accuratissima, Notis Hebraïcis et Lemmatibus Latinis illustrata. A Johanne Leusden, Philosophiae Doctore, & Linguae Sanctae in Academia Ultrajectina Professore,* Amsterdam, Joseph Athias, 1667 (octavo)

University Library, Nijmegen (768 C 37)
**Lit** Fuks/ Fuks-Mansfeld 1984-87, no. 393; Amsterdam 1987, pp. 82-83; Münster 1994, p. 328, no. 113

**Illustrated:** Engraved titlepage of *Biblia Hebraica...,* Amsterdam 1667

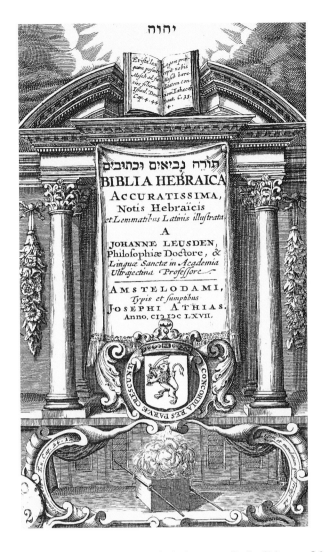

In the Dutch Republic, Christians studied editions of the Old Testament as well as Jews. With the rise of Humanism and the Reformation in the sixteenth century it had become fashionable to examine the Bible in the original languages. For the Old Testament this meant Hebrew. Scholars and publishers tried to compile the original text as accurately as possible.

This *Biblia Hebraica,* edited by the Reformed professor Johannes Leusden and published by the Jewish bookseller Joseph Atthias in an impression of 5,000 copies was promoted as especially accurate, a reputation the book still enjoys. The edition is dedicated to the States General, which is reflected in the titlepage illustration: the decoration - a portico with open Bible and the States coat of arms - is clearly based on the titlepage of the States Bible (*cf.* cat. no. 67). Here, the picture of Elijah is replaced by a representation of the Ark of the Covenant. **PvdC**

*Biblia Sacra Dat is de Geheele Heylige Schrifture Bedeylt in 't Out en Nieu Testament. Oversien en verbetert na den lesten Roomschen text. Verciert met veele schoone figueren. Eerst t'Antwerpen by Ian van Moerentorf, en nu herdruckt by Pieter Iacopsz Paets, Amsterdam, Pieter Jacobsz. Paets, 1657 (folio)*

University Library, Nijmegen (718 a 17)
**Lit** Holl. XXVII, p. 49, no. 49; Lehmann-Haupt 1975, pp. 290-291; Poortman 1983-86, Vol. 1, pp. 129-134; Leiden 1990, p. 20, no. 1; Utrecht 1991-92, p. 92, no. 81; De Bruin 1993, pp. 137-149; Münster 1994, p. 328, no. 114

**Illustrated:** Christoffel van Sichem II/III, *Tobit Burying the Dead; The Blindness of Tobit* (after Hans Holbein the Younger), *Tobit Accused by Anna of Stealing the Kid* (after Jan van de Velde II) in: *Biblia Sacra...*, Amsterdam 1657

With the advent of the Reformation, the Catholic Church needed to state its position regarding the reliability of the various editions of the Bible. Instead of the Hebrew or Greek texts, the Council of Trent declared the Vulgate, the Latin translation of the original by the Church Father Jerome, to be the authorised and canonical text. The definitive text was compiled in 1590-92 under popes Sixtus V and Clemens VIII. In 1599 the Antwerp publisher Jan Moerentorf (Moretus), son-in-law and successor of Christophe Plantin, printed a Dutch translation approved by the Church. The text of this so-called Moerentorf Bible was to remain in use among Dutch Catholics until well into the nineteenth century.

In 1657 the Amsterdam bookseller Pieter Jacobsz. Paets published a new edition of the Moerentorf Bible dedicated to Marius Ambrosius Capello, Bishop of Antwerp. It is not just in the text that this Catholic Bible differs from the States Bible, the design is also different. The text contains no less than 1,200 woodcut illustrations. These were made by Christoffel van Sichem II and his son Christoffel III. Most are simplified versions of well-known prints. The page reproduced here shows three scenes from the Book of Tobit. Above left is *Tobit Burying the Dead* (Tobit 1:17-18). The woodcut, top right, depicting the moment of Tobit's blindness (Tobit 2:7-10) is copied after Hans Holbein's *Icones* print of *c.* 1530. The woodcut, below right, shows Tobit accusing his wife Anna of stealing the kid (Tobit 2:11-14); it is a mirror copy of an etching by Jan van de Velde II after Willem Buytewech (after 1619).[1] Many of Van Sichem's woodcuts had already appeared in previous publications by Paets, including the *Bibels Tresoor* of 1646 (cat. no. 59). **PvdC**

1. Holbein: Holl. German XIVA, pp. 207-212, no. 100 (61); Van de Velde: Holl. XXXIII, p. 10, no. 6.

Propheet: V feeft-daghen sullen verkeert worden in beklaginghe ende droefheyt.

7 Doen de sonne onder was / soo is hy wech gegaen / ende heeft hem begraven.

8 Ende alle sijn naesten berispten hem / seggende: Het was nu korts geboden dat men u dooden soude om dese saecke / ende naeuwelijcr en spdy ontbloden 't gebot des doots / ende begraefdy weder de dooden?

9 Maer Tobias meer vreesende Godt dan den Koninck / nam de lichamen der verslagenen wech / ende verberchdese in zijn huys / ende ten middernacht soo begroef hy die.

10 Ende het geschiede dat hy op eenen dach vermoeyt vander begravenisse te huys komende / hem geworpen hadde aen den want / ende ontslapen was /

11 Ende dat uyt den nest der swaluwen wermen dreck viele op zijn ooghen doen hy sliep / ende dat hy blint worde.

12 Ende dese bekoringhe heeft de Heere daerom laten op hem komen / dat den nakomelinghen soude gegeven worden een exempel zijnder verduldichept / gelijck oock is vanden Heylighen Job.

ob.1.2.
C

13 Want overmits hy van zijn kintshept altijt Godt gevreest hadde / ende zijn geboden bewaert / soo en is hy niet bedroeft geweest teghen Godt / dat de plaghe der blinthept hem aengekomen was /

14 Maer onberoert is hy in de vreese Godts gebleven / danckende Godt alle de daghen zijns levens.

15 Want gelijck de Koninghen den salighen Job beschimpten / alsoo bespotten het leven van desen / zijn ouders ende maghen seggende.

16 Waer is u hope / daerom dat ghy aelmissen ende begravinghe dedet?

17 Maer Tobias straftese / seggende: En wilt alsoo niet spreecken /

18 Want wy zijn kinderen der Heyli-ghen / ende verwachten dat leven / 't welck

D

Godt geven sal den genen die haerlieder geloove nemmermeer van hem en veranderen.

## 70 Flavius Josephus (Dutch)

*Flavii Iosephi hooghberoemde Joodsche historien ende boecken, noch Egesippus vande Ellendighe verstoringe der Stadt Ierusalem. Van nieus met schone figuren verciert, ende met nootwendighe anteikeningen en summarien verrijckt,* Amsterdam, Jan Evertsz. Kloppenburgh, 1626 (folio)

University Library, Nijmegen (556 b 5)
**Lit** Poortman 1983-86, Vol. 2, pp. 219-222; Münster 1994, p. 329, no. 116

**Illustrated:** Christoffel II van Sichem after Tobias Stimmer, *Joseph and Potiphar's Wife,* woodcut in: *Flavii Iosephi...,* Amsterdam 1626

The Jewish historian Flavius Josephus (*c.* AD 37-100) wrote a series of books on the history of the Jewish people from the Creation to the war against Rome (AD 66-70). A particular favourite was his *Jewish Antiquities* with its numerous embellishments on the biblical stories. In the sixteenth and seventeenth centuries at least twenty-five editions of Josephus' complete works appeared in Dutch. The first translation was published in 1552.

The volume shown here contains the second Dutch translation, which appeared in numerous editions between 1594 and 1659. Everard Bommelius, the translator, based his text on a German translation rather than on Josephus' original Greek (*cf.* cat. no. 71). Christoffel II van Sichem's woodcuts are also based on the German edition, namely on the illustrations by Tobias Stimmer. Reproduced here is fol. 14v with the woodcut depicting the story of Joseph and Potiphar's wife (Gen. 39:6-18). It is a simplified mirror-image copy of Stimmer's original. Jacob Saverij, who published a third translation in 1665 (by Lambert van den Bos), described these illustrations by the Van Sichems as 'old, worn-out wooden plates hardly worth seeing'.[1] He replaced them with prints many of which were based on the famous series by Matthaeus Merian (fig. 70.1). **PvdC**

1. '...oude lamme, en naeuw besiens waerde houte platen...', *Flavii Iosephi Hoochgeroemde Joodsche Historien ende Boecken...,* Dordrecht (Jacob Saverij) 1665 (Amsterdam, University Library, inv. no. 347 B 10). *Cf.* Van der Coelen 1991 & 1994, p. 177.

**70.1**
Anonymous artist after Matthaeus Merian the Elder, *The Sacrifice of Isaac,* etching in: *Flavii Iosephi...,* Dordrecht 1665. University Library, Amsterdam

Putiphars wijf houdt ten anderen mael aen Ioseph met bidden en dreigen. Gen. 39.

noch te vpriger geworde/ en meide Ioseph en soude haer niets weygeren: en also de onbehoorlicke liefde nz na en liet/so versocht sp't te anderen mael aen hē/op hope datse meynde hem ten laetsten daer toe te brengen. Als daer nu eē hooge feest voorhande was/ het welck ooc de vrouwen plegen te houde/ so heeft se haer tegē haren man gestelt als crāc/ en begeerde aē cē stille en heymelicke plaetse/en sochte daerdoor voorsake en gelegētheyt/hoe datse dē Ioseph bedriegen mochte: En als sp hem gesien hadde/ sprac sp hem aen met veel saechte ende schoone woorden/meer als opt te vore/en seyde: Dat het veel beter ware geweest/ dat gp mp vandē beginne mijn begeerē nz en haddet af geslagē/ maer na mijner begeerte mp te wille geweest/ aengesiē ic vrouwe in dē hupse bē/ en mp door uwe liefde so gantsch hebbe in neme/ en overwinnē laten/ dat hoe wel ic vrou vandē hupse bē noehtans u so vriendelicke woorde gegevē hebbe. Is nu eenige wijsheyt in u/so suldp mp noch huypde te wille zijn/en wedero vergoedē/ wat gp voormaels upt onverstant versuymt hebt: Ist u daeromme te doē geweest/ dat gp wilt gebedē zijn/ so doe ic nu dz selve veel vlijtiger als opt te vore? wāt ic mp daerom crāc gemaect heb/ en uwe liefde hooger geacht hebbe/ dā alle vreuchde deses feest-daechs. So gp voormaels gedacht hebt/tē zp mp nz ernst geweest/ so hebt nu lichtelicke te bekennē/ dat ic nz bedriegelicker wijse met u gehādelt hebbe/ aengesien ic in mijn voornemē bestandich blijve. Daerō so meuchdp nu de aen gebodē wellusē gebzupcken/en uwer boelē te wille zijn/ het welcke u in andere sake ooc nut ende goet zijn sal: oftegp moet mijner toornichz en ongenade ōwachtē/wāneer ghp u ōmeynde cupsbz liever laet zijn/ als mijn gūste. Dz suldp ooc seherlic wetē dz uwe cupsheyt weynich helpen sal/wāneer ic u bp mijn mā verclage/en segge dat gp mp hebt willē Geraechtē: en wanneer gp schoo mz waerhz om gaet/so sal nochtās Putiphar mijn woordē meer geloofs gevē/als uwe.

Maer Ioseph liet hē door dese woorden/diese ooc mz trane bevestichde/grēsins bewegē noch mz dreygementen verschzicke/dz hp sijne cupsheyt licht achtede/ en haren wille dede: maer bleef bestendich/ en wilde liever alles lijden en verdzage/dā haer oneerlichept met haer doe/ en dat volbzenge/ daerō hp namaels in eē seker verderve come mochte. Vermaende haer wat haer ampt was/ en wat echtelicke plicht en getrou wich3 vorderde: en seyde dat haer sulcx meer behoorde aē gelegē te zijn/ dā eē snode en ūgāclicke welluste/ daer op altijt vā wege desvolbzachtē werex/rouwe en leetwese volchde/ en ooc de schade niet wederōme te bzenge zp. So moeste sp ooc altijt in sorge staē/ dat de gedaē schāde nz upt en come: zo sp doch daer ētegē de liefde en bp woninge hares māg/ stil en sonder eenich perijckel gebzupckē cā/en daer bp voor God en den mensche/ een vreedsamige en vrolicke conscientie mach behoude. So is het ooc veel beter/datse bp haer eere blijve / ende hem als eenen armen dienaer in aller onderdanichept sijn werc late doen/dan dat hp een wetē hebbe van haer schande ende oneere/ende ooc mede daer inne veel hebbē moeste. Dat het oock veel beter zp/ eener goeder conscientien/ ende der eerlicker wercken hem te vertroostē/ dan na dien de sonde ghescdiet is/ te vergeefs hopen datse versweghen soude blijven.

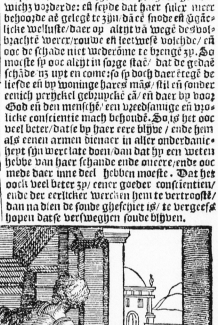

Met dese en diergelijcke andere woorde vele so gedachte Ioseph deser vrouwē de oneerlicke liefde te benemē/ ende haer van haren boosen voornemē/ wederomme op den rechten wech te bzengen: maer sp pielt hoe langer hoe heftiger aē. En nademael sp met woordē bphēniet en conde vercrijgē/en voorder geen middel en wist om hem daer toe te bzengē/ so sloech sp de hant aen hem/en wilde hē met geweit dwingen dz hp haer wille doē moeste. Als nu Ioseph met toorne zijnde/upt de camer spranc/en den roc daer bp sp pielt/achter hē liet/ so verdzoot het haer seer dat sp mis-geschoten hadde/ende moeste in vzeese staen/haer man mochte sulcke boeverie van haer vernemen/ soo nam sp haer

voor den Ioseph valschelicken voorz Putiphar te beclage/ en haer also aen hem te wzeke vā wegē sijns hoochmoets: en gedocht als eē listige vrouwe/dat het haer pzofijtelicker ware / eer te clagē als hp: Daerom so sat sp gātsch dzoevich en onlustich. Ende hoe wel alle hare bedzoeffenisse daer upt was comende/ datse hare derteltept met Ioseph niet en hadde volbzengē connen/so geliet sp haer doch also/ als quame alle haren onwil en toornichept daer hene dat hp haer harer vrouwelicke eere hadde willen benemen ende berooven.

Als haer man nu wederō t'hups quam/ en vā wege haer treurichept verschziete/ende de oorzaecke weten wilde harer bedzoeffenisse/ so

Een schoon exempel der cupscheptae Ioseph. Genes. 39.

Vrouwen list.

viijg

## 71   Flavius Josephus (German)

*Flauij Josephi, deß Hochberühmbten
Jüdischen Geschichtschreibers Historien vnd
Bücher ... mit ... schönen Figuren...,*
Strasbourg, Caspar Dietzel & Christoph
von der Heyden heirs, 1630 (folio)

Museum het Rembrandthuis, Amsterdam
**Lit** Holl. XXVII, p. 35, no. 142; Basel 1984,
nos 58-58a; Poortman 1983-86, Vol. 2, p. 211;
Münster 1994, p. 329, no. 115

**Illustrated:** Tobias Stimmer, *The Death of the
Priest Eli,* woodcut in: *Flauij Josephi...,* Strasbourg
1630

**71.1**
Rembrandt, *Eli Hears that his Sons are Slain and the
Ark of the Covenant is Lost,* c. 1656, pen and bistre,
18.4 x 24.8 cm, Victoria & Albert Museum,
London

Besides the Bible, sixteenth- and seventeenth-century artists also drew
inspiration from the books of Flavius Josephus. His *Jewish Antiquities* was
especially popular among painters looking for extra information about the
stories they wished to depict.[1]

From Rembrandt's inventory of 1656 it appears that besides 'An old Bible'
the master also owned an edition of Josephus, namely 'A High-German
Flavio Jevus illustrated with figures by Tobias Timmerman'.[2] Unusually, he
did not own the popular Dutch translation (cat. no. 70), but the German
edition on which this was based. This was one of the fourteen editions of the
Conrad Lautenbach translation which were printed between 1574 and 1630
in Strasbourg. The Swiss artist Tobias Stimmer had designed 111 illustrations
for this work which were cut by various woodblock cutters, among them
Christoffel van Sichem I.

It was not just the text of the *Antiquities* that inspired Rembrandt, he also
borrowed from one of Stimmer's woodcuts, the print depicting the death of
the priest Eli (1 Samuel 4:10-18). The Israelites had been defeated in battle by
the Philistines. Not only did the enemy capture the Ark of the Covenant;
thirty thousand footmen died fighting for Israel, and among the slain were
the two sons of Eli. Left in the woodcut is a messenger telling the sad news to
the old priest, seated by the wayside. Right, in the main scene Eli is shown
falling off his chair when he hears the news: 'his neck broke and he died, for
he was an old man, and heavy'. Following Stimmer, Rembrandt depicted the
story in a pen-and-bistre sketch in 1656.[3] In fact, he took the theme from
Stimmer's subsidiary scene in which the messenger has just found Eli and
has yet to tell him the bad news (1 Samuel 4:13-15). **PvdC**

1. Cf. Tümpel 1984.
2. 'Een hoogduijtsche Flavio Jevus gestoffeert met figueren van Tobias Timmerman', Strauss/ Van der Meulen 1979,
p. 379, 1656/12, nos 284 and 285.
3. Benesch 1011. Cf. Tümpel 1969, pp. 125-127; Münster 1994, pp. 197-198.

dieweil er es selbs alters halben nicht mehr versehen konte. Da erhub sich nun ein groß frolocken bei den Hebreern/ dann sie verhofften umb der Laden willen ihren Feinden obzusigen: Dargegen entsatzten sich die Philister nicht wenig für der Laden deß HERREN/ welche die Hebreer auff ihrer seiten hatten. Es hat aber viel ein andern außgang genommen/ denn sie sich zu beyden theilen versehen. Sintemal da es ans treffen gangen/ der Sig/ den die Hebreer verhoffet/ auff der Philister seiten bliben/ die Niderlag aber/ dafür sich die Philister besorgt/ auff der Hebreer seiten gerathen ist. Dabei sie dann erfahren/ daß sie vergeblich ihre hoffnung auff die Lade gesetzt haben. Dann sie gleich im ersten angriff in die Flucht geschlagen worden/ vnd dreissig tausent Mann darinn verlohren haben/ vnder welchen auch deß Hohenpriesters Söhne todt bliben/ vnd die Lade in der Feinde Händ kommen ist.

Hophni vnd Phineas erschlagen/ vnd die Lade deß HERREN von den Philistern genomen. 1. Sam. 4.

## Das XII. Cap.

Ein Jüngling so auß der Schlacht war entlauffen/ bringet die Botschafft von der Hebreer Niderlag gen Silo/ darüber sich das Volck hefftig bekümmert.

NAch dem nuhn daß geschrey/ durch einen Jüngling auß dem Stamm BenJamin/ so auß dem Streit entflohen war/ in die Statt Silo kommen/ daß die Hebreer geschlagen/ vnd die Lade Gottes genommen were/ erhub sich ein grosse Klag in der gantzen Statt. Eli aber der Hohepriester saß vnter dem Thor auff einem hohen Sessel/ höret deß Volcks Klag/ vnd gedachte/ es hette sich sonst etwas newes vnter seinen Leuthen zugetragen/ hieß den Jüngling für sich kommen/ welcher ihm erzählet/ beydes seiner Söhne/ vnd deß Kriegsvolcks Niderlag/ darüber er sich nicht so hefftig bekümert/ dieweil ihm Gott solches alles zuvor verkündiget hatte/ daß es also gehen würde. Dann wann einem vngewarnter sach ein vnfall begegnet/ das schmirtzet viel vbeler.

Eli kom̄e die Botschafft von seiner Söhne/ vnd deß Volcks Niderlag.

## Daß XIII. Cap.

Eli erschrickt vber der zeitung von der entwendten Lade Gottes dermassen/ daß er vom Stul zu todt fallet/ vnd Phinees Weib stirbt für leyd.

ALs er aber gehöret/ das die Lade Gottes auch in der Feinde hände kommen were/ ist ihm diser vnversehene Zufall dermassen zu hertzen gangen/ daß er vor ohnmacht von dem Stul herab gefallen/ vnd seinen Geist auffgeben hat/ im acht vnd neuntzigsten Jahr seines Alters/ seiner Regierung aber im viertzigsten.

Eli stürtzt den halß ab. 1. Sam. 4.

N

*De Historie van Joseph de[n] vromen ende Godtvruchtighen Jonghelinc. Allen goeden ende vromen Jonghers tot eenen spieghel ende onderwijsinghe, om Godtvrugtelijc, eerbaerlijc ende deugdelijc te leven,* Rotterdam, Jan van Waesberghe II, 1617 (quarto)

University Library, Amsterdam (2435 E 7 [4])
**Lit** De Booy 1977, p. 285 (under no. 29); Poortman 1983-86, Vol. 2, p. 272; Van Selm 1987, p. 278 (under no. 24); Heimeriks/ Van Toorn 1990, pp. 87, 104, 114, 115, 181- 182

**Illustrated:** Titlepage of *Joseph de[n] vromen...,* Rotterdam 1917, with a woodcut of an anonymous master, illustrating *Joseph Telling his Dreams*

**72.1**
Bernard Salomon, *Joseph Telling his Dreams,* woodcut in: *Wol gerissnen vnd geschnidten figuren Ausz der Bibel,* Lyon (Jean de Tournes) 1554. Herzog August Bibliothek, Wolfenbüttel

Between 1540 and 1560 various religious readers began to appear which were to continue being reprinted for hundreds of years. They were small booklets featuring the stories of biblical characters such as *De Historie van Joseph* and *De historie van den ouden Tobias ende van synen sone den jonghen Tobias* (which also included the stories of Judith, Susanna and Esther).

This 1617 edition of *De Historie van Joseph* contains just 48 pages. It includes the literal text of the thirteen Bible chapters concerning the story of Joseph (Genesis 37; 39-50). The text is set in civilité type. This typeface was designed in the sixteenth century to bring printed type closer to the handwritten letter and was often employed in schoolbooks.

Apart from the text, the book contains 13 woodcuts of identical format of which one -*Joseph Telling his Dreams* (Gen. 37: 1-11) - on the titlepage (see fig.). In style and iconography they closely resemble the Bible prints of the Lyon artist Bernard Salomon (fig. 72.1; see also fig. 42.2). Salomon's woodcuts, with their charming, mannerist elongated figures in panoramic landscapes, began to appear in 1553 in numerous picture Bibles. They exercised an enormous influence on European biblical illustration of the later sixteenth century, reflected not least in the work produced in Antwerp.[1]

This work probably first appeared in that city. In 1587 the Van Waesberghe press began to move to Rotterdam. There Jan van Waesberghe II reprinted many of the titles his father Jan I had already published in Antwerp. He came to dominate the schoolbook market in the early seventeenth century.[2] Although the titlepage does not recommend it as such explicitly, this booklet was certainly intended for use in schools. Of course, it could also be read at home, for example, as indicated in the title, by 'good and pious youngsters' for whom it might be 'a mirror and a guide on how to live a godfearing, honourable and virtuous life'.[3] **PvdC**

1. *Cf.* Cartier 1937-38, no. 267. For the influence of Salomon on Antwerp Bible illustration see: Rosier 1992, Vol. 1, pp. 37, 43.
2. One French-Dutch version of *De Historie van Joseph* is known, published in 1589 (Rotterdam, Jan van Waesberghe II); a French edition probably appeared as early as 1573 (*cf.* Ledeboer 1869, p. 58; Van Selm 1987, p. 278, no. 24). For Jan I and Jan II van Waesberghe see: Briels 1974, pp. 528-537.
3. The 1610 auction catalogue of the bookseller Cornelis Claesz.'s stock mentions a 'Historien van Joseph' together with other biblical readers in the section 'School-goedt' (school materials). See: Van Selm 1987, pp. 234-242, 275-283.

# De Historie van
# Joseph dē vromen
## ende Godtvruchtighen
## Jonghelinc.

Allen goeden end vromen Jongheren tot eenen
spieghel end onderwijsinghe / om Godt=
vruchtelijc / eerbaerlijc end
deuchdelijc te leven.

TOT ROTTERDAM,

## By Jan van Waesberghe / aen
## de Merct inde Fame.
ANNO 1617.

175

## 73 The History of the Royal Prophet David

*De Historie van Den Koninklyken Profete David, Zo van zyn Leven als wonderlyke Werken, en hoe Victorieuzelyk hy tegen zyne Vianden gestreden heeft, Amsterdam, heirs of the widow of Gysbert de Groot and Antony van Dam, 1724 (quarto)*

University Library, Amsterdam (O 89-64)
**Lit** De Booy 1977, pp. 42, 285, no. 28; Poortman 1983-86, Vol. 2, p. 277; Heimeriks/ Van Toorn 1990, pp. 87, 115, 181-182

**Illustrated:** Page in *De Historie van Den Koninklyken Profete David...* with a woodcut of an anonymous master after Christoffel van Sichem, depicting *David and Goliath*

**73.1**
Copy after Christoffel van Sichem, *David and Goliath*, woodcut in: *Bibels Tresoor...*, Amsterdam (Pieter Jacobsz. Paets) 1646. University Library, Nijmegen

),Regum XVII.
Die Philister bald lägern sich
Wider Israel durstiglich/
Israel thut sich fürchten sehr/
Der Goliath trotzt noch viel mehr/

Als solchs David erfahren thut/
Bekompt er bald eins Löwen mut/
Wirfft mit eim Stein durch Gottes gewalt
Den Riesen/daß er nider fallt.
                    M v        1.Regum

**73.2**
Jost Amman, *David and Goliath*, woodcut in *Newe Biblische Figuren...* Frankfurt am Main (Sigmund Feyerabend) 1579. Herzog August Bibliothek, Wolfenbüttel

Instead of using the whole Bible, small volumes of biblical extracts such as *De Historie van Adam, Noach, Abraham, Lot en Isaac, De Historie van Joseph, Simpson, en Jonas, Proverbia ofte Spreuken des alderwysten Konings Salomon* and *Evangelien en epistelen* were employed in the schools of Dutch towns and villages in the seventeenth and eighteenth centuries. In addition to reading primers and abridged catechism volumes, they served as teaching aids in elementary education at Dutch (*Nederduits*) schools, allowing the more advanced pupils to simultaneously improve their literacy and their religious knowledge.[1] *De Historie Van Den Koninklyken Propheet David*, of which the earliest editions appeared in *c.* 1600, was the most popular of all these booklets. It was a steadfast favourite for more than two hundred years, both in the Northern and Southern Netherlands.[2]

This edition is a typical example of the genre, in both form and content. The text comprises extracts from the Bible (after 1637 in the States Bible translation), no more and no less: no commentary, explanation or interpretation, and at first without any omissions either. Passages which were later considered less suitable for minors, like the story of David and Bathsheba, were also included here. *De Historie van Den Koninklyken Profete David* contains chapters 16-31 from 1 Samuel and 1-24 from 2 Samuel.

Bible readers are small in size and have a maximum of 48 pages. The text is set in two columns, generally in gothic type. They usually also contain illustrations, between four and thirty per volume. The illustrations in this volume, which include a titlepage print (*David with his Harp*) and 18 text illustrations, are typical of this genre. They take up around one-third of the page and are therefore quite large. They are simple woodcuts, based on prints by the Van Sichem family (*cf.* cat. nos 59 and 69). The picture of *David and Goliath* (fig.), for example, is a direct copy of a print by Van Sichem (fig. 73.1), which, in its turn, borrows from a print by Jost Amman of 1579 (fig. 73.2).[3]

Copies of copies, that is what these readers usually contain. Compared with these, the woodcuts in the early seventeenth-century volume by Van Waesberghe (cat. no. 72) are high quality, not to mention the type and the paper. In the course of the seventeenth century there was a clear decline in quality. This undoubtedly went hand-in-hand with the increasing popularity of these biblical readers. As more children began to attend school, books had to be affordable for the less affluent sections of society. On average, at the turn of the seventeenth and eighteenth century, the price of a volume such as this *Historie van Den Koninklyken Profete David* would not have been much above three stivers.[4] **PvdC**

1. *Cf.* Boekholt/ De Booy 1987, pp. 27, 34.
2. Buijnsters 1990, pp. 181-182. Between 1700 and 1800, 22 editions were printed by 15 different publishers. *Cf.* Amsterdam 1914, pp. 56-57, nos 1265-1274; Leiden 1932, pp. 36-37.
3. The same format is found in *De Historie van Joseph...* (Jacobus & Jan Bouman, Amsterdam 1703; University Library, Amsterdam: O 84-3) and *De Historie Van Adam, Noach, Abraham, Lot en Isaac...* (Willem Hegerman, Amsterdam 1782; University Library, Amsterdam: Br. 1352-3); these also contain woodcuts copied from the Van Sichems.
4. De Booy 1977, pp. 48, 270-271.

Willem van Swanenburgh after Joachim Wtewael, *Thronvs Ivstitiae. Hoc Est de optimo judice Tractatvs electissimis quibusque exemplis iudiciarijs aeri artificiosissime pulcherrimeque exemplis incisis illustratus. Addita tabularum brevi explicatione tam soluta oratione quam vincta Pictore Ioachimo VVtenvvalio Traiectensi, Et scvlptore VVilhelmo Svvanenbvrgio Leidensi*, Amsterdam, Christoffel I van Sichem, 1607 (quarto)

University Library, Amsterdam (2007 B 3)
**Lit** Holl. XXIX, pp. 37-39, nos. 49-62; Helliesen 1977, *passim*; Lowenthal 1986, pp. 64, 70, 133, figs 58-71; Amsterdam 1993-94A, pp. 560-562, no. 232; Münster 1994, p. 336, no. 134

**Illustrated**: Willem van Swanenburgh after Joachim Wtewael, *The Meeting of Moses and Jethro*, engraving, 30 x 38.5 cm, in: *Thronus Iustitiae…*, Amsterdam 1607

This book contains thirteen engravings designed by Joachim Wtewael (1566-1638) and executed by Willem van Swanenburgh (*c.* 1581/82-1612). Provided with Latin captions, these prints focus on the theme of justice, as the title states: 'The Throne of Justice. That is, a treatise on the supreme judge…'.

Reproduced here is the story of Moses' father-in-law, Jethro, the priest of Midian, who advised Moses to appoint 'able men, such as fear God, men of truth' as judges (Ex. 18:21). The mannerist Wtewael depicted justice, the book's theme, in the background, left (Moses on the throne of judgment), while on the right is the meeting of Moses and Jethro. To their right is Moses' wife Zipporah with their two children. The book contains two other prints on Old Testament themes, *Solomon's Judgement* (1 Kings 3:16-28) and *Susanna and Daniel* (Daniel 13). One illustration shows the Dutch legend of the Good Count William. The remaining prints, two of which have yet to be identified, are based on New Testament themes as well as Graeco-Roman literature and history. The print series was first published in 1606. For this 1607 edition a quire of text was included, printed by Hendrick Lodewijk van Haestens of Leiden.

The way in which the stories are treated is moralistic in tone. While some scenes show good and exemplary judgments, others depict unfair judges. Moreover, the main characters represent particular virtues. For example, Solomon represents *Prudentia* (common sense) and Daniel *Diligentia* (meticulousness). These were themes which had been employed in decorations of buildings which housed courts of justice, such as town halls, since the Middle Ages.[1]

The choice of these, often obscure themes in this series suggests that the *auctor intellectualis* had a sound knowledge of antique literature. And the sophisticated iconographical programme, with its many layers of meaning, indicates that he was a person of considerable erudition. **MH**

1. *Cf.* Huiskamp 1991 & 1994, especially pp. 134-135.

Joost van den Vondel, *Het Pascha Ofte De Verlossinge Israëls uyt Egypten. Trage-Comoedischer-wijse een yeder tot leeringh op 'tTonneel ghestelt...*, Amsterdam, Dirck Cornelisz. Houthaeck, 1636 (quarto)

University Library, Nijmegen (688 C 144 [6])
**Lit** Unger 1888, p. 22, no. 68; Verwey 1986, pp. XI-XII, pp. 6-26; Arpots 1987, pp. 9-10, no. 21; Münster 1994, p. 336, no. 135

**Illustrated:** Titlepage of Vondel's *Het Pascha* with an etching by Pieter Jansz., *The Crossing of the Red Sea*, Amsterdam 1636

During the Dutch Revolt it was common to place events and characters from the Old Testament in contemporary, political settings. For example, the Spanish enemy, Philip II might be compared with biblical antiheroes such as Saul and Goliath, while William of Orange was a latter-day David. The story of the crossing of the Red Sea (Ex. 14:21-31) was employed as a symbol of the deliverance of the Netherlands from the hands of the Spanish oppressors. It was not just a way of praising the Dutch leaders, it was also used to justify the Revolt.[1]

First printed in 1612, Vondel's play *Het Pascha*, was based on the Exodus from Egypt and can also be considered in this light. The message is emphasized in the verses at the end of the drama: 'Comparison of the deliverance of the Children of Israel with the liberation of the United Dutch Provinces'.[2] The etching on the titlepage depicting the crossing of the Red Sea was thought to have been the work of Claes Moeyaert, but is now attributed to Pieter Jansz. (1602 or 1612-1673).[3] **MH**

1. Cf. Münster 1994, p. 59; Huiskamp 1991 & 1994, pp. 147-148.
2. 'Vergelijckinge vande verlossinge der kinderen Israels met de vrijwordinghe der Vereenichde Nederlantsche Provincien'.
3. See for this etching: Holl. XIV, p. 55, no. 16 (as Moeyaert); TIB LIII, no. 026 (*idem*); Schapelhouman 1985, pp. 88-90 (attributed to Pieter Jansz.).

Menasseh ben Israel, *Piedra Gloriosa O De La Estatua De Nebuchadnesar Con muchas y diversas authoridades de la S.S. y antiguos sabios. Compuesto por el Hacham Menasseh Ben Ysrael. Amsterdam. An. 5415*, Amsterdam, Menasseh ben Israel, 1655 (duodecimo)

Museum het Rembrandthuis, Amsterdam
**Lit** Van de Waal 1954-55; Filedt Kok 1972, pp. 43-44; Amsterdam 1987-88, p. 32, no. 15; Van der Coelen 1991 & 1994, pp. 183-184; Dubiez 1992, pp. 26-29; Carstensen 1993, pp. 52-59; Münster 1994, p. 333, no. 127; Amsterdam 1995, p. 26, no. B. 36
[For the prints, see cat. no. 52]

**Illustrated:** Rembrandt, *The Image that Nebuchadnezzar Saw in his Dream*, etching in: *Piedra Gloriosa...*, Amsterdam 1655

In 1655 Rembrandt made four etchings for Menasseh ben Israel's Spanish book *Piedra gloriosa*. As a diplomat, writer and founder of a Jewish printing house in Amsterdam Menasseh (1604-1657) was clearly a man of many talents. He was a central figure in the Jewish world, but also enjoyed respect among Christians, for whom he became a source of information about traditional Jewish opinions on theological questions.

Today, less credence is given to the idea that Rembrandt and the rabbi, who were once thought to have been neighbours, were close friends.[1] However, from the foreword in *Piedra gloriosa*, in which the illustrations are described, it seems likely that Menasseh actually commissioned the four etchings himself.

The book deals with the stone which smashed the image Nebuchadnezzar saw in his dream (Daniel 2:34). In the author's view, this 'glorious stone' symbolized the Messiah, the same stone on which Jacob had slept (Gen. 28:11) and with which David had killed Goliath (1 Samuel 17). These three scenes were illustrated by Rembrandt together with *Daniel's Vision of the Four Beasts* (Daniel 7:3; cf. fig. 52.1). **PvdC**

1. *Cf.* Dubiez 1992; Dudok van Heel 1993.

*Haggadah shel Pesach*, Amsterdam,
Solomon Proops, 1712 (folio)

Bibliotheca Rosenthaliana, University Library,
Amsterdam (3808 A 2)
**Lit** Yerushalmi 1975, figs 66-69; Wischnitzer
1990, pp. 29-54; Amsterdam 1990, no. 68;
Van der Coelen 1991 & 1994, pp. 179, 182, 187;
Van der Coelen 1992, pp. 110-111; Münster
1994, p. 332, no. 126

**Illustrated**: Abraham ben Jacob after Matthaeus
Merian the Elder, *The Temple of Solomon*, etching
in: *Haggadah…*, Amsterdam 1712

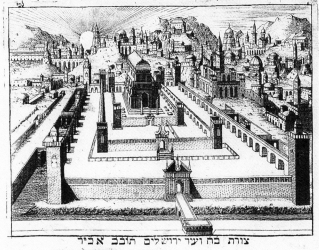

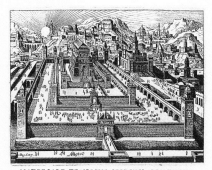

**77.1**
Anonymous after Matthaeus Merian the Elder,
*The Temple of Solomon*, etching in: *Bybel
Printen…*, Amsterdam s.a. University Library,
Amsterdam

The series of biblical prints by the Swiss-German artist Matthaeus Merian
the Elder (1593-1650) was the most popular in the Dutch Republic. Copies
were included in countless picture Bibles, but also in editions of Flavius
Josephus' *Jewish Antiquities* (cf. cat. nos 61, 62, 70). Moreover, Merian's series
was a major influence on Jewish book illustration. The Christian Old
Testament illustrations exhibited no religious bias and could therefore be
employed by Jewish booksellers.

A number of prints from Merian's series, such as the *Temple of Solomon*
(1 Kings 6 and 7), were copied by Abraham ben Jacob and from 1695
included in Amsterdam editions of the *Haggadah*, the order of service for the
Jewish festival of Passover (*Pesach*). Although there are few differences
between Christian and Jewish iconographical traditions regarding the
Temple's appearance, there is a major difference in interpretation. For Jews,
the Temple is a real building that once existed in the past and which, when
the Messiah comes, will be rebuilt. While the copy of Merian's illustration in
the *Haggadah* depicts the Temple in the messianic era - which perhaps
explains the absence of people - in Visscher's picture Bible it is accompanied
by a text offering a specifically Christian perspective on the building
(fig. 77.1). **PvdC**

# Bibliography

## A

**Ackley 1981**
C.S. Ackley, *Printmaking in the Age of Rembrandt*, exh. cat. Museum of Fine Arts, Boston/ The St. Louis Art Museum/ St. Louis, Boston 1981

**AKL**
*Allgemeines Künstler-Lexikon. Die bildenden Künstler aller Zeiten und Völker*, Vol. 1-, Leipzig 1983-

**Amsterdam 1934-36**
*Catalogus der Kunsthistorische Bibliotheek in het Rijksmuseum te Amsterdam*, 3 vols, Amsterdam 1934-36

**Amsterdam 1955**
*De triomf van het Maniërisme. De Europese stijl van Michelangelo tot El Greco*, exh. cat. Rijksmuseum

**Amsterdam 1964-65**
*Bijbelse inspiratie. Tekeningen en prenten van Lucas van Leyden en Rembrandt*, exh. cat. Rijksmuseum

**Amsterdam 1967**
*Hercules Seghers. Grafiek*, exh. cat. Rijksprentenkabinet

**Amsterdam 1984-85**
P. Schatborn and E. Ornstein-van Slooten, *Bij Rembrandt in de leer / Rembrandt as Teacher*, exh. cat. Museum het Rembrandthuis

**Amsterdam 1985-86**
B. Broos, *Rembrandt and his Sources*, exh. cat. Museum het Rembrandthuis

**Amsterdam 1986**
J.P. Filedt Kok, W. Halsema-Kubes and W.Th. Kloek (eds), *Kunst voor de beelden-storm. Noordnederlandse kunst 1525-1580*, exh. cat. Rijksmuseum

**Amsterdam 1986-87**
R.E.O. Ekkart and E. Ornstein-van Slooten, *Oog in oog met de modellen van Rembrandts portret-etsen / Face to Face with the sitters for Rembrandt's etched portraits*, exh. cat. Museum het Rembrandthuis

**Amsterdam 1987**
R. Kistemaker and T. Levie (eds), *Exodo. Portugezen in Amsterdam, 1600-1680*, exh. cat. Amsterdams Historisch Museum

**Amsterdam 1987-88**
S.A.C. Dudok van Heel, P. Schatborn and E. Ornstein-van Slooten, *The Rembrandt Papers. Documents, Drawings and Prints*, exh. cat. Museum het Rembrandthuis

**Amsterdam 1988-89**
P. Schatborn and E. Ornstein-van Slooten, *Jan Lievens. Prints and Drawings*, exh. cat. Museum het Rembrandthuis

**Amsterdam 1989A**
P. van den Brink and J. Werner (eds), *Gesneden en gedrukt in de Kalverstraat. De kaarten- en atlassendrukkerij in Amsterdam tot in de 19e eeuw*, exh. cat. Amsterdams Historisch Museum

**Amsterdam 1989B**
*Het kunstbedrijf van de familie Vingboons. Schilders, architecten en kaartmakers in de Gouden Eeuw*, exh. cat. Koninklijk Paleis op de Dam

**Amsterdam 1990**
*The Image of the Word. Jewish Tradition in Manuscripts and Printed Books*, exh. cat. Joods Historisch Museum

**Amsterdam 1991**
A. Tümpel and P. Schatborn, *Pieter Lastman, leermeester van Rembrandt / Pieter Lastman, the man who taught Rembrandt*, exh. cat. Museum het Rembrandthuis

**Amsterdam 1991-92**
C. Tümpel et al., *Het Oude Testament in de schilderkunst van de Gouden Eeuw*, exh. cat. Joods Historisch Museum

**Amsterdam 1992**
R.E. Jellema and M. Plomp, *Episcopius: Jan de Bisschop (1628-1671), Lawyer and Draughtsman*, exh. cat. Museum het Rembrandthuis

**Amsterdam 1993-94A**
G. Luijten et al. (eds), *Dawn of the Golden Age. Northern Netherlandish Art 1580-1620*, exh. cat. Rijksmuseum

**Amsterdam 1993-94B**
B. Bakker et al., *Nederland naar 't leven. Landschapsprenten uit de Gouden Eeuw*, exh. cat. Museum het Rembrandthuis

**Amsterdam 1995**
E. Ornstein-Van Slooten, M. Holtrop and P. Schatborn, *The Rembrandt House. A Catalogue of Rembrandt Etchings*, Zwolle/ Amsterdam 1995

**Amsterdam 1996**
C. Schuckman, M. Royalton-Kisch and E. Hinterding, *Rembrandt and Van Vliet. A Collaboration on Copper* (Studies in Dutch Graphic Art, 1), exh. cat. Museum het Rembrandthuis

**Amsterdam/ Boston/ Philadelphia 1987-88**
P.C. Sutton et al., *Masters of 17th-Century Dutch Landscape Painting*, exh. cat. Rijksmuseum/ Museum of Fine Arts/ Philadelphia Museum of Art

**Amsterdam/ Gent 1982-83**
J.F. Heijbroek (ed.), *Met Huygens op reis. Tekeningen en dagboeknotities van Constantijn Huygens jr. (1628-1697), secretaris van stadhouder-koning Willem III*, exh. cat. Rijksprentenkabinet/ Museum voor Schone Kunsten

**Andrews 1977**
K. Andrews, *Adam Elsheimer. Paintings, Drawings, Prints*, Oxford 1977

**Antwerp 1993**
*Rubensgrafiek*, exh. cat. Rockoxhuis

**Arpots 1987**
R. Arpots et al., *Vondel in Nijmegen. Catalogus van Vondel-drukken tot en met 1855, aanwezig in de Bibliotheek van de Katholieke Universiteit te Nijmegen*, Nijmegen 1987

**ASC**
L. Hugenholtz (ed.), *Art Sales Catalogues 1600-1825 on Microfiche*, Leiden 1992-

## B

**B. [Bartsch]**
A. Bartsch, *Catalogue raisonné de toutes les estampes qui forment l'oeuvre de Rembrandt, et ceux de ces principaux imitateurs*, Vienna 1797

**Baarsen 1992**
R.J. Baarsen, 'Keuze uit de aanwinsten', *Bulletin van het Rijksmuseum* 40 (1992), pp. 94-121

**Bakhuizen van den Brink 1976**
J.N. Bakhuizen van den Brink, *De Nederlandse belijdenisgeschriften in authentieke teksten*, Amsterdam 1976

**Bakker 1993**
B. Bakker, 'Levenspelgrimage of vrome wandeling? Claes Janszoon Visscher en zijn serie "Plaisante Plaetsen"', *Oud Holland* 107 (1993), pp. 97-115

**Barb 1972**
A.A. Barb, 'Cain's Murder-Weapon and Samson's Jawbone of an Ass', *Journal of the Warburg and Courtauld Institutes* 35 (1972), pp. 386-389

**Basel 1984**
*Tobias Stimmer 1539-1584. Spätrenaissance am Oberrhein*, exh. cat. Kunstmuseum

**Bauch 1935**
K. Bauch, 'Beiträge zum Werk der Vorläufer Rembrandts. I. Die Gemälde des Jan Pynas', *Oud Holland* 52 (1935), pp. 145-158

**Baudrier 1895-1921**
H. and J. Baudrier, *Bibliographie lyonnaise...*, 12 vols, Lyon/ Paris 1895-1921 (reprint Paris 1964)

**BCNI**
*Bibliotheca Catholica Neerlandica impressa 1500-1727*, The Hague 1954

**Beckey 1941**
K. Beckey, 'Merian d.Ä. als Bibelillustrator (1625-1630). Eine bibliographische Übersicht und eine kurze Einführung in sein Schaffen', in: *Festschrift Hans Vollmer zu seinem 70. Geburtstag am 9. Februar 1941*, Potsdam 1941, pp. 58-137

**Beets 1915**
N. Beets, *De houtsneden in Vorsterman's Bijbel van 1528. Afbeeldingen der prenten van Jan Swart, Lucas van Leyden, e.a.*, Amsterdam 1915

**Belobrova 1979**
O.A. Belobrova, 'K istorii biblioteki patriarcha Adriana', *Trudy Otdela drevnerusskoj literatury* 33 (1979), pp. 406-414

**Belobrova 1985**
O.A. Belobrova, 'Biblija Piskatora v sobranii Biblioteki Academii Nauk SSSR', in: *Materialy i soobscenija po fondam otdela pukopisnoj i pedkoj knigi Biblioteki Academii nauk SSSR*, Leningrad 1985, pp. 184-216

**Belobrova 1989**
O.A. Belobrova, 'Illustrirovannyje Biblii v russkom obichode vtoroj poloviny XVII-nacala XVIII stoletija', in: *Pravoslavije v Drevnej Rusi*, Leningrad 1989, pp. 118-124

**Benesch**
O. Benesch, *The Drawings of Rembrandt*, 6 vols, London 1954-57 [second ed., revised by E. Benesch, London/ New York 1973]

**Van den Berg 1993**
A. van den Berg, *Hier komt Urbanus bij een hoer. Volk en volkslectuur in de achttiende-eeuwse Amsterdamse Nes*, Amsterdam 1993

**Van den Berg 1995**
A. van den Berg, 'Prentgeschenk en letter-spel. ABC-prenten in de Nederlanden tussen 1700 en 1900', in: J. ter Linden, A. de Vries and D. Welsink (eds), *A is een aapje. Opstellen over ABC-boeken van de vijftiende eeuw tot heden*, Amsterdam 1995, pp. 31-53

**Bergvelt/ Kistemaker 1992**
E. Bergvelt and R. Kistemaker (eds), *De wereld binnen handbereik. Nederlandse kunst- en rariteitenverzamelingen, 1585-1735*, Zwolle/ Amsterdam 1992

**Berkvens-Stevelinck et al. 1992**
C. Berkvens-Stevelinck et al. (eds), *Le Magasin de l'Univers. The Dutch Republic as the Centre of the European Book Trade*, Leiden etc. 1992

**Berlin/ Amsterdam/ London 1991-92A**
H. Bevers, P. Schatborn and B. Welzel, *Rembrandt: de meester en zijn werkplaats. Tekeningen en etsen*, exh. cat. Kupferstichkabinett SMPK/ Rijksmuseum/ The National Gallery

183

Berlin/ Amsterdam/ London 1991-92B
C. Brown, J. Kelch and P. van Thiel, *Rembrandt: de meester en zijn werkplaats. Schilderijen*, exh. cat. Gemäldegalerie SMPK/ Rijksmuseum/ The National Gallery

Bialostocki 1984
J. Bialostocki, 'Doctus Artifex and the Library of the Artist in XVIth and XVIIth Century', in: A. Horodisch (ed.), *De arte et libris: Festschrift Erasmus*, Amsterdam 1984, pp. 11-22

De Bie 1661-62
C. de Bie, *Het Gulden Cabinet Vande Edele Vry Schilder Const...*, Antwerp 1661-62 [reprint Soest 1971]

Biörklund 1968
G. Biörklund. *Rembrandt's Etchings True And False*, Stockholm 1968

Blanc 1854-89
C. le Blanc, *Manuel de l'Amateur des Estampes*, 4 vols, Paris 1854-89

Blankert 1976
A. Blankert, *Ferdinand Bol 1616-1680 een leerling van Rembrandt*, The Hague 1976 (diss.)

Blankert 1982
A. Blankert, *Ferdinand Bol (1616-1680). Rembrandt's Pupil* (Monographs on Dutch & Flemish Painting, 2), Doornspijk 1982

Blok 1918-19
I. Blok, 'Tentoonstelling van prenten door Cl.J. Visscher in 's Rijks Prentenkabinet te Amsterdam', *Oude Kunst* 4 (1918-19), pp. 107-109

Boccazzi 1974
F.Z. Boccazzi, 'Le incisioni originali di Jan Saenredam', *Antichità Viva* 13 (1974), no. 2, pp. 32-49

Boekholt/ De Booy 1987
P.Th.F.M. Boekholt and E.P. de Booy, *Geschiedenis van de school in Nederland vanaf de middeleeuwen tot aan de huidige tijd*, Assen/ Maastricht 1987

Boerma 1980
R.N.H. Boerma, *Religieuze volks- en kinderprenten uit Nederland en België*, exh. cat. Frans Walkate Archief, Kampen 1980

Boon 1953
K.G. Boon, 'Over vroege staten in het werk van Jan Muller', *Bulletin van het Rijksmuseum* 1 (1953), pp. 31-33

Boonen 1991 & 1994
J. Boonen, 'Verhalen van Israëls ballingschap en vrijheidsstrijd', in: Amsterdam 1991-92, pp. 106-121; 'Die Geschichte von Israels Exil und Freiheitskampf', in: Münster 1994, pp. 106-121

De Booy 1977
E.P. de Booy, *De weldaet der scholen. Het plattelandsonderwijs in de provincie Utrecht van 1580 tot het begin der 19de eeuw*, Utrecht 1977 (diss.)

Boston/ New York 1969
*Rembrandt: Experimental Etcher*, exh. cat Museum of Fine Arts/ Pierpont Morgan Library

Bredius
A. Bredius, *Rembrandt. Schilderijen*, Utrecht 1935

Bredius 1911
A. Bredius, 'Het contract van Picart's bijbelprenten', *Oud Holland* 29 (1911), pp. 185-188

Bredius 1915-22
A. Bredius (ed.), *Künstler-Inventare. Urkunden zur Geschichte der holländischen Kunst des XVIten, XVIIten und XVIIIten Jahrhunderts*, 7 vols, The Hague 1915-22

Briels 1974
J.G.C.A. Briels, *Zuidnederlandse boekdrukkers en boekverkopers in de Republiek der Verenigde Nederlanden omstreeks 1570-1630. Een bijdrage tot de kennis van de geschiedenis van het boek*, Nieuwkoop 1974

Briels 1976
J.G.C.A. Briels, *De Zuidnederlandse immigratie in Amsterdam en Haarlem omstreeks 1572-1630*, Utrecht 1976 (diss.)

De Bruin 1993
C.C. de Bruin, *De Statenbijbel en zijn voorgangers. Nederlandse bijbelvertalingen vanaf de Reformatie tot 1637*, Haarlem/ Brussels 1993

Brunswick 1979
*Jan Lievens. Ein Maler im Schatten Rembrandts*, exh. cat. Herzog Anton Ulrich-Museum

Bruyn 1982
J. Bruyn, 'The Documentary Value of Early Graphic Reproductions', in: RRP, Vol. 1, pp. 35-51

BSC
B. van Selm and J.A. Gruys (eds), *Book Sales Catalogues of the Dutch Republic 1599-1800 on Microfiche*, Leiden 1990-

Buchelius/ Hoogewerff/ Van Regteren Altena 1928
G.H. Hoogewerff and J.Q. van Regteren Altena (eds), *Arnoldus Buchelius 'Res pictoriae'. Aanteekeningen over kunstenaars en kunstwerken voorkomende in zijn Diarum*, Res Pictoriae, Notae Quotidianae en Descriptio Urbis Ultrajectinae (1583-1639), The Hague 1928

Buijnsters 1990
P.J. Buijnsters, 'Nederlandse kinderboeken uit de achttiende eeuw', in: Heimeriks/ Van Toorn 1990, pp. 169-228

Burchard 1917
L. Burchard, *Die holländischen Radierer vor Rembrandt*, Berlin 1917

Busch 1982
W. Busch, 'Lucas van Leydens "Große Hagar" und die augustinische Typologieauffassung der Vorreformation', *Zeitschrift für Kunstgeschichte* 45 (1982), pp. 97-129

## C

Carstensen 1993
H.T. Carstensen, *Empirie als Bildsprache. Überlegungen zum jüdischen Einfluß auf Rembrandts Kunst*, Ammersbek bei Hamburg 1993

Cartier 1937-38
A. Cartier, *Bibliographie des éditions des De Tournes, imprimeurs lyonnais*, 2 vols, Paris 1937-38 [reprint Geneva 1970]

Catalogue Claesz.
*Const ende Caert-Register, In welcke gheteyckent staen, alderhande soorten van Caerten ende Mappen... alle de Prenten ende Coper-stucken, van de beroemste Meesters: Welckers Platen alle by Cornelis Claesz. te becomen, ende daghelijcx tot zijne groote costen ghedruckt worden...*, Amsterdam (Cornelis Claesz.) 1609

Catalogue Visscher
*Catalogus Van groote en kleene Land-Kaerten, Steden, Print-Kunst En Boecken. Van Nicolaes Visscher*, Amsterdam (Nicolaus Visscher) s.a. [c. 1680]

Chartier 1994
R. Chartier, *The Order of Books. Readers, Authors, and Libraries in Europe between the Fourteenth and Eighteenth Centuries*, Cambridge 1994

Clark 1966
K. Clark, *Rembrandt and the Italian Renaissance*, London 1966

Van der Coelen 1991 & 1994
P. van der Coelen, 'Thesauri en trezoren. Boeken en bundels met oudtestamentische prenten', in: Amsterdam 1991-92, pp. 168-193; 'Das Alte Testament in Bilderbibeln des 16. und 17. Jahrhunderts', in: Münster 1994, pp. 168-193

Van der Coelen 1992
P. van der Coelen, 'Het Oude Testament geïllustreerd en geïnterpreteerd in prentenboeken uit de Gouden Eeuw', *Spiegel Historiael* 27 (1992), pp. 106-111

Van der Coelen 1993
P. van der Coelen, 'De Apocalyps als prentenboek. Van Dürer tot Duvet', in: W. Denslagen et al. (eds), *Bouwkunst. Studies in vriendschap voor Kees Peeters*, Amsterdam 1993, pp. 112-123

Van der Coelen 1994-95
P. van der Coelen, 'Claes Jansz. Visschers bijbelse prentenboeken', *De Boekenwereld* 11 (1994-95), pp. 106-120

Van der Coelen 1995
P. van der Coelen, 'Cornelis Bos - Where Did He Go? Some New Discoveries and Hypotheses about a Sixteenth-Century Engraver and Publisher', *Simiolus* 23 (1995), pp. 119-146

Van der Coelen 1996-97
P. van der Coelen, 'Het Oude Testament in prent. Voorstellingen van de Verstoting van Hagar en Ismaël', *Antiek* 31 (1996-97), no. 6 (forthcoming, January 1997)

Van der Coelen 1997
P. van der Coelen, 'Bijbelprenten en prentenbijbels voor het hele "Kristenryk". Over het fonds van de uitgeversfamilie Visscher', *Desipientia - zin en waan* 4 (1997), no. 1 (forthcoming)

Cologne 1981
H.-J. Raupp et al., *Wort und Bild. Buchdruck und Druckgraphik in den Niederlanden im 16. und 17. Jahrhundert*, exh. cat. Belgisches Haus

Cologne/ Vienna/ Antwerp 1992
E. Mai and H. Vlieghe (eds), *Von Bruegel bis Rubens. Das Goldene Jahrhundert der flämischen Malerei*, exh. cat. Wallraf-Richartz-Museum/ Kunsthistorisches Museum/ Koninklijk Museum voor Schone Kunsten

Consagra 1992
F. Consagra, *The De Rossi Family Print Publishing Shop. A Study in the History of the Print Industry in Seventeenth-Century Rome*, Baltimore 1992 (diss.)

Croiset van Uchelen 1976
A.R.A. Croiset van Uchelen, 'Dutch Writing-Masters and the "Prix de la Plume Couronnée"', *Quaerendo* 6 (1976), pp. 319-346

## D

B.F. Davidson, *Raphael's Bible: A Study of the Vatican Logge*, University Park/ London 1985

Davis 1988
B. Davis, *Mannerist Prints. International Style in the Sixteenth Century*, Los Angeles 1988

Dearborn 1994
S.K. Perlove et al., *Renaissance, Reform, Reflections in the Age of Dürer, Bruegel, and Rembrandt. Master Prints from the Albion College Collection*, exh. cat. University of Michigan-Dearborn

Delano-Smith/ Ingram 1991
C. Delano-Smith and E.M. Ingram, *Maps in Bibles 1500-1600. An Illustrated Catalogue*, Geneva 1991

Van Deursen 1974
A.Th. van Deursen, *Bavianen en Slijkgeuzen. Kerk en kerkvolk ten tijde van Maurits en Oldebarnevelt*, Assen 1974

Dierker 1983
M. Dierker, 'Rembrandt - ein protestantischer Künstler', in: Hamburg 1983, pp. 322-347

Dubiez 1992
F.J. Dubiez, 'Drie beeldende kunstenaars en drie rabbijnen te Amsterdam in de zeventiende eeuw', *Kroniek van het Rembrandthuis* (1992), no. 2, pp. 23-32

Dudok van Heel 1993
S.A.C. Dudok van Heel, 'Rembrandt en Menasseh Ben Israël', *Kroniek van het Rembrandthuis* (1993), no. 1, pp. 22-29

Duverger
E. Duverger, *Antwerpse kunstinventarissen uit de zeventiende eeuw* (Fontes Historiae Artis Neerlandicae, 1), Vol. 1-, Brussels 1984-

## E

Van Eeghen 1960-78
I.H. van Eeghen, *De Amsterdamse boekhandel 1680-1725*, 5 vols, Amsterdam 1960-78

Van Eeghen 1969
I.H. van Eeghen, 'Het Amsterdamse Sint Lucasgilde in de 17de eeuw', *Jaarboek van het Genootschap Amstelodamum* 61 (1969), pp. 65-102

Van Eeghen 1985
I.H. van Eeghen, 'Rembrandt en de veilingen (Titus van Rijn, Clement de Jonghe en Samuel Smijters)', *Jaarboek van het Genootschap Amstelodamum* 77 (1985), pp. 54-69

**Van Eeghen 1990**
I.H. van Eeghen, 'De familie van de plaatsnijder Claes Jansz Visscher', *Amstelodamum* 77 (1990), pp. 73-82

**Van Eeghen/ Van der Kellen 1905**
P. van Eeghen and J.Ph. van der Kellen, *Het werk van Jan en Casper Luyken*, 2 vols, Amsterdam 1905

**Ehrle 1908**
F. Ehrle, *Roma prima di Sisto V. La Pianta di Roma Du Pérac-Lafréry del 1577*, Rome 1908

**Engammare 1994**
M. Engammare, 'Les Figures de la Bible. Le destin oublié d'un genre littéraire en image (XVIe-XVIIe s.)', *Mélanges de l'École française de Rome. Italie et Méditerranée* 106 (1994), pp. 549-591

**Enklaar 1993**
M.E.A. Enklaar, 'Een nieuw bruikleen in het Rembrandthuis: "De verstoting van Hagar en Ismaël" (1614) door Jan Pynas', *Kroniek van het Rembrandthuis* (1993), no. 2, pp. 2-8

**Enschedé 1904**
J.W. Enschedé, 'Aanteekeningen over de boekverkoopers Colijn en Colom', *Amsterdamsch Jaarboekje* (1904), pp. 42-61

**Evanston 1993**
T. Riggs and L. Silver, *Graven Images. The Rise of Professional Printmakers in Antwerp and Haarlem, 1540-1640*, exh. cat. Mary and Leigh Block Gallery, Northwestern University

# F

**Faber 1980**
J.A. Faber, 'Inhabitants of Amsterdam and their Possessions, 1701-1710', in: A. van der Woude and A. Schuurman (eds), *Probate Inventories. A New Source for the Historical Study of Wealth, Material Culture and Agricultural Development* (A.A.G. Bijdragen, 23), Wageningen 1980, pp. 149-155

**Falkenburg/ Filedt Kok/ Leeflang 1993**
R. Falkenburg, J.P. Filedt Kok and H. Leeflang (eds), *Goltzius-Studies: Hendrick Goltzius (1558-1617)* (Nederlands Kunsthistorisch Jaarboek 42-43, 1991-92). Zwolle 1993

**Filedt Kok 1972**
J.P. Filedt Kok, *Rembrandt. Etchings and Drawings in the Rembrandt House. A catalogue*, Amsterdam/ Maarssen 1972

**Filedt Kok 1978**
J.P. Filedt Kok, *Lucas van Leyden - grafiek*, exh. cat. Rijksprentenkabinet, Amsterdam 1978

**Filedt Kok 1988**
J.P. Filedt Kok, 'Een "Biblia pauperum" met houtsneden van Jacob Cornelisz. en Lucas van Leyden gereconstrueerd', *Bulletin van het Rijksmuseum* 36 (1988), pp. 83-116

**Filedt Kok 1990**
J.P. Filedt Kok, 'Jacques de Gheyn II. Engraver, Designer and Publisher', *Print Quarterly* 7 (1990), pp. 248-281, 370-396

**Filedt Kok 1993**
J.P. Filedt Kok, 'Hendrick Goltzius - Engraver, Designer and Publisher 1582-1600', in: Falkenburg/ Filedt Kok/ Leeflang 1993, pp. 159-218

**Filedt Kok 1994-95**
J.P. Filedt Kok, 'Jan Harmensz. Muller as Printmaker, I-III', *Print Quarterly* 11 (1994), pp. 223-264, 351-378; 12 (1995), pp. 3-29

**De la Fontaine Verwey 1934**
E. de la Fontaine Verwey, *De illustratie van letterkundige werken in de XVIIIe eeuw. Bijdrage tot de geschiedenis van het Nederlandsche boek*, Amsterdam 1934

**De la Fontaine Verwey 1941**
E. de la Fontaine Verwey, 'Gedichten en boekillustraties van Jan Goeree, teekenaar en graveur', *Halcyon* 2 (1941), no. 5, pp. 1-12

**Forssman 1976**
E. Forssman, 'Rembrandts Radierung "Der Triumph des Mardochai"', *Zeitschrift für Kunstgeschichte* 39 (1976), pp. 297-311

**Franken 1881**
D. Franken, *L'oeuvre gravé des Van de Passe*, Amsterdam/ Paris 1881

**Franken/ Van der Kellen 1968**
D. Franken and J.Ph. van der Kellen, *L' oeuvre de Jan van de Velde, graveur hollandais, 1593-1641*, Amsterdam 1968

**Frankenthal 1995**
E.J. Hürkey (ed.), *Kunst, Kommerz, Glaubenskampf. Frankenthal um 1600*, exh. cat. Erkenbert-Museum

**Frankfurt am Main 1966-67**
*Adam Elsheimer. Werk, künstlerische Herkunft und Nachfolge*, exh. cat. Städelsches Kunstinstitut

**Freise 1911**
K. Freise, *Pieter Lastman, sein Leben und seine Kunst. Ein Beitrag zur Geschichte der Holländ. Malerei im XVII. Jahrh.*, Leipzig 1911

**Friedländer 1963**
M.J. Friedländer, *Lucas van Leyden*, Berlin 1963

**Frijhoff 1990**
W. Frijhoff, 'Devotieprentjes als bestanddeel van culturele praktijken', in: P.G.J. Post (ed.), *Verbeelding van vroomheid. De devotieprent als cultuurwetenschappelijke bron* (Volkskundig Bulletin 16 [1990], no. 3), Amsterdam 1990, pp. 350-378

**Frijhoff 1995**
W. Frijhoff, *Wegen van Evert Willemsz. Een Hollands weeskind op zoek naar zichzelf 1607-1647*, Nijmegen 1995

**Fuks/ Fuks-Mansfeld 1984-87**
L. Fuks and R.G. Fuks-Mansfeld, *Hebrew Typography in the Northern Netherlands 1585-1815. Historical Evaluation and Descriptive Bibliography*, 2 vols, Leiden 1984-87

# G

**Gaskell 1974**
Ph. Gaskell, *A New Introduction to Bibliography*, Oxford 1974

**Gawthrop/ Strauss 1984**
R. Gawthrop and G. Strauss, 'Protestantism and Literacy in Early Modern Germany', *Past and Present* (1984), no. 104, pp. 31-55

**Geisberg/ Strauss 1974**
M. Geisberg, *The German Single-Leaf Woodcut: 1500-1550*, rev. and ed. by W.L. Strauss, 4 vols, New York 1974

**Van Gelder 1916**
H.E. van Gelder, 'Ruzie rondom een prentenbijbel', *Oud Holland* 34 (1916), pp. 127-129

**Van Gelder 1931**
J.G. van Gelder, 'De etsen van Willem Buytewech', *Oud Holland* 48 (1931), pp. 49-72

**Van Gelder 1950-51**
J.G. van Gelder, 'Rubens in Holland in de zeventiende eeuw', *Nederlands Kunsthistorisch Jaarboek* 3 (1950-51), pp. 102-150

**Van Gelder 1972**
J.G. van Gelder, *Jan de Bisschop*, The Hague 1972 (= offprint: 'Jan de Bisschop 1628-1671', *Oud Holland* 86 [1971], pp. 201-288)

**Van Gent 1991 & 1994**
J. van Gent, 'De tijd van de koningen en de profeten', in: Amsterdam 1991-92, pp. 88-105; 'Die Zeit der Könige und der Propheten', in: Münster 1994, pp. 88-105

**Van Gent/ Pastoor 1991 & 1994**
J. van Gent and G.M.C. Pastoor, 'Het tijdperk van de rechters', in: Amsterdam 1991-92, pp. 66-87; 'Die Zeit der Richter', in: Münster 1994, pp. 66-87

**Gibson 1983**
W.S. Gibson, 'Lucas van Leyden and the Old Testament', *The Print Collector's Newsletter* 14 (1983), pp. 127-130

**Gibson 1989**
W. Gibson, 'Old Testament Narratives in the Prints of the German Little Masters', *The Register of the Spencer Museum of Art* 6 (1989), no. 6, pp. 9-24

**Göttingen/ Hanover/ Nuremberg 1977**
K. Renger et al., *Rubens in der Grafik*, exh. cat. Kunstsammlung der Universität Göttingen/ Landesmuseum/ Museen der Stadt Nürnberg

**Griffiths 1984**
A. Griffiths, 'A Checklist of Catalogues of British Print Publishers c. 1650-1830', *Print Quarterly* 1 (1984), pp. 4-22

**Grivel 1986**
M. Grivel, *Le commerce de l'estampe à Paris au XVIIe siècle* (Histoire et civilisation du livre, 16), Geneva 1986

**Groenendijk 1989**
L.F. Groenendijk, 'Kerk, school en gezin in dienst van het bibliocratische ideaal bij de gereformeerden tijdens de 17e eeuw', *Pedagogisch Tijdschrift* 14 (1989), pp. 257-268

**Groningen 1994**
*De Bijbel ingeprent. Prenten met bijbelse onderwerpen uit het Fries Museum*, exh. cat. Instituut voor Kunst- en Architectuurgeschiedenis en Archeologie

**Groningen/ Leeuwarden 1988**
*Bloemaert inventor. Prenten naar ontwerp van Abraham Bloemaert (1564-1651)*, exh. cat. Kunsthistorisch Instituut/ Fries Museum

# H

**Haak 1984**
B. Haak, *Hollandse schilders in de Gouden Eeuw*, Amsterdam 1984

**Hänsel 1991**
S. Hänsel, *Der spanische Humanist Benito Arias Montano (1527-1598) und die Kunst*, Münster 1991

**Hamann 1936**
R. Hamann, *Hagars Abschied bei Rembrandt und im Rembrandt-Kreise* (offprint from the Marburger Jahrbuch für Kunstwissenschaft 8-9), s.a. [1936]

**Hamburg 1983**
W. Hofmann (ed.), *Luther und die Folgen für die Kunst*, exh. cat. Hamburger Kunsthalle

**Hamburg 1992**
E. Schaar and H. Broeker, *Invenit et sculpsit. Zeichnungen und Graphik des niederländischen Manierismus*, exh. cat. Hamburger Kunsthalle

**Hamilton 1981**
A. Hamilton, 'From Familism to Pietism. The Fortunes of Pieter van der Borcht's Biblical Illustrations and Hiël's Commentaries from 1584 to 1717', *Quaerendo* 11 (1981), pp. 271-301

**Haverkamp Begemann 1959**
E. Haverkamp Begemann, *Willem Buytewech*, Amsterdam 1959

**Haverkamp Begemann 1962**
E. Haverkamp Begemann, 'The Etchings of Willem Buytewech', in: C. Zigrosser (ed.), *Prints. Thirteen Illustrated Essays on the Art of the Print, Selected for the Print Council of America*, New York/ Chicago/ San Francisco, pp. 55-81

**Haverkamp Begemann 1973**
E. Haverkamp Begemann, *Hercules Segers. The Complete Etchings*, Amsterdam/ The Hague 1973

**Haverkorn van Rijsewijk 1905**
P. Haverkorn van Rijsewijk, 'Maria Strick', *Oud Holland* 23 (1905), pp. 52-62

**Hazeleger 1979**
R. Hazeleger, *Pieter Fransz. de Grebber. Schilder tot Haerlem*, Utrecht 1979 (unpublished graduate thesis)

**Heimeriks/ Van Toorn 1990**
N. Heimeriks and W. van Toorn (eds), *De hele Bibelebontse berg. De geschiedenis van het kinderboek in Nederland en Vlaanderen van de middeleeuwen tot heden*, Amsterdam 1990

**Helliesen 1977**
S. Helliesen, 'Thronus Justitiae. A Series of Pictures of Justice by Joachim Wtewael', *Oud Holland* 91 (1977), pp. 232-266

**Henderson 1961**
G. Henderson, 'Cain's Jaw-Bone', *Journal of the Warburg and Courtauld Institutes* 24 (1961), pp. 108-114

**Henkel 1926**
M.D. Henkel, 'Romeijn de Hooghe als illustrator', *Maandblad voor beeldende kunsten* 3 (1926), pp. 261-272, 300-309

**Henry 1987**
A. Henry, *Biblia Pauperum. A Facsimile and Edition*, Aldershot 1987

Hind 1912
A. M. Hind, *Rembrandt's Etchings. An Essay and a Catalogue With some Notes on the Drawings*, 2 vols., London 1912

Hindman 1977
S. Hindman, *Text and Image in Fifteenth-Century Illustrated Dutch Bibles*, Leiden 1977

Hinterding 1993-94
E. Hinterding, 'The history of Rembrandt's copperplates, with a catalogue of those that survive', *Simiolus* 22 (1993-94), pp. 253-315

Hirschmann 1919
O. Hirschmann, *Hendrick Goltzius* (Meister der Graphik, 7), Leipzig 1919

Hirschmann 1921
O. Hirschmann, *Verzeichnis des graphischen Werks von Hendrick Goltzius 1558-1617*, Leipzig 1921

Hoekstra 1996-97
F. Hoekstra, 'Het "ideale paar" van Rembrandt', *Antiek* 31 (1996-97), pp. 59-65

Hofstede de Groot 1906
C. Hofstede de Groot, *Die Urkunden über Rembrandt (1575-1721)* (Quellenstudien zur Holländischen Kunstgeschichte, 3), The Hague 1906

Holl.
*F.W.H. Hollstein's Dutch and Flemish Etchings, Engravings and Woodcuts ca. 1450-1700*, Vol. 1-, Amsterdam 1949-

Holl., German
*F.W.H. Hollstein's German Engravings, Etchings and Woodcuts ca. 1400-1700*, Vol. 1-, Amsterdam 1954-

De Hoop Scheffer/ Boon 1971
D. de Hoop Scheffer and K.G. Boon, 'De inventaris-lijst van Clement de Jonghe en Rembrandts etsplaten', *Kroniek van het Rembrandthuis* 25 (1971), pp. 1-17

Huiskamp 1991 & 1994
M. Huiskamp, 'Openbare lessen in geschiedenis en moraal. Het Oude Testament in stadhuizen en andere openbare gebouwen', in: Amsterdam 1991-92, pp. 134-155; 'Öffentlicher Unterricht in Geschichte und Moral. Das Alte Testament in Rathäusern und anderen öffentlichen Gebäuden', in: Münster 1994, pp. 134-155

D'Hulst/ Vandenven 1989
R.-A. D'Hulst and M. Vandenven, *Rubens. The Old Testament (Corpus Rubenianum Ludwig Burchard, 3)*, London 1989

Huygens 1888-1950
*Oeuvres complètes de Christiaan Huygens*, 22 vols, The Hague 1888-1950

Huygens/ Heesakkers 1987
C.L. Heesakkers (ed.), *Constantijn Huygens, Mijn jeugd*, Amsterdam 1987

## J

Jordan 1893
A. Jordan, 'Bemerkungen zu Rembrandts Radierungen', *Repertorium für Kunstwissenschaft* 16 (1893), pp. 296-302

Judson 1964
J.R. Judson, 'Marine Symbols of Salvation in the Sixteenth Century', in: L. Freeman Sandler (ed.), *Essays in Memory of Karl Lehmann*, New York 1964, pp. 136-152

Judson 1969
J.R. Judson, 'Martin de Vos' Representations of "Jonah Cast Over the Side"', in: *Miscellanea I.Q. van Regteren Altena*, Amsterdam 1969, pp. 82-87

## K

Kahn-Gerzon 1992
B.S. Kahn-Gerzon, 'Biografische gegevens over Anthonie Waterloo', *Oud Holland* 106 (1992), pp. 94-98

Kahr 1966
M. Kahr, 'Rembrandt's Esther. A Painting and an Etching newly interpreted and dated', *Oud Holland* 81 (1966), pp. 228-244

Van de Kamp 1991 & 1994
N. van de Kamp, 'Genesis: de oergeschiedenis en de verhalen van de aartsvaders', in: Amsterdam 1991-92, pp. 24-53; 'Die Genesis: die Urgeschichte und die Geschichte der Erzväter', in: Münster 1994, pp. 24-53

Kapp 1886
F. Kapp, *Geschichte des Deutschen Buchhandels bis in das siebzehnte Jahrhundert*, Leipzig 1886

Kerrich 1829
J. Kerrich, *A Catalogue of the Prints Which Have Been Engraved after Martin Heemskerck*, Cambridge 1829

Kleerkooper/ Van Stockum 1914-16
M.M. Kleerkooper and W.P van Stockum, *De Boekhandel te Amsterdam voornamelijk in de 17e Eeuw. Biographische en Geschiedkundige Aanteekeningen* (Bijdragen tot de Geschiedenis van den Nederlandschen Boekhandel, 10), 2 vols, The Hague 1914-16

Knipping 1974
J.B. Knipping, *Iconography of the Counter Reformation in the Netherlands. Heaven on Earth*, 2 vols, Nieuwkoop/ Leiden 1974

Koch 1991
R. Koch (ed.), *Brücke zwischen den Völkern. Zur Geschichte der Frankfurter Messe*, 3 vols, Frankfurt am Main 1991

Köhne 1932A
C.E. Köhne, *Studien zur Graphik von Ferdinand Bol und Jan Lievens*, Bottrop 1932

Köhne 1932B
C.E. Köhne, 'An unpublished Ferdinand Bol', *Burlington Magazine* 60 (1932), p. 224

Koeman 1961
C. Koeman, *Collections of Maps and Atlases in the Netherlands. Their History and Present State*, Leiden 1961

Koeman 1967-85
C. Koeman, *Atlantes Neerlandici. Bibliography of Terrestrial, Maritime and Celestial Atlases and Pilot Books Published in the Netherlands up to 1880*, 6 vols, Amsterdam 1967-85

Van der Krogt 1985
P.C.J. van der Krogt, *Advertenties voor kaarten, atlassen, globes e.d. in Amsterdamse kranten 1621-1811*, Utrecht 1985

Krücke 1959
A. Krücke, 'Der Protestantismus und die bildliche Darstellung Gottes', *Zeitschrift für Kunstwissenschaft* 13 (1959), pp. 59-90

Krüger 1993
P. Krüger, 'Rembrandts "Adam und Eva"-Radierung - Eine Aemulatio mit Dürer', *Jahrbuch der Berliner Museen* 35 (1993), pp. 215-226

De Kruif 1994
J. de Kruif, ' "En nog enige boeken van weinig waarde". Boeken in Haagse boedelinventarissen halverwege de 18e eeuw', *Holland* 26 (1994), pp. 314-327

Kunstreich 1959
J.S. Kunstreich, *Der 'Geistreiche Willem'. Studien zu Willem Buytewech*, Kiel 1959

## L

Landwehr 1970
J. Landwehr, *Romeyn de Hooghe (1645-1708) as Book Illustrator. A Bibliography*, Amsterdam/ New York 1970

Lawrence 1988
S.H. Goddard (ed.), *The World in Miniature. Engravings by the German Little Masters 1500-1550*, exh. cat. Spencer Museum of Art

Ledeboer 1869
A.M. Ledeboer, *Het geslacht Van Waesberghe. Eene bijdrage tot de geschiedenis der boekdrukkunst en van den boekhandel in Nederland*, The Hague/ Utrecht 1869

Lehmann-Haupt 1975
H. Lehmann-Haupt, 'Christoffel van Sichem. A Family of Dutch 17th Century Woodcut Artists', *Gutenberg Jahrbuch* (1975), pp. 274-306

Leiden 1932
A.A. van Rijnbach, *Bibliotheek van de Maatschappij der Nederlandsche Letterkunde te Leiden. Catalogus van de Verzameling-Boekenoogen*, Leiden 1932

Leiden 1990
'Doorgaens verciert met kopere platen'. *Nederlandse geïllustreerde boeken uit de zeventiende eeuw* (Kleine publikaties van de Leidse Universiteitsbibliotheek, 8), exh. cat. Universiteitsbibliotheek

Lowenthal 1986
A.W. Lowenthal, *Joachim Wtewael and Dutch Mannerism*, Doornspijk/ Groningen 1986

Lugt
F. Lugt, *Répertoire des catalogues de ventes publiques intéressant l'art ou la curiosité. Première période vers 1600-1825*, The Hague 1938

## M

Mainz 1991
*Blockbücher des Mittelalters. Bilderfolgen als Lektüre*, exh. cat. Gutenberg-Museum

Van Mander/ Floerke 1906
K. van Mander, *Das Leben der niederländischen und deutschen Maler*, 2 vols, ed. by H. Floerke, Leipzig 1906

Van Mander/ Miedema 1973
K. van Mander, *Den grondt der edel vry schilder-const*, 2 vols, ed. by H. Miedema, Utrecht 1973

Van Mander/ Miedema 1994-95
K. van Mander, *The Lives of the Illustrious Netherlandish and German Painters*, 2 vols, ed. by H. Miedema, Doornspijk 1994-95

Manuth 1993-94
V. Manuth, 'Denomination and Iconography: the Choice of Subject Matter in the Biblical Painting of the Rembrandt Circle', *Simiolus* 22 (1993-94), pp. 235-252

Martin 1911
W. Martin, 'Ausstellung Altholländischer Bilder in Pariser Privatbesitz', *Monatshefte für Kunstwissenschaft* 4 (1911), pp. 433 ff.

Mauquoy-Hendrickx 1978-83
M. Mauquoy-Hendrickx, *Les estampes des Wierix conservées au Cabinet des Estampes de la Bibliothèque Royale Albert Ier. Catalogue raisonné*, 3 vols, Brussels 1978-83

McGee 1991
J.L. McGee, *Cornelis Corneliszoon van Haarlem (1562-1638). Patrons, Friends and Dutch Humanists* (Bibliotheca Humanistica & Reformatorica, 48), Nieuwkoop 1991

McGrath 1984
E. McGrath, 'Rubens's "Susanna and the Elders" and Moralizing Inscriptions on Prints', in: Vekeman/ Müller Hofstede 1984, pp. 73-90

W.L. Meijer, *Kleinood en aanstoot. De Honderdguldenprent en andere bijbelse historiën van Rembrandt*, Leiden 1995

De Meyer 1962
M. de Meyer, *De volks- en kinderprent in de Nederlanden van de 15e tot de 20e eeuw*, Antwerp/ Amsterdam 1962

De Meyer 1970
M. de Meyer, *Volksprenten in de Nederlanden 1400-1900*, Amsterdam/ Antwerp 1970

Middleton 1878
Ch.H. Middleton, *A Descriptive Catalogue of the Etched Work of Rembrandt van Rhyn*, London 1878

Mielke 1967
H. Mielke, *Hans Vredeman de Vries. Verzeichnis der Stichwerke und Beschreibung seines Stils sowie Beiträge zum Werk Gerard Groennings*, Berlin 1967

Mielke 1975
H. Mielke, 'Antwerpener Graphik in der 2. Hälfte des 16. Jahrhunderts. Der Thesaurus veteris et novi Testamenti des Gerard de Jode (1585) und seine Künstler', *Zeitschrift für Kunstgeschichte* 38 (1975), pp. 29-83

Mielke 1979
H. Mielke, *Manierismus in Holland um 1600. Kupferstiche, Holzschnitte und Zeichnungen aus dem Berliner Kupferstichkabinett*, exh. cat. Staatliche Museen Preußischer Kulturbesitz, Berlin 1979

Mielke 1995
U. Mielke (ed.), 'Gerard Groenning, ein Antwerpener Künstler um 1570. I.

Verzeichnis seiner Zeichnungen und Stichwerke aus dem wissenschaftlichen Nachlaß von Hans Mielke', *Jahrbuch der Berliner Museen* 37 (1995), pp. 143-157

Möhle 1951
H. Möhle, 'Beiträge zu Johann Heinrich Schönfeld', *Zeitschrift für Kunstwissenschaft* 5 (1951), pp. 101-124

Montias 1982
J.M. Montias, *Artists and Artisans in Delft. A Socio-Economic Study of the Seventeenth Century*, Princeton 1982

Münster 1976
G. Langemeyer and R. Schleier, *Bilder nach Bildern. Druckgrafik und die Vermittlung von Kunst*, exh. cat. Westfälisches Landesmuseum

Münster 1994
C. Tümpel (ed.), *Im Lichte Rembrandts. Das Alte Testament im Goldenen Zeitalter der niederländischen Kunst*, exh. cat. Westfälisches Landesmuseum

Münz 1952
L. Münz, *A Critical Catalogue of Rembrandt's Etchings and the Etchings of his School Formerly Attributed to the Master*, 2 vols, London 1952

Munich 1979
K. Renger and C. Syre, *Graphik der Niederlande 1508-1617. Kupferstiche und Radierungen von Lucas van Leyden bis Hendrik Goltzius*, exh. cat. Staatliche Graphische Sammlung

Munich 1982
K. Renger and D. Schmidt, *Graphik in Holland. Esaias und Jan van de Velde, Rembrandt, Ostade und ihr Kreis. Radierung, Kupferstich, Schabkunst*, exh. cat. Staatliche Graphische Sammlung/ Neue Pinakothek

## N

Nagler
G.K. Nagler, *Neues allgemeines Künstler-Lexikon oder Nachrichten von dem Leben und den Werken der Maler, Bildhauer, Baumeister, Kupferstecher, Lithographen, Formschneider, Zeichner, Medailleure, Elfenbeinarbeiter etc.*, Linz 1913 [reprint]

New Hollstein, Heemskerck
I.M. Veldman, *Maarten van Heemskerck* (The New Hollstein Dutch & Flemish Etchings, Engravings and Woodcuts 1450-1700), 2 vols, Roosendaal 1993-94

New Hollstein, Hondius
N. Orenstein, *Hendrick Hondius* (The New Hollstein Dutch & Flemish Etchings, Engravings and Woodcuts 1450-1700), Roosendaal 1994

New Hollstein, Lucas van Leyden
J.P. Filedt Kok, *Lucas van Leyden* (The New Hollstein Dutch & Flemish Etchings, Engravings and Woodcuts 1450-1700), Rotterdam 1996

Nice 1996
*Adam et Eve de Dürer à Chagall. Gravures de la Bibliothèque Nationale*, exh. cat. Musée National Message Biblique Marc Chagall

## O

Obreen 1877-90
F.D.O. Obreen, *Archief voor Nederlandsche kunstgeschiedenis*, 7 vols, Rotterdam 1877-90

Orenstein 1995
N. Orenstein, 'Prints and the Politics of the Publisher: the Case of Hendrick Hondius', *Simiolus* 23 (1995), pp. 240-250

Orenstein 1996
N.M. Orenstein, *Hendrick Hondius and the Business of Prints in Seventeenth-Century Holland* (Studies in Prints and Print-making, 1), Rotterdam 1996

Orenstein et al. 1993-94
N. Orenstein et al., 'Print Publishers in the Netherlands 1580-1620', in: Amsterdam 1993-94A, pp. 167-200

## P

Parshall 1978
P. Parshall, 'Lucas van Leyden's Narrative Style', *Nederlands Kunsthistorisch Jaarboek* 29 (1978), pp. 185-237

Pepper 1984
D.S. Pepper, *Guido Reni*, Oxford 1984

Perlove 1993
S. Perlove, 'An Irenic Vision of Utopia: Rembrandt's "Triumph of Mordecai" and the New Jerusalem', *Zeitschrift für Kunstgeschichte* 56 (1993), pp. 38-60

Pijzel-Dommisse 1988
J. Pijzel-Dommisse, *Het poppenhuis van het Haags Gemeentemuseum*, The Hague 1988

Pinder 1929
W. Pinder, *Die deutsche Plastik vom ausgehenden Mittelalter bis zum Ende der Renaissance* (Handbuch der Kunstwissenschaft), Wildpark/ Potsdam 1929

Pluis 1994
J. Pluis, *Bijbeltegels. Bijbelse voorstellingen op Nederlandse wandtegels van de 17e tot de 20e eeuw. Bibelfliesen. Biblische Darstellungen auf Niederländischen Wandfliesen vom 17. bis zum 20. Jahrhundert* (Schriftenreihe zur religiösen Kultur, 3), Münster 1994

Pohlen 1985
I. Pohlen, *Untersuchungen zur Reproduktionsgraphik der Rubenswerkstatt* (Beiträge zur Kunstwissenschaft, 6), Munich 1985

Poortman 1980
W.C. Poortman, *De prentbijbel van Romeyn de Hooghe. Inleiding op de facsimile-uitgave van de serie bijbelprenten van Romeyn de Hooghe*, Franeker/ Amsterdam 1980

Poortman 1983-86
W.C. Poortman, *Bijbel en Prent*, 2 vols, The Hague 1983-86

Poortman/ Augusteijn 1995
W.C. Poortman and J. Augusteijn, *Kaarten in Bijbels*, Zoetermeer 1995

## R

Raupp 1994
H.-J. Raupp, 'Rembrandts Radierungen mit biblischen Themen 1640-1650 und das "Hundertguldenblatt" ', *Zeitschrift für Kunstgeschichte* 57 (1994), pp. 403-420

Réau 1921
L. Réau, *L'art russe des origines à Pierre le Grand*, Paris 1921

Reznicek 1956
E.K.J. Reznicek, 'Jan Harmensz. Muller als tekenaar', *Nederlands Kunsthistorisch Jaarboek* 7 (1956), pp. 65-120

Riggs 1977
T.A. Riggs, *Hieronymus Cock. Printmaker and Publisher*, New York/ London 1977

Robinson 1981
W.W. Robinson, '"This Passion for Prints": Collecting and Connoisseurship in Northern Europe during the Seventeenth Century', in: Ackley 1981, pp. xxvii-xlviii

Rockville 1981
S.W. Morgenstein and R.E. Levine, *The Jews in the Age of Rembrandt*, exh. cat. The Judiac Museum of the Jewish Community Center of Greater Washington

Roethlisberger 1981
M. Roethlisberger, *Bartholomeus Breenbergh. The Paintings*, Berlin/ New York 1981

Roethlisberger 1993
M.G. Roethlisberger, *Abraham Bloemaert and his Sons. Paintings and Prints*, 2 vols, Doornspijk 1993

Rome 1985
G.B. Pezzini et al., *Raphael invenit. Stampe da Raffaello nelle collezioni dell'Istituto Nazionale per la Grafica*, Rome 1985

Roscam Abbing 1993
M. Roscam Abbing, '"Abraham onthaalt de Heer en twee engelen". Opmerkingen over de titel van de Rembrandt-ets B 29', *Kroniek van het Rembrandthuis* (1993), no. 2, pp. 28-33

Rosenberg 1968
J. Rosenberg, *Rembrandt Life & Work*, London 1968

Rosier 1992
B.A. Rosier, *De Nederlandse bijbelillustratie in de zestiende eeuw. De illustraties in de bijbels gedrukt in de Nederlanden en in de Nederlandstalige bijbels gedrukt in het buitenland van 1522 tot 1599*, 2 vols, Amsterdam 1992 (diss.)

Rotermund 1963
H.M. Rotermund, *Rembrandts Handzeichnungen und Radierungen zur Bibel*, Lahr/ Schwarzwald/ Stuttgart 1963

Rotterdam 1994
*Van Eyck to Bruegel 1400-1550. Dutch and Flemish Painting in the Collection of the Museum Boymans-van Beuningen*, exh. cat. Museum Boijmans Van Beuningen

Rotterdam/ Paris 1974-75
*Willem Buytewech 1591-1624*, exh. cat. Museum Boijmans Van Beuningen/ Institut Néerlandais

Rovinski 1890
D. Rovinski, *L'Oeuvre gravé de Rembrandt. Reproduction des planches originales dans tous leurs états successifs avec un catalogue raisonné*, St. Petersburg 1890

## S

Roy 1992
A. Roy, *Gérard de Lairesse (1640-1711)*, Paris 1992

Royalton-Kisch 1992
M. Royalton-Kisch, *Drawings by Rembrandt and his Circle in the British Museum*, London 1992

RRP (Rembrandt Research Project)
J. Bruyn et al., *A Corpus of Rembrandt Paintings*, Vol. 1-, The Hague etc. 1982-

Ruffo 1916
V. Ruffo, 'Galleria Ruffo nel secolo XVII in Messina', *Bolletino d'Arte* 10 (1916), pp. 21-192, 237-388

## S

Saunders 1978
E.A. Saunders, *Old Testament Subjects in the Prints of Maarten van Heemskerck: 'Als een claere spiegele der tegenwoordige tijden'*, Ann Arbor 1984 (diss. Yale 1978)

Savelsberg 1992
W. Savelsberg, 'Flämische Druckgraphik in der zweiten Hälfte des 16. Jahrhunderts', in: Cologne/ Vienna/ Antwerp 1992, pp. 225-234

Schaeps 1994
J. Schaeps, 'Prenten uit de Bibliotheca Thysiana', *Leids Kunsthistorisch Jaarboek* 9 (1994), pp. 247-310

Schapelhouman 1985
M. Schapelhouman, 'Tekeningen van Pieter Jansz. Konstig Glasschrijver', *Bulletin van het Rijksmuseum* 33 (1985), pp. 71-92

Schapelhouman 1987
M. Schapelhouman, *Nederlandse tekeningen omstreeks 1600* (Catalogus van de Nederlandse tekeningen in het Rijksprentenkabinet, Rijksmuseum, Amsterdam, 3), Amsterdam/ The Hague 1987

Scheller 1969
R.W. Scheller, 'Rembrandt en de encyclopedische kunstkamer', *Oud Holland* 84 (1969), pp. 81-147

Schenda 1987
R. Schenda, 'Bilder vom Lesen - Lesen von Bildern', *Internationales Archiv für Sozialgeschichte der deutschen Literatur* 12 (1987), pp. 82-106

Schillemans 1989
R. Schillemans, *Bijbelschilderkunst rond Rembrandt*, Utrecht 1989

Schneider 1932
H. Schneider, *Jan Lievens, sein Leben und seine Werke*, Haarlem 1932

Schubart 1932
H. Schubart, *Die Bibelillustration des Bernard Salomon*, Hamburg 1932 (diss.)

Schuckman 1989
C. Schuckman, 'Dutch Prints and Printmaking', in: R.P. Maccubbin and M. Hamilton Phillips (eds), *The Age of William III & Mary II. Power, Politics, and Patronage 1688-1702. A Reference Encyclopedia and Exhibition Catalogue*, Williamsburg 1989, pp. 281-292

Schuckman 1990
   C. Schuckman, 'Jan Philipsz. Schabaelje (1592-1656) and his "Bibles in Prints"', *Print Quarterly* 7 (1990), pp. 66-69
Schuckman 1993
   C. Schuckman, 'Antoni Waterloo', *Print Quarterly* 10 (1993), pp. 68-75
Von Seidlitz 1922
   W. von Seidlitz, *Die Radierungen Rembrandts mit einem kritischen Verzeichnis und Abbildung sämtlicher Radierungen*, 2 vols., Leipzig 1922
Sellink 1992
   M. Sellink, 'Philips Galle als uitgever van prenten aan het einde van de zestiende eeuw', *De zeventiende eeuw* 8 (1992), pp. 13-26
Van Selm 1987
   B. van Selm, *Een menighte treffelijcke Boecken. Nederlandse boekhandelscatalogi in het begin van de zeventiende eeuw*, Utrecht 1987
Van Selm 1992
   B. van Selm, *Inzichten en vergezichten. Zes beschouwingen over het onderzoek naar de geschiedenis van de Nederlandse boekhandel*, Amsterdam 1992
Silver/ Smith 1978
   L. Silver and S. Smith, 'Carnal Knowledge: the Late Engravings of Lucas van Leyden', *Nederlands Kunsthistorisch Jaarboek* 29 (1978), pp. 239-298
Simon 1958
   M. Simon, *Claes Jansz. Visscher*, Freiburg 1958 (diss.)
Singer 1906
   H. Singer, *Rembrandt's Radierungen in 402 Abbildungen* (Klassiker der Kunst), Stuttgart 1906
De Smet 1977
   R. De Smet, 'Een nauwkeuriger datering van Rubens' eerste reis naar Holland in 1612', *Jaarboek van het Koninklijk Museum voor Schone Kunsten Antwerpen* (1977), pp. 199-220
Smith 1985
   D.R. Smith, 'Towards a Protestant Aesthetics: Rembrandt's 1655 "Sacrifice of Isaac"', *Art History* 8 (1985), pp. 290-302
Smith 1987
   D.R. Smith, 'Raphael's Creation, Rembrandt's Fall', *Zeitschrift für Kunstgeschichte* 50 (1987), pp. 496-508
Spicer 1989
   J. Spicer, 'A Drawing of "David with the Head of Goliath" by Hendrick Goltzius', *Burlington Magazine* 131 (1989), pp. 407-410
Spicer 1991
   J. Spicer, 'Nicolaus Braeu and Gilles van Breen. Two Printmakers or One?', *Print Quarterly* 8 (1991), pp. 275-280
Stechow 1927
   W. Stechow, 'Zu Rubens' erster Reise nach Holland', *Oud Holland* 44 (1927), pp. 138-139
Sterck 1932
   J.F.M. Sterck, *Oud en nieuw over Joost van den Vondel*, Amsterdam 1932
Stirm 1977
   M. Stirm, *Die Bilderfrage in der Reformation* (Quellen und Forschungen zur Reformationsgeschichte, 45), Gütersloh 1977

Van der Stock 1985
   J. Van der Stock, *Cornelis Matsys 1510/11-1556/57. Grafisch werk*, exh. cat. Koninlijke Bibliotheek Albert I, Brussels 1985
Strauss/ Van der Meulen 1979
   W.L. Strauss and M. van der Meulen, *The Rembrandt Documents*, New York 1979
Sumowski
   W. Sumowski, *Gemälde der Rembrandt-Schüler*, 6 vols, Landau/ Pfalz 1983-
Van Swigchem/ Brouwer/ Van Os 1984
   C.A. van Swigchem, T. Brouwer and W. van Os, *Een huis voor het Woord. Het protestantse kerkinterieur in Nederland tot 1900*, The Hague 1984

## T

Van Thiel 1965
   P.J.J. van Thiel, 'De Grebbers regels van de kunst', *Oud Holland* 80 (1965), pp. 126-131
Van Thiel 1978
   P.J.J. van Thiel, 'Houtsneden van Werner van den Valckert en Mozes van Uyttenbroeck. De Hollandse houtsnede in het eerste kwart van de zeventiende eeuw', *Oud Holland* 92 (1978), pp. 7-42
Van Thiel 1983
   P.J.J. van Thiel, 'Werner Jacobsz. van den Valckert', *Oud Holland* 97 (1983), pp. 128-195
Thieme/ Becker 1907-50
   U. Thieme and F. Becker (eds), *Allgemeines Lexikon der bildenden Künstler von der Antike bis zur Gegenwart*, 37 vols, Leipzig 1907-50
Thijs 1993
   A.K.L. Thijs, *Antwerpen, internationaal uitgeverscentrum van devotieprenten (17de-18de eeuw)*, Leuven 1993
TIB
   *The Illustrated Bartsch*, Vol. 1-, New York 1978-
Tsuritani 1974
   D.M. Tsuritani, *The Etchings of Ferdinand Bol*, Oberlin College 1974 (thesis)
Tsuritani 1975-76
   D.M. Tsuritani, 'The Etchings of Ferdinand Bol', *Allen Memorial Art Bulletin* 33 (1975/76), pp. 46-47
Tümpel
   A. Tümpel, *The Complete Work of Pieter Lastman* (forthcoming)
Tümpel 1974A
   A. Tümpel, *The Pre-Rembrandtists*, exh. cat. A.B. Crocker Art Gallery, Sacramento 1974
Tümpel 1974B
   A. Tümpel, 'Claes Cornelisz. Moeyaert', *Oud Holland* 88 (1974), pp. 1-163, 245-290
Tümpel 1978
   A. Tümpel, '"Ruth erklärt Naemi die Treue" von Pieter Lastman. Zur Genese eines typischen Barockthemas', *Niederdeutsche Beiträge zur Kunstgeschichte* 17 (1978), pp. 87-101
Tümpel 1968A
   C. Tümpel, *Studien zur Ikonographie der Historien Rembrandts*, Hamburg 1968 (diss.)

Tümpel 1968B
   C. Tümpel, 'Ikonographische Beiträge zu Rembrandt. Zur Deutung und Interpretation seiner Historien [I]', *Jahrbuch der Hamburger Kunstsammlungen* 13 (1968), pp. 95-126
Tümpel 1969
   C. Tümpel, 'Studien zur Ikonographie der Historien Rembrandts. Deutung und Interpretation der Bildinhalte', *Nederlands Kunsthistorisch Jaarboek* 20 (1969), pp. 107-198
Tümpel 1970
   C. Tümpel, *Rembrandt legt die Bibel aus. Zeichnungen und Radierungen aus dem Kupferstichkabinett der Staatlichen Museen Preußischer Kulturbesitz Berlin*, Berlin 1970
Tümpel 1971
   C. Tümpel, 'Ikonographische Beiträge zu Rembrandt. Zur Deutung und Interpretation einzelner Werke (II)', *Jahrbuch der Hamburger Kunstsammlungen* 16 (1971), pp. 20-38
Tümpel 1977
   C. Tümpel, *Rembrandt*, Reinbek bei Hamburg 1977
Tümpel 1980
   C. Tümpel, 'Die Ikonographie der Amsterdamer Historienmalerei in der ersten Hälfte des 17. Jahrhunderts und die Reformation', *Vestigia Bibliae. Jahrbuch des Deutschen Bibel-Archivs Hamburg* 2 (1980), pp. 127-158
Tümpel 1984
   C. Tümpel, 'Die Rezeption der Jüdischen Altertümer des Flavius Josephus in den holländischen Historiendarstellungen des 16. und 17. Jahrhunderts', in: Vekeman/ Müller Hofstede 1984, pp. 173-204
Tümpel 1986
   C. Tümpel, *Rembrandt. Mythos und Methode*, Antwerp 1986
Tümpel 1991 & 1994
   C. Tümpel, 'De oudtestamentische historieschilderkunst in de Gouden Eeuw', in: Amsterdam 1991-92, pp. 8-23; 'Die alttestamentliche Historienmalerei im Zeitalter Rembrandts', in: Münster 1994, pp. 8-23
Tümpel 1993
   C. & A. Tümpel, *Rembrandt. All Paintings in Colour*, Antwerp 1993

## U

Unger 1888
   J.H.W. Unger, *Bibliographie van Vondels Werken*, Amsterdam 1888
Utrecht 1991-92
   T.G. Kootte (ed.), *De bijbel in huis. Bijbelse verhalen op huisraad en meubilair in de zeventiende en achttiende eeuw*, exh. cat. Museum het Catharijneconvent
Utrecht 1994
   T.G. Kootte, *Rekkelijk of precies. Remonstranten en contraremonstranten ten tijde van Maurits en Oldenbarnevelt*, exh. cat. Museum het Catharijneconvent

## V

Valentiner 1930
   E. Valentiner, *Karel van Mander als Maler*, Strasbourg 1930
Van Veen 1976
   C.F. van Veen, *Catchpennyprints. Dutch Popular- and Childrenprints*, exh. cat. Rijksprentenkabinet, Amsterdam 1976
Vekeman/ Müller Hofstede 1984
   H. Vekeman and J. Müller Hofstede (eds), *Wort und Bild in der niederländischen Kunst und Literatur des 16. und 17. Jahrhunderts*, Erftstadt 1984
Van de Velde 1975
   C. Van de Velde, *Frans Floris (1519/20-1570). Leven en werken*, 2 vols, Brussels 1975
Veldman 1977
   I.M. Veldman, *Maarten van Heemskerck and Dutch Humanism in the Sixteenth Century*, Maarssen 1977
Veldman 1986A
   I.M. Veldman, *Leerrijke reeksen van Maarten van Heemskerck*, exh. cat. Frans Halsmuseum, Haarlem 1986
Veldman 1986B
   I.M. Veldman, 'De boekillustratie als inspiratiebron voor de Nederlandse prentkunst van de zestiende eeuw', in: H. Duits, A.J. Gelderblom and M.B. Smits-Veldt (eds), *Eer is het lof des deuchts. Opstellen over renaissance en classicisme aangeboden aan dr. Fokke Veenstra*, Amsterdam 1986, pp. 261-277
Veldman 1987A
   I.M. Veldman, 'Nederlandse bijbelillustraties voor en tijdens de uitgave van de Statenvertaling', *Met andere woorden. Kwartaalblad over bijbelwerk* 6 (1987), no. 4, pp. 28-38
Veldman 1987B
   I.M. Veldman, 'Maarten van Heemskerks visie op het geloof', *Bulletin van het Rijksmuseum* 35 (1987), pp. 193-210
Veldman 1989
   I.M. Veldman, 'Coornhert en de prentkunst', in: H. Bonger et al. (eds), *Dirck Volckertszoon Coornhert. Dwars maar recht*, Zutphen 1989, pp. 115-143, 178-179
Veldman 1991-92
   I.M. Veldman, 'Bijbelse thema's in de Nederlandse prentkunst van de 16de en het begin van de 17de eeuw', in: Utrecht 1991-92, pp. 29-42
Veldman 1995
   I.M. Veldman, 'The Old Testament as a Moral Code: Old Testament Stories as Exempla of the Ten Commandments', *Simiolus* 23 (1995), pp. 215-239
Veldman/ De Jonge 1985
   I.M. Veldman and H.J. de Jonge, 'The Sons of Jacob: the Twelve Patriarchs in Sixteenth-Century Netherlandish Prints and Popular Literature', *Simiolus* 15 (1985), pp. 176-196
Venlo 1993
   A.A.J.J. van Pinxteren et al. (eds), *Pronkstukken. Venlo 650 jaar stad*, exh. cat. Goltziusmuseum

Vermeeren 1978
K. Vermeeren, 'Constantijn Daniël van Renesse, zijn leven en zijn werken (I)', *Kroniek van het Rembrandthuis* 30 (1978), no. 1, pp. 2-23

Vermeeren 1979
K. Vermeeren, 'Constantijn Daniël van Renesse, zijn leven en zijn werken (II)', *Kroniek van het Rembrandthuis* 31 (1979), no. 1, pp. 27-33

Verwey 1986
A. Verwey (ed.), *Vondel. Volledige dichtwerken en oorspronkelijk proza*, Amsterdam 1986

Visser 1988
P. Visser, *Broeders in de geest. De doopsgezinde bijdragen van Dierick en Jan Philipsz. Schabaelje tot de Nederlandse stichtelijke literatuur in de zeventiende eeuw*, 2 vols, Deventer 1988

Van Voolen 1994
E. van Voolen, 'Juden im Amsterdam Rembrandts', in: Münster 1994, pp. 207-218

Voorhelm Schneevoogt 1873
C.G. Voorhelm Schneevoogt, *Catalogue des estampes gravées d'après P.P. Rubens*, Haarlem 1873

Vos 1978
R. Vos, *Lucas van Leyden*, Bentveld/ Maarssen 1978

De Vries/ Van der Woude 1995
J. de Vries and A. van der Woude, *Nederland 1500-1815. De eerste ronde van moderne economische groei*, Amsterdam 1995

# W

Van de Waal 1947
H. van de Waal, ' "Hagar in de woestijn" door Rembrandt en zijn school', *Nederlands Kunsthistorisch Jaarboek* 1 (1947), pp. 144-169

Van de Waal 1954-55
H. van de Waal, 'Rembrandts Radierungen zur "Piedra gloriosa" des Menasseh ben Israel', *Imprimatur. Ein Jahrbuch für Bücherfreunde* 12 (1954-55), pp. 52- 61

Van de Waal 1969
H. van de Waal, 'Rembrandt and the Feast of Purim', *Oud Holland* 84 (1969), pp. 199-223

Van der Waals 1988
J. van der Waals, *De prentschat van Michiel Hinloopen. Een reconstructie van de eerste openbare papierkunstverzameling in Nederland*, exh. cat. Rijksprentenkabinet, Amsterdam 1988

Van der Waals 1997
J. van der Waals, 'Royal-Size Biblical History Prints. Nicolaus Visscher's "Royaal Bijbel" and Related Prints', in: *Proceedings of the XXIXth International Congress of the History of Art (Amsterdam 1996)*, 1997 (forthcoming)

Washington/ Boston 1983
E.S. Jacobowitz and S.L. Stepanek, *The Prints of Lucas van Leyden and his Contempories*, exh. cat. National Gallery of Art/ Museum of Fine Arts

Watt 1991
T. Watt, *Cheap Print and Popular Piety 1550-1640 (Cambridge Studies in Early Modern British History)*, Cambridge etc. 1991

Weisner 1963
U. Weisner, *Moyses van Uyttenbroeck. Studien und kritischer Katalog seiner Gemälde und Zeichnungen*, Kiel 1963 (diss.)

Welzel 1996
B. Welzel, 'Nordniederländische Druckgraphik und ihre Verleger', *Kunstchronik* 49 (1996), pp. 65-74

Wheelock 1983
A.K. Wheelock, 'The Influence of Lucas van Leyden on Rembrandt's Narrative Etchings', in: A.-M. Logan (ed.), *Essays in Northern European Art Presented to Egbert Haverkamp-Begemann on his Sixtieth Birthday*, Doornspijk 1983, pp. 291-296

White 1969
Chr. White, *Rembrandt as an Etcher. A study of the artist at work*, 2 vols, London 1969

Widerkehr 1993
L. Widerkehr, 'Jacob Matham Goltzij Privignus. Jacob Matham graveur et ses rapports avec Hendrick Goltzius', in: Falkenburg/ Filedt Kok/ Leeflang 1993, pp. 219-260

Van den Wijngaert 1940
F. van den Wijngaert, *Inventaris der Rubeniaansche prentkunst*, Antwerp 1940

Wijsenbeek-Olthuis 1987
T. Wijsenbeek-Olthuis, *Achter de gevels van Delft. Bezit en bestaan van rijk en arm in een periode van achteruitgang (1700-1800)*, Hilversum 1987

Wilson/ Wilson 1984
A. and J.L. Wilson, *A Medieval Mirror. Speculum Humanae Salvationis 1324-1500*, Berkeley/ Los Angeles/ London 1984

Wischnitzer 1990
R. Wischnitzer, *From Dura to Rembrandt. Studies in the History of Art*, Milwaukee/ Vienna/ Jerusalem 1990

Worthen 1993
A.N. Worthen, 'Calligraphic Inscriptions on Dutch Mannerist Prints', in: Falkenburg/ Filedt Kok/ Leeflang 1993, pp. 261-396

Wuestman 1995
G. Wuestman, 'The Mezzotint in Holland: "Easily Learned, Neat and Convenient"', *Simiolus* 23 (1995), pp. 63-89

Wüthrich 1993
L.H. Wüthrich, *Das druckgraphische Werk von Matthaeus Merian d. Ae.*, Vol. 3, Hamburg 1993

# Y

Yerushalmi 1975
Y.H. Yerushalmi, *Haggadah and History. A Panorama in Facsimile of Five Centuries of the Printed Haggadah from the Collections of Harvard University and the Jewish Theological Seminary of America*, Philadelphia 1975

# Z

Zilkens 1982
I. Zilkens, *Druckgraphik der Rembrandtschule*, Aachen 1982 (diss.)

Zilkens 1984
I. Zilkens, *Rembrandt (1606-1669) und sein Kreis. Radierungen*, exh. cat. Suermondt-Ludwig-Museum, Aachen 1984

Zoege von Manteuffel 1926
K. Zoege von Manteuffel, *Die niederländische Radierung. Von den Anfängen bis zum Ende des 17. Jahrhunderts*, Munich 1926

Zweite 1980
A. Zweite, *Marten de Vos als Maler. Ein Beitrag zur Geschichte der Antwerpener Malerei in der zweiten Hälfte des 16. Jahrhunderts*, Berlin 1980

# Index of Artists

**Lenders to the exhibition**

Amsterdam: Amsterdams Historisch Museum cat. no. 65

Amsterdam: Museum het Rembrandthuis cat. nos 2, 4, 5, 6, 9, 11, 12, 17, 18, 19, 21, 32, 33, 41, 49, 50, 71, 76

Amsterdam: Rijksmuseum Library cat. nos 54, 60

Amsterdam: Rijksprentenkabinet, Rijksmuseum cat. nos 1, 3, 7, 15, 23, 24, 26, 27, 31, 34, 35, 36, 37, 38, 42, 44, 46, 48, 51, 52

Amsterdam: Prof. dr L.H. van der Tweel: 43

Amsterdam: University Library cat. nos 55, 61, 64, 67, 72, 73, 74, 77

Arnhem: Nederlands Openluchtmuseum cat. no. 66

Haarlem: Teylers Museum cat. no. 28

The Hague: Museum van het Boek cat. no. 57

Landsmeer: R.N.H. Boerma cat. no. 53

Leiden: Prentenkabinet der Rijksuniversiteit Leiden cat. nos 22, 56

Nijmegen: University Library cat. nos. 59, 62, 63, 68, 69, 70, 75

Rotterdam: Museum Boijmans Van Beuningen cat. nos 8, 10, 13, 14, 16, 25, 29, 30, 39, 40, 45, 47

Tilburg: Library Theological Faculty cat. no. 58

Voorschoten: Th. Laurentius cat. no. 20

**Authors** Peter van der Coelen, with the assistance of Christian Tümpel

**Contributors** Gerlinde de Beer, Marlies Enklaar, Judith van Gent, Aernout Hagen, Marloes Huiskamp, Petra Jeroense, Netty van de Kamp, Jeroen Kuppens, Gabriël Pastoor, Astrid Tümpel

**Editors** Peter van der Coelen, Christian Tümpel

**Final editors** Marlies Enklaar, with the assistance of Peter van der Coelen

**Photo editor** Marlies Enklaar

**Translators** Sammy Herman, Donald Gardner & Bob Ordish (Tibbon Translations, Amsterdam), Harry Lake (Bussum) and Bill Mickens (Cologne)

**Designer** Vincent van Baar, Barlock, The Hague

**Publisher** Museum het Rembrandthuis - Rembrandt Information Centre, Amsterdam

**Printing** Drukkerij Orientaliste, Herent (Belgium)

**Distribution** Primavera Press, Burggravenlaan 7, 2313 HM Leiden

Tel. 071-5144482   FAX 071-5144372

CIP-DATA KONINKLIJKE BIBLIOTHEEK, DEN HAAG

Van der Coelen, Peter *et al.*

Patriarchs, Angels & Prophets. The Old Testament in Netherlandish Printmaking from Lucas van Leyden to Rembrandt (Studies in Dutch Graphic Art, Vol. II)/ Peter van der Coelen, Christian Tümpel, Gerlinde de Beer, Marlies Enklaar, Judith van Gent, Aernout Hagen, Marloes Huiskamp, Petra Jeroense, Netty van de Kamp, Jeroen Kuppens, Gabriël Pastoor, Astrid Tümpel

[ed. Marlies Enklaar; trans. Sammy Herman *et al.*]

Museum het Rembrandthuis - Rembrandt Information Centre, Amsterdam 1996.

Distr. Primavera Press, Leiden. Ill.

ISBN 90-74310-32-x

1. prentkunst  2. Oude Testament  3. Nederlanden  4. 16de-17de eeuw  5. Rembrandt